Warrior Mountains Indian Heritage

Teacher's Edition

By Rickey Butch Walker
August 2008

© Copyright 2008
Bluewater Publications
Protected

All rights reserved. No part of this publication may be reproduced or transmitted in any form or by any means, electronic or mechanical, including photocopying, recording, or by any information storage and retrieval system, without prior written permission from the Publisher.

Published by:
Bluewater Publications
1812 CR 111
Killen, Alabama 35645
www.BluewaterPublications.com

Table of Contents

Preface

LESSON 1 - INTRODUCTION / PRE-TEST	1
LESSON 2 – FAMILY HISTORY AND ANCESTRY	11
LESSON 3 – ECHOTA CHEROKEE TRIBE OF ALABAMA	22
LESSON 4 – PERIODS OF PREHISTORIC INDIANS	33
LESSON 5 – LIFESTYLES OF EARLY INDIAN PEOPLE	50
LESSON 6 – EARLY SURVIVAL NEEDS	62
LESSON 7 – REGALIA	77
LESSON 8 – CEREMONIAL ACTIVITIES	89
LESSON 9 – TENNESSEE RIVER	101
LESSON 10 – EUROPEAN CONTACT	114
LESSON 11 – FIVE TRIBES OF LAWRENCE COUNTY / MID-TEST	126
LESSON 12 – CREEK TRIBE	137
LESSON 13 – CHICKASAW TRIBE	148
LESSON 14 – CHEROKEE TRIBE	158
LESSON 15 – SEVEN CLANS OF THE CHEROKEE	169
LESSON 16 – INDIAN TRAILS AND PATHS	180
LESSON 17 – INDIAN VILLAGES	198
LESSON 18 – LOCAL INDIAN LEADERS	218
LESSON 19 – INDIAN BATTLES	238
LESSON 20 – INDIAN TREATIES	253
LESSON 21 – INDIAN REMOVAL	264
LESSON 22 – TRADITIONAL CULTURAL PROPERTIES	276
LESSON 23 – STATE RECOGNIZED INDIAN TRIBES OF ALABAMA	292
LESSON 24 – REVIEW	304
LESSON 25 – Post-Test	305
Appendix 1: Reading and Social Studies Individual Performance Reports	306
Appendix 2: Alabama Course of Study (2004 Edition)	315
Appendix 3: Reading and Social Studies Teacher-made Pre/Mid/Post Tests	336
Appendix 4: Activities and Crafts	350
Appendix 5: Lesson Activities	352
Appendix 6: End of the Year Performance Report	359
Appendix 7: Checklist for Instructor Improvement	361
Index	363

Preface

Warrior Mountains Indian Heritage was written for the academic and cultural enrichment of Indian students attending Lawrence County Schools' Indian Education Program. This work is a culmination of four years of research and development of educational plans that specifically address the reading and social studies objectives of our Indian education program. The lesson plans are designed to meet the state standards of Alabama and are based on the criteria required in the standardized assessment of all students attending Lawrence County Schools. Lessons are historically specific to the Indian heritage of the Warrior Mountains of North Alabama. These lesson plans were written from an Indian perspective for Indian children in our school system.

In addition to the lessons, state standards, and standardized assessment criteria, Warrior Mountains Indian Heritage also contains individual performance reports, teacher-made pre/mid/post tests, activities for grades Kindergarten through seven, and a checklist for instructor improvement in team teaching. The state standards were taken from the August 2004 edition of the Alabama Course of Study. The standardized assessment criteria are based on Dynamic Indicators of Basic Early Literacy Skills (Dibels) for grades Kindergarten through three and the Stanford Achievement Test (SAT 10) for grades four through seven.

Warrior Mountain Indian Heritage has local, regional, and national significance since it addresses standardized assessment criteria used throughout the United States. The text can be a guide to other Indian programs across the nation who wish to develop their own lesson plans based on their specific history and culture. In addition, teachers of various grades can incorporate historically important details into their reading objectives.

LESSON 1 - INTRODUCTION / PRE-TEST

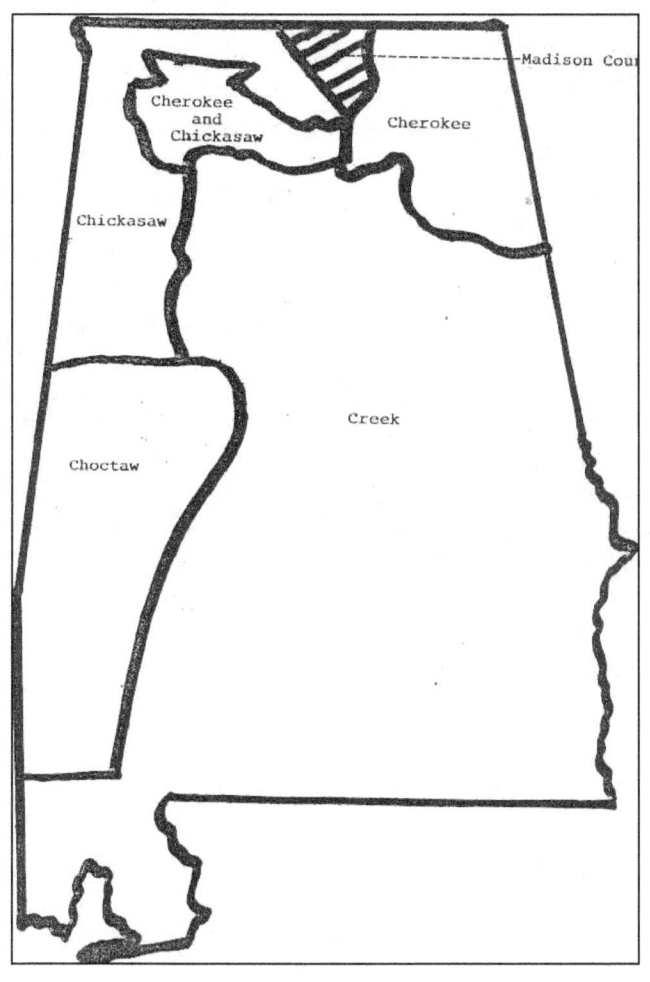

1806 Map of Alabama

Introduce yourself to class. Tell students that you work for Lawrence County Schools' Indian Education Program, which started in 1986. Have the students tell you their names. (Use handout "Getting to Know You")

Prior to Indian removal, our European ancestors moved into Indian lands where they intermarried with Indian people. These mixed families lived in harmony until the United States government started forced removal. During these difficult years of removal, many of our ancestors started denying their Indian race and calling themselves Black Dutch or Black Irish. After the Trail of Tears ended in March 1839, our Indigenous ancestors remaining in Alabama began a long and tragic period of ethnic denial.

Many Indian people in Lawrence County left the area in the early 1800s. Prior to 1840, many of our Indian people left their homes in our area but many others hid their true identity. Both Creeks and Cherokees were removed from here and passed through Oakville, along the Tennessee River, or by the first railroad through Hillsboro, Courtland, and Town Creek. During these times of removal, many of our Indian people escaped and avoided being sent west. Many of our ancestors went on the forced removal but later returned to their homelands in this area.

From the early 1840s to 1968, it was illegal for people to be Indian in the State of Alabama; therefore, our Indian ancestors had to deny their rightful heritage. Sections two through seven of the Civil Rights Act of 1968 allowed people in Alabama to reclaim their Indian heritage. In 1972, the U.S. Congress passed the Indian Education Act which ultimately funded Indian programs across the country. The program primarily provided for cultural based education for Indian students. In 1981, the Echota Cherokee Tribe of Alabama was incorporated and organized by the descendants of Cherokee people who migrated into Alabama from the northwestern corner of Georgia. The Cherokee capital in Georgia was at New Echota; thus, the Indian descendants with ties to this portion of the Cherokee Nation called themselves Echota Cherokee.

In 1986, two members of the Echota Cherokee Tribe, Joe Stewart and Charlotte Stewart Hallmark, helped Lawrence County start their Indian education program for children that were members of the tribe. Rickey Butch Walker was hired as the first coordinator of the Indian program. Initially, the program started an in-house Indian museum and in 1987 held the first Indian festival in Lawrence County. In 1990, the late Congressman, Tom Bevill, through the Appalachian Regional Commission, funded an Indian Youth Leadership Project for Lawrence County Schools' Indian Education Program. During

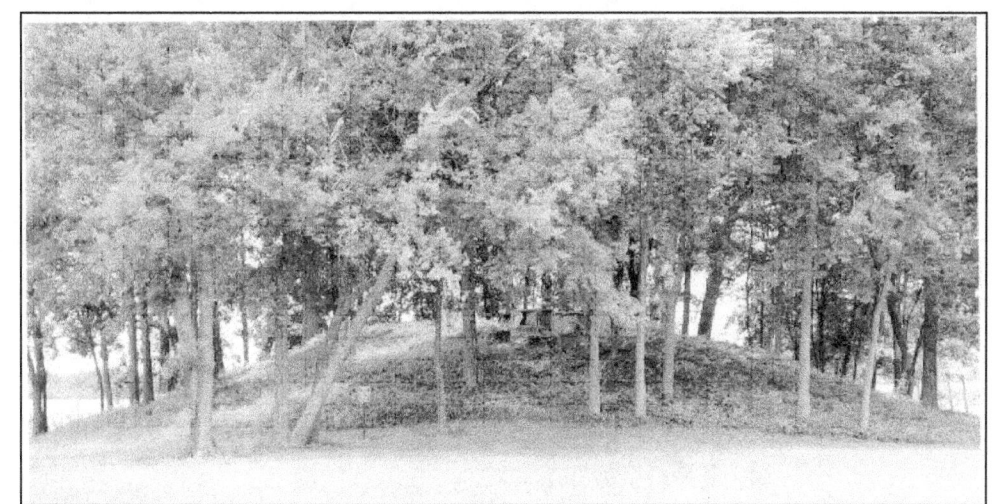

Burial Mound at Oakville

LESSON 1 - INTRODUCTION / PRE-TEST

Ceremonial Indian Mound at Oakville

1991, a land purchase was made for 26 acres containing two ancient Indian mounds and was named Oakville Indian Mounds Park. The facility was later renamed the Oakville Indian Mounds Education Center, which would complement and enhance our county's rich Indian culture and heritage. The Oakville museum and offices were opened in 1995 which was the year the Indian program was recognized as a National Showcase Project. Today, the Indian education offices and festival are held at the Center. Presently, the facility houses thousands of local artifacts and consists of some 116 acres.

Welcome to Indian education! We are glad to have you in our Indian education classes and we are excited about teaching you about your Indian ancestors. All of you have Indian ancestors or otherwise you would not be enrolled in this class. The majority of our Indian students or their parents are members of the Echota Cherokee Tribe of Alabama.

CLASSROOM RULES
Review class rules for all students in the class and post these rules on poster board visible in your classroom.

1. Walk in a straight line to and from the classroom.
2. Keep your hands to yourself.
3. Listen very carefully.
4. Treat others the way you want to be treated.
5. Raise your hand if you have a question or something to say and wait until I call your name to speak.

ADMINISTER PRE-TEST (Read each question and make sure the students are keeping up with you and know how to mark their answers.)

LESSON ACTIVITY: Students will pick clan names for each grade. Teacher will let students choose an Indian name.
Give examples and call roll by Indian names. Encourage students to pick names that personally relate to them, example: someone who likes to run could be named running deer, sing-singing bird.

LESSON 1 - INTRODUCTION / PRE-TEST

KINDERGARTEN

DIBELS Reading Objective: PHONEMIC AWARENESS
Objective: After the teacher directs this lesson, Kindergarten Indian students will orally identify five out of ten terms based on knowledge gained from text.

Objective Activity: Word sort using the following terms: Indian–who we are; ancestors–grandparents, great-grandparents; question-when someone asks you something; name-what you answer to; student-children being taught; teacher-person who teaches you; line-single file when you get ready to go; listen-to hear what to do when teacher is talking; walk-how we go down the hall; and, rules-what we obey. After completing the word sort, the teacher should break apart each word and have the students identify how many word parts are in each. (Ex: t-ea-ch-er or t-augh-t)

STATE STANDARDS Reading Objective:

PG. 14 #9   Begin to use pictures and text to gain meaning from written material.
- Show various pictures of Native Americans related to some of the students.
- Have students to individually introduce themselves to the class.
- Have them to repeat classroom rules in unison
- Have students chose Indian name and explain why they want that particular name.
  - *What part of Alabama did most of our Indian ancestors come from?* <u>North Alabama</u> *(which is the top or north part of the state)*

PG. 15 #15   Use appropriate listening and speaking behaviors
- Have students repeat Echota Cherokee Tribe to which most students belong.
- Each class will be given a clan or family name.
  - *What is the clan name of your class?*
  - *Why did you all chose that name?*

STATE STANDARDS Social Studies Objective:

PG. 11 #3   Develop initial map and globe skills
- Show Alabama map that divides the tribes to show students where most of their Indian ancestors lived.
  - *What part of North Alabama did your Cherokee ancestors live?* <u>North and Northeast part of Alabama</u> *(might be better to color code map)*

Review Questions

1. You are in this class because you, your parents, or grandparents are what race? (Indian or Native American)
2. Most of you are members of which Indian tribe? (Echota Cherokee)
3. In what county do our Indian children live? (Lawrence County)
4. Where are our Indian education program, museum, and mounds located? (Oakville)
5. What is an ancestor? (grandparent, great-grandparent, etc.)

LESSON 1 - INTRODUCTION / PRE-TEST

FIRST GRADE

DIBELS Reading Objective: PHONEME SEGMENTATION FLUENCY

Objective: After the teacher directs this lesson, first grade Indian students will develop an understanding of their classroom rules, learn new vocabulary words, and utilize phoneme segmentation fluency.

Objective Activity: Choose a variety of vocabulary terms from the text. Next, hold up flash cards, use board, or other visuals revealing individual letters of the term. (Ex: I-N-D-I-A-N=Indian) Use the following terms: line, hands, teacher, listen, Indian, etc.)

STATE STANDARDS Reading Objective:

PG. 17 #3   Exhibit phonemic awareness
- Choose five vocabulary terms from the lesson and write the words on the board. Say the word, count the number of sounds in the word, sound out each letter, blend sounds together and say word again. Use the word in a sentence with the class. (Ex: NAME (3 sounds), LINE (3 sounds)
  ∾ *Of what tribe are you a member? (Echota Cherokee Tribe)*

STATE STANDARDS Social Studies Objective:

PG. 18 #9   Compare feature of communities
- Compare where we live to the location of where our ancestors lived. (rural or urban) Ex: We live in a <u>rural</u> area. Do you think our ancestors lived in the country like us or in a city like Decatur or Huntsville? Our ancestors also lived in a <u>rural</u> area. (<u>mountains</u> or country)
  ∾ *Do we live in the same kind of place our ancestors did? (yes-country or rural area)*

Review Questions
1. What year did our Indian program begin? (1986)
2. What is an ancestor? (Grandparent)
3. Where is the Indian education festival held? (Oakville)
4. Do you live in Lawrence County? (yes)
5. Do you have to have Indian blood to be in Indian Education? (yes)

LESSON 1 - INTRODUCTION / PRE-TEST

SECOND GRADE

DIBELS Reading Objective: ORAL READING FLUENCY

Objective: After the teacher directs this lesson, second grade Indian students will be able to use their comprehension skills in knowing how to behave in the classroom and practice oral reading fluency.

Objective Activity: The teacher will write the classroom rules on the board. Then she will read the rules aloud while the students are reading aloud also. Next, the teacher will make sure everyone understands by asking questions concerning the rules. He/she will also have the students echo read throughout the lesson and/or individual students read aloud the text.

STATE STANDARDS Reading Objective:

PG. 25 #13   Demonstrate appropriate listening and communicating behaviors
- The teacher will introduce him/herself to the class. While he/she is doing this, he/she will model appropriate communication skills. Then he/she will have students use the same communication skills to introduce themselves to the teacher and the class. Everyone else should listen and be respectful.

STATE STANDARDS Social Studies Objective:

PG. 25 #21   Develop a sense of history through the examination of family histories
- Ask students if they know what Indian tribe was a part of their family history. Explain the migration of Celtic people (Irish, Scots-Irish, or Scots) into Indian country where intermarriage occurred with our tribal ancestors.
  - *To what tribe do most of our students belong? (Echota Cherokee Tribe of Alabama)*
  - *How did we become a people of mixed family histories? (Intermarriage-Celtic and Indian)*

Review Questions
1. What is the name of the Cherokee capital located in Georgia? (New Echota)
2. Who are our ancestors? (parents, grandparents, great-grandparents, etc.)
3. Of what tribe are you a member? (Cherokee)
4. Where are the Indian education program, museum, and mounds located in Lawrence County? (Oakville)
5. What year was the Indian program started? (1986)

LESSON 1 - INTRODUCTION / PRE-TEST

THIRD GRADE

DIBELS Reading Objective: LISTENING SKILLS

Objective: After the teacher directs this lesson, third grade Indian students will be able to introduce themselves and apply their cultural knowledge to verbally develop their personal connection to the class.

Objective Activity: The teacher will introduce the lesson and rules of the class. Then the teacher will introduce herself and the students will introduce themselves. Next, students will apply their knowledge of their culture and personal characteristics to develop their own Indian name to be used during class discussion.

STATE STANDARDS Reading Objective:

PG. 33 #12   Apply strategies of a skillful listener
- Apply strategies of a skillful listener. The teacher will introduce himself/herself to the students, and tell the students the classroom rules. Also tell the students about the Indian Education Program. Last, let the students introduce themselves. Let them ask questions, if they know anything about their Indian heritage.
    - What is the name of your tribe? (Echota Cherokee Tribe)

STATE STANDARDS Social Studies Objective:

PG. 29 # 1   Extend their development of map and globe skills
- Relate the elements of geography to the time of the early Native Americans and the location of their settlements. After the introduction, show the students a map of where the different tribes were located in the state of Alabama.
    - What clan are you a part of? (Blue Clan)

Review Questions

1. What act in 1968 allows people in Alabama to be Indian? (Civil Rights Act)
2. What clan are you a part of? (Blue Clan)
3. What is another name for the Indian Removal? (Trail of Tears)
4. What year did the Echota Cherokee Tribe become organized? (1980)
5. What two people helped start the Indian program in Lawrence County? (Joe and Charlotte Stewart)

LESSON 1 - INTRODUCTION / PRE-TEST

FOURTH GRADE

<u>SAT</u> Reading Objective: WORD RECOGNITION

Objective: After the teacher directs this lesson, fourth grade Indian students will be able to recognize and identify the terms. (Terms: Indian, ancestors, majority, Echota, tribe, rules, clan, relate)

Objective Activity: After utilizing word games (*Hangman, Jeopardy, or Wheel of Fortune*), Indian students will participate by identifying and recognizing important terms found in this lesson.

<u>STATE STANDARDS</u> Reading Objective:

PG. 40 #20   Demonstrate vocabulary growth developed through reading and listening to literature.
- Play *Jeopardy* and for one of the row/column choices it could be vocabulary from lesson.
- *What year was the Indian education program started? (1986)*

<u>STATE STANDARDS</u> Social Studies Objective:

PG. 35 #5   Describe the natural environment of Alabama
- Show different environmental features of Alabama such as: Bankhead Forest, Kinlock Falls, etc., to teach the kids what areas they will learn about throughout the semester.
- *What is the name of our forest? (Bankhead National Forest or Warrior Mountains)*

Review Questions

1. What did mixed Indian people call themselves? (Black Dutch or Black Irish)
2. When did the Trail of Tears end? (March 1839)
3. How many Indian mounds are located at Oakville? (two-ceremonial and burial)
4. Who was the first coordinator of the Indian program in Lawrence County? (Rickey Butch Walker)
5. What year was the Oakville museum opened? (1995)

LESSON 1 - INTRODUCTION / PRE-TEST

FIFTH GRADE

SAT Reading Objective: LISTENING SKILLS

Objective: After the teacher directs this lesson, fifth grade Indian students will utilize their listening skills to help them identify the following terms: ancestors, majority, Echota, clan. The students will identify the terms from this lesson through word games such as Hangman.

Objective Activity: Students will play Hangman or Wheel of Fortune with the terms. Give clues that include meaning of the word.

STATE STANDARDS Reading Objective:

PG. 47 #13   Apply strategies of a skillful listener
- The teacher will introduce the class to the Indian education program. On the board, the teacher will draw or outline a table of contents to show the students what they will cover during the year.
- ∾ *What is the name of our tribe? (Echota Cherokee Tribe)*

STATE STANDARDS Social Studies Objective:

PG. 46 #4   Describe the natural environment of North Alabama
- Use a map of the state of Alabama to show the location of Georgia.
- Show pictures of Oakville Park, mounds, Black Warriors' Path, museum, etc.
- Use world map to locate the path of the Indian removal (Trail of Tears).
- ∾ *Bankhead Forest is also known as what? (Warrior Mountains)*

Review Questions

1. What two main tribes were removed from Lawrence County? (Creeks and Cherokees)
2. What year was land bought for Oakville Indian mounds to become a park? (1992)
3. What year was the Indian education program started? (1986)
4. What are the names used by Indian mixed bloods after removal? (Black Dutch or Black Irish)
5. How many acres consist of the Oakville Indian Mounds Park? (116)

LESSON 1 - INTRODUCTION / PRE-TEST

SIXTH GRADE

SAT Reading Objective: COMPREHENSION

Objective: After the teacher directs this lesson, sixth grade Indian students will be able to relate to the information learned from the lesson and identify the following terms: ancestors, Echota, descendants, clan, Dutch, heritage.

Objective Activity: Students will play Hangman or Wheel of Fortune with the terms. Give clues that include the meaning of the word.

STATE STANDARDS Reading Objective:

PG. 52 #2 Read with ease textual, functional, and recreational materials encountered in daily life
- After the teacher introduces himself/herself to the students, the teacher will have the students read aloud from either "Warrior Mountain Folklore" or some other text. The students will discuss the text and answer questions about the text to show comprehension of the material.
  - *What is the name of our tribe? (Echota Cherokee Tribe)*
  - *What is "folklore?" (The traditional beliefs, practices, and legends of a people handed down orally)*

STATE STANDARDS Social Studies Objective:

PG. 54 #1 Extend the development of map and globe skills
- Show the location of the capital (New Echota) in GA, the State of Alabama, and the path traveled during the Trail of Tears on a world map.
- Show Lawrence County and Oakville on the Alabama map.
  - *Where is the Indian education office located? (Oakville)*

Review Questions

1. What was the 1968 Act that recognized Indian people in Alabama? (Civil Rights Act)
2. What year was the Indian Education Program started? (1986)
3. What is folklore? (traditional beliefs, practices, and legends of a people handed down orally)
4. Where is the Indian education office located? (Oakville)
5. What year was the Oakville office opened? (1995)

LESSON 1 - INTRODUCTION / PRE-TEST

SEVENTH GRADE

SAT Reading Objective: LISTENING SKILLS

Objective: After the teacher directs this lesson, seventh grade Indian students will gain a better understanding about the Indian education program and their Indian heritage

Objective Activity: The teacher will review the lesson and ask questions. In your own words, explain to me what an ancestor is. What mixed ancestry are most students in Lawrence County? Why do you think you are in Indian education? Why do you think it was illegal to say you were an Indian during 1840 to 1968?

STATE STANDARDS Reading Objective:

PG. 58 #11   Refine general listening behaviors
- After the teacher directs the lesson; the students will be able to retell the content in their own words and answer questions related to the lesson.
  - *What mixed ancestry are most students in Lawrence County? (Celtic and Indian)*

STATE STANDARDS Social Studies Objective:

Online Alex #6   Describe how people organize economic systems for the production and consumptions of goods and services to address the basic economic questions of which goods and services will be produced, how they will be produced, and who will consume them
- Explain economic concepts of historical and current development in local contexts-Lawrence County and Alabama.
  - *Why do you think you are in Indian education? (you have Indian ancestors)*

Review Questions
1. What year was the Indian Education Program started? (1986)
2. What years was it illegal to be an Indian in the State of Alabama? (1840-1968)
3. What allowed people the right to be able to say they were Indian again? (Civil Rights Act of 1968)
4. In 1991, 26 acres with two ancient Indian mounds was purchased to become what park? (Oakville Indian Mounds Park)
5. What year was the Echota Cherokee Tribe started? (1980)

LESSON 2 – FAMILY HISTORY AND ANCESTRY

Today, we are going to talk about our ancestors. Do you know what an ancestor is? Your ancestors are your direct family members who are older than you. For example: your parents, your grandparents, their parents and on and on. So, somewhere down the line you have an Indian ancestor, and we want to teach you about how your Indian ancestors lived.

Most Lawrence County Indian students are of mixed ancestry of Celtic and Indian. The Celtic (Kel'Tic') people are Irish, Scotch, Welsh, and/or Scots-Irish. The Indian people are mostly Cherokee, Creek, or Chickasaw. Celtic people are fair complected, blue eyes, red or blonde hair, and sometimes have little spots called freckles. Indian people are olive complected, black eyes, and black hair. Indians in Alabama also mixed to some degree with African descendants. Anytime a question of race is asked, you should identify yourself as Indian. Be proud to claim your Indian ancestry, but also claim your other heritage, since we are all mixed. Mixed Indian people are referred to as "metis" (me'te') which means American Indian mixed with European especially French in Canada. It is important to understand that most of our ancestors are of mixed or metis ancestry. The word metis (pronounced as me'ta' or me'ti') means people of mixed European and American Indian ancestry.

As already discussed, most of our Indian students belong to the Echota Cherokee Tribe and is the reason they are allowed to attend Indian education classes. Most of our students are of mixed ancestry, usually Celtic and Indian. Celtic is a person of Irish, Scotch, Scotch-Irish, or Welsh ancestry and Indian is usually Cherokee, Creek, or Chickasaw.

Many people may question the fact that you are Indian. Some of our features do not meet their expectations of what an "Indian" looks like. Since most of our Indian students are of mixed Celtic origin, we are not supposed to look like full bloods. We have a unique culture here in Lawrence County like no other in the world; therefore, be proud you are a mixed or metis Indian person. Being Indian is not based on what you look like. Television and movies have given society a false view of Indian people. All Indian people do not have dark skin, black eyes, and black hair. A great number of Indian people do but not all.

Look around the room at each other. How many of you have blue eyes? How about freckles? How about red or blond hair? Even though these are Celtic features, never deny your true Indian heritage. One of the most feared Cherokee Warriors of the Appalachian frontier was the half-brother of Sequoyah, Robert Benge, also known as The Bench, or The Benge. Bob Benge was red headed, blue eyed, fair complected, and spoke perfect English.

It is important to understand that most of our ancestors were of mixed ancestry. As the southern portion of the United States became inhabited with Celtic people, intermarriage became common with the Indian races; therefore, the majority of our students are Celtic Indians.

By 1800, two of the three major tribes in Alabama were controlled by ½ Celtic and ½ Indian leaders. John Watts, Jr. was ½ Celtic (Scotch) and ½ Cherokee. Levi and George Colbert were ½ Celtic (Scotch) and ½ Chickasaw. Alexander McGillivray was ½ Celtic (Scotch), ¼ Creek, and ¼ French. Robert (Bob) Benge was the son of Scots trader John Benge and Wurteh Watts, who was ½ Cherokee and ½ Scotch; therefore, Bob Benge was ¼ Cherokee and ¾ Scotch. The Governor of Virginia presented a rifle for his red scalp.

Chickasaw mixed bloods lived at Breed Camp and guided pack trains through North Alabama to the Chickasaw Towns on the Tombigbee.

During the 1600s, Celtic people came into the Lawrence County area as traders for the English merchants in Old Charles Town, SC. They followed Indian trails and roads. These Celtic people were Irish, Scotch, Welsh, Cornish, or Scots-Irish descent. Many Celtic men married these young, beautiful Indian women. In the 1700s, many more Celtic men married Indian maidens and made their home here. The

LESSON 2 – FAMILY HISTORY AND ANCESTRY

Chickasaws were the first to form communities of mixed ancestry. One such town was known as McIntoshville in northeastern Mississippi and another was known as **Breed Town** on the Coosa River in Alabama.

In 1729, James Logan Colbert, Scotch, married three Chickasaw wives who bore him many children. Over the years, mixed-blood settlements separated themselves more and more from primitive full bloods. By the 1800s, the mixed-bloods had completely taken over management of Chickasaw tribal affairs.

John Melton, Irish, came into Lawrence County in the 1780s with the Cherokee Indians. He married a Cherokee woman. Melton had several children by his Indian wife, most of whom married white people. The Cherokee Indian Town of Melton's Bluff was named after John Melton. The town was located between Mallard Creek and Spring Creek on the south bank of the Tennessee River in Lawrence County, Alabama.

Since you are enrolled in Indian education, you or your parents are members of an Indian tribe. Most of you are members of the ***Echota Cherokee Tribe of Alabama***, which has thousands of members in Alabama and in other states. Just think, you are a member of an Indian tribe, which has thousands of members. If you are an Echota Cherokee, you are also a member of the Blue Clan, since you live in Lawrence County. There are seven clans of the Echota Cherokee.

Most of our Indian students are members of the Echota Cherokee Tribe of Alabama; however, your Indian heritage may come from other tribes. To be a card carrying tribal member, most tribes require at least 1/32 American Indian blood. In 1980, a new tribe called the Echota Cherokee Tribe of Alabama was formed by people of Cherokee Indian heritage who lived in North Alabama that had migrated out of northwestern Georgia near the Cherokee capital of New Echota; thus, Echota Cherokees.

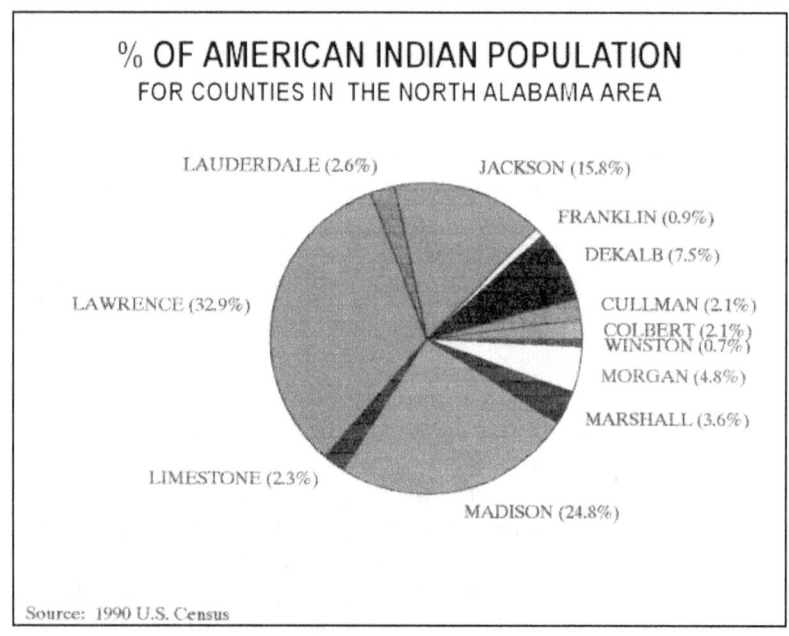

The Echota Cherokee Tribe is the largest and most active tribe in Alabama today. It has thousands of members in Alabama and surrounding states. According to the 1990 Census, Lawrence County has the highest population of Echota Indian people in Alabama with 6.7% claiming Indian heritage. In the 2000 Census, Lawrence County had the second highest Indian population with 5.2% claiming Indian heritage. The vast majority of Indians in Lawrence County is Echota Cherokee.

The Cherokee Indian people recognize the number "seven" as sacred because of the seven clans and the seven directions it represents. The seven clans of the original Cherokee were: Bird, Wolf, Deer, Paint, Long Hair, Wild Potato, and Blue. Out of these, the Blue Clan represents Lawrence, Walker, and Winston Counties. Therefore, if you are an Echota Cherokee from Lawrence County, your clan is the Blue Clan. The seven directions of the Cherokee are East, North, West, South, Up, Down, and from within you as the center (where ever you are) because you are the center of your universe, and only you can decide your eventual destiny. The direction you choose is your sacred direction from life to death. Only you can walk in your shoes down your path of life.

As children of mixed ancestry grew older, they were told of their Indian ancestors, but were not allowed to claim their rightful heritage. Since Indian removal, the degree of Indian blood of Lawrence County's people has steadily diminished and will continue to do so throughout future generations. With the passage of Section 2 through 7 of the Civil Right Act of 1968, it became legal to be Indian and live in Alabama. Many Indian descendants of mixed ancestry began to seek and reclaim their Indian heritage, but for many it was too late. In 1972, the Indian Education Act passed the U.S. Congress. In 1980, the Echota Cherokee Tribe was organized. In 1986, we began Lawrence County Schools' Indian Education Program. In 1995, we moved to the Oakville Indian Mounds Education Center.

LESSON 2 – FAMILY HISTORY AND ANCESTRY

Presently, about one-fifth (20%) of Lawrence County's children are state recognized Indians of mixed-Celtic ancestry. Lawrence County's Indian children have mostly Cherokee, Chickasaw, or Creek bloodlines. As an Indian person, you have a right to claim your race as Indian and should do so, but never deny any of your other previous ancestors of different ethnic backgrounds.

Remarkable advancement of the Cherokee as a people came about largely through the mixing with Celtic families of Irish, Welsh, Scotch, Scots-Irish, and Cornish. During the Indian Removal, mixed-blood inhabitants remained in North Alabama because they were married to whites or were able to identify themselves with white ancestry. They sometimes called themselves Black Dutch or Black Irish in order to remain in the land they loved.

Fearing not only for their personal property but also their lives, the remaining Indian people in Lawrence County denied their Indian race and held to white man's ways. As the times changed, both their Indian culture and Celtic culture blended in with the general population. Both cultures became assimilated into the general lifestyle of the North Alabama area.

LESSON 2 – FAMILY HISTORY AND ANCESTRY

KINDERGARTEN

DIBELS Reading Objective: **INITIAL SOUND FLUENCY**

Objective: After the teacher directs this lesson, Kindergarten Indian students will develop initial sound fluency by recognizing letters and sounding out the names of the letters.

Objective Activity: Write words on the board and let students sound out the initial sound. (Ex: ancestors, family, parents, Indian, Celtic, Irish, and Echota) The teacher will show pictures, objects, and drawings on the board and have students identify initial sounds of the things they see.

STATE STANDARDS Reading Objective:

PG. 14 #9 Begin to use pictures and text to gain meaning from written material.
- Ask students to imagine what they think their ancestors might have looked like. This helps them create mental images while you are teaching. Make sure the students identify the initial sound in **a**ncestors.
- Ask students questions about their Indian ancestor. Ask them if they got their Indian blood from their mother, father, or both parents. This allows their peers to ask those questions as well as the teacher. Allow the students time to identify the initial sounds in the words: **I**ndian, **m**other, **f**ather, and **p**arents.
  - *Do you think your ancestors looked more like the Celtic people or Native Americans?*

STATE STANDARDS Social Studies Objective:

PG. 15 #34 Develop an awareness of the uniqueness of individuals.
- Have students look around the room at one another and see what is unique about each other.
- Have students describe their similarities (ex: Mary has blue eyes like Joe)
  - *What is the same about you that is the same as the person sitting next to you?*

PG. 15 #35 Develop an awareness of how people are the same and yet different
- Teacher can explain Indian and Celtic traits about each individual student aloud to the whole class.
  - *How are you the same?*
  - *How are you different?*

Review Questions

1. How many clans make up the Echota Cherokee Tribe? (seven)
2. What is an ancestor? (parent, grandparent, etc.)
3. Which clan are the Echota Cherokee Indians living in Lawrence County a part of? (Blue)
4. What are the Indian traits? (black hair, black eyes, dark skin)
5. A Celtic person is: (Irish, Scotch, Scots-Irish, or Welsh)

LESSON 2 – FAMILY HISTORY AND ANCESTRY

FIRST GRADE

DIBELS Reading Objective: PHONICS

Objective: After the teacher directs this lesson, first grade Indian students will develop an understanding of certain letter sounds by naming letters derived from words within the text and identifying the sounds of those particular letters.

Objective Activity: The teacher will write terms on the board. Students will then identify each letter in the term. Next, the teacher will ask them what sound that letter makes. Finally, the teacher will ask the students to pronounce the entire word. (Ex: ancestors, Indian, parents, people, and olive)

STATE STANDARDS Reading Objective:

PG. 17 #4   Demonstrate understanding of letter sound relationships
- Throughout the lesson, the teacher will write terms on board and have students identify each letter and make a sound out of the letter. The teacher will then ask him/her to blend sounds together and pronounce entire word. (Ex: Indian, Echota)
  - *Most of our people are mixed with Indian and _____? (Celtic)*

STATE STANDARDS Social Studies Objective:

PG. 18 #3   Extend initial ability to locate new information
- Show location of Alabama on the United States map.
- Show location of Lawrence County on the state map.
- Point out the southern part of the United States (where Celtic lived)
  - *Did Celtic people live in the southern or northern part of the United States? (southern)*

Review Questions
1. To what Indian tribe do most of you or your parents belong? (Echota Cherokee Tribe)
2. Who was the Cherokee Indian town, Melton's Bluff, named after? (John Melton)
3. Who was one of the most feared, red headed, Cherokee warriors? (Bob Benge)
4. Which direction means "within you" or "wherever you are?" (north or center)
5. Celtic families sometimes called themselves what? (Black Dutch or Black Irish)

LESSON 2 – FAMILY HISTORY AND ANCESTRY

SECOND GRADE

DIBELS Reading Objective: NONSENSE WORD FLUENCY

Objective: After the teacher directs this lesson, second grade Indian students will know new words and have the ability to detect understandable words from the text by the usage of nonsense words.

Objective Activity: The teacher will write the nonsense words on the board that are related to the lesson. (Ex: marents-parents, treek-creek, etc.) Then the teacher will ask for the word from the lesson that corresponds to the nonsense word and stating the sentence that the understandable word originates. Also, new words will be written on the board and reviewed with students.

STATE STANDARDS Reading Objective:

PG. 23 #2   Demonstrate the ability to use decoding skills to blend sounds and form words
- The teacher will talk about family history and ancestry. He/she will choose some vocabulary words such as: history, children, and ancestor, etc. and write them on the board. The teacher will use them correctly in a sentence and ask students if the word was used correctly. Use all of them correctly and then throw in some incorrect ways to use the words. (Ex: <u>correct</u>-History is created everyday, <u>incorrect</u>-I'm going to eat history for supper.)
- *What are the two ethnic groups that form our mixed ancestry? (Indian and Celtic)*

PG. 26 #14   Exhibit expanded vocabulary and sentence awareness
- The teacher will explain Celtic and Indian traits and show examples of them using students in the room. Celtic traits and Indian traits will also be written on the board as vocabulary words. Once the students have learned the words have them respond to questions to check for understanding.
- *Name a Celtic trait. (red or blonde hair, blue or green eyes, fair skin, freckles)*
- *Name an Indian trait. (dark hair, dark eyes, and skin)*

STATE STANDARDS Social Studies Objective:

PG. 23 #3   Develop the ability to locate new information and to express understanding of this information in various classroom project
- After talking about ancestry and Celtic and Indian traits, have the students draw a person with Celtic traits and draw a picture of a person with Indian traits. This will be done as a classroom project to illustrate understanding of the new concepts learned.
- *What did Bob Benge look like? (red hair, blue eyes, fair skin, and freckles)*

Review Questions
1. What is the name of the tribe that most of our Indian students are members? (Echota Cherokee Tribe of Alabama)
2. Which Celtic man married three Chickasaw wives? (James Logan Colbert)
3. What number is sacred to our Indian ancestors? (seven)
4. What clan are you a member of? (Blue)
5. What are the seven directions? (east, north, west, south, up, down, center [within you] - your path in life)

LESSON 2 – FAMILY HISTORY AND ANCESTRY

THIRD GRADE

DIBELS Reading Objective: INTERPRETING READING MATERIALS

Objective: After the teacher directs this lesson, third grade Indian students will be able to discuss and identify the difference in family members that are culturally relevant to the lesson.

Objective Activity: The teacher will discuss with students about their own ancestors and how you distinguish direct ancestors from other family members. This will lead to oral discussion about each student's ancestors. (Ex: write what students call their ancestors—great-grandparents, grandparents--on the board) Have each student do the family tree step by step.

STATE STANDARDS Reading Objective:

PG. 33 #12   Apply strategies of a skillful listener
- While the teacher is directing a lesson, he/she should be certain that the students are focusing on the speaker. Ask students questions to make sure they are focusing on the main idea of the lesson.
  - *Our mixed ancestry is made up of Indian and _____? (Celtic)*

PG. 33 #14   Develop an understanding of cultural similarities
- Discuss with the students how the characteristics of our ancestors are similar to ours today. Tell them to look around the room and see.
  - *List the characteristics of the Celtic and Indian people. (Celtic-blonde hair, blue eyes, freckles, Indian-dark hair, dark eyes, dark complexion)*

STATE STANDARDS Social Studies Objective:

PG. 30 #4   Describe the natural environment of North America
- Discuss with the students the various rivers and the trails/paths used by our early ancestors. (Ex: Coosa River, Tennessee River, Spring Creek, Mallard Creek)
  - *What number was sacred to the Cherokee? (seven)*

Review Questions
1. What is the name of the most abundant Celtic group? (Scotch, Irish, Scotch-Irish, Cornish, and/or Welsh)
2. What are the seven clans? (Bird, Wolf, Deer, Paint, Long Hair, Wild Potato, and Blue)
3. What was the name of the town named after John Melton? (Melton's Bluff)
4. Did the Civil Rights Act of 1968 make it legal or illegal for Indians to claim their heritage and live in Alabama? (legal)
5. Name one ½ Celtic and ½ Indian leader during the 1800s. (John Watts Jr.)

LESSON 2 – FAMILY HISTORY AND ANCESTRY

FOURTH GRADE

<u>SAT</u> Reading Objective: VOCABULARY

Objective: After the teacher directs this lesson, fourth grade Indian students will be able to gain meaning of vocabulary words from the text. (Terms: remarkable, advancement, influence, removal, denied, diminished, heritage, recognize, sacred, universe, destiny, population, ancestry, origin, culture, Warrior, intermarriage, and communities)

Objective Activity: Utilizing word games (*Hangman, Jeopardy, and Wheel of Fortune*), Indian students will participate by identifying and recognizing important terms found in this lesson.

<u>STATE STANDARDS</u> Reading Objective:

PG. 38 #4   Demonstrate literal understanding of print material (Identify important details)
- As the teacher directs the lesson, check for literal understanding by asking questions to the students.
  - *We are of mixed ancestry of Celtic and _____? (Indian)*

<u>STATE STANDARDS</u> Social Studies Objective:

PG. 36 #10   Describe aspects of the lives of historic Indians of Alabama
- The teacher will direct the lesson, the class will discuss the mixed ancestry of Levi and George Colbert.
  - *Levi and George Colbert were ½ Celtic and ½ _____? (Chickasaw)*

<u>Review Questions</u>

1. What is the largest tribe in Alabama today? (Echota Cherokee Tribe of Alabama)
2. Explain why mixed-blood inhabitants (Celtic and Indian) called themselves Black Dutch or black Irish during the Indian removal. (Because they feared losing their personal property, belongings, and lives.)
3. In order to be an Echota Cherokee tribal member, a person must have at least what amount of Indian blood? (1/32)
4. What was Bob Benge's real name? (Robert Benge)
5. Who was the most feared Celtic Cherokee Warrior? (Bob Benge)

LESSON 2 – FAMILY HISTORY AND ANCESTRY

FIFTH GRADE

SAT Reading Objective: VOCABULARY

Objective: After the teacher directs this lesson, fifth grade Indian students will be able to gain meaning of the vocabulary words from the text. (Terms: intermarriage, heritage, settlement, etc.)

Objective Activity: Write the vocabulary words and definitions on the board and let individuals match the correct answer. You could also have several fill-in-the-blank questions.

STATE STANDARDS Reading Objective:

PG. 44 #1   Use a wide range of strategies to interpret, evaluate, appreciate, and construct meaning from print materials
- The teacher will have incorrect sentences written on the board for the students to correct using the vocabulary terms.

STATE STANDARDS Social Studies Objective:

PG. 46 #7   Analyze the different cultures of Native American groups by geographic regions
- The teacher will direct the lesson about family history and ancestry. Explaining to the students their occupations, trading patterns, tools and weapons. How are they different and similar today? Explain to the class about the different clans.
  - *What is the Cherokee Indian people's sacred number? (seven)*
  - *What clan represents Lawrence County? (Blue)*

Review Questions

1. What are some traits of a Celtic Indian? (blonde to red hair, green or blue eyes, fair skin, and freckles)
2. Name the law passed in 1968 that allowed Indians to claim their heritage and live in Alabama? (Civil Rights Act of 1968)
3. Identify the tribe that most of the American Indians in Lawrence County are descendants of. (Cherokee)
4. According to the 2000 Census, did Lawrence County have the second or fifth highest Indian population? (second)
5. What tribe was the first to form communities of mixed ancestry? (Chickasaw)

LESSON 2 – FAMILY HISTORY AND ANCESTRY

SIXTH GRADE

SAT Reading Objective: LISTENING SKILLS

Objective: After the teacher directs this lesson, sixth grade Indian students will gain a better understanding of our Cherokee ancestors.

Objective Activity: Students read the lesson aloud and explain in their own words various characteristics of the Lawrence County Indian people.

STATE STANDARDS Reading Objective:

PG. 53 #12   Develop general listening behaviors for different purposes and situations
- After the teacher directs the lesson, every student should be able to retell the information discussed throughout the lesson in their own words and answer teacher or student generated questions.
  - *What are the characteristics of Celtic and Indian descendents? (Celtic/light skin, blue eyes, blonde hair, freckles – Indian/dark skin, dark eyes, dark hair)*

STATE STANDARDS Social Studies Objective:

PG. 54 #1   Extend the development of map and globe skills
- After showing an Alabama map, students will show the location of historic Alabama tribes that include Chickasaw, Cherokee, and Creek.
  - *What three historic tribes claimed Lawrence County as home? (Chickasaw, Cherokee, and Creek)*

Review Questions

1. Today, what tribe has thousands of members in Alabama? (Echota Cherokee Tribe)
2. Most tribes require at least how much Indian blood in order to be a member: (1/32)
3. What law was passed that made it legal to be an Indian in Alabama? (Civil Rights Act of 1968)
4. What is the approximate percentage of Lawrence County's students that are state recognized Indians of mixed Celtic ancestry? (20%)
5. What county has the largest population of Indian people according to the 1990 U.S. Census? (Lawrence County)

LESSON 2 – FAMILY HISTORY AND ANCESTRY

SEVENTH GRADE

SAT Reading Objective: LITERARY ELEMENTS

Objective: After the teacher directs this lesson, seventh grade Indian students will listen to cultural literary works and be able to identify main idea, summarize the text and give significant details about Cherokee history.

Objective Activity: The teacher will have students to read the lesson aloud and then ask questions. Ask students to identify a specific Celtic and Indian trait and give an example of someone who can be traced back to this area that is Celtic or Indian.

STATE STANDARDS Reading Objective:

PG. 58 #7   Appreciate the characteristics, literary elements, and cultural influences of literary works representative of various eras
- After the teacher directs the lesson, the students will have an assignment of going home and interviewing their grandparents or older aunts and uncles about their family history. Then the following week the students will come back and tell the teacher and students what they learned.
    - *Name the Celtic traits: (blonde or fair complected, blue eyes, red or blonde hair, freckles)*
    - *Name the Indian traits: (olive complected, black eyes, black hair)*

STATE STANDARDS Social Studies Objective:

Online Alex #6   Describe how people organize economic systems for the production, and consumption of goods and services to address the basic economic questions of which goods and services will be produced, how they will be produced, and who will consume them.

Review Questions

1. What is the combination of Lawrence County student's mixed ancestry? (Celtic and Indian)
2. Which three counties represent the Blue Clan? (Lawrence, Winston, and Walker)
3. In Lawrence County, most of the Indian people are from what three tribes? (Cherokee, Creek, and Chickasaw)
4. Indians in Alabama are mixed to some degree with what other race? (African descendants)
5. Which tribe first formed towns of mixed ancestry? (Chickasaw)

LESSON 3 – ECHOTA CHEROKEE TRIBE OF ALABAMA

Most of our Indian students are members of the Echota Cherokee Tribe of Alabama, which represents Lawrence County; however, your Indian heritage may come from other tribes. To be a card carrying tribal member, the Echota Cherokee Tribe of Alabama requires at least 1/32 American Indian. In 1980, the Echota Cherokee Tribe of Alabama was formed by people of Cherokee Indian heritage who lived in North Alabama. Lawrence County Schools' Indian Education Program began in 1986 with some 600 Echota Cherokee children enrolled in the program. The Echota Cherokee Tribe of Alabama is recognized by the State of Alabama; therefore, if this is your tribe, you are a state recognized Indian.

The Echota Cherokee Tribe is the largest and most active tribe in Alabama today. It has thousands of members in Alabama and surrounding states. According to the 1990 Census, Lawrence County had the highest population of Indian people in Alabama with 6.7% claiming Indian heritage. In the 2000 Census, Lawrence County had the second highest Indian population in Alabama with 5.2% claiming Indian heritage. If you are a card carrying tribal member, you should always count yourself as Indian on the U.S. Census which is taken every 10 years.

The Cherokee Indian people recognize the number seven as sacred because of the seven clans and the seven directions it represents. The seven clans of the original Cherokee were: Bird, Wolf, Deer, Paint, Long Hair, Wild Potato, and Blue. Out of these, the Blue Clan represents Lawrence, Walker, and Winston Counties. Therefore, if you are an Echota Cherokee from Lawrence County, your clan is the Blue Clan. The seven directions of the Cherokee are East (Red), North (Blue), West (Black), South (White), Up (Yellow), Down (Green), and from within you as the center (where ever you are) because you are the center of your universe and only you can decide your eventual destiny.

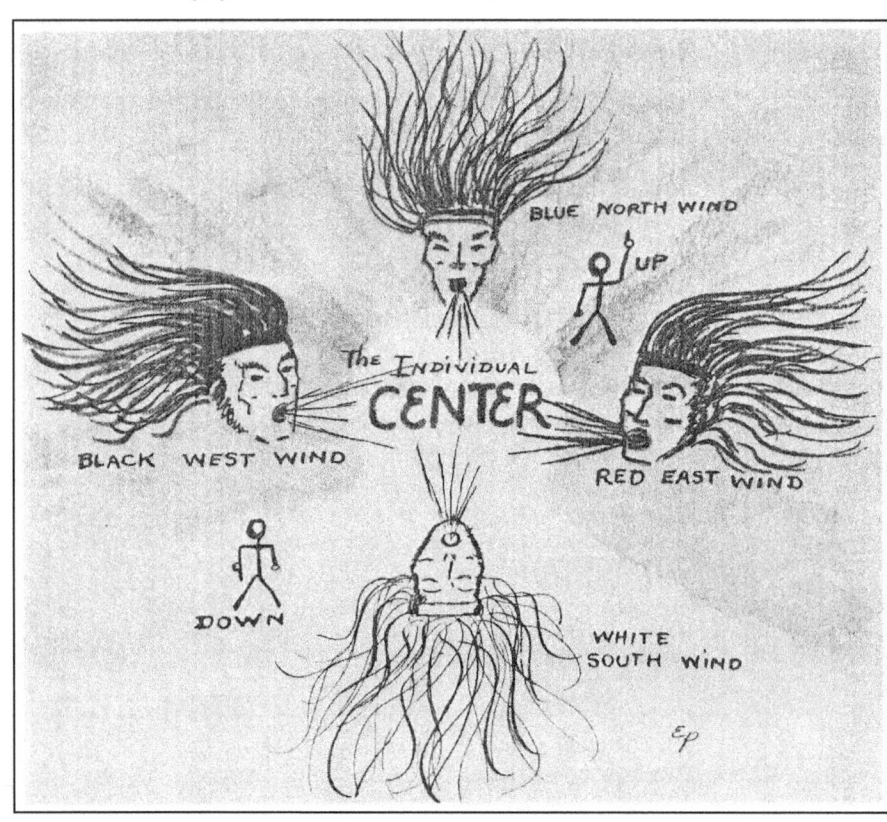

Cherokee Directions

Most of our Indian students are members of the Echota Cherokee Tribe and is the reason you are allowed to attend Indian education classes. It is very important to realize that we are people of mixed ancestry, usually Celtic and Indian. Anytime a question of race is brought up or asked, you should identify yourself as Indian and identify your tribe. Be proud to claim your Indian ancestry, but also be proud of your other lineage and other ethnic backgrounds.

The word Echota was originally derived from the over-hill town of our Cherokee Indian ancestors known as Chota. Chota was located on the Little Tennessee River in Monroe County of East Tennessee. Chota was the capital of the Cherokee Nation until white settlers forced the Cherokees south and west into southeast Tennessee, northwest Georgia, and northeast Alabama. By 1800, all the Cherokees were forced out of the valley of the Little Tennessee River which they had called home for hundreds of years. The capital of the Cherokees was moved into northwest Georgia and was called New Echota. Since most of our Indian people were descendants of the Cherokees who lived in Cherokee County that comprised the northwestern quarter of Georgia, our tribe chose the name of the Cherokee capital of New Echota; thus, the Echota Cherokee Tribe of Alabama was organized.

LESSON 3 – ECHOTA CHEROKEE TRIBE OF ALABAMA

Map of Chota on the Little Tennessee River

The United Cherokee Tribe of Alabama was organized on June 14, 1978, at Daleville, Alabama. B. J. Faulkner was elected principal chief, and Thomas McCloski was elected vice-principal chief. A council of nine people was formed, and the Secretary and Treasurer positions were filled.

In 1978, Chief Faulkner opposed the development plans for an industrial park near Northport that would disturb a 1,000-year-old Indian village site and burial ground. In January of 1980, he sought the reburial of 3,000 Indians along the route to be flooded by the Tennessee - Tombigbee Waterway. In 1980, disenchanted members of the United Cherokee Tribe of Alabama formed a new tribe called Echota Cherokee Tribe, Inc.

Joseph "Two Eagles" Stewart was elected principal chief, and Letter of Incorporation was filed in Shelby County and their seal was registered. The tribe filed for and received non-profit status and clans were organized over the State. A newsletter, *Smoke Signals*, was mailed to members. Regular monthly meetings were held at the Alabaster Community Center. The governing body of the tribe, consisting of tribal council members, elected officers, principal chief and vice-principal chief, was set in to serve a four-year term. (Cromer, 1984)

The tribe has a land fund established for the purpose of purchasing land to build a Cherokee meeting ground and museum. Tribal members are active in voter registration drives around the state. The tribe, represented by the principal chief, is a member of the Alabama Indian Affairs Commission and the National Congress of American Indian (Cromer, 1984). Explain Echota is a tribe we are affiliated with (show shield or picture of symbol of the Cherokee). The vast majority of our Indian students are members of the Echota Cherokee Tribe of Alabama.

LESSON 3 – ECHOTA CHEROKEE TRIBE OF ALABAMA

Today, the Echota Cherokee Tribe of Alabama has their office on tribal land just south of Falkville, Alabama. The tribe is affiliated with several Indian education programs in Madison County, DeKalb County, Jackson County, and Lawrence County. These counties comprised historic Cherokee lands in the Tennessee Valley. Lawrence County Schools' Indian Education Program has been affiliated with the Echota Cherokee Tribe of Alabama since 1986, which is the year our program began.

One of the most common characteristics of the true Warrior Mountains Celtic Indian people that are members of the Echota Cherokee Tribe, is the direct line of descent from the Chickasaw, Cherokee or Creek originating around the 1830s just prior to the Great Removal. Another common occurrence was the intermarriage within family units, where cousins married cousins, sisters of one family married brothers of another family, two different families intermarried over several years, and children from the same mother and different fathers took the mother's last name. One would be amazed at the number of people having the same great-grandparents on two sides of their family. An original Warrior Mountain Celtic-Indian, who is at least a quarter blood Indian, will many times have the same great-grandparents on more than one side of the family.

Another common thread is the migration of their Celtic ancestors from the Carolinas, to Georgia or Tennessee, and then into Alabama. Intermarriage between Celtic and Indian people most often occurred in the Carolinas, East Tennessee, North Georgia, and Northeast Alabama, which made up the Cherokee Nation until 1838.

Indian students enjoy friendship dance at annual Multicultural Indian Event

The remnants of the Warrior Mountain Celtic Indian mixed-bloods (who are members of the Echota Cherokee Tribe of Alabama) survive in Lawrence County under common family names. Today, the most common occurrence of surnames of Indian children in Lawrence County Schools are: Alexander, Black, Blankenship, Borden, Bradford, Dutton, England, Gillespie, Green(e), Hill, Hood, Jackson, Johnson, Jones, Kerby, Kelsoe, LouAllen, Owens, Parker, Riddle, Rutherford, Smith, Terry, Walker, White, and many other family names not as prevalent.

LESSON 3 – ECHOTA CHEROKEE TRIBE OF ALABAMA

KINDERGARTEN

DIBELS Reading Objective: PHONICS INSTRUCTION

Objective: After the teacher directs this lesson, Kindergarten Indian students will recognize phonemes (sounds) and graphemes (letters) in the selected terms that are related to the text and/or short story.

Objective Activity: Ask students to identify the letter that matches the sounds of each letter in the words: bird, wolf, deer, paint, seven, etc.

STATE STANDARDS Reading Objective:

PG. 14 #6 Demonstrate an initial understanding of letter sound relationships
- Take words from the lesson such as Cherokee, Tribe, Indian, Alabama, etc.
- Write the words on the board using capital letters.
- Let the students sound out each individual letter and then say the word together at the end.
  - *In the word Indian, what sound does the letter "I" make? (short i sound)*

PG. 14 #9 Begin to use pictures and text to gain meaning from written material
- Show students a picture of the Cherokee council house. Use different colored construction paper to place individual clan names on separate pages. Under the name paste a picture of something that represents that clan. For example, use blue construction paper to describe the Blue Clan place "Blue Clan" at the top of the page.
  - *Hold up the "Blue Clan" picture and ask what clan is represented? (Blue Clan)*

PG 15 #14 Demonstrate an interest in an enjoyment of literature in a variety of forms, context, and media
- Read the book "If you lived with the Cherokee", or material from any other book. Make sure students listen carefully so that they identify with what was discussed in the lesson. After the book is read conduct a whole class discussion about the similarities.
  - *What is the name of the river where Cherokees make their homes? (Tennessee River)*

STATE STANDARDS Social Studies Objective:

PG. 11 #1 Develop initial map and globe skills
- Explain cardinal directions using a map, pointing them out individually.
  - *What are the four cardinal directions? (North, South, East, West)*

PG. 15 #36 Build an understanding of different cultures through the exploration of holidays, customs, and traditions
- After discussing clans, sing the "Clan song" using the tune of "1 little, 2 little, 3 little Indian."
  - *Everybody sing the "Clan Song" one more time.*

Review Questions

1. Echota Cherokee Indian students in Lawrence County are members of which clan? (Blue)
2. What number was sacred to the early Indians? (seven)
3. What tribe is the largest and most active today? (The Echota Cherokee Tribe)
4. Where is the capital, New Echota, located? (Georgia)
5. According to the 2000 Census, what county has the second highest Indian population? (Lawrence Co.)

LESSON 3 – ECHOTA CHEROKEE TRIBE OF ALABAMA

FIRST GRADE

DIBELS Reading Objective: LETTER NAMING FLUENCY

Objective: After the teacher directs this lesson, first grade Indian students will gain the ability to pronounce and recognize letters while using flashcards, board, objects, or other visual aids.

Objective Activity: Use alphabet flashcards or other visual aids and present a letter (any letter) to one individual student. If that student identifies the correct letter and is able to pronounce the sound of that particular letter they gain the opportunity to participate in the bean toss game. Then go to the next student giving each child a chance to play.

STATE STANDARDS Reading Objective:

PG. 17 #4 Demonstrate understanding of letter sound relationships
- Throughout the lesson, the teacher will write the words on the board. He/she will have a student to recognize each letter, blend the sounds together, and pronounce the entire word. (Ex: BLUE, CLAN, SEVEN, ECHOTA)
  ∾ *What is your clan in Lawrence County? (Blue)*

STATE STANDARDS Social Studies Objective:

PG. 18 #3 Extend initial ability to locate new information
- Locate Lawrence and Winston Counties on the Alabama map.
- Locate Alabama on the state map.
- Show the four cardinal directions on the map. (North, South. East, West)
  ∾ *What counties does the blue clan represent? (Lawrence, Winston, and Walker)*
  ∾ *The Echota Cherokee Tribe is located in what state? (Alabama)*

Review Questions

1. What is the name of the river in Lawrence County that our Cherokee ancestors lived near? (Tennessee)
2. What are the seven clans of the Cherokee? (Bird, Wolf, Deer, Paint, Blue, Wild Potato, Long Hair)
3. What are the seven directions of the Cherokee? (north, south, east, west, up, down, center)
4. What clan represents Lawrence and Winston Counties? (Blue)
5. A person with mixed ancestry is part Celtic and what? (Indian)

LESSON 3 – ECHOTA CHEROKEE TRIBE OF ALABAMA

SECOND GRADE

DIBELS Reading Objective: TEXT COMPREHENSION

Objective: After the teacher directs this lesson, second grade Indian students will be able to relate to the information learned from an orally read text. The students will also read selected sentences aloud and be asked various questions to ensure their understanding.

Objective Activity: The teacher will read text from lesson. Then the teacher will ask comprehension questions that come directly from the orally read text. Play the game *Who Wants to be a Millionaire* and allow students to decode the answer using this format: What is one of the seven clans of the Cherokee? a) <u>bird</u> b) dog c) red d) clay. Place the students on teams and allow one point for that team if they answer correctly. Students will read selected sentences from the lesson aloud and tell in their own words what they read.

STATE STANDARDS Reading Objective:

PG. 25 #10   Read orally with accuracy, fluency, and comprehension
- Throughout the lesson, the teacher will write the vocabulary words on the board. He/she will have a student to identify each word and its correct definition, population, heritage, and ancestry.
  - *What tribe are most of our Indian student's members of? (Echota Cherokee Tribe)*

STATE STANDARDS Social Studies Objective:

PG.22 #1   Develop map and globe skills appropriate to develop mental level and grade level
- The teacher will discuss the number seven and how important that number is to the Echota Cherokee. Then the teacher will discuss the seven directions locating the four cardinal directions on the "Cherokee clans and sacred symbols compass" handout. (in activity book)
- Have a class discussion of our Indian heritage.
  - *The Echota Cherokee Tribe is recognized by what state? (Alabama)*

PG. 25 #21   Develop a sense of history through the examination of family history
- Have students draw a family tree and list family members.
- Have a class discussion of our Indian heritage.
  - *What number is sacred to the Cherokee? (seven)*

Review Questions
1. What is the name of the Cherokee capital located in Georgia? (New Echota)
2. Why are you allowed to come to Indian Education? (you, your parents, or your grandparents are members of the Echota Cherokee Tribe)
3. What is the largest tribe in Alabama today? (Echota Cherokee Tribe)
4. What clan are you a member of? (Blue)
5. What do Celtic people look like? (red or blonde hair, green or blue eyes, and fair skin and freckles)

LESSON 3 – ECHOTA CHEROKEE TRIBE OF ALABAMA

THIRD GRADE

DIBELS Reading Objective: COMPREHENSION

Objective: After the teacher directs this lesson, third grade Indian students will be able to apply, recognize, and better understand the Echota Cherokee Tribe of Alabama.

Objective Activity: The students will color a picture of the Echota Cherokee symbol and glue it on a square piece of construction paper. The teacher will illuminate the student's work and use yarn to piece the squares together and create a quilt to hang in the classroom..

STATE STANDARDS Reading Objective:

PG. 32 #8   Read grade level texts aloud and silently with fluency and comprehension
- After the teacher directs the lesson, have the students read sections of the lesson aloud making sure the class comprehends and speaks fluent.
  - *Did our Native American ancestors believe/practice intermarriage? (yes, they married family members)*

STATE STANDARDS Social Studies Objective:

PG. 30 #5   Environment and Society
- The teacher will direct the lesson explaining part of the Echota Cherokee Tribe. The class will then discuss how we (the Echota) are similar to the other tribes such as clothing, food, housing, etc.
  - *The Echota Cherokee Tribe is the largest and most active tribe in what state? (Alabama)*

Review Questions

1. What tribe represents most of Lawrence County Indian people? (Echota Cherokee)
2. Where is the office of the Echota Cherokee Tribe of Alabama located? (Oakville)
3. What is the name of your clan? (Blue)
4. What year did the Indian Education Program of Lawrence County begin? (1986)
5. Where is the capital of the Cherokees located? (New Echota, GA)

LESSON 3 – ECHOTA CHEROKEE TRIBE OF ALABAMA

FOURTH GRADE

SAT Reading Objective: COMPREHENSION

Objective: After the teacher directs this lesson, fourth grade Indian students will be able to interpret and demonstrate an understanding of the Echota Cherokee Tribe of Alabama.

Objective Activity: After students read paragraphs aloud from the lesson, the teacher will ask questions about what the student read.

STATE STANDARDS Reading Objective:

PG. 38 #4   Demonstrate literal understanding of print material
- As the teacher directs the lesson, he/she will check for literal understanding by asking questions to the students. Have the students split into two groups and whoever is the first to write the correct answer on the board will score a point for their team.
  - *What tribe are you a member of? (Echota Cherokee Tribe)*

STATE STANDARDS Social Studies Objective:

PG. 22 #1   Extend the development of map and globe skills
- The teacher will direct the lesson and will talk about the tribe being the largest in Alabama today.
- Have a student locate Lawrence County; New Echota, GA; and the Tennessee River on the map.
- Have teacher to point out where North Alabama is on the map.
- Show where Winston and Walker County is (Blue Clan)
- Talk about four cardinal directions on the map and point out compass rose map.
  - *Identify the seven directions of the Cherokee and the colors that represent each: (east-red, north-blue, west-black, south-white, up-yellow, down-green, center-X)*

Review Questions

1. What year was the Echota Cherokee Tribe formed? (1980)
2. When did the Lawrence County Indian Education Program begin? (1986)
3. What number is considered sacred to the Cherokee? (seven)
4. What is mixed ancestry? (a mixture of two or more different blood lines)
5. What is the name of the seven clans? (Bird, Wolf, Deer, Paint, Long Hair, Wild Potato, and Blue)

LESSON 3 – ECHOTA CHEROKEE TRIBE OF ALABAMA

FIFTH GRADE

<u>SAT</u> Reading Objective: COMPREHENSION

Objective: After the teacher directs this lesson, fifth grade Indian students will be able to relate to the information learned from the lesson and answer various questions to ensure comprehension.

Objective Activity: Direct students to stand and point to the seven directions and verbally identify the seven clans.

<u>STATE STANDARDS</u> Reading Objective:

PG. 45 #5   Interpret passages in print material
- The students will identify the main idea of this lesson and summarize it using their own words.
  - *What is the largest and most active tribe in Alabama? (Echota Cherokee Tribe)*

<u>STATE STANDARDS</u> Social Studies Objective:

PG. 46 #7   Analyze the different cultures of Native American groups by geographic regions
- After the teacher directs a lesson, the class will have a group discussion about the similarities and the differences of our ancestors and the people today.
  - *What are the seven directions of the Cherokee? (north, south, east, west, up, down, within yourself)*
  - *Which of those directions are still used today? (4)*

Review Questions

1. What was the Cherokee's most sacred number? (seven)
2. List the seven directions: (north, south, east, west, up, down, within yourself)
3. What counties represent the blue clan of the Echota Cherokee Tribe? (Winston, Lawrence, and Walker)
4. What is the name of the capital in Georgia? (New Echota)
5. What is a U.S. census? (an official count of the population carried out in set intervals, usually done every ten years, by the United States)

LESSON 3 – ECHOTA CHEROKEE TRIBE OF ALABAMA

SIXTH GRADE

SAT Reading Objective: LITERARY ELEMENTS

Objective: After the teacher directs this lesson, sixth grade Indian students will be able to construct and interpret meaning and appreciate literary elements in the lesson.

Objective Activity: The teacher will have students to participate in reading the lesson aloud. Afterwards, each student will identify the main idea of the lesson, and summarize those important details in their own words.

STATE STANDARDS Reading Objective:

PG. 52 #1 Interpret and construct meaning by applying appropriate strategies to materials across the curriculum
- Allow each student to make a prediction about who started Echota Cherokee Tribe, how it got started, and what part of Alabama is the tribe located, etc. After the lesson, have students go back and decide whether or not their prediction was right.
  - *Where is Oakville located? (Danville)*

STATE STANDARDS Social Studies Objective:

PG. 54 #1 Extend the development of map and globe skills
- Show the students a map of where the Echota Cherokee Tribe of Alabama is located in the north western part of Alabama, south eastern part of Lawrence County.
- Ask students to located Lawrence County.
- Ask students to locate the Tennessee River.
- Point out North Alabama on the map.
- Show where Winston County is located.
- Talk about the four cardinal directions and point out the compass rose on the map.
  - *The Echota Cherokee Tribe of Alabama represents most of what county? (Lawrence)*

Review Questions

1. The Echota Cherokee tribe is recognized by: (state)
2. What is the largest and most active tribe in Alabama? (Echota Cherokee Tribe)
3. Where does the word Echota come from? (derived from the over-hill town of our Cherokee Indian ancestors known as Chota)
4. What does intermarriage mean? (marriage between members of the same people, clan, or other kinship group)
5. How many Indians had to be reburied along the route of the Tennessee-Tombigbee Waterway? (3000)

LESSON 3 – ECHOTA CHEROKEE TRIBE OF ALABAMA

SEVENTH GRADE

SAT Reading Objective: LITERARY GENRES

Objective: After the teacher directs this lesson, seventh grade Indian students will be able to identify geographic and culturally diverse terms used in literary genres.

Objective Activity: After the teacher reviews the lesson, students must identify words while playing *Hangman, Jeopardy,* or *Wheel of Fortune*.

STATE STANDARDS Reading Objective:

PG. 57 #5 Recognize various forms of literature according to characteristics
- After the teacher directs the lesson, the students will summarize the information discussed throughout the lesson in their own words and answer questions.
  - How much American Indian must you be to be in the Echota Cherokee Tribe? (1/32)

STATE STANDARDS Social Studies Objective:

Online Alex #11 Describe examples of conflict, cooperation and interdependence of groups, societies, and notions, using past and current events
- After the teacher directs the lesson, the students will discuss the cooperation of many groups for the Echota Cherokee Tribe to form.
  - What county has the highest population of Indian people in Alabama? (Lawrence)

Review Questions

1. Where was the first Cherokee capital in Georgia? (Chota)
2. What is the Cherokees sacred number? (seven)
3. What are the seven directions? (north, south, east, west, up, down, within yourself)
4. What form of government recognizes the Echota Cherokee Tribe? (state)
5. Name the three other counties that also have Indian education programs affiliated with the Echota Cherokee Tribe: (Madison County, Dekalb County, Jackson County)

LESSON 4 – PERIODS OF PREHISTORIC INDIANS

Prehistoric Periods

Paleo Indians 10,000 B.C.-8,000 B.C. - The oldest group of people or the first known group to live in Alabama were called Paleo Indians because "Paleo" means "early" or "earliest." Paleo people were hunters.

- Cave dwellers
- Meat eaters
- Lived and traveled in small bands
- Hunted ice age animals
- Spear points long and narrow with fluted sides
- More Paleo points found in Alabama than in western states
- Pleistocene overkill
- Lived on Tennessee River Valley of Lawrence County

Archaic Indians 8,000 B.C.-1,000 B.C. - The next group of people was called Archaic because that is a term commonly used to describe an early stage in the development of a civilization. Archaic Indian people were hunters and gatherers of wild food.

- Semi-permanent settlements
    a) Rivers during summer
    b) Caves, bluff shelters, and mountainous areas during winter
- Meat eaters and gatherers
- Foods: mussels (shell mounds), deer, acorns, and nuts
- Form of religion (burial of dead)
- Atlatl important weapon (throwing spears)
- Made soapstone and sandstone bowls
- First pottery made from clay
- Hides used as clothing
- Used hunting dogs
- Lived all over Lawrence County

Woodland Indians 1,000 B.C.-1,000 A.D. - The third group is called Woodland simply because that group lived in the eastern woodland section of North America. Woodland Indian people were hunters and gatherers, and they also built burial mounds, made pottery, and to a small degree practiced agriculture.

- Lived in more permanent settlements
- Improved pottery
- Began hunting with bow and arrow
- Meat eaters, gatherers, and farmers
- Grew and stored many vegetables
- Began elaborate religious customs
- Mound building, Copena
- Most abundant points found in Lawrence County

Mississippian Indians 1,000 A.D.-1540 A.D. - The fourth group of people or the last prehistoric group to live in Alabama were called Mississippian because archaeologists first identified its culture along the Mississippi Valley. Mississippian Indian people built platform mounds as bases for the buildings of their priests and rulers, made a distinctive kind of pottery, and, for food, depended heavily on agriculture. It was the Mississippian Indians that Desoto found when he came to Alabama in 1540.

- Permanent towns, fortified settlements and religious centers
- Fine pottery
- Excellent farmers---potatoes, corn, squash and beans
- Bow and arrow became very important weapon
- Small game hunted: deer, raccoons, turkeys, beavers, pigeons, opossums, mussels
- Muscle Shoals in Lawrence County on the Tennessee River extremely important

LESSON 4 – PERIODS OF PREHISTORIC INDIANS

Paleo - Our early Indian people lived during a period called "Paleo." About 12,000 years ago, Indian people and their families lived here in Lawrence County, Alabama, but they lived differently than we live today. They could not go to the grocery store for food or to the mall for clothes.

QUESTION: Where do you think our early ancestors got their food? (animals, berries, roots). Where do you think they got their clothes? (animal hides and woven plant fibers).

Beringa migration into America

After a group of Indian people had lived in the same place for a while, they soon had to move because they had hunted all the animals around and they had eaten all the berries and roots; therefore, they had to move to look for more. What did they look for? (animals, nuts, berries, roots, and other foods). The early Paleo Indian people were called *nomads* because they *moved* around searching for food and animals. They came from a continent called Asia into North America. (Show this on a world globe if you have it). They followed the animals across a huge land bridge called the Bering Strait and known as Beringa.

Today, we are going to learn about our very first Indian ancestors. They were called Paleo Indians. They came across the land bridge called the Beringa, in the Bering Strait, from Asia. (show map of Bering Strait) They were nomadic which meant they wandered from place to place searching for food. Around 12,000 years ago, Paleo Indians were living along the Tennessee River in Lawrence County, Alabama; therefore, our Indian ancestors have been here for thousands of years.

The Paleo Indians were hunters and meat eaters. They hunted large ice age animals like the mammoth, mastodons, wild horses, and saber-toothed tigers. (show pictures) The Paleo Indians usually traveled and lived in small bands. Typical bands were usually 20 to 25 people who were generally related. Both men and women within the band had particular jobs. Men were responsible for the preparation of tools and weapons as well as hunting. Women were responsible for childcare, crafts and cooking. The Paleo Indians did not live in permanent settlements, but were nomadic and moved from camp to camp. They located their camps where they could find plenty of animals--their primary source of food. Their shelters were natural caves and bluffs as well as lean-tos and skin tents.

The Paleo Indians were known as big game hunters. They hunted large animals by driving them into traps, over cliffs, or into enclosures. When hunting the animals, someone would distract the animal while others attacked with their weapons. Because of a lack of transportation and refrigeration, the animal had to be butchered on the spot and often eaten raw.

The early Indian people hunted the big wooly mammoths by driving them into traps and over big cliffs. After the animal was killed the Indians would cut the animal up with stone knives and eat it immediately. Some of it they would carry back to the village and use different parts to make clothes from animal skins. The brains were used to tan the hides and smooth the animal skins to make them soft.

After the animal was killed, all parts of the animal were used. Brains and bone marrow of the animals were eaten. Brains were used in curing the skins for use as clothing. Although the Paleo Indians are commonly recognized as big game hunters, they also included a wide variety of plants and animal foods in their diet.

LESSON 4 – PERIODS OF PREHISTORIC INDIANS

The spear was probably the Indians' first weapon--The spear was made from flint rock that had been sharpened and attached to a long handle. Also, the early Indians hunted wild horses, camels, giant ground sloths, saber tooth tigers, rhinoceroses, deer, and bison; some of which are not extinct.

The Paleo Indians made spears from flint. They used a rock to chip off pieces until they formed a sharp point. The flakes of the flint stones were often ready to use as knives. Scrapers were made from the flakes by chipping a steep cutting edge. The scraper was used to prepare the hides. The scraper was also used in working wood, bone, and antler. Gravers were tools of small flakes with one or more finely chipped, delicate points. The gravers may have been used for engraving. Gravers were also used for punching small holes in skins to allow them to be laced together to make clothing and other equipment. The Paleo Indians had no known stone or ceramic

Mammoth and Mastodon

vessels, but probably had baskets. Much evidence of Paleo habitation is found all across Lawrence County, especially along the Tennessee River.

Now close your eyes and imagine how life was back then. Imagine how you would look, what you would eat, how you would live. Can someone tell me what this place would look like? Now, keep in mind that we are talking about a very long time ago. Have a picture of Bering Strait when they open their eyes and tell about Beringa.

Explain that our ancient Indian people walked from Asia to North America by a land bridge known as Beringa or the Bering Strait, which was covered with ice. If you went there today you would have to travel by water. Most of the land at that time was covered with ice. It was called the Ice Age.

The Paleo Indian people had to move each time the herd did. As you know, some of these animals are now extinct. How do you think they killed such large animals? Can anyone name a prehistoric animal? (mastodon, mammoth, saber-tooth tiger, bison, deer, rhinos--show picture of wooly mammoth and saber-tooth tiger)Think about what they had to hunt with. (wait for response--spear). Before you do anything, you need to have a plan and a leader. Some members of the tribe could distract the animals while others would kill it. Another way would be to drive them over cliffs, drive them into traps or into enclosed areas.

Remember, we are talking about a long time ago. Sometimes, when the animals were killed, they were eaten on the spot because they didn't have refrigerators to keep the food from ruining and most often the meat was eaten raw. The meat they could carry and store was dried or placed in cool caves, underground, or in the cold spring water. Although, we are talking about a pre-historic time and a pre-historic people, they were very intelligent. They knew how to use every part of the animal. (Example: brains and bone marrow to eat). How many of you have eaten pig brains? Brains were also used to cure and tan skins, which were used for clothes. They also used bones for different tools and weapons.

For each time period that we cover, a different style of projectile point was used. Who knows what a point is? (stone projectile point-on end of spear or arrow. Show picture of Paleo points. Describe Paleo points--they have curved indentation on top that have been ground down smooth. They have a fluted depression, which is a groove out of the middle point.)

Spear points were made by the flaking process. First, a flat surface was made, using a hammerstone, they knocked off the edge of the flat stone making a long and narrow flake, which was razor sharp. Some of the tools made with flint included scrapers, knives, and gravers. Paleo Indians had no stone or ceramic vessels such as bowls, but they probably had baskets. Clovis points were named for a town called Clovis, New Mexico. These points have also been found throughout the Tennessee Valley. Based on Clovis projectile points, Paleo people were living and roaming the area of Lawrence County, Alabama, some 12,000 years ago.

LESSON 4 – PERIODS OF PREHISTORIC INDIANS

Archaic - The last section we studied was the Paleo period. Today, we're studying about the Archaic period and how they were different. Based on artifacts, archaic people lived throughout Lawrence County. They were the people who discarded mussel shells that eventually formed shell middens along the Tennessee River. The Archaic Indian people were forced to adapt to new and changing food sources, because the climate was beginning to get warmer. Although, the Archaic Indians continued to hunt, they no longer hunted large ice age animals.

Near the end of the Ice Age as the earth began to warm, the Archaic people no longer wandered over great areas. The mammoths and mastodons began to die out. The Archaic people were forced to change their eating habits. They became more of a gatherer than just a hunter. Now they found plants with nuts, seeds, roots, and berries, and they found other meats of animals such as deer, rabbit, mussel, fish, and squirrel. Deer became the most important game animal to Indians in this area. Chestnuts and acorns became important food sources for Archaic people as well as the deer. Chestnuts and acorns could be ground to make flour.

The change from eating Ice Age animals to smaller animals, nuts, and berries led to new methods of preparing the food. Nuts were cracked and picked, seeds and roots were ground, and even bark was beaten for fiber to eat. There are many more methods that were used in the production of foods.

Stone boiling was used to cook their food. They would heat rocks in the fire and then move them to a pit, which was lined with rawhide and filled with water. A soup mixture in this rawhide bowl was boiled by the hot rocks. Mortar, pestles, stone bowls, and nutting stones were some utensils used.

The largest animals hunted by the Archaic Indians were elk and bear. Other game was deer, rabbits, squirrel, wild turkey, fish, mussels, and grub worms. Also, they became gatherers of nuts, berries, seeds, roots, and other plants. Acorns became an important food, since they learned a method of making flour from the nuts. In addition, the American chestnut, which was destroyed by blight in the 1930s, was a major source of food to our Southeastern Indian ancestors and those that lived in Lawrence County. The American chestnut was the largest nut-producing tree in North America.

During the Archaic period, mussels became an important source of food. Does anyone know what a mussel is? (show mussel shell if you have one) Mussels are found on riverbanks inside a shell. The Mussel Shoals starting in Lawrence County near Mallard Creek in the Tennessee River contained more mussels than any place in the world. This area consisted of four major Mussel Shoals: Elk River Shoals; Big Mussel Shoals; Little Mussel Shoals; and Colbert Shoals. Two other Shoals that could be navigated were Bee Tree Shoals and Waterloo Shoals.

ARCHAIC HUNTER WITH SPEAR-THROWER

Discarded mussel shells formed a midden along with flood deposits which created shell mounds. Shell mounds became incidental burial spots. The mounds were created by centuries of activity. Many large shell mounds bigger than football fields were flooded by Wilson and Wheeler Dams on the Tennessee River.

Archaic people possessed a common burial ground. They were very careful with their dead implying emotions of strong affections as well as a belief in an afterlife. Sometime personal possessions were placed with the body (weapons, tools, or even bodies of their dogs). The graves were small circular pits dug into the shell mounds. The graves must have been marked in some way since they were seldom disturbed until later digging. These circular pits were usually sealed with a mud putty mixture consisting of clay, ash, and shell.

Archaic Indians developed new weapons, tools and utensils. The atlatl, a throwing lever, was probably the greatest improvement in weaponry. This allowed the hunter to throw a spear with greater force from a farther distance (show picture of atlatl). The atlatl, or throwing stick, was made from wood, 2-3 ft. long with a deer bone or antler hook. There was a rock placed in the center of the throwing stick called a banner stone. The banner stone was either fixed or moved freely to give the spear more power. The spear was placed on the throwing stick against the antler hook. A

LESSON 4 – PERIODS OF PREHISTORIC INDIANS

quick flip of the lever gave the spear great power and distance.

The Archaic Indians also found it necessary to develop new weapons, tools and utensils as well as ornaments. One of the great weapon improvements was the Atlatl (At-lat-l). It allowed the hunter of the Archaic period to throw a long distance and with more force. A weight was placed in the middle of the throwing stick to give added power. The hunter held the spear resting on the atlatl and against the notched end; then he lifted the atlatl over his shoulder and with a whip like motion, sent the spear hurtling toward the target.

Archaic Indians had distinct characteristics. They seldom lived to be middle age and most died in their twenties and thirties. In appearance, there were at least two distinct types of Indian.

1. One was broad-headed, broad-faced, squared jaw and had a narrow, high-bridged nose.
2. The other type had a narrower and longer head, a narrow face and was generally less rugged in bone structure.
3. The women had a more jutting jaw than the men and were smaller in size.

Archaic Indian people were probably the first to domesticate dogs. Skeletons of rather large dogs, possibly hunting dogs, have been discovered in burial sites. A need for material not found locally led to increased trade as well as social and religious interaction.

During Archaic time period, we are going to cover 8,000 B.C. to 1,000 B.C.. During each time period, changes occurred in the environment and also in Indian lifestyles. With each passing period, American Indian people became more civilized and settled. The Archaic people settled along the Tennessee River and consumed large quantities of fresh water mussels. The discarded mussel shells eventually formed large shell middens or heaps. These middens or heaps of shells became the first mounds to be built in Lawrence County, Alabama.

There is evidence of religion among Archaic Indians. The medicine man used a tube pipe for curing illness. Burials were accompanied with animals, possessions or ornaments. Burials indicate a form of religion. The Archaic people were the first to domesticate dogs. They felt the medicine man was a direct link to the Great Spirit. Some of the burials of the Archaic people were in shell middens. A shell midden is a mound of shells that have been discarded after eating the mussel. Has anyone ever eaten mussels?

Many of the tools were made from flint as in the Paleo period. Flint tools were used to work antler, bone, and hides. Flint could be sharpened for knives and scrapers. Also, it could be ground into a point to make a drill and a variety of weapon points. Fishnets, spears, traps, and hook and line were used to catch fish. Fishhooks were made from deer toe bones. Traps were made by weaving reeds and oak splints. Nets were made by fibers from plants. To create spears, cane was used with sharpened points.

In the late Archaic period, they began making pottery. For the first time, early man had lightweight waterproof containers to store food and water. With pottery, the Indian people were able to stabilize their food supply and settle in more permanent areas. The grooved ax was developed during the archaic time period from rocks tied to a wooden shaft. These axes were used to drive stakes, chop meat, dress hides, break animal bones for marrow, and chop charcoal from burned trees.

Projectile points during the Archaic period were unique because they were beveled, sharp on one side only, serrated on edges (depression), and notched end.

Woodland - Today, we are learning about a more advanced period of our Indian ancestors. They are known as the Woodland Indian people. It is believed the Middle Woodland Indians, about the time of Jesus Christ, built the Oakville Mounds in Lawrence County.

The third era of prehistoric time is called the Woodland period. It dates from 1,000 B.C. to 1,000 A.D. The Woodland Indians were more advanced and lived in smaller settlements, which were more permanent than those of the Archaic period. Improvement of pottery, led to cooking by boiling. The saving, storing, and sowing of seeds to ensure the next years harvest encouraged the

LESSON 4 – PERIODS OF PREHISTORIC INDIANS

growth of more permanent groups of people. Based on artifacts, the Woodland people were very abundant in the Lawrence County area.

Ample food supply encouraged the growth of people living in towns and hamlets. Hamlets were farming families who shared hunting and gathering grounds. Towns had a market, a religious place, and administrative office. The Woodlands had a more formalized leadership. The local and regional leaders guided religion and settled disputes. In the beginning, leaders earned their leadership. Later, these leadership skills were passed to children.

Early Woodland Indians were farmers, gatherers, and hunters. Farmers grew gourds, beans, potatoes, squash, and corn. Vegetables could be stored or traded; therefore, surplus became possible (surplus means extra). Storing and saving food allowed the people more time for trade, crafts, politics, or religion. Vegetables could be traded or easily stored in clay pots.

Burial customs were important to Woodland Indians. People were often buried with their personal possessions. A warrior was buried with weapons. A farmer was buried with agricultural tools. A woman was buried with household items. The grooved stone axes were replaced with ungrooved ones. Human skulls were one of their most treasured cult symbols.

During Woodland time, dugout canoes were made from yellow poplar or yellow pine. Poplar was more common because termites would not eat the poplar wood. The dugouts enabled Woodland people to travel on water for the first time and increase their trade routes. During the process of making a dugout canoe, the stone axes were used. Dugout canoes were made with a burning and scraping process. First, the tree was selected and clay was packed at the base of the tree. A fire was then started to burn the tree down (show picture of dugout). The ax was used to chip away the charred wood. It was also used to dig out the opening to the canoe (show picture of stone ax). Some of the other tools used during the Woodland period were stone hoes, deer bone scrapers, grindstones, and flaked tools. The bow and arrow gradually replaced the spear as a hunting weapon.

Near their secluded village sites, the Woodland people constructed burial mounds to hold their dead. These relatively small mounds, often conical in shape, were sometimes near a river. Frequently there were two or more such mounds together. The number of burials in a mound varied from one to several dozen. Some were single interments; however, others were multiple burials on the same or different prepared surfaces. Some of the burial mounds were constructed over a period of time and built up in several layers. Occasionally shells, clay, logs, or stone slabs separated the layers or were placed around the individual or mass graves. A prominent feature of this specialized burial custom was the placement of ornaments and tools with the bodies.

The Oakville Indian Mounds in Lawrence County are considered Woodland mounds. Has anyone ever seen these mounds? One of the mounds is a burial mound located at the Oakville site.

The tools and ornaments of the Woodland people were similar to those of the Archaic cultures, but they were more varied and often showed finer workmanship. Their tools included chipped drills, knives, celts, scrapers, axes, and a variety of smaller projectile points. The projectile points made during the Woodland period were stem based and cruder looking (example--Swan Lake or Bakers Creek).

Mississippian - They were a more advanced group, but the Mississippians improved all phases of life. Based on Mississippian artifacts, these people lived throughout Lawrence County but seemed to be most abundant along the creeks and streams. The population increased and towns were larger and more permanent. The Mississippians were also known as the mound builders because all important religious practices were associated with their mounds. The Mississippians were known for their decorated pottery and stone pipes.

LESSON 4 – PERIODS OF PREHISTORIC INDIANS

The last prehistoric time period we will cover is the Mississippian period. The period existed from 1000 A.D. to 1540 A.D. and was unique because of the distinctive form of pottery made with crushed shells and clay. During the Mississippian, the people became much more organized in their government and lifestyle. Houses became permanent structures made from cut saplings and branches. Religious ceremonies were connected with agriculture production. In other words, they had ceremonies for planting and harvesting foods. The Mississippian culture had planned communities. People were living in villages with public buildings, stockades, and plazas. Fortified settlements appeared during this time period. Wooden stockades surrounded the fort and often dry moats were built with thorn hedges placed in these.

Their houses contained only a single room measuring about 16 feet by 16 feet. Cane mats were used to divide the room. The houses had a hearth and sleeping benches that served as sofas. There was a centrally located fireplace to provide warmth in winter and protection from insects in the summer. The houses were formed by placing cut saplings in trenches and pulling over at the top to form a roof. The walls were woven with cut branches, covered with clay, and the roof was covered with grass or bark. The cooking was done outside or in a cooking shed.

Cherokee town of Chota around 1762 (Tellico Archaeology)

The Mississippian people were involved in long distance trade. Fortified settlements appeared during the Mississippian period. What does fortified mean? (Wooden stockades or earthen embankments were built around the village.) The Indian mound at Florence was a fortified village.

Religious ceremonies were very important to the Mississippian Indians. In early times, family members were buried in a shallow hole in the floor of the house with each burial, the floor rose higher. Ceremonial pipes were among the most sacred possessions of a tribe. The pipe was carved from stone and decorated with animals or human figures. The ceremonial pipe was passed around the council and each member took a puff before handing the pipe to the person on his left. The pipe came to be referred to as a peace pipe because they often smoked with former enemies as a peace treaty was made. Another belief relating to the spirit world concerns the black drink. It was brewed like tea from the leaves of the holly plant. The black drink contained large amounts of caffeine and when heated and drunk in large quantities caused vomiting. They believed that by emptying their stomachs, they rid themselves of evil.

LESSON 4 – PERIODS OF PREHISTORIC INDIANS

Indian people considered the land sacred and could not be bought or sold. This idea was difficult for the white man to understand. Indians believed that tobacco was a sacred plant. They believed it was a gift from the spirit world with mystical powers. They smoked to ward off evil spirits. They smoked to curb appetites and cure infection. They smoked before they waged war.

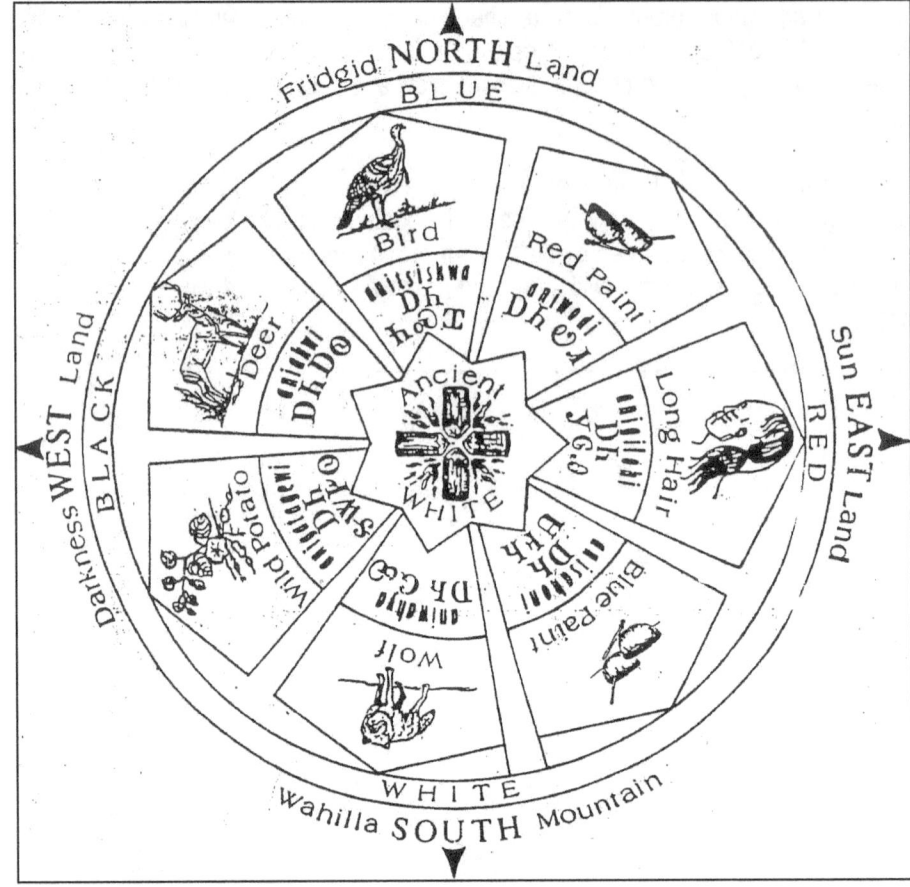

The most important ceremony was the Green Corn Ceremony. The festival was like our Thanksgiving and New Year rolled into one. It was a time to give thanks for a successful harvest, to settle differences, and to begin a new year.

Games were an important part of Indian culture. Indians spent much of their time farming. They grew corn, beans, squash, pumpkins, and sweet potatoes. Art forms were more advanced than that of the previous culture.

Mounds were built around the plaza with some for temples and some for burial. The temples were usually divided into two rooms and contained images of animals or birds on the entrance. One room was for worship and one for burials. The Southern Indians believed the universe was made of three separate but related worlds - the upper world, lower world, and this world.

During ceremonies each of the four directions were recognized.
1. East was associated with the color red, according to the Cherokee doctrine, because it was the direction of the rising sun. East was also associated with the sacred fire, blood, and the color of success.
2. North was the direction of the cold winds of winter and its color was blue (sometimes purple) and it represented trouble and defeat.
3. West was the moon segment and because it was associated with the setting of the sun and the absence of warmth, it was thus associated with the color black, which was the region of the souls and of death itself.
4. South was the direction of the warm winter sun, its color was white, and it was associated with peace and happiness.

Vegetables, wild fruits, nuts, wild animals, and fish were main sources of food. Hunting took second place to farming. Indians grew corn, beans, squash, pumpkins, potatoes, and sweet potatoes. They also gathered nuts, seeds, roots, and fruits and stored them.

The men showed skill in stalking and killing game. Fishing was done with spears and arrows, but most often by dragging seines made of brush fastened together with vines. Seine means to drag the bottom of a lake or pond with a net to get the fish out.

Clothing of the Mississippian was very decorative. Among the Southeastern Indians, young children ran unclothed until their tenth or twelfth birthday. This was accepted in their society just as wearing clothes are expected in our society.

Mississippian religious symbols were engraved, painted and sculptured on shells and dyed cloth. The points during this time period were small and triangular because hunting was second to farming. The bow and arrow were the primary weapons. The Mississippi triangles were the most prevalent point during this time period (show picture of Madison point).

LESSON 4 – PERIODS OF PREHISTORIC INDIANS

KINDERGARTEN

<u>DIBLES</u> Reading Objective: COMPREHENSION

Objective: After the teacher directs this lesson, Kindergarten Indian students will develop an understanding and be able to recognize the difference between prehistoric time periods and how our ancestors once lived.

Objective Activity: Play *Jeopardy* with the students using the information taught in the lesson about all four time periods.

<u>STATE STANDARDS</u> Reading Objective:

PG. 14 #9   Use pictures and text to gain meaning from written materials
- Show pictures of Kinlock Shelter from the Alabama Canyon Book, where the students will understand where the Paleo Indians lived.
- Show pictures of Ice age animals and spear where they will understand what they hunted and what they hunted with. (relate to ice age movie)
  - *Name two ice age animals? (mammoth, sloth, bison)*
  - *What is the name of the animal with the two long teeth that looks like a cat? (saber-tooth tiger)*

PG 15 #17   Exhibit expanded vocabulary and sentence awareness
- Show examples of spear, atlatl, bow and arrow, and blowgun.
  - *Did your Indian ancestors use the bow and arrow to hunt animals? (yes)*
  - *Do people still hunt deer today with Indian weapons? (yes-bow and arrow)*

<u>STATE STANDARDS</u> Social Studies Objective:

PG. 11 #3   Develop initial ability to display information in graphic form
- Use a map to show students where the Tennessee River is located, Lawrence County as well.
  - *Where on this map is the Tennessee River located?(North Alabama)*

PG. 13 #16   Increase awareness of various environments
- Discuss the different homes during all four time periods.
- Discuss farming during Woodland and Mississippian.
  - *Do people still live in caves? (no)*
  - *What was the most important vegetable? (corn)*

PG. 14 #26   Identify human-made and natural-resources
- Why did our ancestors live near the Tennessee River? (Rich soil, supply of H_2O, wood from trees to make canoes and weapons/tools)
  - *Do we still get our water from the river like our Indian ancestors did? (yes)*

PG. 15 #35   Develop an awareness of how people are the same and yet different
- Have a group discussion about how people are the same/different today verses during the four time periods.
  - *What weapon do we still use today to hunt deer with that they used back then? (bow and arrow)*

<u>Review Questions</u>

1. What did the Paleo people live in? (caves)
2. What group used dogs for hunting? (Archaic)
3. What group grew and stored vegetables? (Woodland)
4. What group were excellent farmers? (Mississippian)
5. What group hunted ice age animals? (Paleo)

LESSON 4 – PERIODS OF PREHISTORIC INDIANS

FIRST GRADE

DIBELS Reading Objective: NONSENSE WORD FLUENCY

Objective: After the teacher directs this lesson, first grade Indian students will develop an understanding of family history through learning about the four prehistoric time periods.

Objective Activity: Take words from the text and write them on the board changing the first letter of the word to a nonsense word. Then, orally say the word and ask students if the word sounds right? Finally, have students relate the word to the lesson and explain what letter and sound should be at the beginning of that word. (Ex: dog-bog, hides-bides, people-deople, red-ged)

STATE STANDARDS Reading Objective:

PG. 17 #4   Demonstrate understanding of letter-sound relationships
- After the lesson, the teacher will pick terms from the lesson and write the word on the board. The teacher can write the correct word and nonsense word and let the students determine which one is correct.
  - What was the first prehistoric period? (Paleo)
  - What was the second prehistoric period? (Archaic)

STATE STANDARDS Social Studies Objective:

PG. 18 #3   Extend initial ability to locate new information
- After discussing the Paleo Period, show a map of "Beringa" to the students, so that they see how our Indian ancestors came into America. Also use the globe to show the students the "Bering Strait" and that it is now a body of water.
  - Is the Bering Strait covered with Ice today or is it a body of water? (body of water)

PG. 18 #11   Describe the impact of cultural changes on the locality over time
- After the lesson about the prehistoric time periods, have a discussion with the students about life today as opposed to then. Make a chart on the board and post student responses in "past" and "present."
  - Did our ancestors have a place that they could go to shop for clothes or shoes? (no)

Review Questions

1. Name one ice age animal: (mammoth)
2. Where did the Paleo people live? (cave)
3. What time period used hunting dogs? (Archaic)
4. What time period used the bow and arrow? (Woodland)
5. Which people were excellent farmers? (Mississippian)

LESSON 4 – PERIODS OF PREHISTORIC INDIANS

SECOND GRADE

DIBELS Reading Objective: VOCABULARY

Objective: After the teacher directs this lesson, second grade Indian students will be able to read and identify terms from the text (Example: Paleo, spear, dwellers, Woodland, Archaic, Mississippian).

Objective Activity: The teacher will say the terms and students will repeat them. Next, the teacher will write the terms on the board and the students will say the words out loud as a group.

STATE STANDARDS Reading Objective:

PG. 23 #2 Demonstrate the ability to use decoding skills to blend sound and form words
- The teacher will use the vocabulary words previously learned.
- The teacher will substitute incorrect words in sentences and students will correct the sentence using the correct word. (Ex: They used a bow and arrow during the Paleo period. False it should be spear.)
  - *What weapon did our ancestors use during the Paleo period? (spear)*

PG. 26 #14 Exhibit expanded vocabulary and sentence awareness
- The teacher will conduct a lesson about the four prehistoric periods telling the characteristics of each. Then he/she will ask questions related to the material taught. Vocabulary could include: Paleo, Archaic, Woodland, Mississippian, spear, bow and arrow, etc. Make sure students know each word and how to use them in a sentence. Place the words on the board, point to each one, and have students use words in a sentence.
  - *Name the four prehistoric time periods? (Paleo, Archaic, Woodland, Mississippian)*

STATE STANDARDS Social Studies Objective:

PG. 22 #2 Develop the ability to interpret and display information in graphic form
- After discussing characteristics of each prehistoric period the teacher will discuss forms of living today. Students will compare present-day living to those that lived during the prehistoric time periods. A chart can be written on the board to show the comparison.
  - *The mound at Oakville was built during which time period? (Woodland)*

PG. 25 #22 Compare transportation methods of families now to those used long ago
- After discussion, the teacher will ask students to draw and compare two methods of transportation.
  - *What is one way that our ancestors traveled by water that we still use today? (canoe)*

Review Questions
1. What are two of the four prehistoric time periods? (Paleo, Archaic, Woodland, Mississippian)
2. Which was the most advanced time period? (Mississippian)
3. Name three ice age animals? (saber-tooth tiger, mammoth, mastodon)
4. What did the Archaic Indians hunt with? (atlatl)
5. What did the Woodland Indians hunt with? (bow and arrow)

LESSON 4 – PERIODS OF PREHISTORIC INDIANS

THIRD GRADE

DIBELS Reading Objective: WORD RECOGNITION

Objective: After the teacher directs this lesson, third grade Indian students will be able to identify important vocabulary words associated with the specific time period.

Objective Activity: The students will play hangman using the vocabulary words discussed throughout the lesson and define each word after solving the word.

STATE STANDARDS Reading Objective

PG. 32 #8   Read grade level texts aloud and silently with fluency and comprehension
- The teacher will have the students to take turns reading aloud from the lesson. The student will read the text about the four time periods and discuss the text to show their comprehension of what was read.
  - ∾ *What group of people were cave dwellers? (Paleo)*

PG. 33 #14   Develop an understanding of cultural similarities and differences noted through exposure to multicultural literature
- The teacher will make four columns on the board and label them Paleo, Archaic, Woodland, Mississippian. After the teacher presents the lesson, the students will tell the teacher characteristics of each time period. After the students have listed the different characteristics, the class will notice the similarities and differences between the four periods.
  - ∾ *What were the four time periods of prehistoric Indians? (Paleo, Archaic, Woodland, Mississippian)*

STATE STANDARDS Social Studies Objective:

PG. 31 #9   Compare cultural aspects of selected Native American groups
- After the teacher presents the lesson to the students, the class will recognize the cultural characteristics of each group. Then discuss the cultural traditions of today and how they relate to those of our Native American ancestors.
  - ∾ *The Copena mound was built by our ancestors during what time period? (Woodland)*

Review Questions

1. What custom was considered important to the Woodland Indians? (burial)
2. What animal did Archaic people domesticate? (dog)
3. Name one characteristic about the Paleo Indians? (meat eaters, hunted ice age animals, lived in caves)
4. Who lived in permanent towns? (Mississippian)
5. What is the Green Corn Ceremony? (A time where they gave thanks for a successful harvest to settle differences, and to begin a new year.)

LESSON 4 – PERIODS OF PREHISTORIC INDIANS

FOURTH GRADE

<u>SAT</u> Reading Objective: LITERARY ELEMENTS

Objective: After the teacher directs this lesson, fourth grade Indian students will be able to identify the theme, plot, setting, characters, and point of view of all the prehistoric periods.

Objective Activity: Create a story using the content in this lesson about the pre-historic periods. Then, ask the following questions to check for the students understanding. What is the theme of this story? What is the main idea main idea of this story? Who was this story about? When did it take place? Where did it take place?

<u>STATE STANDARDS</u> Reading Objective:

PG. 37 #1   Use a wide range of strategies to interpret, evaluate, appreciate, and construct meaning from print materials
- What weapon did the early Cherokee have to kill ice age animals? (spear)

PG. 39 #15   Describe cultural similarities/differences
- The teacher will use the big arrowheads to introduce the four periods of prehistoric Indians. After the lesson, the students will discuss the similarities/differences of each time period. The teacher will relate the four time periods to how things still continue to change or improve with time. (Ex: technology, vehicles, schools, clothing, jobs, etc.)
- During what time period did our early ancestors live in caves? (Paleo)

PG. 40 #20   Demonstrate vocabulary growth developed through reading and listening to literature
- After instruction, take class outside to demonstrate tools/weapons. Let each child have the opportunity to experience using tools/weapons in order to gain an appreciation of their early ancestors' way of life. During this hands-on activity, ask each child a question before letting him/her throw weapons. These questions should relate to the lesson and help demonstrate their vocabulary growth. Ex: What was the most important weapon during the Archaic period? (Atlatl) What time period did our ancestors begin farming? (Woodland) When did they hunt ice age animals? (Paleo) What period did everything improve? (Woodland or Mississippian)
1. During the Archaic period, where did they live during the summer (river) and winter? (mountains)

<u>STATE STANDARDS</u> Social Studies Objective:

PG. 34 #1   Expand the development of map and globe skills
- Locate Lawrence County on a state map.
- Locate the Tennessee River.
- Locate the land bridge, Beringa in Bering Strait, from Asia on the globe or map.
2. What kind of bridge did the Paleo Indians cross to get to America? (land bridge)

PG. 35 #7   Identify the major characteristics of prehistoric Indians
- Discuss various characteristics of Paleo, Archaic, Woodland, and Mississippian Indian. (no government to control them/ the economy-hunting, farming)
- Tell the class the time periods of each.
- Explain contributions still used today made by our early Cherokee ancestors. (such as bow and arrow-since Woodland Indians during 1,000 BC-1,000 AD, spear-since Paleo time period during 10,000 BC-8,000 BC, pottery-started making from clay during Archaic period 8,000 BC-1,000 BC)
3. What weapon do most hunters still use today that the Cherokee also used starting during the Woodland time period? (bow and arrow)
4. What county did the Cherokee Indians live in during the four time periods? (Lawrence County, AL)

LESSON 4 – PERIODS OF PREHISTORIC INDIANS

Review Questions

1. What period of early Indians were farmers, gatherers, and hunters? (Mississippian)
2. What does Paleo mean? (early/earliest)
3. Who improved pottery? (Woodland)
4. What period of early Indians were known as mound builders (Explain why)? (Mississippian, all of their important religious practices were associated with their mounds)
5. Who hunted large ice age animals? (Paleo)

LESSON 4 – PERIODS OF PREHISTORIC INDIANS

FIFTH GRADE

SAT Reading Objective: LITERARY ELEMENTS

OBJECTIVE: After the teacher directs this lesson, fifth grade Indian students will identify and analyze the plot, theme, main idea, characters, setting, and point of view.

OBJECTIVE ACTIVITY: Create a story about the prehistoric periods using the information from the lesson and present it to the students. Ask them the following questions to check for comprehension. (*What is the main idea of this story? Who was this story about? What did they do that was of great importance? When did this story take place? How? Why?*)

STATE STANDARDS Reading Objective:

PG. 45 #7   Use literary analysis
- After the teacher directs the lesson, the students will read aloud from "Warrior Mountain Folklore" about the prehistoric Indians. Also, the teacher will have pictures from each time period from encyclopedias showing students the different things.
  - ∾ *What is the second time period? (Archaic)*

STATE STANDARDS Social Studies Objective:

PG. 46 #6   Discuss the progression of culture of the early American people
- The teacher will direct the lesson and discuss with the students the progression of each time period. They will discuss how each time period bettered themselves.
5. *What is the fourth time period? (Mississippian)*
6. *Name something about this time period.*

Review Questions

1. What is one characteristic of the Mississippian people? (permanent towns)
2. Name the four prehistoric time periods? (Paleo, Archaic, Mississippian, Woodland)
3. Who built the Oakville mounds? (Woodland)
4. Who were cave dwellers? (Paleo)
5. Who used hunting dogs? (Archaic)

LESSON 4 – PERIODS OF PREHISTORIC INDIANS

SIXTH GRADE

SAT Reading Objective: PHONETIC PRINCIPLES

Objective: After the teacher directs this lesson, sixth grade Indian students will be able to recognize, understand, and apply different terms discussed in the lesson about the four prehistoric time periods.

Objective Activity: The teacher will allow the students to look up any challenging terms in the dictionary and tell the class what the term means and how it is pronounced. (Ex: elaborate, fortified, dwellers)

STATE STANDARDS Reading Objective:

PG. 52 #4   Demonstrate reading improvement gained through substantial amounts of daily reading
- After the teacher directs the lesson, the students will read aloud from "Trails of the Warrior Mountains" about the prehistoric Indians.
  - What are the four prehistoric time periods? (Paleo, Archaic, Woodland, Mississippian)

STATE STANDARDS Social Studies Objective:

PG. 54 #1   Extend the development of map and globe skills
- The teacher will discuss the directions with the students and show them the compass rose on a map. The teacher will ask the students to stand up and point to each direction.
7. Which direction is north? south? east? west? (have students point to the correct direction)
8. What color goes with west? (black)

Review Questions

1. What style of projectile point was most prevalent during the Mississippian period? (Clovis point)
2. Which group of Indians did Desoto find when he came to Alabama in 1540? (Mississippian)
3. What did the Archaic people live in? (semi-permanent settlements)
4. What group improved pottery? (Woodland)
5. Who had fortified settlements? (Mississippian)

LESSON 4 – PERIODS OF PREHISTORIC INDIANS

SEVENTH GRADE

SAT Reading Objective: VOCABULARY

Objective: After the teacher directs this lesson, seventh grade Indian students will gain an understanding of various terms encountered in the lesson about periods of prehistoric Indians.

Objective Activity: After the teacher reviews this week's lesson, students will be asked questions. During what time period did the Cherokees become excellent farmers? Did the Paleo Indians or Woodland Indians begin using the bow and arrow?

STATE STANDARDS Reading Objective:

PG. 58 #11   Refine general listening behaviors
- After the teacher directs this lesson, the students will gain respect for cultural informational textual materials encountered in the lesson about the four periods of prehistoric Indians. The teacher will ask questions to assure understanding.
  - *Name the prehistoric periods? (Paleo, Archaic, Woodland, Mississippian)*

STATE STANDARDS Social Studies Objective:

Online Alex #9   Identify individual and civic responsibilities
- Ask the students describe the rights, privileges, duties and responsibilities. Explain how each time period is different.
9. *Name some responsibilities of each of the time periods? (Paleo-hunters, Archaic-hunters and gatherer of wild food; Woodland-hunters and gatherers, built burial mounds, made pottery, some agriculture; Mississippian-built platform mounds made distinctive pottery, heavily depended on agriculture)*

Review Questions

1. Name the four prehistoric time periods in order from the oldest? (Paleo, Archaic, Woodland, Mississippian)
2. What group used the atlatl? (Archaic)
3. What group were hunters, gatherers, and farmers? (Woodland)
4. What group used the spear as a weapon? (Paleo)
5. What was the most advanced time period? (Mississippian)

LESSON 5 – LIFESTYLES OF EARLY INDIAN PEOPLE

LESSON 5 – LIFESTYLES OF EARLY INDIAN PEOPLE

There were five Indian tribes of early Lawrence County, Alabama. They were the Yuchi, Creek, Shawnee, Chickasaw, and Cherokee. The Creek, Chickasaw, and Cherokee all lived for a long time in Lawrence County, Alabama. The Cherokees and Chickasaws shared land in our county. The Cherokee and the Chickasaws both lived in the northern part of our state.

Early Cherokee Houses

Indian people were from different tribes but they were a lot alike. Many people think that Indian people just went to war and hunted, but they did much more than that. Every village had big gardens. Men and women both worked in the garden and the food was for everyone in the village. Can anyone tell me what they think our Indian ancestors probably grew? (potatoes, corn, and beans). After working in the gardens, the men and women had different jobs. The men would hunt, build buildings, and make weapons and tools to work with. The women raised children, cooked and made clothing.

How have our Indian people of long ago affected us today? (say names of towns, rivers, and even states--examples: Tuscaloosa, Cherokee, Coosa, Tuscumbia... Show map of state with counties named after Indian names)

Some of the Cherokees that moved into Lawrence County had big farms with lots of livestock. They also planted crops for money such as cotton and corn. The Cherokee Chief Doublehead owned a lot of livestock and had some 30 slaves at the time of his death.

Settlements - Our Cherokee Indian people lived in houses not tipis. They had two types of houses: a summer house-"ge-tsa'di" and a winter house-"asi'." The summer house was like a long shed built from small trees, which they lived in during the hot summer months (show picture). The winter house, also built from logs, had a cone shaped roof. Clay was packed on the outside of the logs to fill in the cracks and keep out the cold air. A fire was built in the center of the room with beds lining the walls.

The Cherokee of Lawrence County lived in farming villages which consisted of either log cabins or plank houses. These Cherokees were living similar to the settlers with houses containing chimneys and fireplaces.

Cherokee Parents - Cherokee fathers were responsible for providing food by hunting and fishing. He also made tools and weapons and helped protect his family and village. The mother tended the garden, cooked, made clothes and crafts, cleaned the house and raised the children. The children were primarily the responsibility of the mother. The mother disciplined the girls and was responsible for their up-bringing. The elders of the village took responsibility for the care and instruction of the boys. Traditionally, boys were disciplined by the oldest uncle of the mother's family, not their father.

The Cherokee mother had more responsibility in the upbringing of the children than the father. Why do you think that the mother was responsible more than the father? (Let students give their opinions.) The father was busy hunting, farming and sometimes defending his village. The mother was at the village cooking and making clothes for the family. Indian girls were disciplined by their mothers and the boys were disciplined by their uncle which was the mother's brother.

LESSON 5 – LIFESTYLES OF EARLY INDIAN PEOPLE

The Cherokee Indians believed that the children were only kin to the mother's family, probably, because the mother gave birth to her children. The woman owned the home. Today, our mothers and fathers are equal in the raising of the family.

When Cherokees moved into Lawrence County, many Cherokee women were married to Celtic traders of Scotch, Irish, or Scots-Irish ancestry. The Celtic men tried to teach the children the ways of the Europeans. Most all of you are descendants of these people.

Cherokee Clan - The clan was a unit of family, kin folks, or relatives and the most important aspect in the life of our Cherokee people. A person belonged to his mother's clan. His only kinsmen were those who could be traced through his mother. The most important and powerful man in a Cherokee's life was his mother's brother. The maternal uncle was responsible for the discipline of his

Cherokee Indian Family

sister's child. The uncle was the one who taught the child to hunt and wage war. The woman owned the dwellings. An ousted husband simply went back to his clan until he remarried. His children remained with his wife.

Since kinship was matrilineal, Cherokee women probably decided the matter of adoption and often had the power to determine the fate of captives. The Beloved Woman, Nancy Ward, saved the life of Mrs. William Bean who was about to be burned at the stake. The Cherokee extended the same privileges to those who married or were adopted into the tribe as those who were born into the tribe.

Mary Hughes eventually married her husband's murderer and refused to leave the tribe even after she was ransomed. Twenty boys captured during the French and Indian War cried and refused to eat when they were returned to their families. Some captives were never adopted into a clan. These people, called the atsi nahsa'i, had no personal or legal protection. Their very existence depended on their master's good will.

Clan membership was essential to one's existence as a human being within the Cherokee society. Since clans were divided into peace or war clans, a Cherokee's clan determined his political alignment and his role in society.

Children's Toys and Games (show handout) - Cherokee girls had dolls made of cornhusks and the boys had other toys like balls and shells. They also had dogs to play with. The children played games. Usually the games helped develop skills that could be used later on: counting and throwing, for example. At the first Thanksgiving feast in 1621, Indian people there taught the settlers their games, and together they raced, wrestled, sang, and danced.

Deer - How many of you have a dad or granddad that likes to hunt? What kind of animals do they hunt? (example: deer, rabbit, raccoons, squirrel, birds) Have any of you ever seen a deer? Where? (zoo, forest) Long ago, our Indian ancestors hunted many different kinds of animals for survival. Deer was their main source of meat and hides (skins). When a Cherokee hunter killed a deer he always asked its spirit for pardon (this was to show honor). During early European settlement, long rifles were used by our metis Indian people to exploit a trade in deer skins. Thirty deer skins could be traded for a new rifle.

LESSON 5 – LIFESTYLES OF EARLY INDIAN PEOPLE

Our Cherokee people not only used the deer for food and clothing, they used all different parts of the deer to make tools and weapons. The points of antlers were used to make wedges to pry things apart, to split wood into thin layers for basket making, and to chip flint arrowheads. Antlers were also used to make garden rakes (show example with deer pictures).

Deer bones were made into scrapers, needles, awls, and fishhooks. Bone scrapers had many uses. Deer jaws could be used to scrape green corn from the cob. This tool was used to take the hair from hides being tanned. Bone needles were made from the ribs. They were large, flat, and curved (show picture). The hole was in the middle. These were used for sewing rush mats. Fine pointed bone awls were used for embroidery stitches and sewing clothing.

Fishhooks were made from round deer bones. First, the bones were sliced with flint knives. Then, the slice was cut into two half-inch circles. Each half was rubbed on sandstone until it was shaped and sharpened. Other fishhooks were made from bone splinters. They were much easier to make than the rounded ones.

Can anyone tell me what glue is used for? (to hold things together). Our Indian folks made glue from boiled deer hooves (show picture-point to hooves). This glue was used to secure sinew. Sinews (or tendons) are the tough fibers that hold a muscle to a bone. The long band of sinew was taken from a deer leg or from the top of the deer's back. It was dried to use as thread. Sinew was used for making moccasins, bowstrings, arrows, and to hold axes to their handles.

Warrior Mountains - We are going to talk about a very special place! A place filled with majestic mountains, peaceful valleys, and very special people. We are going to study Lawrence County, your home. Let's talk about some special features of Lawrence County. We have the Bankhead Forest, also called the Warrior Mountains, which is a national forest. Sometimes we don't stop to think about how lucky we are to have a national forest near our home. The Bankhead Forest serves many purposes for us. Who can name some reasons we go into the mountains? (picnic, fish, hunt, hike, camp, ride horses, swim)

Our Indian ancestors also enjoyed the mountains and their beauty, but more importantly they needed the mountains for their survival. The mountains had natural caves and bluffs that provided shelter for our Indian people. Many prehistoric bluff shelters exist throughout the county, but mainly in the Warrior Mountains. Many sites of prehistoric Indian villages have been found in Lawrence County. Bluff shelters, usually facing a southern direction, were used during winter months. Numerous bluff shelters are located in Bankhead National Forest where the gathering of nuts, fruits, and other foods were practicable. Some of the many bluff shelters in Bankhead National Forest are known as Kinlock, McDougal, and Corral. Petroglyphs (rock drawings) are found on rocks in some shelters. A total of 237 Indian sites were identified in Wheeler Basin. These sites give insight into the times and lifestyles of Indians that once lived in and around the Lawrence County area.

Map of Shoal Town on Big Muscle Shoals

LESSON 5 – LIFESTYLES OF EARLY INDIAN PEOPLE

Muscle Shoals - Many of the early stone tools used by Indian people were chipped and flaked from flint found in Lawrence County at Elk River Shoals and Big Muscle Shoals. The Tennessee River played an important part in providing the things our ancestors needed to survive. The Tennessee River was used as a major transportation route through North Alabama. From the river, the early man could obtain a great variety of plants and animals that were a major source of food. There was also rich soil suitable for farming.

The freshwater mussels found in the shoals were an important food supply for the tribes that settled in this region. This bountiful supply of mussels caused many Indian tribes to settle in this area along the Tennessee River. Large shell mounds or middens have been found along the banks of the Tennessee River. The Paleo Indians and the shell-mound Archaic Indians were among the earliest Indians in Lawrence County. Early Lawrence County Indians were shell-midden people and bluff dwellers. Shell middens were primarily used during the summer months when low water levels made the gathering of mussels easy.

Foods - The foods our Indian ancestors ate are very different from the foods you eat today. Mainly because of the way it was prepared. They did not have grocery stores, microwaves, refrigerators, stoves, electricity, and many more conveniences we have today. Vegetables, wild fruits and nuts, wild animals and fish were their main sources of food. Deer was their main source of meat.

Our Indian ancestors used common food preservation methods. Drying was the most common preservation method. Beans were dried in the pod or shelled. Pumpkins and squash were cut into strips and put in the sun to dry. Meat was dried over the fire, and they also smoked their meats to preserve them.

Indian people spent much of their time farming. They grew corn, beans, squash, melons, pumpkins, and sweet potatoes. Indians made mush, dumplings, hominy, and succotash from corn. Corn was the main food for Indians. Corn could be used in many different ways. The women and girls spent many hours grinding corn. Corn could be parched, boiled, roasted and made into corn cakes. Corn was stored in cribs built of poles about eight feet off the ground. What is one of the foods the Indians gave us that we often eat today? (Potatoes)

Cherokee Plowing With a Steer

Cooking - Cooking was done over fires built having forks of wood driven into the ground, a stick laid across it, and a pot in which meat boiled hung from a stick. The Indians cooked their food in clay pots and they also put pieces of meat on a stick and held it over a fire. Boiling was the most common method of cooking with different foods combined to make a thick stew. Bread and sometimes meat was baked by wrapping the food in cornhusks or leaves and covering it with hot coals.

Historic Farming - By the time the first Cherokees moved into Lawrence County, they were using farming methods adopted from the Europeans. These Cherokees had metal plows, mules, horses, cattle, hogs, sheep, goats, and chickens. Some Cherokees were plantation owners with many slaves. At the time of his death, Doublehead owned some 30 slaves and much livestock.

LESSON 5 – LIFESTYLES OF EARLY INDIAN PEOPLE

KINDERGARTEN

DIBELS Reading Objective: VOCABULARY / LETTER NAMING

Objective: After the teacher directs this lesson, Kindergarten Indian students will verbally identify the main vocabulary terms presented.

Objective Activity: The teacher will write several words on the board from the lesson. Teacher will say each word aloud. With the help of the teacher, students will pronounce the letters in each word. (Ex: home, family, race, and man)

STATE STANDARDS Reading Objective:

PG. 15 #15   Use appropriate listening and speaking behaviors
- Explain to students appropriate listening and speaking behaviors such as: keeping eye contact, speak loudly and clearly, talk slowly.
- Demonstrate talking to another person.
- Have students turn to neighbor and tell something about early Indian people using appropriate listening and speaking skills.
- ∽ *Did Cherokee Indian people live in tipis? (no)*

PG. 15 #17   Exhibit expanded vocabulary and sentence awareness
- Choose five words from the lesson for example: clan-group or family, mussel-shell, blue eye, etc. Tell definition and use in sentence.
- ∽ *What clan are you a member of?(Blue)*

STATE STANDARDS Social Studies Objective:

PG. 13 #16   Increase awareness of various environments
- Show pictures of bluff shelters where early Indian people had their homes.
- Show pictures of summer and winter homes, foods, games, and animals hunted.
- ∽ *What was the main animal our ancestors hunted for food and clothes? (deer)*

PG. 14 #20   Demonstrate the ability to construct models of physical structures in the immediate environment
- Use paper or Popsicle sticks to construct a model of a house.
- ∽ *What were the two kinds of homes of our Cherokee people? (summer and winter)*

Review Questions

1. Who owned the home and was responsible for the children in early Indian time? (women)
2. How many tribes lived in Lawrence County? (five)
3. How many homes did the Cherokee live in? (two)
4. What were the two homes called? (summer and winter)
5. What were early historic homes made from? (logs and planks)

LESSON 5 – LIFESTYLES OF EARLY INDIAN PEOPLE

FIRST GRADE

DIBELS Reading Objective: TEXT COMPREHENSION

Objective: After the teacher directs this lesson, first grade Indian students will use prior knowledge to develop an awareness of the mixed ancestry of our Indian people and use their insights to join into the activity.

Objective Activity: The teacher will read text from the lesson. Then, the teacher will ask comprehension questions that come directly from the orally read text. Play the game "Who wants to be a Millionaire" and allow students to decode the answer using this format: Who was responsible for providing food? (mother, father, children) Place students on teams and allow one point for that team if they answer correctly.

STATE STANDARDS Reading Objective:

PG. 20 #10   Recognize values, beliefs, and interests reflected in literature
- Talk to students about our early Indian ancestors. Be sure that students understand how our ancestors lived and how it is different from today. Use books to show pictures of settlements, clothing, games, etc. This way students have a mental image. Also use books to read about parenting and other cultural aspects of our early Indian ancestors.
  - *What animal did our ancestors make their clothes from? (deer, buckskin)*

PG. 22 #24   Exhibit increased participation in self-expression in a variety of forms
- After discussing lifestyles of early Indian ancestors put students in groups. Have them discuss the homes of our early Indian ancestors and how they are alike/different from the homes we live in today. Open discussion among groups. Teacher should monitor groups to make sure students stay on task.
  - *Name one type of home our early Indian ancestors lived in? (summer or winter)*

STATE STANDARDS Social Studies Objective:

PG. 18 #10   Relate land use in their locality to the physical features of the land
- Discuss how important the Mussel Shoals was to our ancestors and the types of foods that they ate to survive. Also mention how they used soil to farm and how they needed an abundant water supply.
  - *What was our ancestor's important food supply found in rivers? (mussels)*

Review Questions
1. What is another name for Bankhead National Forest? (Black Warrior Mountains)
2. How many different kinds of homes did the Cherokees live in? (two)
3. Name the only job men and women worked together? (gardening)
4. Who was responsible for providing food by hunting and fishing? (father)
5. Who was mainly responsible for raising the children? (mother)

LESSON 5 – LIFESTYLES OF EARLY INDIAN PEOPLE

SECOND GRADE

DIBELS Reading Objective: LISTENING AND COMMMUNICATING

Objective: After the teacher directs this lesson, second grade Indian students will be able to identify and orally communicate the terms listed from the text.

Objective Activity: The teacher will say the word orally and the students will repeat the term. The teacher will write the term on the board. Then the students will say the term as a group. (Terms: Celtic, Irish, uncle, membership, flint, etc.)

STATE STANDARDS Reading Objective:

PG. 25 #10   Read orally with accuracy, fluency, and comprehension
- Students will read about our early Indian ancestors from a resource book. The teacher will monitor student reading to ensure they are correcting their own mistakes. That way the teacher can help students if they have no intention of making corrections on their own.
- *What type of homes did our ancestors live in log cabins or tipis? (log cabins)*

PG. 25 #13   Demonstrate appropriate listening and communicating behaviors
- The teacher will conduct a lesson about early Indian people and their lifestyles. After the lesson, the teacher will ask questions to check for understanding. The teacher will also monitor the students, making sure they are using appropriate oral language behaviors.
- *How many Indian tribes were there in Lawrence County? (5)*

STATE STANDARDS Social Studies Objective:

Pg. 25 #21   Develop a sense of history through the examination of family history
- The teacher will discuss our early ancestors describing the environments in which they lived, their use of water, land, their housing and means of survival. Questions will be asked to check for understanding.
- *What was our Indian ancestors' main source of meat? (deer)*

Pg. 25 #23   Compare occupations of family members now to those family members long ago.
- After the teacher discusses the occupations of our Cherokee ancestors, the class will orally compare past to present family members occupations.
- *Where is the Warrior Mountains/Bankhead Forest located? (Lawrence County)*

Review Questions
1. The elders of the village took responsibility for care and instruction of whom? (boys)
2. Did the Cherokee believe the children were only related to the mother's side of the family or father's family? (mother's)
3. What were the Cherokee dolls made from? (cornhusks or corncobs)
4. What animal was important to the Cherokees? (deer)
5. Name some of the foods important to the Cherokee. (vegetables, wild fruits, nuts, wild animals, and fish)

LESSON 5 – LIFESTYLES OF EARLY INDIAN PEOPLE

THIRD GRADE

DIBELS Reading Objective: ORAL READING FLUENCY

Objective: After the teacher directs this lesson, third grade Indian students will read a Cherokee legend and gain understanding of the lesson.

Objective Activity: The students will orally read a Cherokee legend. After they read the first paragraph, ask students what they think will happen next. The teacher may let each student read a couple of sentences orally, then discuss characters and sequence of events from the story.

STATE STANDARDS Reading Objective:

PG. 32 #8   Read grade level texts aloud and silently with fluency and comprehension

PG. 32 #10   Monitor own reading
- After the teacher directs the lesson, the students will read from the book "Alabama Canyons" about the Warrior Mountains. The teacher will then ask the students questions to check comprehension skills. Also the students will monitor their own reading and adjust their speed accordingly with the teachers help.
  - ∾ *The Warrior Mountains is also called what? (The Bankhead Forest)*

STATE STANDARDS Social Studies Objective:

PG. 30 #6   Compare different groups of Native Americans (food, shelter, clothing)
- After the teacher directs the lesson, the teacher will direct a discussion about different tribes. The teacher will show pictures of the tribes that lived in our county and the other side of tribes that didn't live in our county and compare them.
  - ∾ *What type of homes did our ancestors live in? (summer and winter)*

Review Questions
1. What were fish hooks made from? (deer bones)
2. Who cooked, made clothes, and raised the children? (mother)
3. Identify the father's responsibilities: (hunted, farmed, fought defending his family/village)
4. What were the Cherokee girls dolls made from? (corn husks/corn cob)
5. Name two animals the Cherokee farmed with. (mules, horses, cattle, hogs, sheep, goats, and chickens)

LESSON 5 – LIFESTYLES OF EARLY INDIAN PEOPLE

FOURTH GRADE

<u>SAT</u> Reading Objective: LISTENING SKILLS

Objective: After the teacher directs this lesson, fourth grade Indian students will gain a better understanding about our early ancestors' lifestyle.

Objective Activity: After a review and discussion of this lesson, the teacher will ask students the following questions to check for comprehension. What were the two types of homes our ancestors lived in? (summer and winter) What were early historic homes made from? (logs and plants) etc.

<u>STATE STANDARDS</u> Reading Objective:

PG. 39 #11   Read materials encountered in daily lives
- After the teacher directs the lesson, the students will read material from the lesson.
  - *Name one thing from the lesson we talked about today. (Cherokee homes)*

<u>STATE STANDARDS</u> Social Studies Objective:

PG. 35 #5   Describe the natural environment of Alabama including significant geographical features
- As the teacher directs the lesson, he/she will discuss the Warrior Mountains with the students and all the beautiful places and show the students the Alabama Canyons book for reference as a visual for the students. (Ex: Kinlock Falls, etc.)
  - *Name a bluff shelter in the Warrior Mountains we talked about today. (Kinlock, McDougal, and/or Corral)*

Review Questions

1. What river played an important role in providing things our ancestors in Lawrence County needed to survive? (Tennessee River)
2. Name two of the five tribes. (Yuchi, Creek, Shawnee, Chickasaw, and Cherokee)
3. What did our ancestors' houses look like? (summer/long shed built from small trees, winter/built from logs and a cone shaped roof)
4. Who disciplined the boys? (uncle, mother's brother)
5. Who disciplined the girls? (mother)

LESSON 5 – LIFESTYLES OF EARLY INDIAN PEOPLE

FIFTH GRADE

SAT Reading Objective: GENRES

Objective: After the teacher directs this lesson, fifth grade Indian students will be able to identify geographic and culturally diverse terms used in literary genres.

Objective Activity: After the lesson, play *Wheel of Fortune, Hangman, or Jeopardy* with students. Give clues from the text so that the students can answer the questions.

STATE STANDARDS Reading Objective:

PG. 46 #12   Read a variety of materials and genres encountered in daily lives
- Emphasize that this lesson is made up of nonfiction material
- Describe the different features of the early Indian people such as: parental duties, roles of different members of clans, responsibilities of children, types of homes, etc.
- Explain the diversity in foods that our Indian ancestors used compared to the foods we eat today.
  - *Cherokee girls played with dolls made of what? (cornhusks)*

PG. 46 #13   Apply strategies of a skillful listener
- Read orally text from the lesson and have the students answer questions concerning the text. Be sure the students have an extensive comprehension of the material in the lesson.
  - *Who was responsible for the upbringing of the children in the Cherokee tribe? (mother)*

STATE STANDARDS Social Studies Objective:

PG. 46 #6   Discuss the progression of culture of the early American people
- Have the students color the picture of a deer. While the students are coloring, explain the importance of deer to the early Indian people.
  - *Name three crops that the Cherokees grew. (corn, beans, squash, pumpkin)*

Review Questions

1. What were found in the shoals that were food supply to early Indians? (fresh water mussels)
2. Identify several important characteristics of the mother: (owned the dwellings, probably decided the matter of adoption, often had power to determine the fate of captives, cooked, cleaned, raised children, made crafts and clothes, etc.)
3. What were needles made from? (deer bones)
4. How did our ancestors make glue? (boiled deer hooves)
5. How many deer skins were traded for a new rifle? (30)

LESSON 5 – LIFESTYLES OF EARLY INDIAN PEOPLE

SIXTH GRADE

SAT Reading Objective: VOCABULARY

Objective: After the teacher directs this lesson, sixth grade Indian students will be able to recognize and identify different culturally diverse geographical terms and vocabulary terms listed from the lesson on lifestyles of early Indian people. (Terms: mussels, agriculture, petroglyphs, plantation, etc.)

Objective Activity: After students read the lesson aloud, they will pick several words and explain what they mean. The students will play *Jeopardy, Hangman, or Wheel of Fortune* and include these new vocabulary words.

STATE STANDARDS Reading Objective:

PG. 53 #12   Develop general listening behaviors for different purposes and situations
- Use lesson text to explain the cultural diversity. Have the students discuss the geography and the way of life of the early Indian people.
- Ask questions to check for understanding of the material.
  - Who did the first Cherokees in Lawrence County adopt farming methods from? *(Europeans)*

STATE STANDARDS Social Studies Objective:

PG. 54 #1   Extend the development of map and globe skills
- Use a map of Alabama to show the different locations of the early Indian people. Show the different locations and explain the geography of the areas.
  - Why were Indian villages located near creeks or rivers? *(food, water, etc.)*

Review Questions
1. Kinlock in the Bankhead National Forest is known as a : (bluff shelter)
2. What part of the deer was used to make a rake? (deer antlers)
3. What material was used to make moccasins and bowstrings? (sinew or tendons-tough fiber that hold a muscle to a bone)
4. What did our Indian ancestors cook their food in? (clay pots)
5. Who owned 30 slaves? (Doublehead)

LESSON 5 – LIFESTYLES OF EARLY INDIAN PEOPLE

SEVENTH GRADE

SAT Reading Objective: COMPREHENSION

Objective: After the teacher directs this lesson, seventh grade Indian students will respond and apply basic principles of how information is properly conveyed in visual, auditory or orally presented materials, in order to ensure comprehension on the lesson being taught.

Objective Activity: The teacher will choose selected stories from local history books. Students will conduct popcorn reading from Warrior Mountains Folklore, Indians of the Warrior Mountains, or Indian Trails of the Warrior Mountains in your classroom. Next, ask the students comprehensive questions about the selected text.

STATE STANDARDS Reading Objective:

PG. 58 #11   Refine general listening behaviors
- As the teacher directs the lesson, the students will discuss orally what the main idea of the section is and the students will summarize what the teacher taught them.
  - *Name three things we discussed in today's lesson. (five tribes, settlements, parents, clans, toys and games, deer, Warrior Mountains, Muscle Shoals, foods, cooking, historic farming)*

STATE STANDARDS Social Studies Objective:

Online Alex #10   Describe changes in social and economic conditions in the United States during the 20th and 21st centuries
- After the teacher directs the lesson, the students will discuss how the times of the people have changed. The students will discuss the lifestyle of the early Indian people versus the lifestyle of people today.
  - *What were the settlements like back then? (log cabins or plank houses)*

Review Questions
1. How did our Indian ancestors make glue? (boiled deer hooves)
2. When was the first thanksgiving? (1621)
3. Who was known as the "Beloved Woman" that saved the life of captive, Mrs. William Bean, who was about to be burned at the stake? (Nancy Ward)
4. Deer toe bones were used for what? (fish hooks, scrapers, needles, and awls)
5. Explain why children only belonged to their mother's clan: (Cherokees believed the children were only kin or related to those who could be traced through their mother.)

LESSON 6 – EARLY SURVIVAL NEEDS

Cherokee Foods - We are going to talk about the Cherokee Indians who were ancestors to most of you. The Cherokee were farmers and grew beans, pumpkins, squash, and *most importantly corn and potatoes*. Some food they gathered was: wild grapes, persimmons, plums, blackberries, chestnuts, walnuts, hickory nuts, acorns, and wild onions. (Do color sheets of gathered foods.)

The Cherokee hunted smaller animals for food such as: deer, wild turkey, bear, squirrel, rabbit, and quail. The main source of meat and hides was deer. (Do color sheet of animals they hunted). Some of the rivers and streams produced foods for the Indians such as fish, turtles, and mussels. Indians used fish hooks made of bone. They also used nets, traps, and spears to catch fish.

Cherokees in Lawrence County were farmers who raised all kind of crops. Some also had livestock including horses, cattle, hogs, and chickens.

Indian survival depended on a generous supply of food. The Southeastern environment had many sources to offer. Crops of beans, pumpkins, squash, cucumbers, radishes, and most importantly corn and potatoes were utilized in their daily diet. Corn was used for various foods. It could be ground for corn meal. Hominy, grits and several methods of cooking corn provided a variety of tastes. Many plants yielded fruits, berries, and nuts. Some of these included: wild grapes, persimmons, plums, blackberries, chestnuts, walnuts, hickory nuts, and acorns. Acorns could be pounded into a powder and processed for flour. Foods were preserved with a drying process.

Animals provided a meat source to their diet also. Deer, rabbit, bear, squirrel, wild turkey and quail were commonly hunted. Their main source of meat was deer. How many of you have ever tasted deer or rabbit meat? Do any of you have a relative that hunts for meat today? It's important to remember the Indian people respect animals and never hunted just for sport. Every part of the animals killed was put to use.

The cattail was like the supermarket of the swamp. The roots of the cattail were dried then pounded into flour (show a cattail stalk that has been split open). The white substance was pounded for flour. Young plants were eaten like celery. Also, the yellow pollen was used with corn flour to make very good bread.

Cherokee Homes - Our Indian ancestors in Lawrence County, Alabama lived in villages. They always located their villages near a spring, creek, or river, which provided an abundant water supply, and forest. Why do you think they wanted to be near water? Let students answer, then tell them-(They needed water to drink, cook, and wash). Why do you think that our Indian people wanted to live near a forest? (Let students answer). Then say, (so they could hunt animals in the forest for food.)

What kind of houses did our early Indian people have? Students answer. Then tell them that our people in Alabama never lived in tipis (show picture of the summer home and winter homes--describe each one) Why do you think they had two homes? Explain that in the summer, their summer homes were made with walls constructed of upright saplings imbedded closely together in the ground. Smaller branches were woven around the saplings. A mixture of clay and grass was used to plaster the walls. The roof

LESSON 6 – EARLY SURVIVAL NEEDS

was covered with bark or thinly split wood shingles. The door, which was the only opening except for the small hole in the roof, was about two feet wide.

The winter house had walls built of logs standing on end and woven together with white oak strips that made solid walls. The roof was cone shaped. A clay mixture was used to plaster the inside and outside of the house which was covered with bark or grass. A fire burned in the center of the house with beds lining the walls. The door of the winter house was about four feet high, and it was so narrow that only one person could enter at a time. A small peephole was level with the ground so the enemies could be seen. (Show pictures of the summer home) The summer home was called "ge-tsa'di." The winter home was called "Asi'."

Cherokee Dwelling

After the Cherokees moved into Lawrence County, they lived in log cabins or plank houses. Some wealthy Cherokees and Chickasaw had plantations with slaves. They owned horses, mules, cattle, hogs, sheep, goats, and chickens. They also raised cotton, corn, and other crops.

Our Cherokee Indian people lived in villages of several homes built close together. The Cherokee Indians never lived in tipis. The roof of early Cherokee homes was built in the shape of a cone and outside walls were either round or square. (draw on board or show picture)

The time the Cherokees were living in Lawrence County, they were living in log cabins or plank houses. Both Chief Doublehead and Chief George Colbert lived in two story plank houses with fireplaces. Some early Cherokees had plantations with slaves.

In the Cherokee family, the father was responsible for hunting animals for their food. The mother's responsibility was to take care of the children, prepare the food, and to make their clothes.

LESSON 6 – EARLY SURVIVAL NEEDS

Tools and Weapons - We are going to talk about tools and weapons used by our early Indian people so they could survive. One of the main hunting weapons of early Indian people was the bow and arrow. How many of you have ever seen a bow and arrow? (show picture of bow-n-arrow) They made the bow from some type of wood. The guts of a bear were used as the string for the bow. The arrows were made from cane. The sharp point on the arrow was made primarily from flint rock.

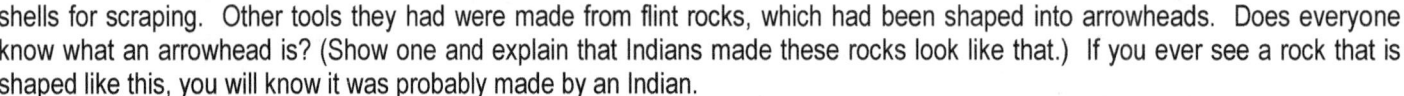

The favorite weapons of the Cherokee were the bow and arrow and blowgun. The blowgun was made from a piece of cane (display cane) cut to a length of seven to nine feet. The cane was hollowed out by dropping hot coals into the cane or by drilling a hole with a smaller cane to which was fixed a flint drill. The cane had to be hollowed out so a dart could be blown through it. The blowgun darts were made of hardwood splinters. The blowgun was used to hunt small animals like rabbits, squirrel, turkey, or birds. Some people think the Cherokees used poison on their darts but there is no evidence of that.

Our Indian people used many tools. One important tool was a stone ax made from a flint rock attached to a handle. They also used mussel shells for scraping. Other tools they had were made from flint rocks, which had been shaped into arrowheads. Does everyone know what an arrowhead is? (Show one and explain that Indians made these rocks look like that.) If you ever see a rock that is shaped like this, you will know it was probably made by an Indian.

Stones were used to heat their water. The stones would be placed into a fire to get hot, and then put into the water to heat it.

Some of the tools they used were the stone ax and deer antler rake. Since our ancestors could not go to the grocery store as we do today, they had to make big gardens. The stone ax and antler rake were used for this purpose. Their very survival depended upon the skillful making and use of their tools and weapons. Early weapons used were spears and the atlatl. Indian people found it necessary to develop new weapons. One of their great improvements was the atlatl which was an extension of the spear. The atlatl allowed the hunter to throw with great force and to keep at a safe distance from animals. The main part of the atlatl besides the spear shaft was the throwing stick. Attached to the throwing stick was a banner stone and deer antler hook.

Early metal tools used by Cherokee *(Tellico Archaeology)*

A lot of time was spent hunting animals for food. The main hunting weapon during the Mississippian Period was the bow and arrow. (Show picture of bow and arrow and blowgun.) The bow was made from many types of trees and the arrow from mountain cane.

When our Cherokee ancestors moved into Lawrence County, they were using weapons made of metal. Long rifles and metal knives were used by Cherokees who lived in this area.

How do you think the early Indians made their clothes? (Sharp pointed pieces of bone called awl were used for sewing leather clothes. Show picture of bone needle and example of a needle we use today.)

What do we use today to cut things? (scissors, knives) Cutting tools and weapons used by early Indians were chipped from flint. Flint also has another name: chert. Flint (chert) was used to make a variety of weapon points. One very important point made was called an arrowhead or spear point. The arrowhead was made by using two methods called pressure flaking and percussion. In percussion flaking, the flint is battered into shape with skillful blows from a hammer stone.

LESSON 6 – EARLY SURVIVAL NEEDS

Figure 7.24. Jar with modeled handles (height 9 cm).

Figure 7.25. Jar with strap handles (height 11.5 cm).

Figure 7.26. Cord impressed jar with pointed rim (height 12.5 cm).

Figure 7.27. This vessel form is referred to as a "hooded" water bottle; the hood is probably an abstract, stylized human head (height 14 cm).

Figure 7.28. Jar with alternating modeled human heads and frogs. The frog may be an iconographic symbol of water or be somehow related to the phenomenon of metamorphosis of life forms (tadpole into frog). In any case, the frog is a common motif and is related to the Mississippian belief system (height 10 cm).

Figure 7.29. Frog effigy bowl (height 8.5 cm).

Pottery from the Overhill Cherokee Towns *(Tellico Archaeology)*

In pressure flaking, a pointed tool of antler or bone is pressed against the edge to remove small flakes. After the arrowhead was completed, it was tied on the end of a piece of cane (show example of cane).

Metal Tools - The first Lawrence County Cherokees were out of the Stone Age. Their weapons, made of steel, were long rifles and knives. By the time they moved to Lawrence County, our Cherokee people were using plows and metal tools like the settlers used. By the time our first Cherokee people came to Lawrence County, they were using metal pots and pans. The metal cookware was an important trade item of the British.

By the time the Cherokees moved into Lawrence County, their favorite weapon was the long rifle. Lawrence County Cherokees used long rifles to hunt and fight with. Thirty deerskins could be traded for a rifle. Metal tools were also an important trade item that Indians got from the British and later the Americans.

Pottery - Remember, Archaic Indian people first developed stone pottery; however, clay pottery was fiber, sand, or shell tempered, which means that fibers (grass, roots, Spanish moss and other materials), sand, or crushed mussel shells were placed in the clay. The clay was then dried and strengthened by firing.

Pottery making was one of the best known Cherokee crafts. There were three basic forms of traditional Cherokee pottery: the bowl; the pot; and a large jar. Most clay used for making Cherokee pottery was found around creek or river banks. It was dug, dried, ground, and sifted. Using an axe head and stone pestle, the lumps of dry clay were broken into fragments, ground to fine flour, and sifted in a basket to remove pebbles. The fine dried clay powder was mixed with water. It was worked with stone and kneaded with the hands. Plant fibers, coarse grit, sand, or crushed shells were added as a tempering agent to aid in hardening. Clay for making pottery had the consistency of putty. Clay has been used for hundreds of years to make cooking vessels.

To begin, a ball was formed and then pressed into the desired beginning shape, like a small bowl. The edges were pressed thin and then built up with rows of clay formed into long thin rolls, in a coiling manner. The last coil formed the rim and was sometimes notched. The firing was done outside. A hot fire was built and the vessel was put close into the embers and covered with dry bark. Heat was added until the vessel turned red. Cornhusk or dried corn cobs were placed inside and allowed to blaze up. The vessel was turned upside down until all the flaming material was burned up. This made it waterproof on the inside. These vessels were extremely important in food preparation and cooking.

LESSON 6 – EARLY SURVIVAL NEEDS

The gorget was made of clay but sometimes from stone during the Woodland period. The gorget was used as decoration for the body such as a neck or an arm piece of jewelry. The word gorget means neck armor. During the Mississippian period, shells were used to make beautifully designed gorgets.

Questions: Hold up some pottery and ask class: "Who knows what this is made from?" (clay)

Clothing - Prehistoric Indians wore clothes made from animal skins. Clothing was usually leather or fur depending on the climate. Men wore a breechcloth which was a strip of skin or cloth about six feet long and one foot wide. The breechcloth was worn between the legs and looped over the belt at the waist. The ends hung down in front and back to the knees. The main item of clothing for the woman was a short, deerskin skirt or dress hanging to the knees. In cold weather, both men and women wore leggings made from buckskin. The woman's leggings usually came to the knee while the man's leggings usually reached from the heel to the hip.

By the time the Cherokee came into Alabama, they had already made contact with the English settlers. Through trade, the Indians were replacing their clothing made from hide with cloth brought by the traders. By the 1800s, all southeastern clothing was made from trade cloth, or from cloth made by Indian women using looms.

Removal era clothing

The traditional clothing worn by today's Cherokees is similar to that made during the removal. The women wear a tear dress made from calico material. During the removal on the Trail of Tears the Indians were unable to trade for materials so they used what was available to them. They used the calico sacks, which flour and meal came in. They would tear the sacks into the pieces that they needed and would sew them together. The men would wear a ribbon shirt. The shirt has bright colored ribbons sewn on it.

Weaving - Some of the first weaving involved the use of animal hair. The weaving loom was made from wood. It was square shaped with strings running from top to bottom. Animal hair was woven in and out of each string. Then a brush was used to pack the hair into place and make it tight. Plant fibers were also used to make yarn. Cotton and wool are still used to make clothing and yarn today. Look at the label in some of your clothes at home.

Fingerweaving - Fingerweaving without a loom is very old and widespread. Generally only fingers are used but needles or weaving frames may be used. Sashes woven in bright geometric patterns were major items made by finger weaving. Before contact with white traders, the sashes were woven of vegetable fibers mixed with animal hair. Wool sashes became popular when yarn and trade sashes were acquired.

Ornamental sashes were worn around the waist with the long fringes trailing or hung over one or both shoulders in bandoleer fashion. They were also wrapped around the head like a turban. Short pieces were tied around the arms or worn on the legs as garters. Sometimes they were used to tie or carry medicine bundles or to decorate a weapon. Glass beads were often woven into the sashes or threaded on the long fringes at each end.

LESSON 6 – EARLY SURVIVAL NEEDS

Cherokee Games

Plants - Perhaps one of the greatest contributions of the American Indian was the use of medicine made out of herbs or plants. Most Indian tribes had a medicine man, which provided not only for the spiritual needs, but also for the medical needs of his people. The place and ritual differed in different tribes and areas of the continent, but to most tribes the gathering and preparation of the herbs or plants was entrusted to the skills of the well trained individual--the medicine man.

The medicine man carried a pouch made out of leather to transport and store fragile plants from the woods to his home. Then, he would gather all needed to begin the process of making his medicine. He would measure, chop, grind, or boil to ensure just the right method of preparation.

Games -Chunkey, stickball, guessing games, stick dice, bowl catch, Cherokee ball game, and other games prepared boys for hunting.

Discuss with class how the games prepared boys for hunting and how games were sometimes used to settle arguments instead of going to war. Describe some of the games to your class and ask if any games played today are similar to those played by Indians.

LESSON 6 – EARLY SURVIVAL NEEDS

KINDERGARTEN

DIBLES Reading Objective: PHONEMIC AWARENESS

Objective: After the teacher directs this lesson, Kindergarten Indian students will orally identify seven out of fifteen terms based on knowledge gained from the text.

Objective Activity: Word sort using the following: weapon-spear, tool-stone, knife; food-nuts, berries, animals; clothes-animal hides, plant fibers; home-villages; animals-deer, bear, rabbit; pottery-clay.

STATE STANDARDS Reading Objective:

PG. 13 #1 Exhibit an awareness of the concept of a story
- After discussing tools, weapons, and games, the teacher will show the students pictures of tools and weapons/games that were used by our ancestors. Then the teacher will guide the students to help them have a better understanding of the relation between games/tools and weapons used by our Native American ancestors and the ones we use today.
  - *What game did our Cherokee ancestors play that is similar to baseball/softball? (stickball)*

PG. 14 #6 Demonstrate an initial understanding of letter-sound relationships
- Choose words from the lesson such as: corn, deer, rabbit, fish, etc. Write the words on the board using capital letters. Let the students sound out each individual letter and say the word together at the end.
  - *What is one thing that your Native American ancestors used to catch fish? (nets, traps, or spears)*

PG. 14 #9 Begin to use pictures and text to gain meaning from written material
- Show students pictures of different types of pottery located in the activity book to help them have a better understanding of what has been discussed.
  - *Name one thing that our ancestors made from clay. (pot)*

PG. 15 #14 Demonstrate an interest in and enjoyment of literature in a variety of forms, contexts, and media
- Let the students draw a summer or winter home using an activity sheet as example. Take summer and winter home sheet out of activity book. Teacher should also model how to draw a summer and winter house on the board.
  - *How many homes did our Indian ancestors have? (2)*

PG. 15 #17 Exhibit expanded vocabulary and sentence awareness
- While discussing clothing, the teacher will teach several new vocabulary words to the class such as: deer skin, leggings, fur, and jacket. We will discuss the new vocabulary words using simple sentences. For example, the teacher could say, "Our ancestors wore leggings on their arms." The students would then say, "No they wore them on their legs."
  - *What did men and women wear on their legs in the winter? (leggings)*

LESSON 6 – EARLY SURVIVAL NEEDS

STATE STANDARDS Social Studies Objective:

PG. 12 #10   Exhibit personal responsibility for the care of the physical environment
- Discuss how farming/gardening was a form of survival for our Native American ancestors. Allow students to plant a seed in a cup and watch it grow in order to understand the responsibility of gardening. Also talk about how the land was taken care of and how sunlight helped in the growing process.
  - *Did the Cherokee Indians ever use guns? (yes)*

PG. 13 #16   Increase awareness of various environments
- Relate how summer months were spent by the river and how winter months were spent in the mountains, in rock shelters and why they chose this type of environment for different months.
  - *Where did our ancestors live during the summer/winter months? (mountains, river)*

PG. 15 #37   Develop an awareness of the lives of children in other places
- Discuss the lives of Native American boys and girls and how boys were raised to go out and hunt, fish, and fight. Girls were made to stay in the village and learn to sew, cook, and clean. If time permits, discuss the difference between the lives of children now and then.
  - *Did the boys or the girls have to learn to hunt, fight, and fish? (boys)*

Review Questions
1. What did men and women wear in the winter? (leggings)
2. Fish hooks were made from what? (deer bones)
3. Cherokee owned what animals? (horses, mules, cows, hogs, sheep, goats, and chickens)
4. What is a bow made from? (wood)
5. What is an arrowhead made from? (flint)

LESSON 6 – EARLY SURVIVAL NEEDS

FIRST GRADE

DIBELS Reading Objective: PHONEME SEGMENTATION FLUENCY

Objective: After the teacher directs this lesson, first grade Indian students will compare the past lifestyles of our American Indian ancestors to present-day lifestyles. In addition, new words will be pointed out for them to say aloud, then segment the word verbally.

Objective Activity: Choose vocabulary terms from the lesson. (river, winter, summer, water, cabin, and forest) Next, hold up flash cards revealing individual letters of the vocabulary term. (Ex: R, I, V, E, R to make River) Then, write each letter on the board as it is identified. Finally, discuss the term orally with the class.

STATE STANDARDS Reading Objective:

PG. 17 #3   Exhibit phonemic awareness
- Once the teacher directs the lesson, pick out five words from the lesson and have the class count the number of sounds by clapping to the syllables. (Ex: sur-vi-val)
  - *What type of rocks were points of weapons made from? (flint)*
  - *What were the two most important foods to our ancestors? (potatoes, corn)*

STATE STANDARDS Social Studies Objective:

PG. 18 #9   Compare features of communities
PG. 18 #10   Relate land use in their locality to the physical features of the land
- Discuss features of our Native American ancestors and the communities in which they lived. Talk about how they used man-made tools and weapons and natural resources as different forms of survival. (Ex: shelter-trees-bluffs, food-soil-vegetation-water, weapons-used cane and arrows made from flint)
  - *Who provided medicine for our ancestors? (medicine man)*

Review Questions

1. What are the names of the homes of our Cherokee ancestors? (summer and winter)
2. The Cherokees most important crops were what? (corn and potatoes)
3. Name three animals the Cherokees hunted. (deer, wild turkey, bear, squirrel, rabbit, quail)
4. What kind of bone did the Cherokee use to make fish hooks? (deer)
5. What were two reasons the Cherokees used water? (drink, cook, wash)

LESSON 6 – EARLY SURVIVAL NEEDS

SECOND GRADE

DIBELS Reading Objective: ORAL READING FLUENCY

Objective: After the teacher directs this lesson, have the students to read aloud and demonstrate oral reading fluency.

Objective Activity: Have the students swap up reading paragraphs aloud to the class. Monitor each student as they read aloud and make necessary corrections.

STATE STANDARDS Reading Objective:

PG. 25 #13   Demonstrate appropriate listening and communicating behaviors
- During a group discussion about survival needs of our early Indian ancestors, he/she will ask teacher generated questions in order for the students to gain a better understanding of the information taught.
  - *How many homes did the early Cherokee have? (two-summer and winter)*

STATE STANDARDS Social Studies Objective:

PG. 22 #2   Develop the ability to interpret and display information in graphic form
- After teacher conducts a lesson about survival needs, he/she will use a chart to compare the features of the past to the present. (Ex: Still use bow and arrow, spears, and guns but not as the only means of survival. Still eat some of the same foods and raise the same crops, but this is not our only food supply.) (Our homes aren't the same-they lived in caves, bluffs, and mountain areas-we live in houses all year round.)
  - *Name one animal we still hunt today. (deer)*

Pg. 24 #12   Develop an initial awareness of geographic concepts related to the food industry
- After the directed lesson, the teacher will ask the class how the climate and soil fertility played a key role in raising crops and food sources.
  - *How were foods preserved? (drying process)*

Review Questions

1. What tool did early Indians use to sew leather clothes? (bone needle)
2. After European contact, what type of homes did the Cherokees of Lawrence County live in? (log cabins or plank houses)
3. What kind of crops did they grow? (beans, pumpkins, squash, corn, and potatoes)
4. What was their pottery made from? (clay from creeks or river banks)
5. What was used to heat water? (stones)

LESSON 6 – EARLY SURVIVAL NEEDS

THIRD GRADE

DIBELS Reading Objective: LISTENING SKILLS

Objective: After the teacher directs this lesson, third grade Indian students will gain information on early survival needs.

Objective Activity: The teacher will read a Cherokee legend orally to the students. Read the first paragraph and ask students what they think will happen next. The teacher may let students read a couple of sentences orally then discuss characters and sequence of events from the story. Then, ask students to identify key terms from the text in order to check for understanding.

STATE STANDARDS Reading Objective:

PG. 32 #8   Read grade level texts aloud and silently with fluency and comprehension
- The students will read aloud from a book about tools and weapons. The students will be asked questions from the teacher to test comprehension.
  - *What weapon did the Cherokees use that we still have today? (bow and arrow)*

STATE STANDARDS Social Studies Objective:

PG. 30 #6   Compare different groups of Native Americans
- The teacher will teach the lesson and then compare the food, shelter, and clothing of the Cherokees to another tribe.
  - *What was the Cherokees most important crop? (corn)*

Review Questions

1. What object was used by our early Indian ancestors to cook food? (clay pots)
2. What was the sting on a bow and arrow made from? (bear guts)
3. Describe an important tool used by our early ancestors: (stone ax made from flint rock attached to a handle)
4. What was a game the children played? (chunkey, stickball, guessing games, stick dice, bowl catch, Cherokee ball games)
5. Identify an important trade item of the British: (metal cookware and/or tools)

LESSON 6 – EARLY SURVIVAL NEEDS

FOURTH GRADE

<u>SAT</u> Reading Objective: WORD RECOGNITION

Objective: After the teacher directs this lesson, fourth grade Indian students will recognize and comprehend words relating to the Cherokee's early survival needs. They will recognize the following words: villages, livestock, flint (chert), cane, atlatl, and vessel.

Objective Activity: The students will exhibit their understanding of the words by explaining in their own words the meaning of the selected terms found in the lesson and/or showing the class what the term is for example: an atlatl, flint (arrowhead), or cane (blowgun).

<u>STATE STANDARDS</u> Reading Objective:

PG. 39 #11   Read materials encountered in daily lives
- While the teacher directs the lesson, the students will read books on survival needs for the Cherokee people.
  - *What were the two most important foods to the Cherokee? (corn and potatoes)*

<u>STATE STANDARDS</u> Social Studies Objective:

PG. 36 #10   Describe aspects of the lives of historical Indians of Alabama

PG. 36 #11   Explain lasting contributions made by Alabama's earliest inhabitants
- Discuss with the students about what types of weapons our early ancestors used and discuss which ones we still use today. (atlatl, bow and arrow, etc.)
  - *Describe some of the games of Cherokees that were played. (Chunkey, stickball, guessing games, stick dice, bowl catch, Cherokee ballgame)*

Review Questions

1. What was used to heat water in early Indian times? (stones)
2. Name some tools our ancestors used. (stone ax and deer antler rake)
3. What were some early weapons used? (spears and atlatl)
4. What were some weapons used by the first Lawrence County Cherokees? (long rifles and knives)
5. Who provided medicine for our ancestors? (medicine man)

LESSON 6 – EARLY SURVIVAL NEEDS

FIFTH GRADE

<u>SAT</u> Reading Objective: LISTENING SKILLS

Objective: After the teacher directs this lesson, fifth grade Indian students will comprehend and identify the terms related to the Cherokee's early survival needs. (livestock, ancestors, plantations, breech cloth, persimmons)

Objective Activity: After a review of the lesson, divide the students into teams and play Hangman with the terms. Put vocabulary word blanks on the board and give clues that include the meaning of the word from the text.

<u>STATE STANDARDS</u> Reading Objective:

PG. 46 #13   Apply strategies of a skillful listener
- The teacher will read a legend to the students and then ask questions to ensure they were listening.
  - *What was the greatest contribution of the American Indians? (use of medicine made out of herbs or plants)*

<u>STATE STANDARDS</u> Social Studies Objective:

PG. 46 #4   Describe the natural environment of North America
- While the teacher directs the lesson, the students and the teacher will discuss how and where early ancestors used the natural environment. (hunted what animals, use of Tennessee River, food they ate, etc.)
  - *What do we use today to cut things? (knife, saw, etc.)*

Review Questions

1. What was the favorite hunting weapon of the Mississippian Indians? (bow and arrow)
2. What was used to settle arguments instead of going to war? (games)
3. Some early weaving involved the use of what? (animal hair)
4. What was the main item of clothing for women? (deerskin skirt or dress)
5. After European contact, what did Indian women make their clothes from? (cloth brought by traders)

LESSON 6 – EARLY SURVIVAL NEEDS

SIXTH GRADE

SAT Reading Objective: COMPREHENSION

Objective: After the teacher directs this lesson, sixth grade Indian students will read and gain an understanding of materials that they will encounter in the lesson on early survival needs.

Objective Activity: Read a Cherokee legend. Tell me the meaning of the story. What is the main idea? Have students read the lesson aloud and discuss each paragraph to check for comprehension.

STATE STANDARDS Reading Objective:

PG. 52 #1   Interpret and construct meaning by applying appropriate strategies to materials across the curriculum
- After the conducted lesson, the Indian students will be able to recognize various forms of literature that include cultural diverse materials through their characteristics from Lawrence County Indian people. Students can read this lesson aloud and explain in their own words characteristics of Lawrence County Indian people. While talking about the lesson, the teacher will allow the students to make a pony bead bracelet using clan colors, and explain to the students why the colors were important.
  - *What part of the animal killed was put to use? (every part)*

STATE STANDARDS Social Studies Objective:

PG. 54 #1   Extend the development of map and globe skills
- Show students a map of the Tennessee River and discuss with the class that it was essential for them to live close to the river because it provided different things for survival. (mussel shells)
  - *What river was essential for survival? (Tennessee River)*

Review Questions

1. In most early Indian tribes who provides for the spiritual needs of the people? (medicine man)
2. What were the homes located near? (spring, creek, or river)
3. Explain the importance of games. (prepared boys for hunting and sometimes were used to settle arguments instead of going to war)
4. Why do you think they wanted to be near water? (abundant water supply and forest)
5. The sharp point on the arrow was made primarily from what? (flint rock)

LESSON 6 – EARLY SURVIVAL NEEDS

SEVENTH GRADE

SAT Reading Objective: COMPREHENSION

Objective: After the teacher directs this lesson, seventh grade Indian students will read and gain an understanding of materials that they will encounter in the lesson on early survival needs.

Objective Activity: Read a Cherokee legend. Tell me the meaning of the story. What is the main idea? Have students read the lesson aloud and discuss each paragraph to check for comprehension.

STATE STANDARDS Reading Objective:

PG. 52 #1   Interpret and construct meaning by applying appropriate strategies to materials across the curriculum
- After the conducted lesson, the Indian students will be able to recognize various forms of literature that include culturally diverse materials through their characteristics from Lawrence County Indian people. Students can read this lesson aloud and explain in their own words characteristics of Lawrence County Indian people. While talking about the lesson, the teacher will allow the students to make a pony bead bracelet using clan colors, and explain to the students why the colors were important.
    - ∽ *What part of the animal killed was put to use? (every part)*

STATE STANDARDS Social Studies Objective:

PG. 54 #1   Extend the development of map and globe skills
- Show students a map of the Tennessee River and discuss with the class that it was essential for them to live close to the river because it provided different things for survival. (mussel shells)
    - ∽ *What river was essential for survival? (Tennessee River)*

Review Questions
1. In most early Indian tribes who provides for the spiritual needs of the people? (medicine man)
2. What were the homes located near? (spring, creek, or river)
3. Explain the importance of games. (prepared boys for hunting and sometimes were used to settle arguments instead of going to war)
4. Why do you think they wanted to be near water? (abundant water supply and forest)
5. The sharp point on the arrow was made primarily from what? (flint rock)

LESSON 7 – REGALIA

The early Indian men and women didn't have clothing like we do today. Can anyone tell me what they think Indians might have worn? They didn't have stores or sewing machines to buy or sew their clothing. I would like for everyone to look around the room for just a minute. Also look at your clothes and the things you are wearing. Some of you may be wearing something that is made out of leather or buckskin. Do you know what leather or buckskin is? (Leather or buckskin is something we get from different kinds of animal skins. Buckskin is made from deer hides.)

A long time ago, our Indian people used many kinds of animal skins to make leather and buckskin such as: deer, rabbit, bear, beaver, buffalo, and elk. How do you think our ancestors made leather or buckskin? First, they would take the animal skin and scrape all the fur off. Next, they would wet it, stretch it, and let it dry. Then, they would take a rock and rub it over the skin until it became smooth and soft (show different pieces of leather and differences in leather and buckskin). Then they rubbed the skin with the animal's brains. The brain of an animal was enough to tan its hide.

Our Indian ancestors used leather and buckskin to make their clothes, shoes, blankets, and bags to carry water from the stream. What are some things we have now that are made from leather or buckskin? (Your mom may have a purse made out of leather. Your dad may have a billfold or belt made out of leather). Can you think of anything else that is made out of leather? (saddles, bridles, furniture, car seats, gloves, shoes)

Buckskin Clothes - Our early Cherokee Indian people made their clothes out of deer skins (show piece of deerskin or leather). The women made all of the clothing for the family. The Cherokee men wore three different kinds of clothes; a breechcloth, buckskin leggings, and a jacket made of buckskin. Buckskin leggings were made in pairs and covered the whole leg, but were not sewn together (show picture). A buckskin jacket, which hung to the knees, and leggings were worn in the winter and a breechcloth was worn in the summer to stay cool. The Cherokee women wore a short deerskin skirt, which hung to the knees (show picture, women w/deerskin skirt).

They had to kill animals to get their clothes. When the Indians killed an animal, they would use every part. Nothing was wasted. Most of their hides came from deer and bear. The men would kill and skin the animals. The women would start the process of hides. (show picture of Indian man and woman) Sometimes they would wear a deerskin or woven mantles to show that they were important. In winter months, the men would add a deerskin shirt and leggings tucked into the high, laced moccasins worn by everyone (show the class a piece of leather).

Early Indian Clothing (*History of Alabama for Junior High Schools*)

The clothing of our early Indian people was different from what you wear. The breechcloth was a strip of skin or cloth about six feet long and one foot wide. They wore buckskin leggings as protection from the underbrush and from the cold in winter. They fitted the whole length of the leg and were held up by a cord tied to the waist string. A jacket made of buckskin, reaching to the knees, was also worn; in cold weather a bearskin or blanket was thrown around the shoulders.

Leather came from animal hides. Hides were processed and fashioned into clothing and footwear. They were also responsible for preparing the hides. Women were probably engaged almost continuously in the processing of hides (show picture of woman working hide on rack).

Preparation of Skins - Leather today comes mostly from cow or pig. People usually buy their leather from companies that buy large quantities. Today, hides are tanned by machines. It took a lot of work to prepare an animal hide so that it could be used as clothing, footwear, or blankets. (1) The flesh was removed with a stone, bone, or antler scraper; (2) The hair of the hides was removed with flint scrapers; (3) Tanning was merely a matter of smearing the hide with fat, brains, and liver; (4) The hides were then soaked in water; (5) The skin was sometimes smoked; (6) The hide was then stretched on a framework to dry; (7) The leather was finally made pliable by working between the hands or sliding back and forth across a pole. Hides were processed and

LESSON 7 – REGALIA

fashioned into clothing and footwear. (1) Women were responsible for making the clothes from hides; (2) Women were probably engaged, almost continuously, in the processing of hides.

Historic Clothes - By the time Cherokees moved into Lawrence County, they were wearing traditional clothing of the settlers and pioneers. Cherokee women learned to make clothes using looms. They traded with the British and later Americans for cloth, shoes, hats, shirts, pants, dresses, and other clothing items. Some dressed like rich plantation owners in fine clothes of the planters and society. By the time our Cherokee people moved into Lawrence County, they were wearing clothes made of cloth. Today, you are an Indian and look at your clothes.

The first Cherokees in Lawrence County wore clothes made from cloth. The cloth was a trade item of the British. Indian women using a loom also weaved cloth for making clothes.

Our Indian people did not always wear skins, but for thousands of years they did. Skins (also called leather) provided the best type of clothing they could find until the Europeans arrived in North America and started trading with Indian people. The Europeans wore clothing made of cloth (like we wear today). When the European traders traded with our Indian ancestors, they would swap cloth for skins. This is how they got cloth material to make their clothes. Indian women also had looms on which they wove their own cloth to make clothes. Many Indians and Celtic people intermarried in this area of Lawrence County, Alabama; therefore, their clothing changed to a blend of Indian and Celtic.

Today, Cherokee women wear tear dresses as tribal regalia. The dress is made from cotton with a small floral design. The dress is trimmed with bright ribbons or a diamond design appliquéd to the fabric. The men wear shirts decorated with brightly colored ribbons. This is called a ribbon shirt. We have talked about the different dress of our ancestors but, remember you are Indians, but you are wearing the clothes that are in fashion or comfortable for you.

Jewelry - Jewelry has always been important to our Indian people. Both men and women wore jewelry for decoration. The men liked to wear necklaces to show that they had a good hunt and were proud. Our Indian people used different things to make necklaces such as beads, animal teeth and bear claws (show picture). They also wore earrings and bracelets to show they had won a fight against other people. Do you have any jewelry that you like to wear? Maybe you have a special person in your life that you really like a lot. You might want to make them a bracelet or necklace and give it to them to let them know that they are special to you. Sometimes we call these friendship bracelets or necklaces.

Silver Cherokee Jewelry and Body Ornaments (*Tellico Archaeology*)

Our Indian ancestors used another way to decorate themselves and their belongings. They used different things to make paint such as, sand rocks (show example), different kinds of berries (blackberries, blueberries, strawberries, plums, and cherries), and different plants (bloodroot and yellow root). The paint was used to decorate their faces and bodies before going to war or if they had won a battle. Also, Indians used paint to make pictures on animal skins.

Silver ornaments became important to wear by Cherokees of Lawrence County. Sequoyah was considered a great Cherokee silversmith.

LESSON 7 – REGALIA

Early Beads

The earliest of our ancestors decorated their bodies with ornaments and tattoos. This usually demonstrated their position in society. This still has some effects on people today. Some people believe you need to wear name brand jeans or certain T-shirts to fit in. You should remember that it is important to be yourself. But we all like to dress up because it makes us feel good. How many of you are wearing a ring or watch? This is an example of jewelry. But where did your ring or watch come from?

The first jewelry or ornaments were made from things in nature. For example, the Indian people used shells, rocks, and even clay. They also used plants to create dyes for tattoos on their body. Another source for jewelry was from teeth, claws, and bones of animals that were killed. After European contact, the Indian people began to trade for various glass beads; therefore, making their adornment even more colorful.

Beads - They also used beads as money. They called their money wampum. The different colors represented their value. The purple beads were the most valuable because they were harder to get.

Cherokee men and women wore jewelry and used tattooing as adornment. How many of you have thought about wearing jewelry or having tattoos? As a matter of fact, that was the way the men could show that they had been successful in battle or hunting. It was like having trophies.

Who can name some things that our Indian ancestors might have used to adorn themselves? A lot of you may think that all our people wore a feather head dress, but they didn't. Only a few did. Other things they used were animal bone, teeth and shells.

Body Paint - Sometimes Cherokee Indians would paint their faces and bodies for different reasons such as battle or a cause of celebration. Where do you think they got their paints and dyes? They found berries, bark from trees, and from sand rocks. (Use a sand rock to show the way that they could rub them together to get the color to paint their face). They also used paint for pictures on stones to tell stories.

Tattooing - The men also used tattooing as a mark of personal identification and to designate honors. Tattooing was common among Cherokee men. Designs of animal figures, serpents, stars, the moon, the sun, and scrolls were used. Designs were made by pricking the skin with a sharp object like a garfish tooth, bone, or a needle. Sometimes they would paint their faces or body with paint. Where did they get their dye or paint? They had to make it. They would mix iron ore with bear grease, berry stain or ashes from the fire. Face and body painting was seen as a means of obtaining magic. The colors and symbols make them look and feel powerful. Different face paint colors meant different things to different tribes.

Some boys and girls think Indians always wore animal skins for clothes. How many of you know better?

Hair - Boys and Girls, you all look very nice today! I'm looking around the room and I see many different types of clothing and hairstyles. We all wear our hair and our clothes the way we have been taught, don't we. Well, today, we are going to discuss how our Indian ancestors dressed and wore their hair. They also dressed the way they had been taught. And let's remember, they didn't have clothing stores, barbershops, or beauty shops like we do.

Indian men plucked or pulled all the hair from their bodies except for their eyebrows, and sometimes they removed their eyebrows. However, since this was a custom from childhood the nerves became accustomed to the shock and little pain was experienced. The items used in removing the hair was tweezers made from attaching two mussel shells together, sharp side of a mussel shell,

LESSON 7 – REGALIA

rocks and projectile points. Burning the hair with hot stones was also used.

Reasons for Cutting Hair

1. Cleanliness--The hair became tangled and dirty. It would get caught on limbs and branches, OUCH!!
2. Certain hairstyles represented a custom from certain tribes (example-Mohawk, Cherokee, and other examples of different tribes and their hairstyles).
3. A symbol of belief or superstition in a magical power.

Dyes and Colors - Look around the room and count how many different colors you see. The Native American people loved beautiful and colorful things. The clothes we have today are dyed cloth with various colors and patterns. Our ancestors also learned ways to dye the various objects they wore. How do you think they did this? Well, they used things that were natural to their surroundings. For example, how many of you have ever picked some blackberries and it turned your fingers purple? Blackberries were just one of the many things used for dyeing. Also, green walnuts make a great dye that will last a long time.

Native Americans used plant materials to make beautiful, soft colors to dye wool, cotton, and other fibers. They made almost every color, though shades of yellow were the easiest to produce. Listed below are some of the plants Native Americans used for coloring. As a general rule, if the plant part is hard, like bark or sticks, pound or grind it to loosen the fibers; if it's soft, like flower petals or berries, use it as is.

Wash the plant material first. Then put it, ground up or whole, in a large pot and fill the pot with water. (Metal pots may change the color, though sometimes that produces an interesting result.) Boil until the color is a little darker than you'd like. Strain the dye material out and add a little salt and baking soda to the colored water of dye bath. For a more permanent dye, add a teaspoon of alum, available from a hardware or crafts store.

To dye wool or heavy cloth, soak it in warm water before putting it in the dye bath. Let it boil in the dye bath for about an hour and then let it cool in the pot. To dye raffia, thread, or thin cloth, soak them in the dye bath for several hours. Rinse all dyed materials several times in cold water. Then hang them up to dry, away from direct sunlight or heat, which may cause bleaching.

Color--Plant Material
- Blacks--wild grapes, hickory bark, alder bark, and dogwood bark.
- Blues--larkspur petals, alfalfa flowers, sunflower seeds.
- Browns--walnut shells, birch bark, oak bark.
- Greens--moss, algae, lily-of-the-valley leaves, cedar berries.
- Purples--blueberries, raspberries, blackberries, and rotten maple wood.
- Reds--sumac berries, dogwood berries, beets, cranberries, bloodroot.
- Yellows--onion skins, goldenrod stems and flowers, sunflower petals, dock roots, marigold petals, moss, peach leaves, birch leaves, sagebrush, yellow root.

Some of the common plants used for color from the Warrior Mountains include bloodroot and yellow root. Bloodroot has a very deep red color and yellow root has a golden color. These were dug from the ground and boiled to produce their color.

Pottery - Early Cherokee Indians used the coiled method, which is still used by many Cherokee potters today. Amanda Swimmer, noted Cherokee potter, explains the process: "For coiled pottery, start with a disk of clay, placing ropes of clay on top of each other until you reach the desired height. Then you mold these coils together using your fingers. Now, set the pots out in the sun to dry. When they become dry, polish them with smooth river stones. Make your design, then let them dry to a chalky white. First preheat the pottery until it becomes bluish in color. It then should be put directly into the fire until the fire goes out. The type of wood you use in the firing determines the color of the finish. For the lighter colors you use hardwoods, which give off more flames and less smoke, while for dark colors use a softwood, which gives off more smoke and less flame."

LESSON 7 – REGALIA

KINDERGARTEN

DIBELS Reading Objective: INITIAL SOUND FLUENCY

Objective: After the teacher directs this lesson, Kindergarten Indian students will develop initial sound fluency by recognizing symbols and sounding out the names of those symbols.

Objective Activity: Draw symbols on the board or show objects/pictures and teach the meaning of those symbols or objects/pictures by helping students sound out the names of symbols. Ex: teeth, fur, food, clay, fire, red, shells. (f-u-r/f-oo-d/r-e-d)

STATE STANDARDS Reading Objective:

PG. 14 #6   Demonstrate an initial understanding of letter-sound relationships
- Choose unfamiliar words from text such as buckskin, leggings, deer, and cloth. Have children sound out each beginning sound and everyone say it in unison.
  - *What kind of animal did our Indian ancestors use to make their clothes? (deer)*

PG. 14 #9   Begin to use text to gain meaning from written material
- Show students pictures of the various styles of jewelry that our Indian ancestors wore. (necklaces, bearclaw, beads, bracelets)
- Also show pictures of body art.
- Draw different designs on board and have students design their own body art on paper and color or do face painting with students if allowed.
- Relate the colors with the plant/fruits/vegetables being discussed in lesson and while face painting.
  - *Did both men and women wear jewelry? (yes)*
  - *Did the men or women have tattoos? (men)*

STATE STANDARDS Social Studies Objective:

PG. 14 #26   Identify human made and natural resources
- Use the book, *Indian Trails of the Warrior Mountains,* or any other material to show pictures of trees, rivers, and plants. Have students identify the plants and locate different area in which they grow.
  - *What type of root was used to make the color red? (bloodroot)*

Review Questions

1. The Cherokee Indian clothes were made from what animal? (deer)
2. Did they call their money dollars or wampum? (wampum)
3. What part of an animal was used to tan its hide? (brain)
4. Where did leather come from? (animal hide)
5. What was used to give our Indian ancestors purple? (blueberries, raspberries, blackberries, and rotten Maplewood)

LESSON 7 – REGALIA

FIRST GRADE

DIBELS Reading Objective: PHONICS

Objective: After the teacher directs this lesson, first grade Indian students will develop an understanding of certain letter sounds by naming letters derived from words within the text and identifying the sounds of those particular letters.

Objective Activity: Ask students to name types of regalia mentioned in the lesson. Write the words on the board as students call them out. Then, point to the first letter of the first word and ask students to pronounce that particular letter. After the letter is identified, ask them what sound that letter makes. Finally, pronounce the entire word.

STATE STANDARDS Reading Objective:

PG. 17 #3   Exhibit phonemic awareness
- Discuss clothing and rhyming words with students. Pick words such as: deer, bear, wet, brain, etc. Write these words on the board and have students come up with rhyming words. Write the rhyming word on the board next to the original word. (Ex: dear-near, bear-hair-wear, brain-train)
- ∞ *Name one type of skin besides deer that our ancestors used. (rabbit, bear, beaver, buffalo, elk)*

PG. 21 #16   Demonstrate appropriate listening and speaking behaviors
- Discuss preparation of skins with children thoroughly and ask questions about the different steps used by our ancestors when preparing skins. While discussing, write the steps on the board and explain each one in terms that they can understand. Check for understanding by asking questions that clarify information previously learned.
- ∞ *What was the flesh of animals removed with? (stone, bone, antler scraper)*

STATE STANDARDS Social Studies Objective:

PG. 19 #20   Become acquainted with various cultures encountered in stories from literature
- Talk to students about tattooing, which would be a form of art used in a specific community. Also discuss how our ancestors traded goods and used beads as a form of money. Make sure students understand that this was the way of life for our ancestors during a particular time in history. (Ex: in the beginning our ancestors used natural resources to survive and when they were influenced by Europeans they began to trade, use body paint, to make different kinds of jewelry, and also started using a form of money (beads).
- ∞ *Who had tattoos men or women? (men)*

Review Questions
1. What type of fruit makes the color purple? (berries)
2. What was a form of money, also called wampum? (beads)
3. What was jewelry made from? (animal teeth, bear claws, mussel shells, and stones)
4. Explain reasons for the men cutting their hair. (to be clean/would get tangled and dirty, hairstyles represented customs, symbol of belief or superstition in a magical power)
5. Why were tattoos important? (show honor)

LESSON 7 – REGALIA

SECOND GRADE

DIBELS Reading Objective: NONSENSE WORD FLUENCY

Objective: After the teacher directs this lesson, second grade Indian students will have the ability to detect understandable words from the text by the usage of nonsense words.

Objective Activity: The teacher will write nonsense words on the board that are related to the lesson. (Ex: dribes for tribes, treek for creek, Slabama for Alabama, etc.). Then the teacher will ask for the word from the lesson that corresponds to the nonsense word stating the sentence that the understandable word originates.

STATE STANDARDS Reading Objective:

PG. 25 #10   Read orally with accuracy, fluency, and comprehension
- While the teacher directs the lesson, the students will read parts of the lesson aloud making self corrections (if they don't correct themselves, the teacher will). This will give the students the ability to comprehend the material read, such as, words, sentences, paragraphs, etc.
  - *Why did the Indian men wear tattoos? (show honor)*

STATE STANDARDS Social Studies Objective:

PG. 22 #2   Develop the ability to interpret and display information in graphic form
- After the teacher directs the lesson, he/she will guide the students while he/she makes a chart on the board of similarities/differences of today and the past, using things from the lesson (Ex: buckskin, jewelry, tattoos, etc.)
  - *What type of root was used to make the color red? (bloodroot)*

Review Questions

1. What are leggings made from? (buckskin)
2. What animal does leather come from today? (deer, pigs, cattle)
3. Why did the men and women wear jewelry? (decoration)
4. What color was the most valuable bead? (purple)
5. Where did our Indian ancestors get their dyes? (Our ancestors used things that were natural to their surroundings such as berries, plants, tree bark, etc.)

LESSON 7 – REGALIA

THIRD GRADE

DIBELS Reading Objective: INTERPRETING READING MATERIALS

Objective: After the teacher directs this lesson, third grade Indian students will recognize and apply text words to show their understanding of Regalia.

Objective Activity: The teacher will call upon a student and ask the student to say a color and ask what produces that color. (Ex: blues-sunflower seeds)

STATE STANDARDS Reading Objective:

PG. 31 #1 Use a wide range of strategies to interpret, evaluate, appreciate, and construct meaning from print materials
- Ask questions to ensure comprehension
  - *Do you know what leather or buckskin is? (animal skin-deer hides)*
  - *What is something that jewelry was made from? (animal teeth, bear claws, mussel shells)*

STATE STANDARDS Social Studies Objective:

PG. 31 #9 Compare cultural aspects of selected Native American groups
- After the teacher directs the lesson, show the class pictures of how our ancestors made pottery and how it is different from today.
  - *What was used to make pottery? (clay, mud)*

Review Questions

1. Why did Indian people wear tattoos? (to designate honor)
2. What type of dress do Cherokee women wear today? (tear dress)
3. What did the men wear that was about six feet long and 1 foot wide? (breech cloth)
4. What determined the color of pottery? (type of wood used when firing)
5. Why did our ancestors cut their hair? (cleanliness, certain styles represented a custom from each tribe, and symbol of belief or superstition)

LESSON 7 – REGALIA

FOURTH GRADE

SAT Reading Objective: VOCABULARY

Objective: After the teacher directs this lesson, fourth grade Indian students will develop an understanding of regalia.

Objective Activity: The students will write a summary of the material learned from the lesson and create an illustration of their writing.

STATE STANDARDS Reading Objective:

PG. 40 #20   Demonstrate vocabulary growth developed through reading and listening to literature
- Have students color a picture of one of the vocabulary words from the lesson. (skins, clothes, buckskin, jewelry, etc.)
  - *What animal did our Native American ancestors use for clothes? (animal hides)*

STATE STANDARDS Social Studies Objective:

PG. 36 #11   Explain lasting contributions made by Alabama's earliest inhabitants
- After the teacher directed the lesson, class will participate in a discussion about how our ancestors contributed to many things that we still use today such as necklaces, bracelets, tattoos, etc.
  - *What did our ancestors use to make bracelets? (shells, rocks, clay, beads)*

Review Questions

1. Who was a famous Cherokee silversmith? (Sequoyah)
2. Identify the various plants used to make shades of red. (bloodroot, cranberries, beets, etc.)
3. What were some things our ancestors used to tattoo themselves? (garfish, tooth, bone, or needle)
4. What did our ancestors call their money? (wampum)
5. What type of wood was used in order to get a lighter color of pottery? (hardwood)

LESSON 7 – REGALIA

FIFTH GRADE

SAT Reading Objective: VOCABULARY

Objective: After the teacher directs this lesson, fifth grade Indian students will gain understanding and be able to identify the terms from regalia.

Objective Activity: The teacher and students will read this lesson for understanding and have an open discussion to determine comprehension.

STATE STANDARDS Reading Objective:

PG. 44 #1   Use a wide range of strategies to interpret, evaluate, appreciate, and construct meaning from print materials
- Have students listen to the lesson and answer questions about the material to show an understanding of the text and terms.
  - What animal did the Cherokees depend on for clothing? (deer)

PG. 45 #6   Demonstrate reading improvement gained through substantial amounts of daily reading
- Have students read the text from the lesson aloud. As the students read, make sure they understand the text they have read.
  - What determines the color of pottery? (type of wood used in the fire)

STATE STANDARDS Social Studies Objective:

PG. 47 #9   Describe the impact of their early European exploration and settlement on Native American cultures
- Discuss the cultural significance that the early Native Americans obtained form the Europeans. (Ex: clothing, jewelry, etc.)
  - Name one reason the Cherokees cut their hair. (cleanliness)
- Explain why Indian men plucked all of their hair out. (That was a custom or belief they practiced since childhood.)
  - Describe how the men removed their hair. (made tweezers from mussel shells and/or rocks and burned hair off using hot stones)

Review Questions

1. What were things our Indian ancestors used to make paint? (sand rocks, berries, plants)
2. Who did our ancestors trade cloth for skins with? (Europeans)
3. How did our ancestors remove their hair? (tweezers, burn with hot stones)
4. What gave our ancestors the color yellow? (yellowroot, onion skins, sunflower petals, peach leaves, etc.)
5. What was the hardest color bead to get? (purple)

LESSON 7 – REGALIA

SIXTH GRADE

SAT Reading Objective: LISTENING SKILLS

Objective: After the teacher directs this lesson, sixth grade Indian students will be able to answer questions pertaining to the lesson due to their listening skills.

Objective Activity: After a review of the lesson, ask students why are we studying Regalia? What did they make jewelry from? (beads, mussel shells, bear claws) Why did they wear masks and jewelry? (ceremonies)

STATE STANDARDS Reading Objective:

PG. 53 #12   Develop general listening behaviors for different purposes
- Read text from the lesson to the students and have them answer questions to show their listening skills. Have them to remember specific details, remember sequence of events, and paraphrase various sections of the material.
  - Why did Cherokee men wear jewelry? (wealth, success in hunting)

STATE STANDARDS Social Studies Objective:

PG. 54 #1   Extend the development of map and globe skills
- After a teacher directed lesson on clothing, jewelry, etc., explain the importance of copper to the process of making jewelry to the Native Americans.
- Explain that east Tennessee was main source of copper and that it was located in Ducktown, Tennessee.
- Also, explain the importance of the Tennessee River to the Native Americans.
- Locate these places on a state map of Tennessee and Alabama.
  - Identify the parts of an animal our ancestors used to tan its hide. (brain, fat, and/or liver)

Review Questions

1. What was our early Indian ancestors money called? (wampum)
2. What method did the early Cherokee Indians use that many Cherokee potters still use today? (coiled method)
3. What two plants were dug from the ground in the Warrior Mountains and boiled to produce their color? (bloodroot, yellowroot)
4. Describe the process our ancestors used to prepare animal hides. (remove flesh and hair, tan hides, soak hides in water, smoke hides, stretch hides to dry, work hides (leather) with both hands or slide back and forth across a pole to make pliable)
5. Who was engaged in the processing of hides? (mainly the women)

LESSON 7 – REGALIA

SEVENTH GRADE

<u>SAT</u> Reading Objective: LITERARY ELEMENTS

Objective: After the teacher directs this lesson, seventh grade Indian students will listen to cultural literary works and be able to identify main idea, summarize the text, and give significant details of Regalia.

Objective Activity: Read from the lesson and ask basic questions. What is the main idea behind our lesson? Let the entire class help summarize the lesson while the teacher writes it on the board.

<u>STATE STANDARDS</u> Reading Objective:

PG. 58 #7   Appreciate the characteristics literary elements, and cultural influences of literary works representative of various eras
- After the directed lesson, the class will have an open discussion about "Regalia." Ask students questions to ensure comprehension. Then let students make bracelets and while doing so talk with students about the colors and what they represent.
  - *Explain how the Cherokee men would tattoo themselves: (prick skin with a sharp object like a tooth, bone, or needle)*

<u>STATE STANDARDS</u> Social Studies Objective:

Online Alex #1   Describe the world in spatial terms using maps
- Show pictures of maps and explain to the students where they got their copper and mussel shells for the jewelry.
  - *Where did they get copper, mussel shells, and pearls to make jewelry? (Tennessee River)*

Review Questions

1. Name two reasons our Indian ancestors cut their hair? (cleanliness and custom)
2. Name the steps our ancestors followed to prepare the animal skins for clothing, footwear, or blankets: (1. Flesh was removed with a stone, bone, or antler 2. Hair was removed with flint scrapers 3. Tanned the hides with fat, brains, or liver 4. Hides were soaked in water 5. Skins were sometimes smoked 6. Hides were then stretched on a framework to dry 7. Leather was made pliable by working between the hands or sliding back and forth against the pole)
3. How did they make dye or paint? (mix bear grease, stain made from nature, and ashes with iron ore)
4. Name several designs that were common for Cherokee men to tattoo on themselves. (animal figure, stars, moon, sun, serpents (snakes), and scrolls)
5. Name a color and the plant material it came from. (Black-grapes, bark; Browns-walnut shells; Purples-blueberries; Blues-sunflower seeds; Greens-moss, algae; Reds-berries; Yellows-onion skins, etc.)

LESSON 8– CEREMONIAL ACTIVITIES

LESSON 8 – CEREMONIAL ACTIVITIES

Our Indian ancestors always had lots of work to do such as hunting, cooking, growing, gathering food, and fishing. But besides all their work, our folks also had lots of fun and enjoyed their lives. They loved making music and playing games just like we do today.

Cherokee Musical Instruments

Cherokee Music - Our Indian ancestors had many musical instruments such as drums, flutes, whistles, and rattles (show examples if you have them), but the most important instrument was the drum.

Drums were made from hollowed out logs and wet skins were stretched across the ends. The drum was a sacred instrument to our people. They believed the beat of the drum carried their prayers to heaven.

Most Indian dancers shook rattles to the rhythm of their dances. The rattles were made from dried gourds or even turtle shells. How many of you know what a gourd is? (a plant--show a gourd if available, let children shake it). The gourd has seeds inside that rattle when you shake it. Traditional Cherokee songs are chants made with a gourd rattle. Gourds and rattles were used to show that Indian dancers were keeping beat to the drum. Rattles were also thought of as objects of great power to be used to summon good spirits or drive away evil ones. Turtle shells were used as rattles in the corn dance. Different types of turtles were used to make the rattle including the snapping or mud turtle, the box turtle, and the water turtle (show example of at least one of the different turtle shells). The shells were laced together to keep the stones from falling out. The Creek woman, prior to performing a dance, would fasten the turtle shells to the calves of her legs.

Flutes were made from cane. They made beautiful music with their flutes.

Oh, how our Indian people loved music! They used musical instruments as a part of their ceremonies as well as for personal enjoyment, such as games. Do you enjoy music? Why? (makes you happy and feel good).

Indian men and women seemed to enjoy life. They held athletic events, played games, danced, held feasts, told stories, and played musical instruments. Many times rattles were carried by dancers as a part of their ceremonial dress.

Cherokee Games - Cherokee Indian boys and girls had lots of work to do. The maternal uncle taught the boys how to fish and hunt and the mothers taught the girls to cook and make crafts, but they still had time for games and music. The girls made dolls from corn cobs. Have you ever seen a corn cob doll? They enjoyed playing with dolls just like you do today. The Indian mother carried her baby on her back in a cradle board.

Games were an important part of our early ancestor's culture. They played a variety of games, such as ballgames and guessing games. Their favorite game was stickball where two teams played against each other using ball

Indian Mother Carrying Infant

LESSON 8– CEREMONIAL ACTIVITIES

sticks to try to score (show ball sticks). Another ballgame they played was called "chunkey" where they threw a pole to see who could throw closer to a stone disk called chunkey stone. Chunkey was a favorite game, which utilized a round stone (like a biscuit) that was rolled.

Another game was the basket and bean game. Each bean would be burned on one side and the other side left white. The six beans were tossed into the air and caught in the basket. If all of the beans land white side up, they got points. Our Indian people enjoyed this on long winter nights.

Besides ballgames, they also played guessing games with moccasins or shells (play game--see directions). Blow gun competitions as well as stickball, were important gatherings for the Cherokee towns.

Although the Indians worked very hard to do their chores in the village, they also took time out to play. One of the first games Indian people played was called "stickball" or "ballplay." Stickball or the ballplay is one Cherokee sport that has lived on throughout the years. Even though today it has been changed to erase some of its dangers, everyone still loves the ball game. The Cherokee in Cherokee, N.C. still play stickball at their Fall festival.

The day before the ball game is played is a day spent in preparation. Special sequences of events are followed to prepare participants for the game. The ball dance, going to water (dipped themselves seven times), and scratching are carefully done to bring strength, speed, courage, endurance, and purification to your team and to weaken your opponents. Sometimes players will draw a cross or a semicircle with a dot in it on their upper body as a sign of good luck. Slippery elm is chewed and the spit was rubbed on their bodies to make themselves slippery.

In the ball game, there are two teams. One village or clan plays against another village or clan. They play in a large field with a goal at each end for each of the teams. The equipment needed to play consists of two ball sticks for each player and a game ball made from soft animal skins, about the size of a walnut.

The object of the game is to be the first team to score twenty points. You score one point each time the ball crosses your goal post. You can only move the ball with your ball sticks. Sometimes it takes all day long for a team to win. Today, the points have been cut back and twelve points wins the game.

Everyone anxiously awaits the signal from the Medicine Man that he has finished the rites and is coming up from the water. One team yells three short calls that are repeated by the opposing team. They are ready to get onto the field. The Medicine Man begins the game by tossing the ball into the air and then the players try to get to the ball, by using their sticks, to score points for their team.

Many would go home with broken arms or legs, cuts, or bruises. Sometimes, players even died in their eagerness to prove their clan was the most skilled. Today, rules are given to help prevent the players from getting hurt.

Before the game began, everyone would bring their possessions to bet with. Ladies would put on all of their clothing and wager skirt against skirt, blouse against blouse with the opposing team's women. Men would wager weapons, animals, whatever they had.

Cherokee Masks - How many of you have ever been trick or treating on Halloween? Did you dress up in a costume? Most children who go trick or treating will wear some kind of mask to cover their face.

A long time ago, our Indian ancestors wore masks for different reasons. They loved to have ceremonies. A ceremony is like a big celebration or party. During these ceremonies, Indian people wore different kinds of masks while they were dancing. Some wore masks while they hunted to give them good luck so they might find many animals to kill for food. Sometimes when hunting deer, they would use a whole deerskin to cover their body so they could get closer to the animal without scaring it away. (show picture)

Our Indian people made many different kinds of masks. Some of these masks were carved from trees or made out of animal furs and some masks, such as the Booger Mask, were made from gourds. Do you know what carved means? It means to cut away

LESSON 8– CEREMONIAL ACTIVITIES

pieces of wood from a tree. The wooden masks were carved into the shape of a man's face and they were pretty ugly (show picture). The Cherokee have wooden masks that represent each of the seven clans.

Green Corn Ceremony

Cherokee Ceremonies - We're going to be learning about ceremonies. Can anyone name a ceremony that we might celebrate today? (wedding, birth, any holiday) One of the most important ceremonies for the Indian was the Green Corn Ceremony. The festival was like our Thanksgiving and New Year rolled into one. It was a time to give thanks for a successful harvest, to settle differences, and to begin a new year. The ceremony took place in July or August depending on when corn ripened. The sacred fire and corn ritual was part of the Green Corn Ceremony. Logs were laid in the form of a cross around a new fire, which the medicine man had started by twirling a fire drill. Then, the medicine man placed four ears of corn in the fire as an offering of thanksgiving to the Breath Maker for another year. Who can tell me who they think the Breath Maker could have been?

From this sacred fire, all household fires will be rekindled anew. The next five days of the festival were spent playing games and dancing. On the last day of the festival, a respected speaker of the tribe told the people to keep the ancient rites and reminded them that they were bound together because they shared the same sacred fire. Another important ceremony was the burial ceremony. There's evidence that Indians had a form of religion. They would bury their dead with ornaments and personal possessions. They were careful in the treatment of their dead implying emotions of strong affections.

Ceremonies were an important part of Indian life. Significant dates and events in the lives of Indian people were times that tribes came together to celebrate. They believed that these ceremonies could affect the outcome of certain events.

One ceremony that held great importance in the Southern tribes was the Green Corn Ceremony. This ceremony could be said to be similar to Thanksgiving.

Ceremonial Objects - Besides ceremonies, our Indian ancestors considered several things sacred. The items were of great importance to the tribe and the people who were the keepers of the items were also of importance. Some of the items considered to be sacred were tobacco, pipe, eagle feathers, and many of the items used in ceremonies. Usually the keeper was the only one

LESSON 8– CEREMONIAL ACTIVITIES

who ever touched the sacred item. It was considered to be disrespectful to touch another person's property, or an item that was in their possession without their permission. Also, in Celtic culture, it was disrespectful to touch another person's belongings without their permission.

Ceremonial pipes were among the most sacred possessions of a tribe (Brown and Owens, 1984). Depending on the person who made the pipe, it usually had things on it to represent the earth, water, and air. Some of the things used were fur from an animal, a feather from a bird, a shell from a river, and a crystal from the earth.

The bowl of the pipe was carved from stone and decorated with animals or human figures. The stem of the pipe was usually made out of red (meaning war) and white (meaning peace) wood of the eastern red cedar. It was then adorned with feathers or other materials. The ceremonial pipe was passed around the council and each member took a puff before handing the pipe to the person on his left. The pipe came to be referred to as a peace pipe because it was smoked with former enemies as a peace treaty.

Cherokee Pipes and Pipe Fragments *(Tellico Archaeology)*

LESSON 8– CEREMONIAL ACTIVITIES

KINDERGARTEN

DIBLES Reading Objective: PHONICS INSTRUCTION

Objective: After the teacher directs this lesson, Kindergarten Indian students will recognize letter sounds in the selected terms that are related to the text and/or short story.

Objective Activity: Ask students to identify each letter of the following words: corn, bean, food, spear, seed, nuts, plums, deer, quail, and fish. Also, have them identify the sound of the beginning letter.

STATE STANDARDS Reading Objective:

PG. 15 #14 Demonstrate an interest in and enjoyment of literature in a variety of forms, contexts, and media
- After the teacher discusses ceremonial customs the students will make a mask out of paper plates/construction paper. The teacher will demonstrate dances using Indian music. This will allow students to use their creativity and imagination to participate in Indian dances.
  - *What was the most important musical instrument to our Indian ancestors? (drums)*

PG. 15 #15 Use appropriate listening and speaking behaviors
- The teacher will direct a lesson about ceremonies and instruct the students to listen. The teacher will show pictures of different types of masks. The teacher will ask students questions to check for understanding.
  - *What was the most important ceremony to our Indian ancestors? (Green Corn)*

STATE STANDARDS Social Studies Objective:

PG. 12 #4 Locate new information and express understanding of the new information in various classroom activities.
- The teacher will introduce the students to Native American customs by playing different types of Indian music.
  - *Name one of the rattles used by our ancestors? (gourd, turtle shell)*

PG. 12 #7 Exhibit behaviors that are part of responsible civic life in the school setting resulting in harmonious and socially satisfying relationships with others
- The teacher will allow students to take turns using musical instruments such as a rattle. This will teach the students the responsibility of sharing.
  - *How did music make our ancestors feel? (good/happy)*

Review Questions
1. What was the most important musical instrument to the Cherokee Indians? (drum)
2. What was a game the Cherokee's played? (stickball)
3. What were the girls' dolls made from? (corn cobs and husks)
4. What were mask made from? (gourds)
5. What were rattles made from? (dried gourds and turtleshells)

LESSON 8– CEREMONIAL ACTIVITIES

FIRST GRADE

DIBELS Reading Objective: LETTER NAMING FLUENCY

Objective: After the teacher directs this lesson, first grade Indian students will develop an understanding of nonsense word fluency and beginning sounds.

Objective Activity: Take words from the text such as: tools, pottery, mussel, war, corn, and harvest. Next, write these words on the board changing the first letter of the word to a nonsense word. (Ex: tools-bools, pottery-mottery, mussel-dussel, etc.) Then orally say the word and ask student if the word sounds right? Finally, have students relate the word to the lesson and explain what letter and sound should be at the beginning of that word.

STATE STANDARDS Reading Objective:

PG. 17 #4   Demonstrate understanding of letter-sound relationships
- The teacher will discuss Native American music with the students. He/she will also talk about consonant and vowel sounds as well as blends. Choose words form the lesson and only review blends and letters used in those particular words. Say the word first, then write the first letter of the word and have students sound it out, as well as tell if it is a consonant or a vowel. Words that contain blends need to be explained and expressed to the students. (Ex: sh<u>oo</u>k, <u>wh</u>istle, ra<u>tt</u>les, <u>sh</u>ells, <u>sn</u>apping, etc.)
- *Name one of our Indian ancestors instruments? (flute, drum, whistles, rattles)*

STATE STANDARDS Social Studies Objective:

PG. 20 #29   Become acquainted with various cultures encountered in stories from literature
- After the teacher directs the lesson about ceremonies. The teacher will read "Dancing Drum" by Cohlene to the students in order for them to become acquainted with the various cultures and beliefs of our ancestors.
- *What was one of the most important ceremonies for the Indians? (Green Corn Ceremony)*

Review Questions

1. What did our early Cherokee wear as a symbol while they were dancing during a ceremony? (masks)
2. What were masks made from? (trees, animal furs, gourds)
3. Besides ballgames, what were some games our ancestors played? (guessing games, bean toss games, blowgun competitions)
4. Usually, who was the only person that touched the sacred items? (the Keeper)
5. Name one important item of a tribe. (tobacco, pipe, eagle feathers, etc.)

LESSON 8– CEREMONIAL ACTIVITIES

SECOND GRADE

DIBELS Reading Objective: TEXT COMPREHENSION

Objective: After the teacher directs this lesson, second grade Indian students will read the information learned from text accompanied by a remedial game.

Objective Activity: The teacher will read the lesson. The teacher will then ask comprehension questions that come directly from the orally read text. Use the game, *Who wants to be a Millionaire,* and allow students to decode the answer using the following format: Creek tribes were often named for their…a) <u>towns</u>, b) name, c) nation, d) people. Place the students on teams and allow one point for that team if they answer correctly.

STATE STANDARDS Reading Objective:

PG. 25 #13   Demonstrate appropriate listening and communicating behaviors
- After the directed lesson, the students will orally answer questions to ensure comprehension.
  - *What was the Cherokee's favorite game? (stickball)*

STATE STANDARDS Social Studies Objective:

Pg. 22 #22   Develop the ability to interpret and display information in graphic form
- After the teacher conducts the lesson, the class will make a chart on the board to compare ceremonies today to our Indian ancestor's ceremonies.
  - *When did the Green Corn Ceremony take place? (July or August)*
  - *When do we celebrate Thanksgiving? (November)*

PG. 25 #24   Identify major celebrations of events in U.S. history
- After the teacher conducts the lesson, the students will relate our ancestors Green Corn Ceremony to our Thanksgiving today.
  - *What did our ancestors give thanks for during the Green Corn Ceremony? (a successful harvest)*

Review Questions

1. What were rattles made from? (turtle shells and dried gourds)
2. Why did the Cherokee wear masks while hunting? (for good luck)
3. How did music make our ancestors feel? (good/happy)
4. What two colors was the stem of the pipe? (red and white)
5. Why didn't anyone touch the sacred possessions of a tribe? (It was considered disrespectful to touch another person's belongings without their permission.)

LESSON 8– CEREMONIAL ACTIVITIES

THIRD GRADE

DIBELS Reading Objective: COMPREHENSION

Objective: After the teacher directs this lesson, third grade Indian students will orally interpret and gain meaning of the selected words from the text. (Terms: stickball, ceremony, pipe, instrument, drum, Cherokee)

Objective Activity: The teacher will read each term orally to students. Discuss terms with students then let students say the words orally and tell teacher meaning of term.

STATE STANDARDS Reading Objective:

PG. 33 #12   Apply strategies of a skillful listener
- The teacher will read any text material pertaining to Cherokee ceremonies. The students will listen as the text is read and will answer questions about the text to ensure comprehension.
  - The _____ _____ Ceremony was to give thanks for the harvest, settle differences, and begin a new year. (Green Corn)

STATE STANDARDS Social Studies Objective:

PG. 31 #9   Compare cultural aspects of selected Native American groups
- Discuss cultural traditions of the Cherokee people and how they affected the societies and how they conducted their day to day life.
  - When did the thankful ceremony take place? (July or August)

Review Questions
1. What was the most sacred possession of a tribe? (ceremonial pipe)
2. What two items were use to play guessing games? (moccasins or shells)
3. Why were gourds and rattles used during ceremonies? (show that the dancers were keeping beat to the drum)
4. Why did the ceremonial pipe come to be known as the peace pipe? (smoked with former enemies as a peace treaty)
5. What did our ancestors use to bet during a game of stickball? (possessions)

LESSON 8– CEREMONIAL ACTIVITIES

FOURTH GRADE

SAT Reading Objective: COMPREHENSION

Objective: After the directed lesson, the students will gain knowledge on the material taught on ceremonial activities.

Objective Activity: The teacher will ask questions to ensure comprehension by playing the *Jeopardy* game.

STATE STANDARDS Reading Objective:

PG. 39 #15 Describe cultural similarities and differences through exposure to multicultural literature
- Discuss with the class the difference in our music and our ancestors. You can give an example such as the drum, turtleshell rattle. Make sure the class has an understanding in the differences in the music.
  - *What was the most important instrument our ancestors used? (drum)*

STATE STANDARDS Social Studies Objective:

PG. 36 #10 Describe aspects of the lives of historic Indians of Alabama
- Discuss cultural traditions of the Cherokee people and how they affected the societies and how they conducted their day to day life.
  - *What was one of the things our ancestors used to make masks? (trees, animal furs, gourds)*

Review Questions

1. What was one game the Cherokee Indians played as a team? (stickball)
2. What was the name of the ceremony like our Thanksgiving? (Green Corn Ceremony)
3. During the game of stickball, everyone awaits signal from who to start the game? (medicine man)
4. Name something our ancestors considered sacred: (eagle feather, tobacco, ceremonial pipe)
5. What did the ceremonial pipe become known as? (peace pipe)

LESSON 8– CEREMONIAL ACTIVITIES

FIFTH GRADE

SAT Reading Objective: COMPREHENSION

Objective: After the teacher directs this lesson, fifth grade Indian students will gain comprehension skills and have an understanding of ceremonial activities.

Objective Activity: Have an open discussion with students about the ceremonial activities. Compare how music and games are different and similar to today.

STATE STANDARDS Reading Objective:

PG. 44 #1   Use a wide range of strategies to interpret, evaluate, appreciate, and construct meaning from print materials
- After the teacher directs the lesson, discuss with the class how music and games are different and similar to today.
  - Name a game that our ancestors might have played? (stickball, bean game)
  - What were flutes made from? (cane)

STATE STANDARDS Social Studies Objective:

PG. 47 #9   Describe the impact of the early European exploration and settlement on Native American cultures
- Discuss with the class about the religious reasons our ancestors wore masks and why they wore them during ceremonies. (Ex: Can anyone name a ceremony that we might celebrate today?)
  - Why did our ancestors use rattles during ceremonies? (believed they could drive away evil spirits)

Review Questions

1. Why did Indians have a Green Corn Ceremony? (give thanks for harvest)
2. Who taught the boys how to fish and hunt? (maternal uncle)
3. Which direction was the ceremonial pipe passed around the council? (left)
4. Explain what took place during the Green Corn Ceremony: (In July or Aug., our ancestors laid logs in the form of a cross around a new fire, which was started by the medicine man. Then, the medicine man placed four ears of corn in the fire as an offering of thanks to the "Breath Maker" for another year. For the next five days, they played games and danced. On the last day, a respected man of the tribe would speak.)
5. What did they bury with their dead? (personal possessions and ornaments)

LESSON 8– CEREMONIAL ACTIVITIES

SIXTH GRADE

SAT Reading Objective: LITERARY ELEMENTS

Objective: After the teacher directs this lesson, sixth grade Indian students will be able to identify the literary elements of this lesson.

Objective Activity: Ask students to identify the main idea, theme, plot, setting, characters, etc. After reading about Cherokee music.

STATE STANDARDS Reading Objective:

PG. 52 #1 Interpret and construct meaning by applying appropriate strategies to material across the curriculum
- After the teacher directs the lesson, the students will read from, "Trails of the Warrior Mountains" to learn about Cherokee games and music.
  - *Describe how our ancestors prepared for a game of stickball: (They spent the day before the game preparing. They had a ball dance, sometimes drew a cross with dot in it on upper body for good luck, and chewed slippery elm bark in order to rub slimy spit on themselves to make body slippery.)*

STATE STANDARDS Social Studies Objective:

PG. 54 #1 Extend the development of map and globe skills
- The teacher will show the students a map of Lawrence County and show the students where the Oakville ceremonial mound is located. The teacher will also tell the students what the mound was used for and show them a picture of the mound. Repeat this instruction for the burial mound. *What were the two mounds called? (ceremonial and burial)*
  - *What were the two mounds used for? (ceremonies and burial)*

Review Questions

1. During the game of stickball everyone awaits the signal from whom before starting the game? (medicine man)
2. What is another name for stickball? (ballplay)
3. What did the Cherokee dancers carry around as a part of their dress? (rattles)
4. Besides wearing masks, what did some Cherokee men do when hunting? (cover body with whole deerskin to disguise themselves so they could get closer to animal without scaring it away)
5. How were the masks carved? (from wood, in the shape of an ugly man's face)

LESSON 8– CEREMONIAL ACTIVITIES

SEVENTH GRADE

<u>SAT</u> Reading Objective: LITERARY GENRES

Objective: After the teacher directs this lesson, seventh grade Indian students will be able to identify geographic and culturally diverse terms used in literary genres. (Terms: traditional, endurance, purification, etc.)

Objective Activity: Read from the "Indians of the Warrior Mountain" on the Cherokee removal from this area. Read on page 62 about Doublehead and Removal. Also, have students read the lesson aloud. Students must identify words (terms) from their reading by playing *Hangman, Jeopardy, or Wheel of Fortune*.

<u>STATE STANDARDS</u> Reading Objective:

PG. 57 #5   Recognize various forms of literature according to characteristics
- After the teacher directs the lesson, the students will be able to identify geographic and culturally diverse terms used in literary genres and their characteristics from ceremonial activities.
  - What was the most important instrument? (drum)

<u>STATE STANDARDS</u> Social Studies Objective:

Online Alex #10   Describe changes in social and economic conditions in the U.S. during the 20th and 21st centuries
- Discuss the Green Corn Ceremony.
- Discuss with the class about how our ancestors played games, what kind of music they had, why they wore mask and why they had ceremonies. Have a class discussion asking the students questions about ceremonial activities making sure they can relate to the materials. Since all important events were celebrated with dances among our Cherokee ancestors, we will do an Indian dance. Demonstrate and show pictures of Indian dances (friendship, quail, or beaver). Allow the students do the dance.
  - What was the most important ceremony that our ancestors celebrated? (Green Corn Ceremony)
  - Explain the significance of the ceremony: (celebrated beginning of new year, gave thanks for harvest, and settled differences among each other)

Review Questions

1. What did our Indian ancestors believe the beat of the drum would do? (carry their prayers to heaven)
2. Why was the "keeper" only allowed to touch someone's sacred possessions? (thought it was disrespectful to touch others personal property without permission)
3. Name several things that could have been carved in their pipes: (things to represent earth, water, and air)
4. How was the game of stickball played? (The day before was spent preparing for the game. The Ball Dance, going to water, and scratching were done to bring strength, speed, courage, endurance, and purification. They had two teams and the object of the game was to be the first team to score 20 point by hitting the ball across the goal with their ballsticks. Which ever team won, they walked away with the other tribes possessions.)
5. Why did the ceremonial pipe became known as the peace pipe? (smoked with former enemies as a peace treaty)

LESSON 9 – TENNESSEE RIVER

Tennessee River - We are going to talk about how our Cherokee Indian ancestors used the Tennessee River. The Tennessee River was first named the Hogohegee (Ho'Go'He'Gee') River of the Cherokees. The Tennessee River is the largest river that flows through North Alabama and forms the north border of Lawrence County. It begins in Tennessee, comes into Alabama in the northeast, and goes out in the northwest. The Tennessee River is a small part of the state line between Alabama and Mississippi. (Look at a map showing the location of the Tennessee River in Alabama.)

How many of you have enjoyed visiting or swimming in the Tennessee River? Some of you may have and just don't know it. If you have ever crossed the Decatur Bridge or visited the Boat Harbor then you have been at the Tennessee River. Also, some other places you may recognize which are located on the Tennessee River are Spring Creek, Mallard Creek, McFarland Park and O'Neal Bridge in Florence, Joe Wheeler Park, Wheeler Dam, Wilson Dam, Champion Park, and Ditto Landing in Huntsville.

"Big Muscle Shoals"

Have you ever wondered about how we know so much about how Indian people used to live? Most of what we know about the pre-historic Indians came from shell mounds beside the Tennessee River. Shell mounds, as you have studied earlier, are huge mounds of mussel shells (which are shells of freshwater mussels) found along the banks of the rivers. The Archaic Indians sometimes buried their dead in the mussel shells. The reason so many mussels were found in the Lawrence County portion of the Tennessee River is because of the Great Muscle Shoals. Elk River Shoals and Big Muscle Shoals lay along the northern border of Lawrence County. In addition, Little Muscle Shoals and Colbert Shoals complete the four shoals that make up the Great Muscle Shoals of North Alabama. Two other lesser Shoals were the Bee Tree Shoals and Waterloo Shoals. The Shoals were known by the Indian name of "Chake Thlocko," meaning Great Crossing Place or Big Ford.

Our Indian ancestors used the river for many things. Besides the food from the mussels, they used the Tennessee River for drinking water, to bathe in, water to cook with, fish for food, flint rocks from the riverbanks, and shells for making jewelry. They also used the river as a means of transportation.

Chert or commonly called flint was responsible for the Shoals because it does not erode. Who can tell me why flint rocks were important to the Indians? (They used flint rocks to make their tools and weapons). Flint is a type of hard rock, which can be shaped into points like arrowheads.

LESSON 9 – TENNESSEE RIVER

Much of the early tools of the Indian people were made from flint. There is an abundance of flint located along the Elk River Shoals on the Tennessee River. It was logical for the Indian people to live along the shoals of the river that contained vast amounts of mussels.

Early Cherokee Indian Trading Settlement

Besides providing our Lawrence County's prehistoric Indian people stone for tools, the Tennessee River was used as a major transportation route through North Alabama. From the river, early man could obtain a great variety of aquatic plants and animals that were an inexhaustible source of food. Along the banks of the river, early inhabitants could also find wide varieties of terrestrial plant and animal foods, rich soil compatible to farming, and protective caves and bluff shelters to make camp.

The freshwater mussels found in the Shoals were an important food supply for the tribes that settled in this region. The Mussel Shoals extended from present-day Lawrence County through Colbert County and had a fall of 134 feet within a distance of thirty-seven miles creating a vast series of rapids. According to Ortmann (1924), the Mussel Shoals received its name from the immense number of species and individuals of fresh-water mussels, which were found at this locality. The official spelling, *Muscle Shoals*, that we use today, came from an 1806 government document that later became the accepted spelling.

The Tennessee River has played an important role in the habitation of North Alabama because numerous trails crossed the shoals of the river. For example, in the Lawrence County area originates Elk River Shoals and Big Muscle Shoals the largest shoals in the Tennessee River. The Shoals consisted of the Elk River Shoals, Big Muscle Shoals, Little Muscle Shoals, Colbert Shoals, Bee Tree Shoals, and Waterloo Shoals. These shoals were known by Indian people as "Chake Thlocko" which means great crossing

LESSON 9 – TENNESSEE RIVER

place or big ford.

The Elk River Shoals includes that portion of the Tennessee River located in Lawrence County between what is now known as Mallard Creek and Spring Creek. The Big Muscle Shoals started in Lawrence County in the area that is now Joe Wheeler State Park and extended into Colbert County. Little Muscle Shoals and Colbert Shoals are not located in Lawrence County. The present-day Wilson Dam is located at the lower end of the Little Muscle Shoals.

These Shoals had an abundance of aquatic life with the fresh water mussels being very numerous. Our Indian ancestors depended upon these mussels as a seasonal source of meat for their diet. This bountiful supply of mussels caused many Indian tribes to settle in this area along the Tennessee River (show map of the Muscle Shoals).

Our Cherokee Indian people called the Tennessee River the Great Bend, the Hogohegee, and River of the Cherokees. The reason was for the shape of the river, which curves into a horseshoe shaped bend through Alabama. From Knoxville, Tennessee it flows to Alabama and winds back into Kentucky and into the Ohio River.

Foot Travel - How did our first Indian ancestors travel on land? Long ago our Indian people did not have cars and trucks to go places like we do today. We can go from place to place very quickly because we have cars and trucks to travel. The only way our Indian ancestors could go from place to place was by foot. They had to walk everywhere they went. Can you imagine how long it took them to get to another place? It took days and sometimes weeks to get to another place. How long do you think it would take you to walk to school or to town from where you live? It might take you all day, from morning to dusk.

We are going to discuss the ways our Indian people traveled. How do you think our first Indian ancestors traveled? Did they have paved roads, cars, or airplanes? No. They were surrounded by woods and streams and had to make a path and travel by foot. So the earliest form of travel was on foot. Traveling by foot was very slow and it took a long time to travel from place to place.

Dugout Canoe - Our Indian ancestors also had another way to go from place to place. They would build a dugout canoe to travel down streams and rivers. The boat was made from trees. Have any of you ever seen a dugout canoe? (Show picture of dugout canoe.) Have you ever ridden in a canoe? Indians would ride in the dugout canoe sitting on their knees, and use a long pole to paddle with.

Since our Indian folks located their villages along streams and rivers, the dugout was a very necessary vehicle to them. The dugout canoe was a much faster way for them to travel. The dugout was also used by the warriors and could carry as many as 15 to 20 men. A paddle was not used like the ones we use today. The canoe was guided by long poles. Sometimes it was guided by the water's current. The dugout canoe was made from the huge poplar tree. To get the tree down, they would start a fire at the trunk of the tree and mud or clay would be dabbed above the place to be burned to keep the tree from burning up. After the tree was down, the top was burned out and the bark peeled from the tree. Then, came the process of hollowing out the log where the men would sit. The log would burn up if the men were not careful. So, this is what was done. Mud or clay dabbed around the area that was not to be burned. This kept the fire from spreading beyond the area they wanted to hollow out. Slowly and carefully the builders of the canoe took the stone ax and chipped away the charred pieces where the fire had burned until it was hollowed out. This process was continued until the canoe was completed. The size of the dugout canoe sometimes reached 30 or 40 feet long and two feet wide.

Indian Dugout
(History of Alabama for Junior High Schools)

Most of you know that the first mode of travel for our Indian ancestors was walking. Well, today, I'm going to tell you about the second way of travel by the Cherokee Indians. This was the dugout canoe, or the tsi-yu' as the Cherokee called it. The dugout was much different from canoes made today.

Since the Cherokee located their villages along streams and rivers, the dugout was a very necessary vehicle to them.

LESSON 9 – TENNESSEE RIVER

Horses - After the first Europeans came to America, the favorite mode of travel became horse. The Spanish were the first to introduce horses into Alabama. The Cherokee eventually loved horses which greatly improved travel.

After the meeting with the first Europeans, our Indian people used horses as another way to travel. The horse was a beautiful animal and our people no longer had to walk long distances and could go a lot faster on land. The first horses in Alabama came from the Spanish explorers led by Desoto in 1540.

LESSON 9 – TENNESSEE RIVER

KINDERGARTEN

<u>**DIBELS**</u> Reading Objective: COMPREHENSION

Objective: After the teacher directs this lesson, Kindergarten Indian students will develop an understanding and be able to recognize travel methods and uses from the Tennessee River used by our ancestors.

Objective Activity: Show pictures and give explanations of Cherokee travel and ways Indians used the Tennessee River. Then, explain them well enough for students to visually recognize them. Read about Cherokee ways to travel, and then ask students to describe one mode of travel.

<u>**STATE STANDARDS**</u> Reading Objective:

PG. 15 #17 Exhibit expanded vocabulary and sentence awareness
- Take the words: river, canoe, flint, etc. from the lesson write the words on the board and sound out each individual letter with students and use them in a separate sentence. For example: We travel in _____ on water. (cars, canoes)
  - *What river was very important to the Cherokee? (Tennessee River)*

PG. 13 #1 Exhibit an awareness of the concept of story
- The teacher will show pictures of various ways of using water (Tennessee River) to the students in order to help them relate their own personal experiences to what is being taught or discussed. Ex: show pictures of Indian people fishing, in caves, etc.
  - *Name one way our Indian ancestors used water from the Tennessee River. (cooking)*

PG. 14 #9 Begin to use pictures and text to gain meaning from written material
- The teacher will show pictures of an actual canoe to the class to help them gain a better understanding of how they were made and used and help them connect what is being discussed with their prior knowledge and personal experiences with traveling in canoes.
  - *What was a canoe made from? (tree)*

<u>**STATE STANDARDS**</u> Social Studies Objective:

PG. 11 #1 Develop initial map and globe skills
- The teacher will locate the Tennessee River on a map.
- The teacher will locate Europe on a globe or world map to show the class where the first Europeans came from, which our Indian ancestors got horses from as another way to travel.
  - *What animal did our ancestors ride to get from place to place? (horse)*

PG. 14 #26 Identify human-made and natural-resources
- Our Indian ancestors used water as a means of transportation, to cook with, to bathe in, for food, for drinking, adornment, etc. They used trees to make canoes, tools, weapons, etc.
  - *Did our Indian ancestors use wood and stone or plastic to make their tools/weapons? (wood and stone)*

PG. 15 #35 Develop an awareness of how people are the same and yet different
- The teacher will lead a class discussion about how some things are still the same today as they were then. Ex: People still use horses, canoes, and foot as a means of transportation, and the Tennessee River for food and drinking water, etc.
  - *Do people still travel by canoe? (yes)*

LESSON 9 – TENNESSEE RIVER

Review Questions

1. How did our Indian ancestors travel on water? (dugout canoe)
2. What shape does the Tennessee River bend look like in Alabama? (horseshoe)
3. How many warriors did the dugout canoe carry? (15-20)
4. What was the canoe guided by? (long poles)
5. How did our Indian ancestors sit in the canoes? (on their knees)

LESSON 9 – TENNESSEE RIVER

FIRST GRADE

DIBELS Reading Objective: NONSENSE WORD FLUENCY

Objective: After the teacher directs this lesson, first grade Indian students will develop an awareness of the Cherokee lifestyle using nonsense word fluency.

Objective Activity: Throughout the lesson, take words from the text and write them on the board. Change the first letter of each word to create a nonsense word. Ask the students if the word sounds silly and explain that it's a nonsense word. Ask them if they know what letter should be at the beginning of the word to make it a real word that relates to the lesson. (Ex: <u>r</u>iver-<u>p</u>iver or <u>c</u>amp-<u>f</u>amp)

STATE STANDARDS Reading Objective:

PG. 17 #3   Exhibit phonemic awareness
- After the teacher directs a lesson about the Tennessee River the teacher will choose terms such as: shell, mussel, food, cook, tools, etc. and write them on the board. Have the students come up with rhyming words and allow them to write the word beside the original word. (Ex: tools-pools)
  - *What was the Cherokee name of the Tennessee River? (Hogohegee)*

STATE STANDARDS Social Studies Objective:

PG. 18 #3   Extend initial ability to locate new information and to express understanding in various forms
- After the teacher directs a lesson about the Tennessee River he/she will show the students where it is located on a map. Also traveling on water and land should be discussed.
  - *Identify the three ways out ancestors traveled: (foot, canoe, horse)*

PG. 19 #21 Compare transportation today to the transportation in the past
- The teacher will discuss canoes, how they were made, and what they were used for. Canoes were used as a form of transportation (talk about horses and how our ancestors walked in the beginning) so a chart could be made on the board to compare transportation then as opposed to now.
  - *How many warriors could a dugout carry? (15-20)*
  - *How long was the dugout? (30-40 feet)*

Review Questions
1. Our early ancestors used what type of material to make their hunting points? (flint)
2. Name one thing the Cherokees used the Tennessee River for. (travel, bathe, food)
3. What is flint? (a hard rock)
4. Name one important food source our ancestors found in the Tennessee River? (mussels)
5. Where is the Tennessee River located in Alabama? (northern part of Alabama)

LESSON 9 – TENNESSEE RIVER

SECOND GRADE

DIBELS Reading Objective: VOCABULARY

Objective: After the teacher directs this lesson, second grade Indian students will be able to read and identify the following terms from the text materials. (Terms: flint, climate, Southeastern, Tennessee River, establish, dugout canoe, ceremonies, and religious)

Objective Activity: The teacher will say the term and student will repeat the term. The teacher will ask students to write each term on the board then say terms as a group.

STATE STANDARDS Reading Objective:

PG. 24 #7   Read and comprehend a variety of material
- After the teacher directs the lesson, the students will be able to identify words used in the lesson.
  - *Who brought horses to America? (Europeans or Canadians)*

STATE STANDARDS Social Studies Objective:

PG. 22 #1   Develop map and globe skills appropriate to developmental level and grade level
- After directed lesson, the teacher will pass a map of Lawrence County. She will then instruct students to label the Tennessee River. (in activity book)
  - *Does the Tennessee River run across the top (north) part of Alabama or the bottom (south)? (north)*

PG. 25 #22   Compare transportation methods of families now to those used by families long ago
- Discuss with the class the difference between the ways of travel today than many of years ago. Have the students make a canoe out of construction paper, making sure the class has a understanding of our ancestors way of travel.
  - *What was the Cherokee second form of transportation? (dugout canoe)*

Review Questions
1. What was the Indian name of the Tennessee River? (Hogohegee)
2. Where are fresh water mussels found? (Muscle Shoals/Tennessee River)
3. What is the largest river that flows through Alabama? (Tennessee)
4. What year did Desoto and the Spanish explorers bring horses to Alabama? (1540)
5. What was the average length of a dugout canoe? (30-40 feet)

LESSON 9 – TENNESSEE RIVER

THIRD GRADE

DIBELS Reading Objective: WORD RECOGNITION

Objective: After the teacher directs this lesson, third grade Indian students will have a group discussion on similarities and differences of present transportation vs. past transportation. In addition, students will identify key words found in the lesson such as flint, horses, Tennessee River, transportation, European, and Spaniards.

Objective Activity: The teacher will have an oral discussion with the students about similarities and differences of foot travel/dugout canoe/horses vs. travel today.

STATE STANDARDS Reading Objective:

PG 31 #1 Use a wide range of strategies to interpret evaluate, appreciate, and construct meaning from print materials
- Using knowledge of letter-sound correspondence
- Using knowledge of word meaning.
  - *What race of people brought the horses to America? (Europeans)*
  - *How did our Indian ancestors travel first? (walking)*

STATE STANDARDS Social Studies Objective:

PG. 30 #5 Relate the elements of geography to the time of the early Native Americans
- The teacher will show the students a map of Lawrence County and the Tennessee River and show all the settlements along the Tennessee River (Ex: Great Mussle Shoals, Elk River Shoals, Big Muscle Shoals)
  - *Name one community on the Tennessee River? (Muscle Shoals)*

Review Questions
1. The dugout canoe is made from what type of wood? (poplar)
2. What river was very important to the Cherokee? (Tennessee)
3. What rock comes from the Tennessee River? (flint)
4. What was another way our ancestors used mussel shells besides food? (jewelry)
5. Flint was used to make what type of hunting point? (arrowhead)

LESSON 9 – TENNESSEE RIVER

FOURTH GRADE

<u>SAT</u> Reading Objective: LITERARY ELEMENTS

Objective: After the teacher directs this lesson, fourth grade Indian students will identify from the lesson the following literary elements: main idea, theme, characters, setting, and plot.

Objective Activity: Create a story about the importance of the Tennessee River using the information from the lesson. Ask the students to identify the main idea, where it took place, when it happened, who it involved, etc.

<u>STATE STANDARDS</u> Reading Objective:

PG 39 #11   Read materials encountered in daily lives
- After the teacher directs the lesson, the students will read from "Trails of the Warrior Mountains" about the Tennessee River.
  - *What was the Tennessee River used for? (food, travel, tools)*
  - *Where is it located? (northern part of Alabama)*

PG 39 #12   Apply strategies of a skillful listener
- As the teacher directs the lesson, the students will listen to the lesson and the teacher will check the students' listening skills by asking comprehension questions about the Tennessee River.
  - *Name three modes of travel: (foot, dugout canoe, and horses)*

<u>STATE STANDARDS</u> Social Studies Objective:

PG. 34 #2   Interpret and display information and data using various graphic organizers
- The teacher will direct the lesson and then show the students a map of Alabama, point out the Tennessee River and allow them to color the map to recognize what part of the state the river runs through.
  - *What counties does the Tennessee River run through in Alabama? (Lawrence and Morgan)*

Review Questions

1. In the Shoals, our Indian ancestors depended on what as a seasonal source of meat for their diet? (mussels)
2. Chert was commonly called? (flint)
3. What does Chake Thlocko mean? (Great Crossing Place or Big Ford)
4. Where was there an abundance of flint located? (Tennessee River)
5. Who was responsible for bringing horses to America? (Desoto and other Spanish explorers)

LESSON 9 – TENNESSEE RIVER

FIFTH GRADE

SAT Reading Objective: LITERARY ELEMENTS

Objective: After the teacher directs this lesson, fifth grade Indian students will be able to recognize the main idea, theme, setting, etc.

Objective Activity: Play *Jeopardy, Hangman or Wheel of Fortune* to review questions about the importance of the Tennessee River.

STATE STANDARDS Reading Objective:

PG 45 #5   Interpret passages in print material
- Direct students to read aloud from the lesson and discuss the literary elements.
  - *What tribe of Indians were discussed in the lesson? (Cherokee)*
  - *Why did they depend on the river so much? (food and travel)*

STATE STANDARDS Social Studies Objective:

PG. 46 #4   Describe the natural environment of North America
- Show the students where Tennessee is located on a state map
- Show the students the four shoals that make up the Great Muscle Shoals of North Alabama and discuss how mussels were an important food supply. (Show them a mussel shell)
  - *What river did our ancestors rely on in Lawrence County? (Tennessee River)*

Review Questions

1. Who first introduced horses into Alabama as a new mode of travel? (Desoto)
2. Define the term "Chake Thlocko": (Great Crossing Place or Big Ford)
3. What does Hogohegee mean? (River of the Cherokees)
4. What were the three names for the Tennessee River? (Great Bend, Hogohegee, River of the Cherokees)
5. Name the three states the Tennessee River runs through? (TN, AL, MS)

LESSON 9 – TENNESSEE RIVER

SIXTH GRADE

SAT Reading Objective: PHONETIC PRINCIPLES

Objective: After the teacher directs this lesson, sixth grade Indian students will be able to recognize, understand, and apply different elements from the text on the Tennessee River.

Objective Activity: The teacher will select terms that students are unfamiliar with and have them to look up the meanings.

STATE STANDARDS Reading Objective:

PG 52 #4   Demonstrate reading improvement gained through the substantial amounts of daily reading
- After the teacher directs a lesson, the students will read "Warrior Mountain Folklore" about the Tennessee River. After they read aloud they will discuss orally preselected questions.
    - There is an abundance of _____ rock found along the Tennessee River? (flint)

STATE STANDARDS Social Studies Objective:

PG. 54 #1   Extend the development of map and globe skills
- The teacher will show the students where the Tennessee River is on a map and what states it runs through.
    - What states does the Tennessee River run through besides Alabama? (Tennessee, and Kentucky)

Review Questions
1. What is the largest river that flows through Alabama and forms the north border of Lawrence County? (Tennessee River)
2. What counties in Alabama does the Tennessee River run through? (Lawrence and Morgan)
3. Explain why the Tennessee River was also called "The Great Bend" by the Cherokee. (it curves into a horseshoe shaped bend through Alabama)
4. What did our ancestors use the mussel shells to build? (shell mounds)
5. What did the Cherokees call the Shoals? (Chake Thlocko--meaning Great Crossing Place or Big Ford)

LESSON 9 – TENNESSEE RIVER

SEVENTH GRADE

SAT Reading Objective: VOCABULARY

Objective: After the teacher directs this lesson, seventh grade Indian students will gain an understanding of various words from the text.

Objective Activity: Allow students to participate in a word game such as *Hangman*. Have them identify the word and meaning. (Ex: erode, vast, inexhaustible, originates, compatible, abundance, logical, inhabitants, immense, terrestrial, aquatic, and bountiful)

STATE STANDARDS Reading Objective:

PG 58 #11   Refine general listening behaviors
- After the teacher directs the lesson, the students will read aloud from "Indian Trails of the Warrior Mountains" about the Tennessee River.
  - *What were the three Indian names for the Tennessee River? (Great Bend, Hogohegee, River of the Cherokees)*

STATE STANDARDS Social Studies Objective:

Online Alex #2   Analyze regional characteristics for factors that contributed to change and for their relative importance
- The teacher will show the students the importance of the Tennessee River to the students by showing the students where the Cherokees got their pearls and copper for jewelry, their mussels to eat, bluff shelters to camp in, and protective caves to live in.
  - *Why was the Tennessee River called the "Great Bend?" (its horseshoe shape)*

Review Questions

1. What place in North Alabama was known by its Indian name of "Chake Thlocko" meaning Great Crossing place or Big Ford? (Shoals)
2. The Tennessee River is a small part of the state line between what two states? (Alabama and Mississippi)
3. What did the Archaic Indian sometimes use the shell mounds for: (bury dead)
4. What state park in Alabama is located on the Tennessee River? (Joe Wheeler State Park)
5. What was the first process of hollowing out the log: (set it on fire)

LESSON 10 – EUROPEAN CONTACT

Meeting of Desoto and Giant Chief Tuscaloosa
(History of Alabama for Junior High Schools)

Desoto - We are learning about Desoto. Who was Hernando Desoto? (He was a Spanish explorer) Desoto was the first European to move inland to the heart of Alabama Indian Country. Desoto's goal was to conquer the Indians, steal their gold and become a very wealthy man.

In 1540, Desoto entered Alabama and crossed the Tennessee River near Guntersville. He was thought to be the first European to discover the Tennessee River. Desoto's party consisted of about 600 men and in addition numerous Indians who went along as guides, laborers, and bearers of burdens. Desoto obtained food by seizing it from the Indians who had stored up small amounts for their own use. It was Desoto's custom to seize Indian chiefs who were then held hostage to ensure that Desoto got what he wanted. One of these was Chief Tuskaloosa. Tuscaloosa is a Creek Indian word that means "Black Warrior." The lusa or loosa means "black" and tusca or tusica means "warrior."

When Desoto and his men first came to Alabama, Indian people welcomed the Spaniards. Desoto was cruel to Indians. Chief Tuskaloosa and his warriors fought a battle with Desoto. Since Desoto and his men had guns, the Indians lost the fight. According to Desoto's reports, about 2500 Indians were killed. Tuskaloosa was one of them. There were only 80 of Desoto's men killed. The Spaniards were willing to fight the Indians, because they had armor to protect themselves from the Indian arrows. The greatest of all advantages was the fact that the Spaniards had horses.

Desoto did not find gold in Alabama. After the battle, he led his group further west. Desoto was the first European who discovered the Mississippi River. Desoto was the first European to discover the Tennessee River, the Coosa, the Tallapoosa, the Alabama, the Black Warrior, the Sipsey, the Tombigbee, and many lesser Creeks and streams of Alabama. After he died, his men buried him in the mighty Mississippi River. They did not want our Indian ancestors to know their leader was dead.

After Desoto, other men from Spain came into Alabama. None of them settled down to stay. Although, Desoto never found the gold that he so desperately sought in Alabama, he became one of the most famous explorers anywhere in the world.

Diseases - New world diseases were among the greatest killers of Southeastern Indian people, both intentionally and unintentionally. The devastation of disease helped break the power of Native Americans and left them vulnerable to cultural changes brought by invading Europeans. Our Indian folks had no immunities to these diseases; therefore, the Indian population diminished.

Smallpox was the worst of the new diseases. Other diseases included measles, typhus, tuberculosis, chicken pox, bubonic plague, diphtheria, and influenza. Smallpox would infect almost every individual who became exposed; 30 percent or more would die. For those who did survive, they would have disfiguring pockmarks on their bodies. Some even became blind.

Later, cholera epidemics came about. Cholera was transmitted by water infected by the disease germ. United States troops often transmitted the disease to Native Americans. Another was scarlet fever, which was not identified by the medical profession as a distinct affliction until the 18th century. Other diseases of lesser significance among the Native Americans were whooping cough, malaria, and mumps. There was also diabetes, which still affects American Indian people today.

LESSON 10 – EUROPEAN CONTACT

Lamar Marshall – Proud of his Celtic-Indian Heritage

Celtic Contact - During the 1600s, Celtic people came into the Lawrence County area as traders following Indian trails and roads. These Celtic people were Irish, Scotch, Welsh, or Scots-Irish descent. Many Celtic men married these young, beautiful Indian women. In the 1700s, many more Celtic men married Indian maidens and made their home here. The Chickasaws were the first to form communities of mixed ancestry, one known as McIntoshville in northeast Mississippi and another known as Breed Town on the Coosa River in Alabama.

Metis (mixed Native Americans) - Between 1816 and 1840, thousands of the southeastern Indians intermingled by marriage with Celtic (Irish, Scotch, Scots-Irish, Welsh) pioneers who rapidly moved into the Indian nations. Many of these mixed-blood Indian people were eventually forced into hiding or denial of their Indian ancestry because of their fear of removal to the west by the United States Government. The newly established southern states, still in their infancy in the early 1800s refused the right of the Cherokee, Creek, or Chickasaw to establish Indian nations within the newly recognized sovereign states of Alabama, Georgia, Mississippi, and Tennessee.

In 1729, James Logan Colbert (Scotch) married three Chickasaw wives who bore him many children. James Colbert was in charge of a large pack train that brought British trade goods to North Alabama. Over the years, mixed-blood settlements separated themselves more and more from primitive full bloods. By the 1800s, the mixed-bloods had taken over management of Chickasaw tribal affairs.

John Melton (Irish) came into Lawrence County in the 1770s with the Cherokee Indians. He married a Cherokee woman. Melton had several children by his Indian wife, most of whom married white people. John Melton lived here in our county until his death in 1815. He founded the Cherokee town known as Melton's Bluff.

Remarkable advancement of the Cherokee as a people came about largely through the influence of Celtic families of mixed ancestry- Irish, Welsh, Scotch, Scots-Irish, and Cornish. During Indian removal, mixed-blood inhabitants remain in North Alabama because they were married to whites or were able to identify themselves with white ancestry. They sometimes called themselves Black Dutch or Black Irish to deny their true Indian blood.

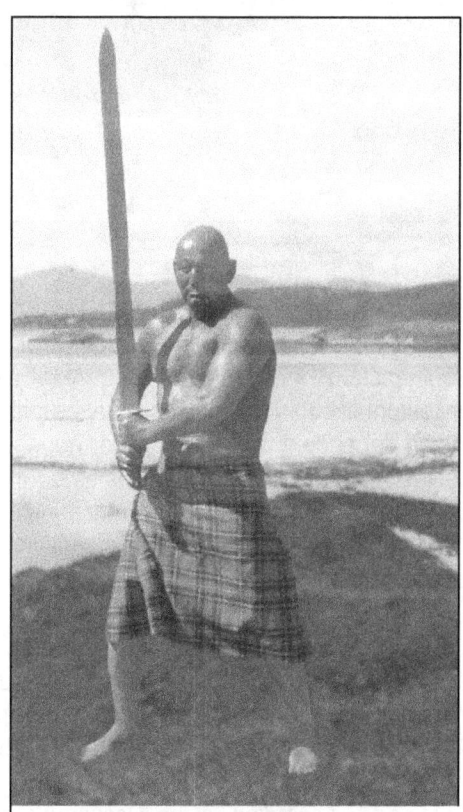

Butch Walker – Proud of his Celtic-Indian Heritage

Fearing not only for their personal property but also their lives, the remaining Indian people in Lawrence County denied their Indian race, held to white man's ways, and blended their Indian and Celtic culture. The two cultures became assimilated in the general population. As children of mixed ancestry grew older, they were told of their Indian ancestors, but were not allowed to claim their rightful heritage. Since Indian removal, the degree of Indian blood of Lawrence County's people has steadily diminished and will continue to do so throughout future generations. With the passage of Section 2 through 7 of the Civil Right Act of 1968, it became legal to be Indian and live in Alabama. Many Indian descendants of mixed ancestry began to seek and reclaim their Indian heritage, but for many it was too late.

LESSON 10 – EUROPEAN CONTACT

Presently, about one-fifth (20%) of Lawrence County's school children are state recognized Indians of mixed Celtic ancestry. The majority of Lawrence County's Indian children have Cherokee, Chickasaw, or Creek bloodlines. As an Indian person, you have a right to claim your race as Indian and should do so, but never deny any of your other previous ancestors.

European Trade - We are going to be talking about trade with our Indian ancestors. Trade was a very important part of their lives, because they didn't have money to buy things. Can anyone name something that they might have traded? (beads, furs, pottery)

The whites would trade strings of cheap beads for deerskins. Trade between Indian people and Europeans was based mostly on animal skins. An Indian could get a rifle for about 30 deerskins.

Trading Party led by Chief Doublehead

Native animals such as whitetail deer, black bear, eastern cougar, timber wolves and eastern elk became depleted throughout the Southeastern United States, because of all the hunting and trading. Trading with the white man changed the way our Indian ancestors lived. Trading wasn't necessarily a good thing for Indian people. Can anyone say why? (Because it was making the Indian dependent on the whites for guns, cloth, and manufactured goods.) The traders found that they could manipulate Indian people. Most of the time, Indians hated them, so the traders usually lived hard and dangerous lives. One of the other items for trade was Indian slaves. The French justified Indian slavery on the grounds that it saved them from cruel deaths at the hands of their enemies. In 1708, the total population of South Carolina was 9,580 including 2,900 blacks and 1,400 Indian slaves. In 1712, an Indian man and woman sold for 18 or 20 pounds.

Doublehead, by the 1800s, was living in Lawrence County at Brown's Ferry. His old home site is still visible across the river from the Brown's Ferry Nuclear Plant. He requested a keelboat in 1802 for cotton trade to New Orleans. In 1805, he signed the Wafford Settlements, which allowed for Gaines Trace. The Trace allowed cotton trade to Cotton Gin Port, MS, and East Port, MS. At Doublehead's death on August 9, 1807, he owned 30 slaves.

Jackson – According to the *Documents on United States Indian Policy*, written by Francis P. Prucha, on December 8, 1829, record that President Andrew Jackson said, "The Southern tribes, having mingled much with the whites and made some progress in the arts of civilized life, have lately attempted to erect an independent government within the limits of Georgia and Alabama.

LESSON 10 – EUROPEAN CONTACT

These States, claiming to be the only sovereigns within their territories, extended their laws over the Indians, which induced the latter to call upon the United States for protection."

Jackson went on to say, "It seems to me visionary to suppose that in this state of things claims can be allowed on tracts of country on which they have neither dwelt nor make improvements, merely because they have seen them from the mountain or passed them in the chase." Jackson, the great Indian fighter of the Southeast, believed in the spoils system, "To the victor belongs the spoils of the war." After the Turkey Town Treaty in September 1816, Jackson laid claim to the Irish-Cherokee Indian farmland at Melton's Bluff in Lawrence County, Alabama, on November 22, 1816. As he acquired from the local Irish-Indian people at Melton's Bluff prior to the time that any legal land claims could be made, Jackson had no reservations about eliminating all Indian lands east of the Mississippi River after becoming President of the United States.

Denial - During the turbulent times in the early history of the Southeastern United States, Celtic people, who have always been somewhat rebellious freedom seekers, migrated into the Southeastern Indian farmlands, mingled with the native people, and married into their tribes. As the Federal Government forced the removal issue during the 1830's under Jackson's administration, mixed-blood Celtic-Indians began moving from the Cherokee Nation in Alabama, the Carolinas, Georgia, and Tennessee into the Warrior Mountains of northern Alabama. The mountains provided isolation and protection as long as they denied their Indian backgrounds. The Celtic-Indians, who were of dark complexion, would many times claim to be Black Dutch or Black Irish and deny their rightful Indian descent in order to stay in their aboriginal lands.

Intermarriage of Celtic and Indian people, who settled primarily on the poor isolated lands found in the Warrior Mountains of Lawrence County as well as other isolated areas of northern Alabama, was common. After looking into their eyes and examining the features of those who make efforts to reclaim links to their Indian past, many common threads appear which not only strengthen but also confirm that the vast majority of these people are truly Celtic-Indians afflicted with over 150 years of denial. Isolationism and intermarriage forced their complexions fairer through the genetic sieve of the Celtic which transcends nearly four centuries. However, from within their hearts they speak with a straight tongue of their Indian ancestors who survived in the Warrior Mountains of Lawrence County, Alabama.

The Trail Of Tears - More than 150 years ago the Southeastern Indians became a conquered people. This did not happen quickly or easily. They had fought to stay and keep their land and had lost. They arrived like ghosts in Oklahoma, their destination. All of them were footsore, sick, and weary of their long journey, which began in October 1838 and ended in March 1839. They had walked more than 800 miles and more than 4,000 died. Many arrived more dead than alive.

Indian Removal Act 1830 - The Cherokee Removal came after years of pressure by white settlers who said they needed the Cherokees' land. And so, they said, the Cherokees must go. President Thomas Jefferson was the first to initiate the removal of some 1,130 Cherokees from our area in the summer of 1808.

On May 28, 1830, congress passed an act authorizing the exchange of lands in the west for those lands east of the Mississippi River held by Indian tribes. President Andrew Jackson was determined to see all Indian people removed from the eastern United States.

LESSON 10 – EUROPEAN CONTACT

KINDERGARTEN

DIBLES Reading Objective: VOCABULARY / LETTER NAMING

Objective: After the teacher directs this lesson, Kindergarten Indian students will verbally identify the main vocabulary terms presented and name the letters in each word.

Objective Activity: The teacher will read aloud short sentences from the lesson and will verbally identify different vocabulary words from the text. The students will recognize if the words are used correctly or incorrectly. The students will identify the letters that make up selected words.

STATE STANDARDS Reading Objective:

PG. 14 #6   Demonstrate an initial understanding of letter-sound relationships
- The teacher will instruct a lesson about Desoto. Take words having to do with Desoto such as: chief, men, warrior, river, etc.
- The teacher will write the words on the board and the students tell what each letter is and the sound it makes.
  - *Who was the first Spanish explorer in Alabama? (Desoto)*

PG. 15 #17 Exhibit expanded vocabulary and sentence awareness
- The teacher will instruct a lesson about European trade and then have a group discussion.
  - *Name one thing our ancestors traded. (beads, fur, pottery)*

STATE STANDARDS Social Studies Objective:

PG. 11 #3   Develop initial ability to display information in graphic form
- The teacher will talk to the students about Andrew Jackson and Lawrence County. then show a map of Lawrence County. Students will color the map of Lawrence County.
  - *Who was the first white land owner in Lawrence County? (Andrew Jackson)*

PG. 12 #11 Discover characters and events from literature that demonstrate the impact of one person's behavior upon another
- After talking about Andrew Jackson and the impact he had on the Trail of Tears, the teacher will discuss the feelings that their ancestors might have had.
  - *How many people died on the Trail of Tears? (about 4,000)*

Review Questions

1. What did our ancestors trade? (skins)
2. Who wanted to steal the Indians gold and become wealthy? (Desoto)
3. Did Desoto and his men have guns? (yes)
4. Did Desoto find gold in Alabama? (no)
5. What was the worst of the New World diseases? (small pox)

LESSON 10 – EUROPEAN CONTACT

FIRST GRADE

DIBELS Reading Objective: TEXT COMPREHENSION

Objective: After the teacher directs this lesson, first grade Indian students will be able to relate to the information learned from an orally read text. The students will also be asked various questions to ensure their comprehension.

Objective Activity: Play *Who wants to be a Millionaire* and allow students to decode the answer using this format: Who was the first European to discover the Tennessee River? (Abraham, <u>Desoto</u>, Sam) Place students on teams and allow one point for each correct answer.

STATE STANDARDS Reading Objective:

PG. 20 #6   Comprehend material read, heard, or viewed
- The teacher will conduct a lesson about diseases carried by our Indian ancestors. When the lesson is over the teacher will check for understanding by asking questions.
  - *Name the worst New World disease? (small pox)*

PG. 21 #16   Demonstrate appropriate listening and speaking behaviors
- The teacher will direct a lesson on Desoto. He/she will model how to listen while someone is speaking and how he/she should speak to the students. When the teacher is finished with the lesson he/she will ask questions to check for understanding.
  - *Was Hernando Desoto Japanese or Spanish? (Spanish)*

STATE STANDARDS Social Studies Objective:

PG. 19 #13   Exhibit an awareness of the ways personal actions benefit or harm the local environment
- The teacher will discuss Andrew Jackson and his contribution to the removal of Indians in the state of Alabama. His actions resulted in a tragic and life altering moment in time known as "The Trail of Tears."
- Make sure students understand the fact that one person's actions can effect the lives of others. Sometimes positive and sometimes negative. Refer to the environment in which our ancestors lived.
  - *Who was responsible for the Indian removal? (Andrew Jackson)*
  - *How many miles did our ancestors walk? (more than 800)*

Review Questions

1. Who was the first Spanish explorer in Alabama? (Hernando Desoto)
2. How many deerskins did our ancestors trade for one rifle? (30)
3. Tuscaloosa is a Creek Indian word meaning what? (Black Warrior)
4. How many men did Desoto have with him? (600)
5. Was Desoto nice to the Indians? (no)

LESSON 10 – EUROPEAN CONTACT

SECOND GRADE

DIBELS Reading Objective: LISTENING AND COMMUNICATING

Objective: After the teacher directs this lesson, second grade Indian students will be able to identify and orally communicate the terms listed from the text. (Terms: settlers, Oklahoma, removal, defeated, declared, Lawrence County)

Objective Activity: The teacher will say the word orally and the students will repeat the term. The teacher will ask students to write a sentence on the board using each term.

STATE STANDARDS Reading Objective:

PG. 24 #7   Read and comprehend a variety of materials
- After the directed lesson, the teacher will ask the students questions to ensure they have comprehended the text that was taught.
  - *Who was Desoto? (first European explorer)*

PG. 25 #10   Read orally with accuracy, fluency, and comprehension
- Have students read a story about the Trail of Tears, and once they are finished ask questions to be sure they understood what they read.
  - *What was the greatest killer of southeastern Indian people? (New World diseases)*

STATE STANDARDS Social Studies Objective:

PG. 22 #2   Develop the ability to interpret and display information in graphic form
- Discuss how the past differs from the present on European contact.
  - *Name some of the diseases: (smallpox, Cholera, bubonic plague, influenza, etc.)*

Pg. 25 #26   Describe the contributions of significant individuals who have affected our lives
- After the teacher conducts the lesson on European contact, he/she can ask students questions about how the Europeans actions affected our Indian ancestors.
  - *Name some things that the Indians traded with the Europeans: (beads, furs, pottery)*
  - *How many miles did our ancestors walk on the Trail of Tears? (over 800 miles)*

Review Questions
1. How many deerskins could an Indian trade for a rifle? (30)
2. Who was the first white land owner in Lawrence County? (Andrew Jackson)
3. Approximately how many people died on the Trail of Tears? (4,000)
4. Where was Desoto buried? (Mississippi River)
5. To what state did our ancestors have to walk during the Trail of Tears? (Oklahoma)

LESSON 10 – EUROPEAN CONTACT

THIRD GRADE

DIBELS Reading Objective: ORAL READING FLUENCY

Objective: After the teacher directs this lesson, third grade Indian students will read aloud and demonstrate oral reading fluency.

Objective Activity: Read a Cherokee lesson. Ask students to read aloud from the lesson and orally discuss the similarities and differences of European contact.

STATE STANDARDS Reading Objective:

PG. 32 #8 Read grade level texts aloud and silently with fluency and comprehension
- Have students read orally using the overhead projector.
  - *Identify several New World diseases. (small pox, measles, chicken pox, typhus, tuberculosis, bubonic plague, influenza, diphtheria, cholera, scarlet fever, whooping cough, malaria, and mumps)*

STATE STANDARDS Social Studies Objective:

PG. 31 #9 Compare cultural aspects of selected Native American groups
- Discuss how the European traded with our Indian ancestors such as the whites would trade strings of cheap beads for deerskins.
  - *Identify several things that the Indians traded with the Europeans? (beads, furs, pottery)*
  - *How many deerskins did our ancestors trade to the white men for a rifle? (30)*

PG. 31 #11 Describe relationships between early settlements and the natural environment
- Explain to the class why our ancestors lost their land by fighting. Also how they walked more than 800 miles which became known as the Trail of Tears.
  - *How many Cherokees died in the "Trail of Tears?" (over 4,000)*
  - *Where did they have to move? (Oklahoma)*

PG. 31 #13 Describe land use by Native Americans and Europeans
- Explain to students what the Indians would trade with the Europeans. (furs, beads, guns)

Review Questions
1. Who was the first European to discover the Tennessee River? (Desoto)
2. What disease killed thousands? (small pox)
3. Which disease was transmitted through the water? (Cholera)
4. Which man had three Chickasaw wives? (James Colbert)
5. What was Andrew Jackson responsible for? (Indian removal)

LESSON 10 – EUROPEAN CONTACT

FOURTH GRADE

<u>SAT</u> Reading Objective: LISTENING SKILLS

Objective: After the teacher directs this lesson, fourth grade Indian students will use their listening skills to comprehend the information about European contact.

Objective Activity: The teacher will show and discuss pictures of the maps in the "Indian Trails of the Warrior Mountains" book and the "Indian Trails and Towns" map in the classroom involving European contact, such as: Lawrence County, Tennessee River, Coosa Path, and Tallapoosa. Students will be asked to identify the Indian trails that went through their area.

<u>STATE STANDARDS</u> Reading Objective:
PG. 39 #11   Read materials encountered in daily lives
- After the conducted lessons have students read sentence/paragraph from the text and ask questions to be sure they comprehend what they read.
  - *Who was the first Spanish explorer in Alabama? (Hernando Desoto)*

PG. 39 #15   Describe cultural similarities and differences through exposure to multicultural literature
- Discuss (open discussion) with the students about different aspects of our ancestors' lives versus our lives today. (schooling, housing, diseases)
  - *What made the Indian population diminish? (New World diseases)*

<u>STATE STANDARDS</u> Social Studies Objective:
PG. 35 #8   Assess the impact of European contact on Native American populations in Alabama
- While teacher directs lesson, he/she should discuss the impact the European contact had on Native Americans.
  - *Approximately how many Cherokees died on the Trail of Tears and how far did they walk? (4,000/800 miles)*

Review Questions
1. What does Métis mean? (mixed Native American)
2. Identify several waterways Desoto discovered. (Tennessee River, Tombigbee, the Black Warrior, the Coosa River, the Tallapoosa, etc.)
3. What tribe of Indians were the first to form communities of mixed ancestry? (Chickasaw)
4. What descent are Celtic people? (Irish, Scotch, Welsh, Scots-Irish)
5. The Celtic-Indians, who were of dark complexion, would many times claim to be? (Black Dutch or Black Irish)

LESSON 10 – EUROPEAN CONTACT

FIFTH GRADE

<u>SAT</u> Reading Objective: GENRES

Objective: After the teacher directs this lesson, fifth grade Indian students will recognize the features of a variety of genres.

Objective Activity: After the lesson, play a game with the students to review questions from the lesson. (ex: *Jeopardy*)

STATE STANDARDS Reading Objective:

PG. 46 #12   Read a variety of materials and genres encountered in daily lives
- Have a discussion on European impact on daily lives of local Indian tribes.
  - *Desoto was the first Spanish to discover what river? (Tennessee)*

STATE STANDARDS Social Studies Objective:

PG. 47 #9   Describe the impact of the early European exploration and settlement on Native American cultures
- After a teacher directed lesson, the students will take part in a class discussion about the impact of the Europeans on the Native Americans such as horses, weapons, etc.
- Show the students where Europe is located, making sure to label the Atlantic Ocean also.
  - *What act was passed in 1830 that caused the Cherokee to move to Oklahoma also known as the Trail of Tears? (Indian Removal Act of 1830)*

Review Questions

1. What was the worst of the New World diseases brought in by invading Europeans? (smallpox)
2. What month did the Trail of Tears begin? (October)
3. What was it called when Celtic's married Indians? (intermarriage)
4. What year did the Trail of Tears begin and end? (began-October 1838, ended-March 1839)
5. Approximately how many Cherokees died of the small pox disease? (30% or more)

LESSON 10 – EUROPEAN CONTACT

SIXTH GRADE

SAT Reading Objective: VOCABULARY

Objective: After the teacher directs this lesson, sixth grade Indian students will be able to recognize and identify different culturally diverse geographical terms and vocabulary terms listed from the text on European contact. (Terms: Cholera, trade, intermarriage, etc.)

Objective Activity: After the teacher reviews the lesson, Indian students will play *Jeopardy* and include the terms selected from the lesson. Teacher will read each new word aloud and define or explain what the word means. Students will then be asked to define the words.

STATE STANDARDS Reading Objective:

PG. 53 #10   Recognize linguistic and cultural diversity
- After the teacher directs the lesson, the students will be able to recognize and identify different culturally diverse geographical terms and vocabulary terms listed from the text on European contact. The students will play *Jeopardy* and include the terms selected from the lesson. The teacher will read each new word aloud and define or explain what the word means. Students will then be asked to define the words.
  - ∞ Explain how the New World diseases hurt the Cherokee Indians. *(They had no medicine, some died or went blind, left them vulnerable to Europeans.)*

STATE STANDARDS Social Studies Objective:

PG. 55 #4   Review major changes in America from 1870 to 1900
- Discuss with the class how our ancestors' cultural changes are similar and different from us today, or either have a class discussion. Since European trade was an important part have the students make a bead bracelet or something made from pottery. Have them understand or visualize what they traded.
  - ∞ How much would an Indian man or woman (slave) sell for in the 1700s? *(18-20 pounds)*

Review Questions
1. How many miles did our Indian ancestors walk on the Trail of Tears? (over 800)
2. What act was passed in 1830 that caused the Cherokee to move to Oklahoma, also known as the Trail of Tears? (Indian Removal Act of 1830)
3. What was the destination of the Cherokee people on the Trail of Tears? (Oklahoma)
4. Where did the Chickasaws first form communities of mixed ancestry? (McIntoshville)
5. How many of Desoto's men were killed? (80)

LESSON 10 – EUROPEAN CONTACT

SEVENTH GRADE

SAT Reading Objective: COMPREHENSION

Objective: After the teacher directs this lesson, seventh grade Indian students will be able to interpret and demonstrate an understanding about the impact of the European contact on the Native Americans.

Objective Activity: Popcorn reading from the lesson in your classroom. Next, ask the students comprehensive questions about the text on European contact.

STATE STANDARDS Reading Objective:

PG. 58 #11   Refine general listening behaviors
- After the teacher directs the lesson, the students will read aloud from "Indian Trails of the Warrior Mountains" about a preselected topic from the lesson.
  - Name eight of the diseases that devastated the southeastern Indians? *(small pox, measles, typhus, tuberculosis, influenza, chicken pox, bubonic plague, diphtheria)*

STATE STANDARDS Social Studies Objective:

Online Alex #10   Describe changes in social and economic conditions in the U.S. during the 20th and 21st centuries
- After the teacher directs the lesson, the students will discuss the changes in the conditions of how our Indian ancestors once lived versus the 20th century when they were able to distinguish themselves as Native Americans.
  - In the 19th century what was Andrew Jackson famous for doing to the Indians? *(removing Native Americans which was known as the Trail of Tears)*

Review Questions

1. What race did the Celtic Indians claim to be in order to stay in Alabama? (Black Dutch or Black Irish)
2. How long did the Trail of Tears last? (5 months)
3. Who was the Irishman that came into Lawrence County in the 1770's with the Cherokee Indians and founded a Cherokee town known as Melton's Bluff? (John Melton)
4. Why did Doublehead request a keelboat in 1802? (for cotton trade to New Orleans)
5. What made the Indian population diminish? (New World diseases)

LESSON 11 – FIVE TRIBES OF LAWRENCE COUNTY / MID-TEST

There were five major Indian tribes of early Lawrence County, Alabama. When the first European settlers came to Alabama, lesser Indian tribes were also found in Alabama. The four major tribes of Alabama: Creek, Choctaw, Chickasaw and Cherokee, along with the Seminoles of Florida, are often referred to as the "five civilized tribes." Their civilization was very advanced according to historic documents about the area and due to the intermarriage with Celtic people and other Europeans.

Tribal Movement according to the Tradition and Earliest Records

The five major Indian tribes of Lawrence County were Yuchi, Creek, Shawnee, Chickasaw, and Cherokee. These were five groups of historic Indian people known by tribal names instead of by cultures. Most Indian people of the historic period lived in villages near rivers or other waterways. They were both farmers and hunters. They believed the land belonged to all people, and they took care of the part they used. They killed only the animals they needed for food, and then used the skins for clothes or cover.

The four major Alabama tribes occupied most of the southeastern United States, but their territories met in Alabama. Each was in a corner of the state. The Cherokees, Creeks, and Chickasaws lived in Lawrence County. The Chickasaw and Cherokee were in the two northern corners. The Cherokees were mainly on the northeast side of Alabama, and the Chickasaws on the northwest. The Choctaws occupied the west and southwest while the Creeks were in the northern side of Alabama, central, and southeastern part of Alabama. Although the four tribes were similar in many ways, they each had their own customs and beliefs. If their differences could have been overcome, perhaps they could have banded together in the nineteenth century and prevented their removal to western lands by the Federal Government.

Andrew Jackson - Andrew Jackson was the first white landowner in Lawrence County, Alabama at Melton's Bluff. He purchased the land from a Cherokee named David Melton, on November 22, 1816. He called the land the Muscle Shoals Plantation and his town, he named Marathon. He sold his Lawrence County land in 1827, probably to the Gilchrist family.

The election of Andrew Jackson as President in 1828 resulted in one of the darkest eras for the American Indians in Alabama. The Alabama Emigrating Company forcefully removed our Indian ancestors from the State of Alabama and surrounding southern states. Thousands of southern Indians died while they were being forced to march on the infamous Trail of Tears.

Water and fire were sacred to the Creeks and most ceremonies centered on one or the other. The first duty of every Creek each morning was to bathe in the nearby river or stream even in very cold weather. In each village, the sacred fire had to be kept burning day and night. This fire was extinguished only at the time of the Green Corn Festival.

Andrew Jackson

LESSON 11 – FIVE TRIBES OF LAWRENCE COUNTY / MID-TEST

Yuchi - The Yuchi were here when five Canadians descended down the Tennessee River in 1701. John R. Swanton in his book, The Indians of the Southeastern United States, shows the Yuchi living in this area at the Mussel Shoals in the early 1700s. For some reason, part of the Yuchi migrated to the Hiwassee River in Tennessee and the rest migrated south to the Chattahoochee River on the Alabama-Georgia border. After fighting the Cherokee in Tennessee, these northern Yuchi also migrated south to the Chattahoochee River Valley.

Creek Indian *(George Catlin)*

Creek - The Creeks were Muscogee people who lived in the central, eastern and southeastern part of our state. The Creeks were a nation of several small tribes joined together to form the Creek Confederacy. Its capital was Tukabachee, not far from present-day Montgomery.

One of the Creek tribes gave us our state's name. Alabama was named for the Alabama River, which was named for the Alibamos Indians. The word "Alabama" comes from the Indian word meaning "thicket clearers."

The Creeks of Lawrence County lived from the Tennessee Divide to South. They were the only tribe to live primarily in Alabama. The Creeks' lifestyle was very similar to other Southeastern Indians; therefore, much of the following information in this lesson can be compared to other Indian tribes that occupied much of the state.

The Creeks divided their towns into the red and white. Red was for war and the war chief always came from a red town. Peace talks were always held in a white town, lead by a chief from a white clan. In a white town, in which the buildings were stained white, no man could be killed. But in times of war, reds and whites fought together against the common enemy.

Creek men were fearless warriors, productive farmers, and skilled hunters. Although the warriors gave no quarter in battle, they did offer their captured foes a chance to join the confederacy. The land that they cultivated belonged to the whole town. Men and women worked together to harvest corn, squash, pumpkins, beans, and sweet potatoes. When hunting, the hunter only killed enough food in order for his family to survive. He never took more than he needed.

Apart from farming, men and women engaged in different jobs. The men hunted, built buildings, made war, and governed; and, the women raised children, cooked, and made clothing. From birth, boys were treated differently from girls. The boys were wrapped in cougar furs to take on that animal's fierceness. The girls were dressed in deer or bison skins. The boys spent most of their day wandering in the woods and practicing with their bow and arrows. The girls had less freedom. They usually stayed with the women and learned to tend the garden, keep the fire going, and make pottery, baskets, mats, and clothing.

Shawnee - These Algonquin Indian people migrated into the Tennessee River Valley after it was vacated by the Yuchi. In the early 1700s, the Shawnee came from the Cumberland (Nashville, TN) and Ohio River Valleys and lived in the Lawrence County area as a tribe until the middle 1700s. Even though the tribe was forced from the Tennessee River area by a combination of Chickasaw and Cherokee forces, the Shawnee hunting parties continued to forage in the area for years afterward. Tecumseh was the great Shawnee leader who tried to unite the southern tribes against white encroachment. He was supposedly half Creek and half Shawnee. Some Shawnee also intermarried with the Cherokee.

Chickasaw - The Chickasaws were also Muscogee people who lived in Northwestern Alabama and in parts of Mississippi and Tennessee. They are mostly remembered as skilled warriors. Chickasaws usually tried to sneak up on their enemies and surprise them. As a surprise tactic, the group of warriors divided into smaller groups of three or four. They would step in each other's tracks so they would appear to be only one. They kept in touch with the other groups by imitating animal sounds--the owl, wolf,

LESSON 11 – FIVE TRIBES OF LAWRENCE COUNTY / MID-TEST

fox, and bird. Often the Chickasaw warriors were satisfied with just touching the victims with a special stick called a coup. Touching was considered as brave an act as killing.

Cherokee - The Cherokee in Alabama were Iroquoian people who lived in the northeastern part of the state and the Tennessee River Valley. They called themselves "the principal people." One historian says the name "Cherokee" was given to them by other Indians and means "people who speak a different language." Another historian says English traders called them cherk, which means fire. This was because fire was sacred to these Indians.

The Cherokee under the leadership of Doublehead moved into Lawrence County about 1780. Doublehead lived in Doublehead's Village at Brown's Ferry for at least 12 years and possibly much longer. He signed the Cotton Gin Treaty of 1806, which placed a cotton gin in Lawrence County at Melton's Bluff. He was assassinated on August 9, 1807, by Major Ridge, Alex Saunders, and John Rogers. Doublehead is supposedly buried in Butler Cemetery on Blue Water Creek in Lauderdale County, Alabama; however, many believe his grave is located in a small mound of chert stones on a knoll just north of Highway 72 and east of Blue Water Creek overlooking the Blue Water Oldfields, now a polo club.

One famous Cherokee was Sequoyah. He was shown how to write his name in English by Charles Hicks who had equal shares of land with Moses Melton

Cherokee Indian *(George Catlin)*

in an early Cherokee Treaty. The Melton's lived in Lawrence County. Sequoyah saw that white men could send news on paper he called "talking leaves." Sequoyah wanted his people to do the same. He spent twelve years creating an alphabet based on the sounds in the Cherokee language. This is called the Cherokee syllabary. The syllabary was finished in 1819. Thousands of Cherokees were taught to read and write. Some Cherokees started a newspaper called the Cherokee Phoenix. It was written in both the English and the Cherokee languages.

Choctaw - The Choctaw tribe did not live in Lawrence County, Alabama; however, they were an important tribe living to the south and west of our area. They lived in southwestern Alabama and in southeastern Mississippi. One of their customs is strange to us. They placed a baby's head against a wooden cradleboard, and then tied it down with leather strips. This pushed the soft bones of the baby's head, and they became flat like the board. The head stayed flat after it was taken off the board. The Indians thought a flattened head was handsome.

Choctaw Indian *(George Catlin)*

The Choctaws also had an unusual burial custom. The body was covered with skins and bark, and placed on a raised platform near the house. Food, drinks, clothing and personal belongings were placed with the body to ride it on its long journey into the next life. A fire, close by, provided warmth on its journey. The body stayed on the platform until it had decomposed. Then, the "buzzard men" or bone pickers came and picked the remaining flesh from the bones. The bones were then placed in a box or basket and taken to the bone house.

LESSON 11 – FIVE TRIBES OF LAWRENCE COUNTY / MID-TEST

KINDERGARTEN

DIBELS Reading Objective: PHONEMIC AWARENESS

Objective: After the teacher directs this lesson, Kindergarten Indian students will orally identify five out of ten terms based on knowledge gained from the text.

Objective Activity: Ask students to break apart each word and identify how many word parts are in each. (Ex: F-U-R and M-E-N have three word parts)

STATE STANDARDS Reading Objective:

PG. 14 #9   Begin to use pictures and text to gain meaning from written material
- The teacher will show pictures of Sequoyah and explain that he was a famous Cherokee man who invented the Cherokee alphabet. This will help the student have a better understanding of the text.
- *What did Sequoyah invent? (Cherokee alphabet or stickball)*

PG. 15 #14   Demonstrate an interest in and enjoyment of literature in a variety of forms, contexts, and media
- The teacher will teach the class a song about the four major tribes of Alabama. Cherokee, Chickasaw, Choctaw, Creek. These are the four major tribes..."
- *Name one of the four tribes talked about besides Cherokee. (Chickasaw, Choctaw, Yuchi, Shawnee, Creek)*

STATE STANDARDS Social Studies Objective:

PG. 11 #1   Develop initial map and globe skills
- The teacher will locate Melton's Bluff on a map when discussing Andrew Jackson.
- The teacher will show Alabama map that divides the tribes.
- Show students the Trail of Tears from Alabama to Oklahoma.
- *Where did Andrew Jackson live? (Melton's Bluff or Moulton)*

PG. 15 #34   Develop an awareness of the uniqueness of individuals
- Discuss the uniqueness and importance of Sequoyah. (How he stood out from others and committed his time to create the alphabet for Cherokee, then taught it to his people).
- *Was Sequoyah Cherokee or Creek? (Cherokee)*

PG. 15 #35   Develop an awareness of how people are the same yet different
- The teacher will lead a class discussion on how our lifestyle is still similar to the lifestyle of our Indian ancestors. Example: we still farm, hunt, use skin for clothes, etc.
- *Do we still use animal skins for clothes? (yes)*

Review Questions

1. What did Sequoyah invent? (Cherokee alphabet)
2. How many tribes lived in Lawrence County? (five)
3. What work did the Indian people do? (hunting and farming)
4. What were animal skins used for? (clothes and cover)
5. Which tribe divided their towns into red & white? (Creeks)

LESSON 11 – FIVE TRIBES OF LAWRENCE COUNTY / MID-TEST

FIRST GRADE

<u>DIBELS</u> Reading Objective: PHONEME SEGMENTATION FLUENCY

Objective: After the teacher directs this lesson, first grade Indian students will develop an understanding of musical instruments used by Indians, increase their vocabulary, and utilize phoneme segmentation fluency.

Objective Activity: Choose a variety of terms from the text. Next, hold up flash cards revealing individual letters of the term. (Ex: R, I, V, E, R = River) Use the following terms: fearless, harvest, Shawnee, chert, bark, plant, rattle, stick, games, dance, shell, men, and drum. Be sure to include visual and auditory aids)

<u>STATE STANDARDS</u> Reading Objective:

PG. 17 #3   Exhibit phonemic awareness
- After the directed lesson, the class can sing a song about the five tribes of Lawrence County.
  - *Name the five tribes of Lawrence County. (Yuchi, Creek, Shawnee, Chickasaw, Cherokee)*

<u>STATE STANDARDS</u> Social Studies Objective:

PG. 18 #3   Extend initial ability to locate new information and to express understanding in various classroom settings.
- After the teacher directs the lesson about the five tribes of Lawrence County. The teacher can show a picture where Andrew Jackson lived at Melton's Bluff. (map)
  - *Where in Lawrence County was Andrew Jackson's land located? (Melton's Bluff)*

<u>Review Questions</u>

1. What did Andrew Jackson name his town? (Marathon)
2. Who was the first white landowner in Lawrence County? (Andrew Jackson)
3. What tribe gave us our state's name? (Creek)
4. What tribe was known as "skilled warriors?" (Chickasaw)
5. What did the two Creek towns stand for? (red-war/white-peace)

LESSON 11 – FIVE TRIBES OF LAWRENCE COUNTY / MID-TEST

SECOND GRADE

DIBELS Reading Objective: ORAL READING FLUENCY

Objective: After the teacher directs this lesson, second grade Indian students will be able to use their comprehension skills to discuss questions asked by the teacher while also demonstrating oral reading fluency.

Objective Activity: The teacher will read the lesson and then read aloud, "Who are the Cherokee," in the book, <u>If you lived with the Cherokee</u>, while the students read silently. Next, the teacher and students will <u>echo read</u> (the teacher reads a sentence or a phrase from the sentence and the students repeat him/her) the passage. Then, the teacher will ask comprehension questions and discuss the passage with the students.

STATE STANDARDS Reading Objective:

PG. 23 #2   Demonstrate the ability to use decoding skills to blend sounds and form words
- While students are reading aloud, make sure they are recognizing and correcting their word-recognition errors. If students do not recognize their errors then the teacher will aide in this process.
  - *Who was the first white land owner in Lawrence County? (Andrew Jackson)*

PG. 25 #13   Demonstrate appropriate listening and communicating behaviors
- (Group discussion) After teacher directs the lesson, ask appropriate questions to gain and clarify information while also having a group discussion with students. (Ex: Have students read aloud from the text-whether it is the lesson or book from museum/classroom.)
  - *What are the five major tribes of Lawrence County? (Yuchi, Creek, Shawnee, Chickasaw, Cherokee)*

STATE STANDARDS Social Studies Objective:

PG. 23 #3   Develop the ability to locate new information and to express understanding of this information in various classroom projects
- After the teacher directs the lesson, have students color code each of the five tribes on an Alabama map.
  - *What were the Cherokee people called? (principle people)*

Review Questions

1. The word "Alabama" comes from the Indian word meaning what? (Thicket Clearers)
2. Which tribe was the only tribe to live primarily in Alabama? (Creeks)
3. Which tribe was known as "skilled warriors?" (Chickasaw)
4. Who was the famous Cherokee that created the Cherokee alphabet? (Sequoyah)
5. Was Tecumseh a great Shawnee or Yuchi leader? (Shawnee)

LESSON 11 – FIVE TRIBES OF LAWRENCE COUNTY / MID-TEST

THIRD GRADE

DIBELS Reading Objective: LISTENING SKILLS

Objective: After the teacher directs this lesson, third grade Indian students will listen to and read the text to gain information and be able to communicate with others about our county.

Objective Activity: The teacher will read the lesson orally to the students. The teacher may let each student orally read a sentence from the lesson then, discuss the story.

STATE STANDARDS Reading Objective:

PG. 32 #3 Demonstrate literal understanding of print materials
- After the teacher directs the lesson, the students will retell the information gained from the lesson in their own words.
- ∾ *What tribe are we a part of? (Echota Cherokee Tribe)*

STATE STANDARDS Social Studies Objective:

PG. 29 #1 Extend development of map and global skills
- After the teacher directs the lesson, he/she will show the students an Alabama map and then show where each tribe lived. The teacher will then show the students it was north, south, east, or west from the other tribes.
- ∾ *Where is the Tennessee River located on the Alabama map? (northern top part of Alabama)*

Review Questions

1. What tribe placed their baby's head against a wooden cradle board to make it flat? (Choctaw)
2. What tribe considered "touching" a very brave act? (Chickasaw)
3. Who was the Cherokee leader that lived at Brown's Ferry? (Doublehead)
4. In a white town, what did it stand for when the buildings were stained white? (no man could be killed)
5. What did the Cherokee people call themselves? (the principle people)

LESSON 11 – FIVE TRIBES OF LAWRENCE COUNTY / MID-TEST

FOURTH GRADE

<u>SAT</u> Reading Objective: WORD RECOGNITION

Objective: After the teacher directs this lesson, fourth grade Indian students will recognize and comprehend terms from the lesson about the five tribes of Lawrence County.

Objective Activity: Students will play *Hangman, Jeopardy, or Wheel of Fortune*, using the following terms from the lesson: Marathon, ceremonies, assassinated, Alibamos, etc.

<u>STATE STANDARDS</u> Reading Objective:

PG. 38 #4   Demonstrate literal understanding of print material
- After the teacher directs the lesson the students will be able to identify one main idea about each tribe.
  - *What tribe was known for being "skilled warriors?" (Chickasaw)*

PG. 39 #11   Read materials encountered in daily lives
- After the teacher directs the lesson the students will read a passage from "Indian Trails of the Warrior Mountains" about the five tribes.
  - *Who was the great Shawnee leader? (Tecumseh)*

<u>STATE STANDARDS</u> Social Studies Objective:

PG. 36 #10   Describe aspects of the lives of historic Indians of Alabama and European contact
- After the teacher directs the lesson, the students will be able to describe one aspect of each tribe.
  - *What tribe is known for naming the State of Alabama? (Creek)*

Review Questions

1. Who was the first legal white landowner in Lawrence County? (Andrew Jackson)
2. What inspired Sequoyah to invent the Cherokee alphabet? (He saw that white men could send news on paper he called "talking leaves.")
3. What did the Cherokee call themselves? (the principal people)
4. Name an unusual custom practices by the Choctaw Indians? (their burial custom)
5. What tribe did not live in Lawrence County? (Choctaw)

LESSON 11 – FIVE TRIBES OF LAWRENCE COUNTY / MID-TEST

FIFTH GRADE

SAT Reading Objective: LISTENING SKILLS

Objective: After the teacher directs this lesson, fifth grade Indian students will utilize their listening skills by identifying the important details from the lesson. (Tribes: Shawnee, Creek, Chickasaw, Yuchi, Cherokee)

Objective Activity: The teacher will check the students listening behaviors by asking questions during a game of *Jeopardy*.

STATE STANDARDS Reading Objective:

PG. 46 #13 Apply strategies of a skillful listener
- After the teacher directs the lesson, the students will read about the Creek, Choctaw, Chickasaw, Cherokee, from the book "Warrior Mountain Folklore."
  - *What tribe gave us the name Alabama? (The Creeks)*

STATE STANDARDS Social Studies Objective:

PG. 46 #7 Analyze the different cultures of Native American groups by geographic regions
- After the teacher directs the lesson, the students will discuss aloud the differences in the tribes.
  - *Name one famous Cherokee. (Sequoyah)*

Review Questions

1. Name the five tribes of Lawrence County. (Yuchi, Creek, Shawnee, Chickasaw, Cherokee)
2. Which tribe lived primarily in Alabama? (Creek)
3. Where did the Yuchi live in the early 1700s? (Area of Muscle Shoals).
4. What was Alabama named for? (It was named for the Alabama River, which was named for the Alibamos Indians.)
5. Which tribe had had an unusual burial custom? Describe. (Choctaw – cover body with skins and bark and place personal belongings with the body. They would build a fire and keep body on platform till decomposed. The buzzards picked remaining flesh from the bones and then the body was placed in a box or basket and taken to bone house.)

LESSON 11 – FIVE TRIBES OF LAWRENCE COUNTY / MID-TEST

SIXTH GRADE

SAT Reading Objective: COMPREHENSION

Objective: After the teacher directs this lesson, sixth grade Indian students will read and gain understanding of materials from studying the five tribes of Lawrence County: Cherokee, Yuchi, Shawnee, Chickasaw, and Creek.

Objective Activity: After the teacher reviews the lesson, students will read selected paragraphs and answer questions concerning the five tribes of Lawrence County.

STATE STANDARDS Reading Objective:

PG. 53 #12   Develop general listening behaviors for different purposes and situations
- After the teacher directs the lesson, the students will read and gain understanding of materials that they will encounter in their daily lives from studying political boundaries. After the teacher reviews the lesson the students will read selected paragraphs and answer questions concerning the five tribes of Lawrence County.
  - *Name the five tribes of Lawrence County? (Yuchi, Shawnee, Cherokee, Chickasaw, Creek)*

STATE STANDARDS Social Studies Objective:

PG. 55 #4   Review major changes in America
- Discuss with the students about the five tribes and their changes over time.
  - *Which tribe did not live in Lawrence County? (Choctaw)*

Review Questions

1. What tribe divided their towns into red and white? (Creek)
2. What year did Andrew Jackson become president and why did it result in one of the darkest eras for the American Indians in Alabama? (1828. Our ancestors were forced to be removed from the state of Alabama and surrounding southern states.)
3. What year was the Cotton Gin Treaty signed and who signed it? (1806; Doublehead)
4. What were the men called that picked the flesh from the bones of the dead? (Buzzard men)
5. Name the four major tribes that occupied most of the southeastern U.S. but their territories met in Alabama. (Cherokees, Creeks, Chickasaws, Choctaws)

LESSON 11 – FIVE TRIBES OF LAWRENCE COUNTY / MID-TEST

SEVENTH GRADE

SAT Reading Objective: LISTENING SKILLS

Objective: After the teacher directs this lesson, seventh grade Indian students will utilize their listening skills to construct and interpret meaning from the text on the five tribes of Lawrence County.

Objective Activity: Divide the class into two teams. Ask random students from both teams a question. If they answer correctly, they earn a point. If not, the other team has a chance to answer and steal a point.

STATE STANDARDS Reading Objective:

PG. 58 #11   Refine general listening behaviors
- Ask students to retell the information discussed bout the five tribes of Lawrence County in their own words.
  - *What did the Cherokee call themselves? (the principal people)*

STATE STANDARDS Social Studies Objective:

Online Alex #10   Describe changes in social and economic conditions in the U.S. during the 20th and 21st centuries
- Show students a map of where the five tribes are located in Lawrence County, Alabama.
  - *Which tribe did not live in Lawrence County? (Choctaw)*

Review Questions

1. What did Sequoyah refer to as "talking leaves?" (newspaper)
2. How long did it take Sequoyah to invent the alphabet? (12 years)
3. Who was the great Shawnee leader? (Tecumseh)
4. What year was the Cherokee syllabary finished? (1819)
5. When was Doublehead assassinated and which three men were responsible? (August 9, 1807; Major Ridge, Alex Saunders, and John Rogers)

LESSON 12 – CREEK TRIBE

Since many of our Indian students have Creek blood, we are going to talk about the Creek Indians and their lifestyle. The Creeks of Lawrence County lived from the Tennessee Divide to the south. They were the only tribe to live primarily in Alabama. The Creeks' lifestyle was very similar to other Southeastern Indians; therefore, they can be compared to other Indian tribes that occupied much of the state.

Creek Towns - The Creeks divided their towns into the red and white. Red was for war and the war chief always came from a red town. Peace talks were always held in a white town, lead by a chief from a white clan. In a white town, in which the buildings were stained white, no man could be killed. But in times of war, reds and whites fought together against the common enemy.

Sacred Indian Marker Tree in Indian Tomb Hollows

White towns were peace towns. People living in the white towns were very peaceful and did not want to fight. In fact, they only participated in ceremonies not related to war. The Creek Nation's most powerful chief was always from the white town. Red towns were war towns. War ceremonies were carried out in red towns. The people in the red towns organized war parties, led raids, and had religious ceremonies related to war.

Creek Farms - Creek men were fearless warriors, productive farmers, and skilled hunters. Although the warriors gave no quarter in battle, they did offer their captured foes a chance to join the confederacy. The land that they cultivated belonged to the whole town. Men and women worked together to harvest corn, squash, pumpkins, beans, and sweet potatoes. When hunting, the hunter only killed enough food in order for his family to survive. He never took more than he needed.

Apart from farming, men and women engaged in different jobs. The men hunted, built buildings, made war, and governed. The women raised their children, cooked, and made clothing. From birth, boys were treated differently from girls. The boys were wrapped in cougar furs to take on that animal's fierceness. The girls were dressed in deer or bison skins. The boys spent most of their day wandering in the woods and practicing with their bow and arrows. The girls had less freedom. They usually stayed with the women and learned to tend the garden, keep the fire going, and make pottery, baskets, mats, and clothing.

Creek Religion - Water and fire were sacred to the Creeks and most ceremonies centered on one or the other. The first duty of each Creek every morning was to bathe in the nearby river or stream even in very cold weather. In each village, the sacred fire had to be kept burning day and night. This fire was extinguished only at the time of the Green Corn Festival.

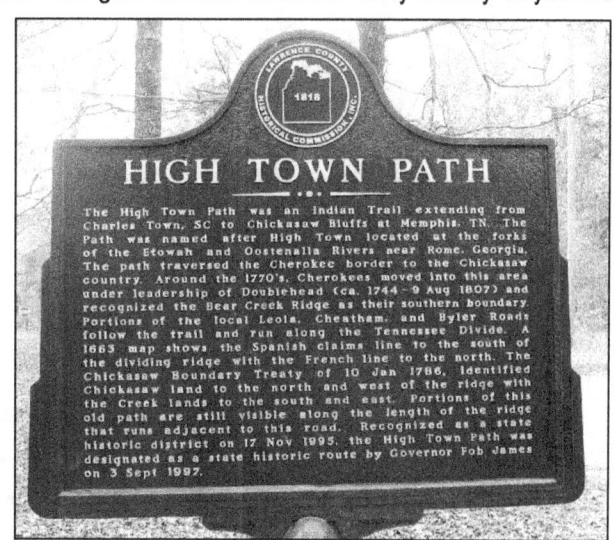
High Town Path marker in Lawrence County

Creek Nation - We are going to talk about the Creek Indians and their lifestyle. Their homes, weapons, clothing, and food are very similar to the Cherokee Indians and other Southeastern tribes because they all lived in the same climate and in the same area. The name Creek was given to these Indians by English traders because they lived on the Ochese Creek in Georgia. Also, Creek tribes were often named for their towns. The southern fourth of Lawrence County, Alabama, was ancestral Creek land and lay from the High Town Path (Tennessee Divide) toward the south and east.

LESSON 12 – CREEK TRIBE

The deep, worn, and old route of the High Town Path runs adjacent to the present day Ridge road and along the Continental Divide in Lawrence County

The Creek domain ran from the High Town Path (Tennessee Divide) in Lawrence County to the south and east into Georgia. The Creeks of Lawrence County, Alabama, helped Doublehead establish towns along the Tennessee River. Creeks fought the Chickasaws in our county at the Battle of Indian Tomb Hollow. Creeks in Lawrence County lost their claim to the land in the 1814 Treaty at Fort Jackson. Andrew Jackson's forces defeated the Creeks at the Battle of Horseshoe Bend. Moulton is named after Lt. Michael Moulton, who was killed at Horseshoe Bend.

Creek Indians brought many different tribes together to form a Creek Nation. Some of the tribes which joined with the Creeks were the Alibamos, Koasatis, Apalachees, Yuchies, and the Shawnees. There were more than 45 Creek towns with a population of 15,000 to 20,000 people. People living in these Creek towns spoke six different languages, had their own customs and their own chiefs.

Creek Government - The Upper Creeks lived in about 40 towns on the Coosa, Tallapoosa, and Alabama Rivers. The Lower Creeks lived in about 20 towns on the Okmulgee, Flint, and Chattahoochee Rivers. Each town had its own chief. Then each division, Upper and Lower Creeks had a head chief (called a micco) who had authority over all the other town chiefs. The micco ruled over the tribal council. The chief would sit on a high platform, which raised him above other men.

Creek War - After the Creek-Indian War was over in 1814, the Creek land in Lawrence County and areas to the south was declared public land. Land-hungry whites rushed in to claim the Creek land. During the war between the Creek Indians and the white settlers, there were several major battles that may be familiar to you: The Battle of Fort Mims and the Battle of Horseshoe

Indian Trails through the Warrior Mountains are shown Crossing the High Town Path

LESSON 12 – CREEK TRIBE

Bend. The fight at Horseshoe Bend was the final battle for the Creeks. The 1,000 mighty Creek warriors could not win against General Jackson and his 3,300 soldiers. After the Battle of Horseshoe Bend, most of the Creek land was taken from them. In 1835 and 1836, with some of their chiefs in chains, approximately 14,000 Creeks were forced to move to Oklahoma.

Lawrence County - Two groups of Creeks came through Lawrence County during removal. Lawrence County has several things in common with Creek people: (1) Creek land lay from the High Town Path to the south. (2) Moulton is named after Lt. Michael Moulton who was killed during the Battle of Horseshoe Bend. (3) Andrew Jackson, who defeated the Creeks, became the first white landowner in Lawrence County, Alabama. (4) The High Town Path, the Creek Nation's northern border, ran across southern Lawrence County. (5) A major Creek trading path, Black Warriors' Path, ran across eastern Lawrence County.

LESSON 12 – CREEK TRIBE

KINDERGARTEN

DIBELS Reading Objective: INITIAL SOUND FLUENCY

OBJECTIVE: After the teacher directs this lesson, Kindergarten Indian students will develop beginning sound fluency by recognizing letters and sounding out the names of those letters.

OBJECTIVE ACTIVITY: Write selected words on board and let students sound out the initial sound. (Example: car, foot, walk, boat, dugout, and water)

STATE STANDARDS Reading Objective:

PG. 14 #6   Demonstrate an initial understanding of letter-sound relationships
- The teacher can write words on the board (red, white, home, path, etc) or use flash cards and let students pronounce the initial sound of the word and then say the entire word.
- ∾ *What two types of towns did they have? (red and white)*

PG. 15 #13   Gain an awareness of others through exposure to written, spoken, and visual forms of communication
- Make sure students understand the lifestyles of Creek Indians using pictures and verbal communication.
- ∾ *Why did the Creek Indians take a bath first thing every morning? (custom)*

STATE STANDARDS Social Studies Objective:

PG. 11 #1   Develop initial map and globe skills
- After discussing Creek Indians, give students a copy of the map of Alabama located in the activity book. Have the class color the portion of Alabama where the Creeks were located.
- ∾ *What two things were most sacred to the Creeks? (fire and water)*

PG. 15 #34   Develop an awareness of the uniqueness of individuals
- Talk with class about the characteristics of the Creeks.
- Show pictures of their towns. (if available)
- Talk about their religion, farms, and nation.
- Ask questions for understanding.
- ∾ *During what ceremony was the fire put out? (green corn)*

Review Questions
1. What was the first thing the Creeks did each morning? (bathed)
2. The Creeks divides their towns into what colors? (red and white)
3. The red towns stood for: (war)
4. The white towns stood for: (peace)
5. What did men and women grow together in their crops? (corn, squash, pumpkins, beans, and sweet potatoes)

LESSON 12 – CREEK TRIBE

FIRST GRADE

DIBELS Reading Objective: PHONICS

Objective: After the teacher directs this lesson, first grade Indian students will develop an understanding of certain letter sounds by naming letters derived from words within the text and identifying the sounds of those particular letters, as well as gain knowledge of Creek towns.

Objective Activity: The teacher will write terms on the board or use other visual aids. Students will then identify each letter in the term. Next, the teacher will ask what sound that letter makes. Finally, the teacher will ask the students to pronounce the entire word. (Ex: red, white, war, farm, hunter, etc.)

STATE STANDARDS Reading Objective:

PG. 17 #4   Demonstrate understanding of letter-sound relationships
- After the teacher directs the lesson, choose some words from the text such as: Creek, chief, clothing, etc. Have students sound out the blending sounds.
  - *What town did all of the fighting take place? (red)*

PG. 20 #6   Comprehend material read, heard, or viewed
- Once the teacher directs the lesson on the Creek Tribe, ask questions to make students understand.
  - *What two things are sacred to the Creek Tribe? (water and fire)*

STATE STANDARDS Social Studies Objective:

PG. 20 #29   Become acquainted with various cultures encountered in stories from literature
- After the teacher directs the lesson, ask students about the Creek religion, farming, and government. (beliefs and customs)
  - *What was the first thing they did every morning? (bathe in the river)*

Review Questions

1. What were two things sacred to the Creeks? (water and fire)
2. How many towns were the Creeks divided into? (two)
3. What did the men and women do together? (harvest a garden)
4. Did the Creek hunter kill more than he needed? (no)
5. What town was the most powerful chief from? (white town)

LESSON 12 – CREEK TRIBE

SECOND GRADE

DIBELS Reading Objective: NONSENSE WORD FLUENCY

Objective: After the teacher directs this lesson, second grade Indian students will have the ability to detect understandable words from the text by the usage of nonsense words.

Objective Activity: The teacher will write nonsense words on the board that are related to the lesson. (Ex: Creek-Dreek, tribe-dribe, ran-gan, etc.) The teacher will ask for the word from the lesson that corresponds to the nonsense words stating the sentence that the understandable word originates.

STATE STANDARDS Reading Objective:

PG. 23 #2 Demonstrate the ability to use decoding skills to blend sounds and form words
- After the lesson, the students will have the ability to detect understandable words from the lesson.
  - *What were the two names of the Creek towns? (red, white)*

STATE STANDARDS Social Studies Objective:

PG. 22 #1 Develop map and globe skills
- After the teacher directs the lesson, the teacher will show the class a map of where the Creek Tribe is located. (Ex: Let kids color on map where the tribe is located and check to make sure they know where it is located.)
  - *What was the first thing they did every morning? (bathe in the river)*

PG. 22 #2 Develop the ability to interpret and display information in graphic form
- Discuss how the Creek Tribes are similar/different with the students. Make sure they understand the difference in time periods and customs.
  - *What two things were sacred to the Creeks? (water and fire)*

Review Questions

1. How many towns was the Creek tribe divided into? (2)
2. Did the Creek hunter kill more food than he needed? (no)
3. During what ceremony was the fire extinguished? (Green Corn Ceremony)
4. What were Creek men known for? (fearless warriors, productive farmers, and skilled hunters)
5. Who ruled the tribal council? (micco)

LESSON 12 – CREEK TRIBE

THIRD GRADE

DIBELS Reading Objective: INTERPRETING READING MATERIALS

Objective: After the teacher directs this lesson, third grade Indian students will recognize and apply their understanding by answering the teacher generated questions.

Objective Activity: Students will silently read from text and then the teacher will ask questions to ensure comprehension.

STATE STANDARDS Reading Objective:

PG. 33 #14   Develop an understanding of cultural similarities and differences noted through exposure to multicultural literature
- The teacher will have a class discussion on the similarities and differences in clothing past and present.
  - *What ceremony was sacred to the Creeks? (Green Corn Ceremony)*

STATE STANDARDS Social Studies Objective:

PG. 29 #1   Extend development of map and globe skills
- Show the students where the Creeks lived and where the battles and/or wars took place.
  - *What was the name of the final battle for the Creeks? (Battle of Horseshoe Bend)*

Review Questions

1. If Creeks divided their towns into red and white, what did the colors stand for? (red-war, white-peace)
2. When was the Creek Indian war over? (1814)
3. What did it mean when the buildings were painted white in a Creek town? (no man could be killed)
4. Which town was the Creek nation's most powerful leader/chief from? (white town)
5. What were the Creek women responsible for? (raising children, cooking, and making clothes)

LESSON 12 – CREEK TRIBE

FOURTH GRADE

SAT Reading Objective: VOCABULARY

Objective: After the teacher directs this lesson, fourth grade Indian students will gain an understanding about the Creek tribe and be able to identify the following terms: fearless, authority, platform, ceremonies, productive, etc.

Objective Activity: The students will write a summary of the material learned from the lesson and create an illustration of their writing.

STATE STANDARDS Reading Objective:

PG. 39 #12   Apply strategies of a skillful listener
- After the teacher directs the lesson, the students will read aloud from the "Warrior Mountains Folklore" book about the Creek Tribe. As the students are reading aloud, the teacher will ask questions to check for skillful listening. Also to ensure comprehension on the vocabulary terms.
  - *Name one fact about how the Creek tribe farmed: (the men and women harvested the crops together)*

STATE STANDARDS Social Studies Objective:

PG. 34 #2   Interpret and display information and data using various graphic organizers
- After the teacher directs the lesson, he/she will show the students a map of Lawrence County and show where Moulton is located and where Back Warriors' Path ran.
  - *Who is the town of Moulton named after? (Lt. Michael Moulton)*

Review Questions

1. Creeks fought the Chickasaws in Lawrence County at what battle? (Battle of Indian Tomb Hollow)
2. Where was Lt. Michael Moulton killed? (Horseshoe Bend)
3. When was the Creek and Indian War over? (1814)
4. How many Creeks fought at Horseshoe Bend? (1,000)
5. The Creeks were often named for their what? (towns)

LESSON 12 – CREEK TRIBE

FIFTH GRADE

SAT Reading Objective: VOCABULARY

Objective: After the teacher directs this lesson, fifth grade Indian students will be able to identify the following terms: tribe, customs, removal, extinguished, raids fierceness, productive, fearless.

Objective Activity: The teacher needs to pick out a passage from the "Indian Trails of the Warrior Mountain" book that is related to Indian removal and ask questions about material read. The teacher and students will read this lesson, and explain in their own words about removal.

STATE STANDARDS Reading Objective:

PG. 44 #1   Use a wide range of strategies to interpret, evaluate, appreciate, and construct meaning from print materials
- After a teacher directed lesson, the students will identify different elements of the text. (Main idea, etc.)
- Have the students summarize the text to simplify the material they have been taught.
  - _____ and fire were sacred to the Creeks. (water)

STATE STANDARDS Social Studies Objective:

PG. 46 #6   Discuss the progression of culture of the early American people
- Discuss the importance of hunting of the Creek tribe. Be sure the students understand the significance of the deer. Ask questions to check for understanding.
  - What year did the Creek-Indian War end? (1814)

Review Questions

1. What was the final battle for the Creeks? (Battle of Horseshoe Bend)
2. How many Creeks were forced to move to Oklahoma and during what year did this happen? (14,000; 1835 & 1836)
3. What was a Creek Indian Chief called and why did he sit on a high platform? (Micco, it raised him above other men)
4. How many towns did the Upper Creeks live in? (about 40)
5. Creeks in Lawrence County lost the claim to their land in the 1814 Treaty of _____. (Fort Jackson)

LESSON 12 – CREEK TRIBE

SIXTH GRADE

SAT Reading Objective: LISTENING SKILLS

Objective: After the teacher directs this lesson, sixth grade Indian students will be able to recognize the importance of the Creek tribe.

Objective Activity: After the students read this lesson, the teacher should divide the class into two teams. Ask an individual from each team a question, if answered correctly, they receive one point. If not, the opposite team gets the opportunity to answer and steal a point.

STATE STANDARDS Reading Objective:

PG. 53 #12   Develop general listening behaviors for different purposes and situations
- After the teacher directs the lesson, the students will be able to identify the location of the Creek Nation and retell the information from the lesson in their own words.
- *Name three crops farmed by Creek Indians. (cotton, corn, squash, beans, pumpkins, sweet potatoes)*

STATE STANDARDS Social Studies Objective:

PG. 55 #4   Review major changes in America from 1870 to 1900
- Discuss the changes in the Creek Tribe over the 30 year time period. (Ex: Advances in farming, hunting, etc.)
- *What were the men's responsibilities in the Creek Tribe? (fearless warriors, productive farmers, skillful hunters)*

Review Questions

1. What was the name of the head chief (of the upper and lower Creeks), who had authority over all town chiefs? (Micco)
2. Where did the Creeks primarily live? (Alabama)
3. Who was the town of Moulton named after? (Lt. Michael Moulton)
4. Which major trading path ran across eastern Lawrence County? (Black Warriors' Path)
5. What is the name of the first major battle of the Creek and Indian War? (Battle of Fort Mims)

LESSON 12 – CREEK TRIBE

SEVENTH GRADE

SAT Reading Objective: LITERARY ELEMENTS

Objective: After the teacher directs this lesson, seventh grade Indian students will listen to cultural literary works and be able to identify main idea, summarize the text, and give significant details about the Creek tribe.

Objective Activity: Allow students to read from the lesson and ask basic questions. What tribe of Indians was this lesson about? Why was water and fire sacred to them? Where did the Creeks lose claim to their land? etc.

STATE STANDARDS Reading Objective:

PG. 58 #7   Appreciate the characteristics, literary elements, and cultural influences, of literary works representative of various areas
- After the teacher directs the lesson, the students will listen to cultural literary works and be able to identify main idea, summarize the text, and give significant details of the text on Creek Tribe.
  - *What were the two most sacred things to the Creeks? (water and fire)*

STATE STANDARDS Social Studies Objective:

Online Alex #9   Identify individual and civic responsibilities of citizens
- Identify individual tribes discussing how they all are similar and different. Discuss the responsibilities of the Creek Tribe.
  - *What were the Creek towns divided into? (red-meaning war/blood, white-meaning peace)*

Review Questions

1. What year did the Creek Indian War end? (1814)
2. Name the five things Lawrence County has in common with the Creek people: (1) Creek land lay from the High Town Path to the south. (2) Moulton is named after Lt. Michael Moulton who was killed during the Battle of Horseshoe Bend. (3) Andrew Jackson, who defeated the Creeks, became the first white landowner in Lawrence County, Alabama. (4) The High Town path, the Creek Nation's northern border, ran across southern Lawrence County. (5) A major Creek trading path, Black Warriors' Path, ran across eastern Lawrence County.
3. Explain the responsibilities of the Creek boys and girls? (boys-spent most of the day wandering in the woods practicing with their bow and arrows, girls-had less freedom, usually stayed at home with the women and learned to tend to a garden, keep fire going, make pottery, baskets, mats, and clothing)
4. Describe the parameters of the Creek domain. (from the High Town Path (Tennessee Divide) in Lawrence county to the south and east into Georgia)
5. Name some of the activities that took place in the red town. (war, war parties, raids, religious ceremonies)

LESSON 13 – CHICKASAW TRIBE

Chickasaw - Today, we are going to talk about the Chickasaw Indians that lived in Lawrence County, Alabama. The Chickasaw Nation owned Lawrence County, Alabama by the Chickasaw Boundary Treaty of January 10, 1786. The Chickasaw tribe claimed a large portion of land covering West Alabama, Northeast Mississippi, Tennessee, Kentucky, and even Ohio (show picture of four tribes divided into their sections). George and Levi Colbert were Chickasaw chiefs who were ½ Celtic (Scotch) and ½ Indian (Chickasaw). Colbert County is named after this Indian family.

High Town Path – South Boundary of the Chickasaw Nation

The Chickasaws were smaller in number than the other Indian tribes in Alabama, yet they claimed a large region of land. Some of the land regions overlapped with the land claims of the Cherokee. The Chickasaws noted for the defense of their land and after the white people came, gained a reputation for being warlike people. They, like the Cherokees and Creeks, intermarried to a large degree with Celtic people.

Warfare was conducted with much ceremony and occurred only in retaliation for attacks made on them. The Chickasaws believed that the success of a raid depended on the prewar ceremonies, which lasted for three days. During this time, the men ate nothing and drank a mixture made from the leaves of a variety of holly called the black drink. Stories of brave deeds were told by the older men and the young warriors painted their bodies with war paint.

Customs - The Chickasaws were known for being warlike people. That means they often participated in battles against other tribes in order to gain their land and possessions. The Chickasaws shared many of the same customs as the other southeastern tribes. One of these was in marriage. A Chickasaw man was allowed to have more than one wife. This marriage custom was also allowed when the Celtic people came and started intermarrying with the Indian.

Chief George Colbert's House at Colbert's Ferry in Colbert County

LESSON 13 – CHICKASAW TRIBE

Have any of you ever been to a wedding or had someone that you know get married? The Chickasaws had weddings that were in some ways similar to the weddings we have today. The boyfriend would send his girlfriend a gift. If she accepted the gift that meant they would get married soon. When the time would come for them to be married, the man and woman would exchange gifts before other people. The man would select a nice ear of corn, divide it in half, give the woman one half and keep the other for himself. He also gave her a deer's foot as a sign that she should be ready to serve him, and in return she would give him some cakes of bread.

Who is responsible for taking care of you in your family? Your mother or daddy? Well, the mother was responsible for the children in the Chickasaw family. One interesting custom practiced by the Chickasaws was the flattening of the infant's (baby's) forehead. The mother would place a block of wood covered with buckskin or a bag of sand fastened to the head. They thought this made the child look pretty. Later, over the years, they stopped doing this.

In the family, the girls were disciplined by the mother. The boys were disciplined by the oldest uncle of the mother's family. Women were responsible for the upbringing of the girls, and the elders (older people in the tribe) took responsibility for the care and instruction of the boys.

Chief George Colbert *(William L. McDonald – Lore of the River)*

Colbert - A well-known Celtic man to the Chickasaws was James Logan Colbert. He had three Chickasaw wives who had sons, which became important men in Chickasaw history. One of these sons was George Colbert (show picture of George Colbert's home). George married two of the Cherokee Chief Doublehead's daughters-Tuskiahooto and Saleechie. He was head chief of the Chickasaws for 12 years and became the wealthiest man in the Chickasaw Nation. Levi Colbert also became Chief of the Chickasaw Nation and is buried in Colbert County west of Cherokee, Alabama.

Many of the Colbert family went west with the Chickasaw tribe during the removal, however; Colbert County in northwest Alabama was the home of this family and bears their name. Today many Chickasaw descendants still call northwest Alabama home. The houses of the Chickasaws in the Lawrence County area were cabins built very much like those of the white people (show picture of George Colbert's house). George Colbert lived in a large two-story house that burned in 1927.

LESSON 13 – CHICKASAW TRIBE

KINDERGARTEN

DIBELS Reading Objective: PHONICS INSTRUCTION

Objective: After the teacher directs this lesson, Kindergarten Indian students will match the letter to the sound of words found within the text.

Objective Activity: Ask student to identify the letter that matches the beginning sounds of selected words. (Example: Indian, man, land, cabins, house, etc.)

STATE STANDARDS Reading Objective:

PG. 14 #9   Begin to use pictures and text to gain meaning from written material
- Discuss Chickasaw lifestyle with the students describing their customs, beliefs, and people of importance.
- Show pictures of George Colbert and his home using a resource book.
- Allow students to examine the pictures while the teacher asks questions about the lesson.
- Also let the students talk about the Chickasaws among one another by pairing up children.
    - *Who disciplined the boys? (mother's brother)*

STATE STANDARDS Social Studies Objective:

PG. 11 #1   Develop initial map and globe skills
- After talking about the Chickasaw Tribe handout the map of Alabama located in the activity book that shows the portion where the Chickasaw were located.
- Let the students color only the Chickasaw portion of Alabama.
    - *From looking at the map, find the place where the Chickasaw lived?*

PG. 15 #36   Build an understanding of different cultures through the exploration of holidays, customs, and traditions
- The teacher will direct a lesson about the Chickasaw that explains the different customs and traditions of this tribe. Pictures can also be shown.
- The students will listen carefully and answer questions about the Chickasaw tribe.
    - *Were the Chickasaw men allowed to have more than one wife? (yes)*

Review Questions
1. Who raised the Chickasaw children? (mother)
2. What does warlike mean? (fought in many battles)
3. Were the Chickasaw warlike people? (yes)
4. Did the Chickasaw own Lawrence County? (yes)
5. What ceremony did they have that we still have today? (weddings)

LESSON 13 – CHICKASAW TRIBE

FIRST GRADE

DIBELS Reading Objective: LETTER NAMING FLUENCY

Objective: After the teacher directs this lesson, first grade Indian students will develop the ability to recognize and pronounce letters using visual aids.

Objective Activity: Use alphabet cards or other visual aids and present a letter to each individual student. If identified correctly and is able to pronounce sound they gain opportunity to participate in activity/craft.

STATE STANDARDS Reading Objective:

PG. 17 #4   Demonstrate understanding of letter-sound relationships
- Throughout the lesson, the teacher will write the terms on the board. He/she will have the students recognize each letter, blend sounds together, and pronounce the entire word.
  - ∾ *Who was a well-known Celtic man to the Chickasaw? (James Logan Colbert)*

STATE STANDARDS Social Studies Objective:

PG. 18 #3   Extend initial ability to locate new information and to express understanding in various classroom
- Show the students a picture of where the Chickasaw Tribe is located and Colbert County.
  - ∾ *What county is named after George and Levi Colbert? (Colbert County)*

Review Questions
1. Who disciplined the boys? (mother's brother-uncle)
2. Name two Chickasaw chiefs? (George and Levi Colbert)
3. Name the two things the man would give the woman during their wedding ceremony? (1/2 ear of corn and a deer's foot)
4. Who married two of Doublehead's daughters? (George Colbert)
5. In what type of housing did Chickasaws in Lawrence County live? (cabins)

LESSON 13 – CHICKASAW TRIBE

SECOND GRADE

DIBELS Reading Objective: TEXT COMPREHENSION

Objective: After the teacher directs this lesson, second grade Indian students will relate information learned from an orally read text accompanied by a remedial game.

Objective Activity: The teacher and the students will read text from the lesson. Then, the teacher will ask comprehension questions that come directly from the orally read text. Play the game, *Who wants to be a Millionaire* and allow students to decode the answer using this format: Who was the wealthiest man in the Chickasaw nation? (George Colbert) Place students on teams and allow one point for that team if they answer correctly.

STATE STANDARDS Reading Objective:

PG. 24 #7   Read and comprehend a variety of material
- After the teacher directs the lesson, the students will gain knowledge learned from an orally read text, accompanied by a remedial game. Ask questions to check for understanding. (Ex: Play the game *Jeopardy*. Make up four or five categories and then have questions for each one that second graders can answer.)
  - *The Chickasaws were known for being what kind of people? (warlike)*

STATE STANDARDS Social Studies Objective:

PG. 22 #1   Develop map and globe skills
- Show students a map of where the Chickasaw Tribe and Colbert County is located on an Alabama map.
  - *Who was a well known Celtic man to the Chickasaw? (James Logan Colbert)*

PG. 25 #24   Identify major celebrations of events in U.S. history
- Discuss how the Chickasaws were similar to our beliefs and customs today. (wedding/ceremonies)
  - *Did the Chickasaws have ceremonies as we do today? (yes)*

Review Questions

1. What kind of houses did the Chickasaws build in Lawrence County? (log cabins)
2. The responsibility of the mother was what? (to raise the children)
3. Doublehead's two daughters married the same man. What was his name? (George Colbert)
4. Name two brothers that were Chickasaw chiefs: (George and Levi Colbert)
5. The mother's brother was responsible for what? (discipline of the boys)

LESSON 13 – CHICKASAW TRIBE

THIRD GRADE

DIBELS Reading Objective: COMPREHENSION

Objective: After the teacher directs this lesson, third grade Indian students will orally be able to interpret and gain meaning from the terms in the text. (Terms: warlike, battles, wedding, attack)

Objective Activity: The teacher will read each term orally to students. Discuss terms with students then let students say the words orally and tell teacher meaning. Have students to read aloud sections of the lesson.

STATE STANDARDS Reading Objective:

PG. 32 #3   Demonstrate literal understanding of print material
- After the teacher directs the lesson have the class identify the important details of the story. To make sure they understand the customs as they were.
  - *What were the names of the two Chickasaw chiefs? (George and Levi Colbert)*

STATE STANDARDS Social Studies Objective:

PG. 29 #1   Extend development of map and globe skills
- Show students a map of Lawrence County, which was owned by the Chickasaw Nation, by using the Chickasaw Boundary Treaty of January 10, 1786.
- Show picture of the four tribes divided into their sections
  - *Who is responsible for taking care of the children? (mother)*
  - *Who were the boys disciplined by? (the oldest uncle, mother's brother)*

Review Questions
1. Who became the wealthiest man in the Chickasaw nation? (George Colbert)
2. What county was named after the Colbert family? (Colbert County)
3. Why did the Chickasaws place a flat board covered with buckskin over a baby's forehead? (to make the forehead flat; they thought it was pretty)
4. Were the Chickasaw men allowed to have more than one wife? (yes)
5. Who was the well-known Celtic man that had three Chickasaw wives? (James Logan Colbert)

LESSON 13 – CHICKASAW TRIBE

FOURTH GRADE

<u>SAT</u> Reading Objective: COMPREHENSION

Objective: After the teacher directs this lesson, fourth grade Indian students will gain knowledge about the Chickasaw tribe.

Objective Activity: Have students read paragraphs from the lesson and select words which they are not familiar. The teacher will explain unfamiliar words to the students and have them repeat the words aloud. Students will then write the word and definition.

<u>STATE STANDARDS</u> Reading Objective:

PG. 39 #11   Read materials encountered in daily lives
- After the teacher directs the lesson, the students will read about George Colbert in "Indian Trails of the Warrior Mountains." The teacher will then ask the class questions to check for comprehension.
  - *Who was George Colbert? (Chickasaw Chief)*

<u>STATE STANDARDS</u> Social Studies Objective:

PG. 35 #9   Describe historic Indians of Alabama after European contact
- After the teacher directs the lesson, the teacher will discuss how the Chickasaw owned Lawrence County by the Chickasaw Boundary Treaty, the Chickasaws were warlike people, etc.
  - *Did the Chickasaws own Lawrence County? (yes)*

Review Questions

1. What Alabama county is named after a Chickasaw chief? (Colbert County)
2. What kind of homes did the Chickasaw build in Lawrence County? (log cabins)
3. What objects were used by the Chickasaw to flatten the baby's forehead? (block of wood or bag of sand)
4. Which of the four tribes were war-like people? (Chickasaws)
5. According to what treaty did the Chickasaw own Lawrence County? (Chickasaw Boundary Treaty of January 10, 1786)

LESSON 13 – CHICKASAW TRIBE

FIFTH GRADE

SAT Reading Objective: COMPREHENSION

Objective: After the teacher directs this lesson, fifth grade Indian students will gain understanding and be able to read and recognize a variety of material in daily lives.

Objective Activity: The teacher will review the lesson and play *Wheel of Fortune* or *Hangman* with students. Give clues from the text that means the same as the questions.

STATE STANDARDS Reading Objective:

PG. 46 #12   Read a variety of materials and genres encountered in daily lives
- After the teacher directs the lesson, the students will read from "Warrior Mountains Folklore" about the Chickasaw Tribe and then discuss what was read.
  - *Who disciplined the Chickasaw boys? (mother's brother -uncle).*

PG. 46 #13   Apply strategies of a skillful listener
- The students will listen to other students as they read aloud.
  - *Name one unusual custom about the Chickasaws. (flattening of baby's forehead)*

STATE STANDARDS Social Studies Objective:

PG. 46 #6   Discuss the progression of culture of the early American people
- The teacher will discuss the Chickasaw Tribe and how it was different from today's people.
  - *What ceremony do we have today that the Chickasaw Tribes also had? (weddings)*

Review Questions
1. What Chickasaw married Cherokee Chief Doublehead's daughters Tuskiahooto and Saleechie? (George Colbert)
2. What ceremony did they practice that we still practice today? (wedding)
3. Did the Chickasaw own Lawrence County? (Yes)
4. What kind of house did George Colbert live in? (large two-story house)
5. Who was a well-known Celtic man to the Chickasaw that had three wives? (James Logan Colbert)

LESSON 13 – CHICKASAW TRIBE

SIXTH GRADE

SAT Reading Objective: LITERARY ELEMENTS

Objective: After the teacher directs this lesson, sixth grade Indian students will be able to recognize various forms of literature that include culturally diverse materials through their characteristics from Lawrence County Indian people and informational materials from the text on the Chickasaw tribe.

Objective Activity: Use the information from this lesson to create a story about the Chickasaw tribe. Ask the students to identify the literary elements of the story. (main idea, setting, characters, etc.)

STATE STANDARDS Reading Objective:

PG. 52 #1   Interpret and construct meaning by applying appropriate strategies to materials across the curriculum
- After the teacher directs the lesson, the students will read aloud from "Warrior Mountain Folklore" and then the class will have a discussion about what they have read.
  - *What was one custom that the Chickasaw's practiced? (flattening the baby's forehead)*

STATE STANDARDS Social Studies Objective:

PG. 54 #1   Extend the development of map and globe skills
- The teacher will show the students where the Chickasaw Tribe lived in Lawrence County and where the Chickasaw Tribe claimed a large portion of land in West Alabama, Northeast Mississippi, Tennessee, Kentucky, and Ohio.
- Show students Colbert County on an Alabama map
  - *Name three states in which the Chickasaw owned land. (Alabama, Tennessee, Mississippi)*
  - *What county is named after George and Levi Colbert? (Colbert County)*

Review Questions

1. What Celtic man had three Chickasaw wives who had sons that became important in Chickasaw history? (James Logan Colbert)
2. Who took responsibility for the care and instruction of the boys? (elders)
3. Who were Doublehead's daughters? (Tuskiahooto and Saleechie)
4. When did Gorge Colbert's house burn? (1927)
5. What county is named after George and Levi Colbert? (Colbert County)

LESSON 13 – CHICKASAW TRIBE

SEVENTH GRADE

SAT Reading Objective: LITERARY GENRES

Objective: After the teacher directs this lesson, seventh grade Indian students will respond and apply basic principles of how information is properly presented in viewed, heard, or read materials from the text on George Colbert and the Chickasaw tribe.

Objective Activity: After the lesson, allow the students to play basketball as a remedial game. Divide the students into two teams. Ask each child a question related to the lesson. If answered correctly, allow him/her to shoot. (can be played inside with paper ball and garbage can)

STATE STANDARDS Reading Objective:

PG. 58 #11   Refine general listening behaviors
- After the teacher directs the lesson, the students will respond and apply basic principles of how information is properly presented in viewed, heard, or read materials from the text on Chickasaw Tribe.
  - *The Chickasaw Indians owned what county? (Lawrence County)*

STATE STANDARDS Social Studies Objective:

Online Alex #11   Describe examples of conflict of groups using past and current events
- The students can read aloud from the lesson. The teacher can discuss with the students the similarities from the Chickasaw Tribes with some of the other tribes. Since the Chickasaw Indians were warlike people if permitted the teacher may paint faces, showing a picture of how the Indians looked during or before war.
  - *What was a reason that the Chickasaw Indians went to war with the other tribes? (to gain their land and possessions)*

Review Questions

1. Who owned Lawrence County by the Boundary Treaty of January 10, 1786? (Chickasaw)
2. What tribe was smaller in number than any other tribe in Alabama? (Chickasaws)
3. Like the Cherokees and Creeks, the Chickasaw intermarried to a large degree with what people? (Celtic)
4. What tribe claimed a large region of land despite their small number? (Chickasaw)
5. Who were Doublehead's daughters and to whom were they married? (Tuskiahooto and Seleechie/George Colbert)

LESSON 14 – CHEROKEE TRIBE

Cherokee Nation - Some of you were born in a different county other than Lawrence. (Name some of them.) Maybe you were born in Colbert or Lauderdale Counties of Alabama. (Show picture of counties in Alabama.) All of these counties are found in the State of Alabama. (Show picture of State of Alabama.) Now, our state and others together, make up what we call the United States. (Show U.S. map.) Long ago, this map did not look this way. Most of the land we live on now belonged to our Indian ancestors.

The Cherokee people lived in mostly three states. (Show state map again.) Most of the Cherokee Nation was located in Georgia, Tennessee, and Alabama. The northern part of Georgia was known as Cherokee County and made up half of the Cherokee Nation in the 1800s. The other half lay approximately between east Tennessee and North Alabama. In 1832, the State of Georgia made it illegal for Cherokees to assemble as a group at their capital at New Echota; therefore, they moved their capital from New Echota, Georgia to Red Clay, Tennessee. In 1838, most of the Cherokees east of the Mississippi were removed to Oklahoma by President Andrew Jackson.

Lawrence County was Cherokee and Chickasaw country until the Turkey Town Treaty of 1816. Our Cherokee people lived in the Lawrence County area from the Tennessee River on the north side of our county to the Warrior Mountains on the south side of our county.

Cherokee Legends - We are going to talk about Indian stories and legends. Legends and myths were an important part of Cherokee life. The mind of the Cherokee storyteller or myth-keeper was a storehouse of Indian traditions. Much of what we know today of our ancient Cherokees, we have learned from their myths and legends. Since our people had no written language, only word of mouth kept alive the traditions of their history, ceremonies, rituals, and their beliefs. The Cherokee stories were handed down from generation to generation. They told stories about animals, famous people, and creation.

A young boy was taken by a storyteller and taught how to tell a legend and be a good storyteller. As the child grew, he was not allowed to do the things other children did. He was given one primary goal in life which was to learn every myth or legend of his people and to eventually pass them on to someone else. A storyteller was a highly respected member of his tribe. No tribal function was considered complete without the presence and assistance of the storyteller. He took pride in his people and strived to preserve their heritage.

Today, many of our older Cherokee descendants (our grandparents and great grandparents) carry on the traditions of storytelling. You need to listen very closely to the stories your grandparents tell and show respect to your elders. Each family usually has one member who is a storyteller designated to pass down family history.

Cherokee Council House Museum at Oakville

LESSON 14 – CHEROKEE TRIBE

Lawrence County Cherokees - The Cherokee lived in Lawrence County from about 1770, under the leadership of Doublehead. The Chickasaws actually owned the land by the Chickasaw Boundary Treaty of January 10, 1786, but the Cherokee lived here. Doublehead's two oldest daughters, Tuskiahooto and Saleechie, married Chickasaw Chief George Colbert. He allowed the Cherokees to live in Lawrence County because they were the people of his wives. Today, we have descendants of Doublehead and George Colbert still living in Lawrence County.

All Cherokee towns usually had a community building known as a council house where the local government was run by the people of the village. Today, at Oakville, we have a council house style building for our Indian education program. How many of you have ever been to the Oakville Mounds? The mounds are in Lawrence County, Alabama and the office and museum of the Indian Education Program is located in the park. The education center also has a beautiful seven-sided building sitting right in the middle of the property. Have you seen the building? It is built just like a Cherokee Council House.

The Cherokee Council House at Oakville has seven sides representing each of the seven matrilineal clans and the seven directions of the world. The seven directions are east, north, west, south, up, down, and inside yourself because you are always the center of your universe. Seven was a sacred number to our Indian people.

The Cherokee Tribe has seven clans. Who can tell me what a clan is? (take student responses) A clan is like a family of close relatives and the tribe is made up of all these seven different clans who are distantly related to each other. The seven clans are Bird, Deer, Long Hair, Paint, Wolf, Wild Potato, and <u>BLUE</u>, of which you are a member.

Cherokee Stickball

Cherokee Stickball - Although Indian people worked very hard to do their chores in the village, they also took time out to play. One of the first games they played was called "stickball" or "ballplay." Stickball or the ballplay is one Cherokee sport that has lived on throughout the years. Even though today it has been changed to erase some of its dangers, everyone still loves the ball game. The Cherokee in Cherokee, N.C. still play stickball at their Fall festival.

The day before the ball game is played is a day spent in preparation. Special sequences of events are followed to prepare participants for the game. The ball dance, going to water (dipped themselves seven times), and scratching are carefully done to bring strength, speed, courage, endurance, and purification to your team and to weaken your opponents. Sometimes players will draw a cross or a semicircle with a dot in it on their upper body as a sign of good luck. Slippery elm is chewed and the spit was rubbed on their bodies to make them slippery.

In the ball game, there are two teams. One village or clan plays against another village or clan. They play in a large field with a goal at each end for each of the teams. The equipment needed to play consists of two ball sticks for each player and a game ball made from soft animal skins, about the size of a walnut.

The object of the game is to be the first team to score twenty points. You score one point each time the ball crosses your goal post. You can only move the ball with your ball sticks. Sometimes it takes all day long for a team to win. Today, the points have been cut back and twelve points wins the game.

Everyone anxiously awaits the signal from the Medicine Man that he has finished the rites and is coming up from the water. One team yells three short calls that are repeated by the opposing team. They are ready to get onto the field. The Medicine Man begins the game by tossing the ball into the air and then the players try to get to the ball, by using their sticks, to score points for their team.

LESSON 14 – CHEROKEE TRIBE

Many would go home with broken arms or legs, cuts, or bruises. Sometimes, players even died in their eagerness to prove their clan was the most skilled. Today, rules are given to help prevent the players from getting hurt.

Before the game began, everyone would bring their possessions to bet with. Ladies would put on all of their clothing and wager skirt against skirt, blouse against blouse with the opposing team's women. Men would wager weapons, animals, whatever they had.

State Recognized Cherokee Tribes - There are nine Indian tribes in the State of Alabama that have enrolled several thousand Indians. These represent about 13% of the 165,416 persons in Alabama who disclosed that they were of Indian ancestry in the Federal Census of 1980. Most of those with Indian ancestry in Alabama are descendants of the Cherokee, Choctaw, and Creek tribes who were the aboriginal inhabitants of the State. While the majority of the members of these tribes were removed to Indian Territory in the 1830s, a significant Indian minority remained in the State, including Cherokees in North Alabama, Creeks in South Alabama, as well as a sizeable community of Choctaws in Southwest Alabama (Alabama Indian Affairs Commission, 1988). Today, four state recognized tribes represent the aboriginal Cherokee people who claimed Alabama as their home. These tribes are the Echota Cherokee Tribe of Alabama, Cherokees of Northeast Alabama, Cher-o-Creek Intra Tribal Indians, and United Cherokee AniyunWiya Nation.

LESSON 14 – CHEROKEE TRIBE

KINDERGARTEN

<u>**DIBELS**</u> Reading Objective: COMPREHENSIVE

Objective: After the teacher directs this lesson, Kindergarten Indian students will develop an understanding and be able to recognize homes used by the Cherokee Indians.

Objective Activity: The teacher will read from the text or short story, and give explanations about the Cherokee homes. Then, show pictures of homes for students to visually recognize. Also, students will identify beginning sounds of words in text. (Examples: hot, log, wall, food, tools, boys)

<u>**STATE STANDARDS**</u> Reading Objective:

PG. 15 #13   Gain an awareness of others through exposure to written, spoken, and visual forms of communication
- Discuss how the number seven was important to the Cherokee (sacred-seven sided council house, clans, directions)
  - *What was the most important number to the Cherokee? (7)*

PG. 14 #9   Begin to use pictures and text to gain meaning from written material
- Show class pictures in order to help them gain a better understanding of what's being discussed. (Doublehead, council house-museum, game of stickball)
  - *Did Cherokee enjoy playing stickball or football? (stickball)*

PG. 15 #14   Demonstrate an interest in and enjoyment of literature in a variety of forms, contexts, and media
- After discussing the importance of legends to the Cherokee, read a legend to the students and ask questions related to story to make sure the students have a chance to participate. (Ex: "How the bear lost its tail")
  - *The Cherokee told stories called _____. (legends)*

<u>**STATE STANDARDS**</u> Social Studies Objective:

PG. 11 #1   Develop initial map and globe skills
- Teacher will show several counties on Alabama map. Show state of Alabama on United States map. Show Georgia, Tennessee, and Mississippi on United States map.
  - *Most of the Cherokee lived in _____ states. (3) GA, TN, AL*

PG. 15 #34   Develop an awareness of the uniqueness of individuals
- Teacher will tell the students about Chickasaw Chief George Colbert and how he allowed Cherokees to live in Lawrence County.
  - *Who was leader of the Cherokees? (Doublehead)*

<u>**Review Questions**</u>

1. What was the Cherokees' favorite game? (stickball)
2. The Cherokee people lived mostly in how many states? (three)
3. What is a storyteller? (a person who tells myths or legends)
4. Name two of the seven clans. (Blue, Wild Potato, Long Hair, Wolf, Bear, Paint, Deer)
5. What clan are you a part of? (Blue)

LESSON 14 – CHEROKEE TRIBE

FIRST GRADE

DIBELS Reading Objective: NONSENSE WORD FLUENCY

Objective: After the teacher directs this lesson, first grade Indian students will gain an understanding of nonsense word fluency.

Objective Activity: The teacher will choose real words from the lesson and change the letter to create nonsense words. (Ex: re<u>d</u>-re<u>f</u> or <u>up</u>-<u>ep</u>) Remember vowels ALWAYS make short vowel sound in nonsense words.

STATE STANDARDS Reading Objective:

PG. 17 #4   Demonstrate understanding of letter-sound relationships
- While the teacher is directing the lesson, he/she will pick words from the text, write on the board, change the first letter, and have students sound out each word, then ask which one is correct. (Ex: <u>C</u>herokee, <u>st</u>ories, etc.)
- Who was the person to pass down family history? (storyteller)

PG. 20 #6   Comprehend material read, heard, or viewed
- After a directed lesson, ask questions to check for understanding about the lesson and the terms pulled from text. (nonsense words)
- Name one of the games the Cherokee loved to play. (stickball)

STATE STANDARDS Social Studies Objective:

PG. 18 #3   Extend initial ability to locate new information and to express understanding in various classrooms
- Read the story "How the Bear Lost His Tail" or any other story/legend to the class, while talking about the Cherokees myths.
- What is a legend? (story passed down from generation to generation)

Review Questions

1. What were the stories/myths called? (legends)
2. Where is the Cherokee capital located? (Red Clay, Tennessee)
3. How many sides does a Cherokee Council House have? (seven)
4. Name four of the seven directions: (east, north, south, west, up, down, center)
5. What was the Cherokee's sacred number? (seven)

LESSON 14 – CHEROKEE TRIBE

SECOND GRADE

DIBELS Reading Objective: VOCABULARY

Objective: After the teacher directs this lesson, second grade Indian students will be able to read and identify terms from the text materials. (Terms: log cabins, war, family, Celtic, Indian, Chickasaw, lifestyle, and tribe)

Objective Activity: The teacher will say the term and the students will repeat the term. The teacher will write the terms on the board, and then the students will say the term as a group.

STATE STANDARDS Reading Objective:

PG. 23 #1   Understand the concept of story
- While the students are reading have them pause between paragraphs and make sure everyone understands the concept of the story and terms used in the story by asking questions dealing with events/characters.
  - *While living in Lawrence County, whose leadership were the Cherokees under? (Doublehead)*

PG. 25 #10   Read orally with accuracy, fluency, and comprehension
- After the directed lesson, let individual students read a story from the book "If you lived with the Cherokee" and while the student is reading the teacher will monitor for any mistakes. If the student doesn't correct him/herself the teacher will make the correction for him/her.
  - *Name one of the games the Cherokee loved to play. (stickball/ballplay)*

STATE STANDARDS Social Studies Objective:

PG. 23 #3   Develop the ability to locate new information and express understanding of this information in various classroom projects (Example-imitating others activities in a different time period)
- During a directed lesson discuss how the time period then is different/similar to the time period today? (Ex: the games they played back then and the games today.)
  - *Name the Cherokees' favorite game. (stickball)*

Review Questions

1. No tribal function was considered complete without the presence and assistance of what person? (storyteller)
2. Explain the importance of a storyteller. (since they had no written language, the storyteller kept alive the traditions of their history)
3. Name the three states the Cherokee people lived in: (Georgia, Tennessee, and Alabama)
4. Where was the local government held? (the council house)
5. The Cherokee capital was moved from where to where? (New Echota, Georgia to Red Clay, Tennessee)

LESSON 14 – CHEROKEE TRIBE

THIRD GRADE

DIBELS Reading Objective: WORD RECOGNITION

Objective: After the teacher directs this lesson, third grade Indian students will be able to orally discuss cultural similarities and differences of the Cherokee then and now and identify various terms used throughout the lesson.

Objective Activity: The teacher will allow the students to play Hangman using terms related to the lesson about the Cherokee tribe.

STATE STANDARDS Reading Objective:

PG. 33 #14   Develop an understanding of cultural similarities and differences noted through exposure to multicultural literature
- The class will have a discussion about the similarities and differences of the Cherokee lifestyle then versus now.
  - *What was the Cherokee storyteller's primary goal in life? (to learn every myth/legend of his people and to pass them on to someone else eventually)*

STATE STANDARDS Social Studies Objective:

PG. 29 #1   Extend development of map and globe skills
- Show students Lawrence County map. Show places such as Doublehead, Oakville, etc. to represent important historical landmarks in Lawrence County.
- Show maps of Alabama and U.S.A.
  - *Where are the Indian mounds in Lawrence County located? (Oakville)*

Review Questions

1. Name one of the seven directions of the Cherokee. (north, south, east, west, up, down, within self)
2. The Cherokee people mostly lived in what three states? (AL, GA, TN)
3. How have the Cherokee people kept alive the traditions of their history, ceremonies, rituals, and beliefs? (through word of mouth or storytelling)
4. What games did the Cherokee love to play? (stickball and chunkey)
5. Name the seven clans of the Cherokee. (Blue, Paint, Bird, Wolf, Long Hair, Wild Potato, Deer)

LESSON 14 – CHEROKEE TRIBE

FOURTH GRADE

SAT Reading Objective: LITERARY ELEMENTS

Objective: After the teacher directs this lesson, fourth grade Indian students will be able to identify the following literary elements: main idea, theme, setting, and plot.

Objective Activity: Create a story about the lifestyles of the Cherokee using the information from this lesson. Ask the students to identify the main idea, setting, characters, etc.

STATE STANDARDS Reading Objective:

PG. 38 #5   Interpret passages in print material
- The students will take turns reading the legend "How the Beaver Lost his Tail." The teacher will ask the students what the main idea of the story was, who the characters were, where did the story take place, etc.
    - *What game did the Cherokee love to play? (stickball)*

STATE STANDARDS Social Studies Objective:

PG. 34 #2   Interpret and display information and data
- The teacher will direct the lesson and show the students where the Cherokee originated (which was Alabama, Tennessee, Georgia) on a U.S. map. Also, the teacher will show the students the *Trail of Tears* and Oklahoma, the location to which Andrew Jackson had our Indian ancestors removed.
    - *What president removed the Cherokee from the south? (Andrew Jackson)*

PG. 35 #9   Describe historic Indians of Alabama after European contact
- After the teacher directs the lesson, he/she will discuss the historic Indians of Lawrence county and demonstrate several games played by the Cherokee with the students.
    - *Name one game we talked about today. (stickball)*

Review Questions
1. Where was the Cherokee capital in Georgia? (New Echota)
2. The community building located in all the Cherokee towns were known as what? (council house)
3. Since our ancestors had no written language how was their past kept alive? (word of mouth)
4. The stories or myths our ancient Cherokee ancestors told were also known as? (legends)
5. Who was the Chickasaw chief that allowed the Cherokees to live in Lawrence County? (George Colbert)

LESSON 14 – CHEROKEE TRIBE

FIFTH GRADE

<u>SAT</u> Reading Objective: LITERARY ELEMENTS

Objective: After the teacher directs this lesson, fifth grade Indian students will identify and analyze the following literary elements: main idea, setting, character(s), point of view, and theme.

Objective Activity: The teacher will create a story about the Cherokee using the information from the lesson. Have the students re-tell the important details and identify the literary elements.

<u>STATE STANDARDS</u> Reading Objective:

PG. 45 #7   Use literary analysis
- After the teacher directs the lesson, the students will read from "Warrior Mountain Folklore" about the Cherokee Tribe and then discuss what they read.
- ∾ What is a legend? (story or myth)

PG. 46 #13   Apply strategies of a skillful listener
- The students will listen to other students as they read aloud.
- ∾ How many tribes represent the aboriginal Cherokee people? (four)

<u>STATE STANDARDS</u> Social Studies Objective:

PG. 46 #6   Discuss the progression of culture of the early American people
- The teacher will discuss the Cherokee Tribe and how it was different from today's people.
- ∾ What is the Cherokee's sacred number? (seven)
- ∾ What are the seven directions? (north, south, east, west, up, down, and within)

<u>Review Questions</u>

1. All Cherokee towns had a community building where local government was held. This building was known as what? (council house)
2. What type of Indians lived mostly in Alabama, Georgia, and Tennessee? (Cherokee)
3. Our Indian ancestors kept their past alive by word of mouth, this is also known as what? (storytelling)
4. Who was the leader of the Cherokees? (Doublehead)
5. Up until the Turkey Town Treaty of 1816, Cherokees and Chickasaws lived in what county? (Lawrence County)

LESSON 14 – CHEROKEE TRIBE

SIXTH GRADE

<u>SAT</u> Reading Objective: PHONETIC PRINCIPLES

Objective: After the teacher directs this lesson, sixth grade Indian students will be able to recognize, understand, and apply different terms discussed in the lesson about the Cherokee Tribe.

Objective Activity: The teacher will allow the students to look up any challenging terms in the dictionary and tell the class what the terms mean and how they should be pronounced. Ex: matrilineal, aboriginal, inhabitants, etc.

<u>STATE STANDARDS</u> Reading Objective:

PG. 52 #4   Demonstrate reading improvement gained through substantial amounts of daily reading
- After the teacher directs the lesson, the students will be able to recognize, understand, and apply different terms from the lesson about the Cherokee Tribe. After the lesson, the teacher will ask the following questions: Can anybody recognize the main idea of the lesson?
  - *Name one game we discussed today, and tell how it was played. (stickball, chunkey, etc.)*
  - *How many tribes represented the aboriginal Cherokee people? (four)*

<u>STATE STANDARDS</u> Social Studies Objective:

PG. 55 #4   Review major changes in America from 1870 to 1900
- After you have a class discussion, discuss how our culture is different from our ancestors. Such as what kind of homes they lived in, and how clothing and our government is different today. Since decoration by painting dyes were used by our Cherokee people, we will paint our clay pots.
  - *What president removed the Cherokee from the south? (Andrew Jackson)*

Review Questions

1. The people of the Cherokee Nation lived in mostly what three states? (AL, GA, TN)
2. The Cherokees' stories usually told about what? (animals, famous people, and creation)
3. Why was storytelling important to the Cherokees? (It kept their past alive even though they had no written language.)
4. Whose leadership was the Cherokee under while living in Lawrence County? (Doublehead)
5. Which president removed most of the Cherokees living east of Mississippi to Oklahoma? (President Andrew Jackson)

LESSON 14 – CHEROKEE TRIBE

SEVENTH GRADE

SAT Reading Objective: VOCABULARY

Objective: After the teacher directs this lesson, seventh grade Indian students will be able to identify and gain meaning of various vocabulary terms from the text. Terms: aboriginal, matrilineal, inhabitants, etc.

Objective Activity: The teacher and students will read from the lesson on pathways from this area. Students will identify the terms from above playing *Hangman, Wheel of Fortune,* or *Jeopardy*.

STATE STANDARDS Reading Objective:

PG. 58 #11   Refine general listening behaviors
- Ask students to retell the information discussed about the Cherokee Tribe in their own words.
  - Which three states did the Cherokees mostly live? (AL, GA, TN)

STATE STANDARDS Social Studies Objective:

Online Alex #9   Identify individual and civic responsibilities of citizens of the United States
- After the teacher directs the lesson, the students will discuss what the responsibilities of the tribe were.
  - How many Indian tribes are represented in the State of Alabama? (nine)

Review Questions

1. What Chickasaw allowed the Cherokees to live in Lawrence County? (George Colbert)
2. How many tribes represent the aboriginal Cherokee people? (four)
3. During the late 1700s who was the leader of the Cherokee people? (Doublehead)
4. How was a Cherokee storyteller chosen? (He was chosen as a young boy by a storyteller and was taught all the stories and legends and when the older storyteller died, the young boy took over.)
5. The Cherokee people used a council house for what purpose? (to run their local government)

LESSON 15 – SEVEN CLANS OF THE CHEROKEE

Does anyone have a special number? (wait for response) Our Cherokee ancestors regarded seven as their sacred number. Cherokee had seven directions. Can anyone name these directions? You should know four of them at least? (east/red, west/black, north/blue, south/white--the other directions were up/yellow, down/green, and center/brown). The center would be the direction pointing toward you. Because you were considered the center of your universe and you must walk your own direction in life.

As I've already said, "seven" was a very significant and sacred number to the Cherokee people. In addition to the seven counselors and seven women, there were seven Cherokee clans, seven mother towns to serve as clan headquarters, and a seven-sided council house with a section of seats for representatives from each clan. The council house held approximately 500 people.

Clan membership was inherited from one's mother and retained for life. Each person had a close relationship with four of the seven clans: the mother's clan (of which he was a member), the father's clan, the paternal grandfather's clan, and the maternal grandfather's clan. A person was expected to marry into one of the latter two of these four clans. Marriages took place in the council house with a priest officiating. In any single town, all of the clans were represented, and all members of any one clan considered themselves to be brothers and sisters. Clan membership was indicated by the color of feathers one wore.

The civil or peace government conducted the religious ceremonies of the tribe and acted in both a judicial and legislative capacity, holding court and making laws. Murder and inter-clan marriage were both punishable by death. Most criminal acts were avenged by members of the wronged family and were seldom left up to the government.

In times of war, a war chief, Kalanu, and his organization replaced the civil-peace organization. The war organization always wore red. The peace chief, though installed in yellow, customarily wore white.

This design is the symbol of the seven clans of the Cherokees and the seven sided council house, which was the center of their governmental and ceremonial life. In the center, burns the sacred fire, kindled with seven kinds of wood. Around this fire, the struggles, victories, and agonies of the Cherokee empire were discussed and many momentous decisions of their history made.

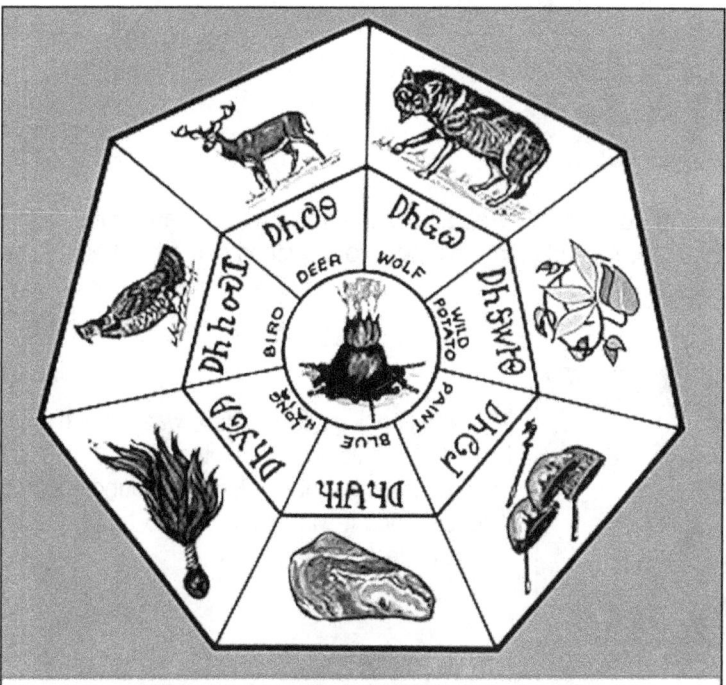

THE CHEROKEE CLANS
The above design symbolizes the seven clans of the Cherokee. The seven-clan system was a relational, social, religious and political structure brought forward from ancient times to have its remnant effect on the Cherokee people today. The number seven was sacred.

One's clan was derived from the mother and his/her only kinsmen were those who could be traced through her. One could not marry within his/her clan and his role in society and his political alignment was determined by his clan. Today the Cherokee communities closely resemble the old clans and representation in the Cherokee council is based on them.

SEVEN CLANS:
LONG HAIR (A NI GI LO HI)
BIRD (A NI TSI S KWA)   WILD POTATO (A NI GA TO GE WI)
BLUE (A NI SA HO NI)   WOLF (A NI WA YAH)
PAINT (A NI WO DI)   DEER (A NI KA WI)

A. Clans-   THE SEVEN CLANS
- Wild Potato .... A NI GA TO GE WI
- Bird .... A NI TSI S KWA
- Long Hair .... A NI GI LO HI
- Blue .... A NI SA HO NI
- Paint .... A NI WO DI
- Deer .... A NI KA WI
- Wolf .... A NI WA YAH

LESSON 15 – SEVEN CLANS OF THE CHEROKEE

The Aniwayah, or **Wolf Clan**, in ancient days hunted like wolves, running after game and attacking in packs. They were fond of wolves and raised them in captivity, training wolf pups just as dogs were trained. It was considered bad luck to kill a wolf, although there is mention of a professional wolf killer who used magic to avoid the bad-luck consequences. Wolf Town is named after the Wolf Clan.

The Anikawi, or **Deer Clan**, members were once like the deer in swiftness. They kept deer in captivity and through special training became skilled in hunting and killing deer. They used prayer formulas and rituals to ward off divine retribution for any mistakes made in following their profession. A portion of Paint Town was once called Deer Place.

The Anitsiskwa, or **Bird Clan**, was fond of birds, and often had captive crows and chicken hawks. Members of the Bird Clan were renowned for their use of snares and blowguns in hunting. Bird Town is named after this clan.

The Aniwodi, or **Red Paint Clan**, members were noted for their skill in ritually employing red iron-oxide paint to attract lovers and gain protection from witches and other harm. They were known as great conjurers in those matters.

The Anisahoni, or **Blue Clan**, was named after a bluish plant that was gathered from swamps and used for food and medicine. The plant was called sakoni or sahoni and was a kind of narrow-leafed grass that produced berries that looked like young cucumbers. The roots of the plant were used to protect children from diseases, and it was customary to bathe the children at the appearance of each new moon in a liquid made from the plant's boiled roots.

The Anigatogewi, or **Wild Potato Clan**, were gatherers of wild potatoes. These grew in swampy places along the rivers and were like sweet potatoes, except that they were round.

The Anigilohi, or Twisters Clan (**Long Hair**), obtained its name in one of two ways. One version has it that the name evolved through the word gagiloha, "one who twists," later changed to ugilaha, "one born twisted" -- referring to the fact that they once were a proud people who strutted when they walked and twisted their shoulders in a haughty manner. A second version maintains that the name was derived from ugilohi, or "long hair," referring to the clan's love of personal adornment and elaborate hairstyles.

LESSON 15 – SEVEN CLANS OF THE CHEROKEE

Seven Festivals -There are other ways that seven is significant to the Cherokee. This includes the seven festivals of the Cherokee.

SEVEN FESTIVALS OF THE CHEROKEE YEAR

Name	Ceremony	When
First New Moon of Spring		March
Solutsunigistisi	Green Corn Ceremony	August
Donagohuni	Ripe Corn Ceremony	September
Nuwatiegwa	Great New Moon Ceremony	October
Atohuna	Friendship Ceremony	October or November
Elawatalegi	Bouncing Bush Feast	September
Uku Dance	The Chief Dance	Every 7th year

Instruments used for music during the festivals and dances were: the drum, gourd rattles, turtle shell rattles, and flutes. The "Square," on a flat ground by the river and near the Council House, was an area designated and prepared for the ceremonies and dances. Green branches tied to high poles provided shade in the dance area, and the river close by provided the water for cold ceremonial plunges.

Things sacred to the Cherokees - Eagle, Eagle Feathers, Rattlesnake, Fire, Smoke, Sun, Moon, Corn, "Seven", Quartz Crystals, The Ark.

LESSON 15 – SEVEN CLANS OF THE CHEROKEE

KINDERGARTEN

DIBELS Reading Objective: VOCABULARY / LETTER NAMING

Objective: After the teacher directs this lesson, Kindergarten Indian students will verbally identify the main vocabulary terms presented and will identify the letters making up the words.

Objective Activity: The teacher will write words on the board from the lesson and ask students to verbally identify each letter. (Ex:, dance, food, fire, eagle, etc.) Students will then identify each word by saying the word aloud. The teacher can also show objects for students to visibly and verbally identify.

STATE STANDARDS Reading Objective:

PG. 14 #9   Begin to use pictures and text to gain meaning from written material
- Use pictures/symbols to help students gain a better understanding of the text. Ex: eagle, rattlesnake, sun, moon, corn, fire, directions.
- Use drawings/pictures to help students remember the seven clans.
- Show pictures of the seven sided council house (museum).
- Show pictures of instruments. (drum, rattles, flute, etc.)
   - ∾ When was the Green Corn Ceremony? (August)

STATE STANDARDS Social Studies Objective:

PG. 15 #34   Develop an awareness of the uniqueness of individuals
- Discuss the importance of the number seven to the Cherokee. (council house, festivals, clans, and direction)
- Discuss other things sacred to the Cherokee such as: rattlesnake, eagle, sun, moon, etc.
   - ∾ What holiday do we celebrate that is like the Green Corn Ceremony? (Thanksgiving or New Year)

PG. 15 #36   Build an understanding of different cultures through the exploration of holidays, customs, and traditions
- Explain how festivals were types of holidays. (Ex: Green Corn Ceremony-Thanksgiving) Also, how festival took place during different months of the year.
- Explain where weddings took place (seven sided council house)
- Another custom would be the use of musical instruments during festivals and dances such as: drum, rattles, flutes, etc.
   - ∾ Name an instrument that we still use today. (drum, flute)

Review Questions

1. What clan are you a member of? (Blue)
2. How many directions are there? (seven)
3. What color is produced when you use blood root? (red)
4. How was the Potato Clan named? (from gatherers of wild potatoes)
5. How many festivals do the Cherokee have? (seven)

LESSON 15 – SEVEN CLANS OF THE CHEROKEE

FIRST GRADE

DIBELS Reading Objective: TEXT COMPREHENSION

Objective: After the teacher directs this lesson, first grade Indian students will use prior knowledge to develop awareness about the seven clans of the Cherokee.

Objective Activity: The teacher will read text from the lesson and ask comprehension questions that come directly from the lesson. Play the game, *Who wants to be a Millionaire,* and allow students to decode the answer using this format: What bird is sacred to the Cherokee? (hawk, eagle, crow)

STATE STANDARDS Reading Objective:

PG. 20 #6   Comprehend material read, heard, or viewed
- After the teacher directs this lesson, ask the students questions to ensure comprehension.
  - *What number was sacred to the Cherokee? (7)*

PG. 20 #10   Recognize values, beliefs, and interests reflected in literature and other materials from various cultures
- After the lesson students will identify the seven clans as a form of recognition in cultural values and beliefs.
  - *Name the seven clans. (Blue, Wolf, Bird, Deer, Long Hair, Wild Potato, Paint)*

STATE STANDARDS Social Studies Objective:

PG. 18 #3   Extend initial ability to locate new information and to express understanding in various classroom
- After directing lesson, ask questions to ensure comprehension of the clans.
  - *What was one of the seven festivals that was like our Thanksgiving? (Green Corn Ceremony)*

Review Questions

1. What ceremony was like our Thanksgiving? (Green Corn Ceremony)
2. What color represents north? (blue)
3. Name three of the seven clans. (Wild Potato, Bird, Long Hair, blue, Paint, Deer, Wolf)
4. When was the Green Corn Ceremony? (August)
5. Name two things sacred to the Cherokee. (eagle, eagle feathers, rattlesnake, fire, smoke, sun, moon, corn, seven, quartz, crystals, The Ark)

LESSON 15 – SEVEN CLANS OF THE CHEROKEE

SECOND GRADE

DIBELS Reading Objective: LISTENING AND COMMUNICATIONS

Objective: After the teacher directs this lesson, second grade Indian students will be able to identify and orally communicate the terms after they have read sentences from the text.

Objective Activity: The teacher will create sentences using terms from the lesson and write them on the board or overhead. He/she will allow students to write the correct term that completes each sentence. Ex: The Long Hair clan loved personal adornment and elaborate hairstyles.

STATE STANDARDS Reading Objective:

PG. 24 #7   Read and comprehend a variety of material
- After the teacher directs the lesson, the students will be able to identify and orally communicate the terms after they have read words/sentences from the text. (Ex: The teacher will say the word and the students will repeat the term. Next, the teacher will write the words on the board. Lastly, the students will say the words as a group. (seven, clans, blue, deer, paint)
  - *What number was sacred to the Cherokee? (7)*

PG. 25 #13   Demonstrate appropriate listening and communicating behaviors
- While the teacher directs the lesson he/she needs to ask questions to ensure comprehension from the students.
  - *What clan are you a part of? (Blue)*

STATE STANDARDS Social Studies Objective:

PG. 23 #3   Develop the ability to locate new information and express understanding of this information in various classroom projects. Example-imitating activities from other time periods (ceremonies)
- Discuss with students how the seven clans were different than how our lifestyles are today. (bathed in the river, married in council house, etc.)
  - *Name some of the things that were sacred to the Cherokee. (water, fire, eagle, seven, etc.)*

Review Questions

1. Name three of seven Cherokee clans. (Blue, Bird, Deer, Wild Potato, Long Hair, Paint, Wolf)
2. During the Cherokees' Green Corn Ceremony, thanks were given for what? (their harvest)
3. What color represents the south? (white)
4. Where did marriages take place? (council house)
5. What were some of the instruments used during the festival and dances? (drum, gourd rattles, turtleshell rattles, and flutes)

LESSON 15 – SEVEN CLANS OF THE CHEROKEE

THIRD GRADE

DIBELS Reading Objective: ORAL READING FLUENCY

Objective: After the teacher directs this lesson, third grade Indian students will orally read aloud and discuss the lesson about seven clans of the Cherokee.

Objective Activity: The teacher will choose various passages from the lesson and randomly choose students to read aloud.

STATE STANDARDS Reading Objective:

PG. 33 #14   Develop an understanding of cultural similarities and differences noted through exposure to multicultural literature
- After the teacher directs the lesson, the students will read orally and discuss the cultural similarities and differences in marriages, clans, festivals, and etc. of ancient to modern times.
  - *Name the seven clans. (Wild Potato, Long Hair, Blue, Deer, Wolf, Paint, Bird)*

STATE STANDARDS Social Studies Objective:

PG. 30 #5   Compare different groups of Native Americans
- Orally discuss with the class what each clan had in common and what was different.
  - *What ceremony was like our Thanksgiving? (Green Corn Ceremony)*

Review Questions

1. What is one of the clans of the Cherokee Tribe? (Blue, Deer, Wolf, Bird, paint, Long Hair, Wild Potato)
2. How was a clan membership obtained? (inherited from one's mother)
3. What color did the peace chief customarily wear? (white)
4. What was the most important instrument to the Cherokee? (drum)
5. The color of one's feathers indicated what? (clan membership)

LESSON 15 – SEVEN CLANS OF THE CHEROKEE

FOURTH GRADE

SAT Reading Objective: LISTENING SKILLS

Objective: While the teacher directs this lesson, fourth grade Indian students will listen to the information regarding the importance of seven to the Cherokee.

Objective Activity: Students will answer comprehension questions during a game of *Jeopardy*. What is another name for wolf clan? Explain. Where did marriage take place? Explain. How were clan members indicated? Explain. When is the Green Corn Ceremony? Explain.

STATE STANDARDS Reading Objective:

PG. 38 #4   Demonstrate literal understanding of printed material
- Ask the students questions pertaining to the lesson to ensure comprehension and good listening skills.
  - *What number was significant to the Cherokee? (seven)*

STATE STANDARDS Social Studies Objective:

PG. 36 #10   Describe aspects of the lives of historic Indians of Alabama
- Discuss the lesson with the students and describe why certain things were sacred to them and why.
  - *Name some things that were sacred to the Cherokee. (water, fire, eagle, feathers, smoke, sun, corn, moon)*

Review Questions

1. What is placed in the center of the council house that kindles seven kinds of wood? (sacred fire)
2. What type of potato is similar to the potatoes the Wild Potato clan gathered? (sweet potatoes)
3. What clan was known as the twister clan? (Long Hair)
4. What colors did the war organization and peace chief wear? (red/white)
5. What color did the war chief always wear? (red)

LESSON 15 – SEVEN CLANS OF THE CHEROKEE

FIFTH GRADE

SAT Reading Objective: GENRES

Objective: After the teacher directs this lesson, fifth grade Indian students will be able to identify the geographic & culturally diverse terms used in literary genres. (Terms: ancestors, clans, ceremonies, Wolf Clan, Deer Clan, Bird Clan)

Objective Activity: After a review of the lesson, select several vocabulary terms to review with the Indian students. Ask if they know what each term means and explain in their own words. Play game of *Hangman, Wheel of Fortune, or Jeopardy* with the students. Give students clues that include meanings of the words from the text.

STATE STANDARDS Reading Objective:

PG. 46 #12   Read a variety of materials and genres encountered in daily lives
- Have the students read aloud about the seven clans making sure they have an understanding of the text. Have a group discussion and ask questions.
  - *Name the seven clans? (Blue, Bird, Wild Potato, Wolf, Long Hair, Deer, Paint)*

STATE STANDARDS Social Studies Objective:

PG. 46 #7   Analyze the different cultures of Native American groups by geographic regions
- The teacher will direct the lesson explaining the seven clans. (Ex: Wolf Clan meaning hunted like wolves, Deer Clan-swiftness, etc.)
  - *How did the Red Paint Clan get its name? (to attract lovers and gain protection)*

Review Questions

1. What clan was known as the twister clan? (Long Hair)
2. What shape was the area close to the council house where ceremonies took place? (square)
3. Name two reasons the Wolf clan obtained its name: (they hunted in packs, and raised wolf pups for hunting dogs)
4. What were the two crimes punishable by death? (murder and inter-clan marriage)
5. Name some things that were sacred to the Cherokee. (water, fire, eagle, feathers, smoke, sun, corn, moon)

LESSON 15 – SEVEN CLANS OF THE CHEROKEE

SIXTH GRADE

<u>SAT</u> Reading Objective: VOCABULARY

Objective: After the teacher directs this lesson, sixth grade Indian students will be able to recognize and identify various vocabulary terms listed from the text about the seven clans of the Cherokee

Objective Activity: After the teacher reviews the lesson, the students will play *Jeopardy, Hangman, or Wheel of Fortune* using terms from the lesson. The teacher will read each word aloud and students will then define words. Terms: significant, paternal, maternal, momentous, retribution, conjurers.

<u>STATE STANDARDS</u> Reading Objective:

PG. 53 #12   Develop general listening behaviors for different purposes and situations
- After the teacher directs the lesson the students will read aloud from "Indian Trails of the Warrior Mountains", and when they are finished they will be able to discuss orally what they read.
- *Name the seven clans. (Blue, Bird, Wild Potato, Wolf, Long Hair, Deer, Paint)*

<u>STATE STANDARDS</u> Social Studies Objective:

PG. 54 #1   Extend the development of map and globe skills
- Show the students a map of Lawrence County and then show them where the Oakville Indian Mounds are located and tell them what the Oakville Indian Mounds were used for and how the museum is built like the council house.
- *Name three of the ceremonies we talked about today. (First New Moon of Spring, Green Corn, Ripe Corn, Great New Moon, Friendship, Bouncing Bush, and the Chief Dance)*

Review Questions

1. What was the flat ground by the river and the council house designated for ceremonies called? (square)
2. What is placed in the center of the council house that kindles seven kinds of wood? (sacred fire)
3. How was clan membership indicated? (by the color of the feathers one wore)
4. What served as the clan headquarters? (the seven mother towns)
5. The Chief Dance was celebrated how often? (every 7th year)

LESSON 15 – SEVEN CLANS OF THE CHEROKEE

SEVENTH GRADE

SAT Reading Objective: COMPREHENSION

Objective: After the teacher directs this lesson, seventh grade Indian students will use their comprehension skills to develop an understanding about the seven clans of the Cherokee.

Objective Activity: Have an open discussion with students about the seven festivals and compare them to the holidays we celebrate.

STATE STANDARDS Reading Objective:

PG. 58 #11 Refine general listening behaviors
- After the teacher directs the lesson the students will gain respect for cultural information concerning the seven clans of the Cherokee. Ask questions for understanding and comprehension.
  - *Name the seven clans of the Cherokee. (Blue, Bird, Deer, Wolf, Long Hair, Wild Potato, Paint)*

STATE STANDARDS Social Studies Objective:

Online Alex #9 Identify individual and civic responsibilities of citizens
- Discuss the individual responsibilities of the different members of the clans. Compare them to the leaders of today's society and their responsibilities.
  - *What two crimes were punishable by death? (murder and inter-clan marriage)*

Review Questions

1. When was the Green Corn Ceremony? (August)
2. How did the Deer clan obtain its name? (their swiftness in hunting, captured deer to learn hunting skills)
3. How did the Bird clan obtain its name? (they were fond of birds and often had captive crows and chicken hawks)
4. What clan was noted for their skill in employing red-oxide paint to attract lovers and gain protection from harm? (Red Paint clan)
5. Every 7th year the Cherokee celebrated what? (The Chief Dance)

LESSON 16 – INDIAN TRAILS AND PATHS

Early Travel - Our Indian ancestors considered the land sacred; therefore, it could not be bought or sold. They believed that the earth was their mother and the sun was their father. They wanted to honor the land, as you are to honor your mother. They believed that the sun watched them with its great blazing eyes and, as long as it was on them, everything was all right. If the sun's eye was not shining on them, they were doomed. As they walked the trails across the land under the sun, they felt the precious land under their feet.

Our Cherokee Indian people traveled long ago by foot and dugout. These were the most common ways. Later on, the Cherokee used horses that were brought from overseas by the Europeans. At that period of time, they did not have the use of wheels, motors, and gasoline. Our Cherokee people were not a nomadic (roam from place to place) tribe and travel was limited to certain areas.

Early Trails - In order for our people to travel from neighbor to neighbor, or village to village, a system of trails was developed for easier traveling. Most of these trails and paths could be followed on foot or horseback but were not suitable for coaches or wagons. These Indian paths became important to white settlements and white development of the North Alabama area.

Some of these trails extended all the way across Alabama. There were a great many short trails and hunting trails, but there were fewer long trails. These trails were determined by the lay of the land. Many of today's highways and railroad lines follow these early trails.

We are going to discuss some important Indian trails that came through Lawrence County. The early trails and paths later became some of the roads we travel today. Why do you think the trails were important to the Indian and white settlers during the 1700s and 1800s? (trade)

Many important Indian trails or roads ran through Lawrence County. Trappers and Indian traders came down the Tennessee River by flatboat to the head of Elk River Shoals at Melton's Bluff. These early white intruders on Indian lands were allowed to remain because most of these Celtic traders had married into and were accepted in the Creek, Chickasaw, and Cherokee Nations.

1839 Map of Indian Roads

LESSON 16 – INDIAN TRAILS AND PATHS

From Melton's Bluff, two early Indian roads ran south through the Warrior Mountains of Lawrence County. Gaines' Trace went through the western part and was established by a treaty negotiated by Doublehead in 1805. Mitchell Trace (Black Warriors' Path) went through the eastern portion of the Warrior Mountains and was named from Fort Mitchell in Russell County, Alabama. Mitchell Trace ran from Ft. Mitchell to Ft. Hampton in Limestone County, Alabama. Many other Indian trails traversed the dividing ridges of the Warrior Mountains creating a north-south network from the Warrior River Valley to the Tennessee River Valley. Doublehead's Trace followed the approximate route of Highway 101 through Lawrence County. Brown's Ferry Road ran from Huntsville to Courtland and crossed the Tennessee River by ferry as early as 1813 while still Indian land.

The High Town Path was an example of a long Indian trail that passed through Lawrence County. (show location on Lawrence County map) This trail was named for the Creek village of High Town in present-day Rome, GA. The High Town Path extended from the site of Charles Town, South Carolina by Atlanta, Georgia, westward through the Cherokee Nation south of Sand Mountain, through the Creek Nation, and into the Chickasaw Nation. The trail passed through the present counties of Lawrence, Franklin, and Marion in Alabama prior to entering Mississippi. The trail ran in an east-west direction along the mountain ridges avoiding lowlands and creek crossings. The Leola Road and Ridge Road in Lawrence County represent the most accurate route of the High Town Path through Lawrence County.

Another major Indian route into the Warrior Mountains portion of Lawrence County was by way of the High Town Path also known as The Path or Ridge Path. The Path ran along the Continental Divide in Lawrence County and followed portions of the Old Corn Road, Leola Road, Cheatham Road, Ridge Road, and Byler Road.

The High Town Path was probably most heavily used as an Indian foot path in prehistoric times and was free of creek crossings and wet weather or water barriers. Major portions of the High Town Path followed high lands, which appear to be the general route of early Indian trails. The trail ran from Charles Town or Charleston, South Carolina, to Chickasaw Bluffs at the junction of the Wolf River and the mighty Mississippi at what is today known as Memphis, Tennessee.

According to the Annals of Northwest Alabama, "before the coming of the white man, the ridge generally separated the lands of the Chickasaws on the west from those of the Creeks to the east and the lands of the Cherokees on the north from the Creeks to the south. During the late 1700s and early 1800s, the ridge top path and the Continental Divide were referred to in treaties with the Chickasaw and Cherokee Indians. Later, The Path was used to divide early counties in the Mississippi Territory.

The High Town Path in addition to an Indian trail became the line of the Chickasaw land claims under the Treaty of January 10, 1786. According to a map of Chickasaw boundaries, the Chickasaw claims line followed the Continental Divide through Lawrence and Cullman Counties and turned north and east of the Chickasaw Oldfields on the Tennessee River near Huntsville.

The High Town Path was one of the most famous Indian trails in the Southeastern United States. The Path traversed across the Continental Divide portion of William B. Bankhead National Forest in Lawrence County, Alabama. The Indian trail completely crossed the southeastern United States in an east-west direction and traveled through Alabama along the dividing watersheds of the Tennessee River to the north and the waters that drain into Mobile Bay to the south." The long Indian trail was some 1000 miles in length with the Indian village of High Town (Rome, GA) located somewhat near the middle of the route.

Indian people, including metis Indian people of mixed Celtic ancestry, and early settlers moving into Lawrence County from east Tennessee and north Georgia, came in contact with the High Town Path and probably followed along its course. The Indian trail crossed Georgia just north of Atlanta and another fork traversed diagonally across Tennessee toward the southwest from the Knoxville area and through the area east of Chattanooga. Portions of the trail crossed Lookout Mountain and Sand Mountain as it proceeded toward the dividing ridges of Bankhead National Forest in the southern portion of Lawrence County.

High Town, which was near present-day Rome, Georgia, and Turkey Town, which was near present-day Gadsden, Alabama, were important Indian towns along the eastern portion of the route. It was by this route that numerous settlers of the Warrior Mountains and many Lawrence County families can trace the western movement of their ancestors.

According to the Annals of Northwest Alabama, "The High Town Path was an Indian trail that extended from near the present site of Atlanta, Georgia, westward through the Cherokee Nation south of Sand Mountain, through the Creek Nation, and into the Chickasaw Nation and the present counties of Lawrence, Franklin, and Marion in Alabama prior to entering Mississippi. Settlers

LESSON 16 – INDIAN TRAILS AND PATHS

from North Georgia and South Carolina could migrate to Winston along this route having good roads until they turned southward to cross the mountains. After the building of the Cheatham Road and Byler's Road, they could have fair roads all the way."(Elliott, 1972:20) It should be noted that the High Town Path probably entered only the northwest corner of Winston County. Settlers traveled from The Path along present-day Highway 41 (Jasper Road), the Cheatham Road (Sipsie Trail) which is present-day Highway 33, and the Byler Road to get into Winston County.

The following is two descriptions of the High Town Path as reported in The Story of Alabama, "High Town Path, from High Shoals on the Apalachee River to High Town in the fork of the Oostenalla and Etowa Rivers, the site of the modern Rome Georgia, thence to Turkey Town of the Cherokee Country, to Coosa, thence to Flat Rock in the northwestern part of the state, thence to Copper Town of the Chickasaw Nation. Two great trails from the east united at Flat Rock in Franklin County, Alabama, and thence-continued west to the Chickasaw Nation. One of these trails comes from the Chattahoochie to Little Okfuskee thence to Flat Rock. The other, the High Town Trail, started from Tellico in Monroe County, East Tennessee, thence southwest to Coosa Town, and from it to Flat Rock."(Owens, 149:240, 244)

The book Alabama History for Schools describes the trail in the following, "One example of a long Indian trail was the High Town Path. This was named for the Creek Indian village of High Town in present-day Etowah County. This trail ran all the way across Alabama from the land of the Chickasaws in the west, through the Creek Country to Turkey Town. From Turkey Town, it ran through the Cherokee Country and across the Chattahoochee River into Georgia." (Summersell, 1981:187)

According to the book, History of Alabama, "The Creeks had numerous paths radiating from eastern Georgia into Alabama, along which Carolina and Georgia traders, and later settlers, penetrated the interior of the state. The most notable of these were the 'High Town Path' and the 'Southern Trail.' The former crossed the Chattahoochee at Shallow Ford, just north of the present city of Atlanta and extended by way of High Town (Etowah), Turkey Town, and other villages along the Cherokee border to the Chickasaw Country." (Moore 1951: 292)

According to the Sesquicentennial Edition 1819-1969 of the Franklin County Times, "Indian trail was first County road: The first account in history of a traveled pathway through Franklin County is of an Indian trail that came from the east and intersected another trail from the north at 'Flat Rock' in Franklin County."

From Brown's Village, the High Town Path followed the Continental Divide through Marshall and Cullman Counties along the "Old Corn Road." The Old Corn Road traversed along the Continental Divide crossing present day Highway 31 at Vinemont and crossed present day Highway 157 at Battleground Mountain in Cullman County.

From Battleground, The Path continued west to an Indian crossroads, which became known as Basham's Gap. Basham's Gap was located near the present-day site of Piney Grove in the southeast corner of Lawrence County. At Basham's Gap, the High Town Path intersected the north-south Indian path, known as Black Warriors' path, from the Tennessee River at Melton's Bluff to Elyton (Birmingham) and on south. The Jasper Road also intersected The Path at Basham Gap and traversed from the Tennessee River (Decatur), to Jasper, then to Tuscaloosa.

From Basham's Gap, the High Town Path traversed westerly along the Leola Road portion of the Continental Divide to the Wren Mountain area where it intersected another southerly divide which was an Indian path, Sipsie Trail. The Sipsie Trail from Muscle Shoals, on the Tennessee River, through the Bankhead Forest to Tuscaloosa became the Cheatham Road (present day Highway 33).

From the Wren Mountain area, The Path continued on westerly along the Ridge Road portion of the Continental Divide to Kinlock. Near Kinlock, the Path intersected an Indian trail known as Doublehead's Trace or the Old Buffalo Trail from the French Lick (Nashville). Doublehead's Trace or the Old Buffalo Trail later became the Byler Road along the mountain ridge in Lawrence County.

It should be noted that another diamond pattern of the High Town Path may begin at The Path's junction with the Old Buffalo Trail. Some think one fork turned northwest along the Old Beulah Motorway with the other fork traversing southwest by Haleyville, Alabama along the Continental Divide between Bear Creek and the upper Tombigbee River system. To continue west along the Old Beulah route would require at least one stream crossing on the western portion of the Bear Creek system. Some early maps

LESSON 16 – INDIAN TRAILS AND PATHS

do indicate a Flat Rock on Little Bear Creek. It appears that both routes were used and probably rejoined at a point on the divide southwest of Bear Creek. From that point, evidence exists both in text and maps that one trail led to Copper Town and one to Chickasaw Bluffs.

In addition to traders and early settlers, the High Town Path was not only a geographic boundary but also used as a tribal boundary and a political boundary. The ridge was a prominent feature or landmark through North Alabama noted in early history as the Continental Divide of the waters draining south into Mobile Bay and the waters draining north into the Tennessee River. According to a report of the Alabama History Commission, "the true Cherokee southern boundary, after following the ridge separating the waters of the Tennessee and Black Warrior to the headwaters of Caney Creek, ran thence down said creek to the Tennessee River."

In identifying the Cherokees' southern boundary the Manual for Writing Alabama State History states, "Consequently we may conclude in a general way that from the lower end of Ten Islands the line followed the most prominent dividing ridge butting on the river in that vicinity, around the headwaters of Canoe Creek, until it reached the height of Blount Mountain, thence northward with said mountain along the ridge dividing the waters of the Coosa from those of the Black Warrior to the top of Raccoon or Sand Mountain near the Town of Boaz in Marshall County. From this point westward to the Chickasaw boundary, wherever that lay, it is quite clear that the line was the ridge dividing the waters of the Tennessee from those of the Black Warrior. Gov. Blount in 1794, writing to the chiefs and headmen of the Creeks said: "In the original division of land amongst the red people, it is well known that the Creek lands were bounded on the north by the ridge which divides the waters of the Mobile and the Tennessee." Judge Haywood, criticizing a Mr. Barnard for some erroneous statements the latter had made to the Governor of Georgia in 1793, says, "And he (Barnard) ought to have known that the Creek claim to lands was bounded by the ridge which divides the waters of the Tennessee and Mobile."

In the Turkey Town Treaty of 1816, which ceded land from both the Chickasaws and Cherokees, the Ridge Path (High Town Path) was used as the southern boundary for the land cession of both Indian nations including Franklin, Lawrence, and Morgan Counties (Jones, 1972:2). Article 2 of the treaty with the Cherokee, 1816, states, "The Cherokee Nation acknowledge the following as their western boundary: South of the Tennessee River, commencing at Camp Coffee, on the south side of the Tennessee River, which is opposite the Chickasaw Island, running from thence a south course to the top of the Dividing Ridge between the waters of the Tennessee and Tombigbee Rivers, thence eastwardly along said ridge, leaving the head waters of the Black Warrior to the right hand, until opposed by the West branch of Well's Creek down the east bank of said creek to the Coosa River, and down said river."(Kappler, 1904:133)

According to the book Myths of the Cherokee, "failing in this, pressure was at once begun to bring about a cession in Alabama, with the result that on September 14 of the same year, a treaty was concluded at the Chickasaw council-house, and afterward ratified in general council at Turkey Town on the Coosa, by which the Cherokee ceded all their claims in that state south of the Tennessee River and west of an irregular line running from Chickasaw Island in that stream, below the entrance of Flint River, to the junction of Wills Creek with the Coosa, at the present Gadsden."(Mooney, 1982:98) It should be noted that the irregular line to the west was on the High Town Path along the ridge top and followed the Chickasaw claims of January 10, 1786. The line ran south from Chickasaw Island to the Continental Divide then west along the dividing Ridge Path.

Several references indicate the Continental Divide through Lawrence County and North Alabama was not only a geographic boundary between major watersheds but also an important political boundary in separating the counties of Blount and Shelby in the Mississippi Territory. The county to the north included what is now the Tennessee Valley portion of Lawrence County in North Alabama. According to the Journal of Muscle Shoals History (1977), the following statement is given, "All that tract country lying south of the Tennessee River, east of the Chickasaw boundary line, north of the highlands that divide the waters of the Tennessee from the water of the Mobile Bay and west of the Cherokee boundary line shall form one other county to be called and known by the name of Blount, the courts of justice where of will be held at Melton"s Bluff." Melton's Bluff is on the south bank of the Tennessee River between Spring and Mallard Creeks in Lawrence County, Alabama.

The Franklin County Times reporting on the history of Franklin County included the following, "It seems from Ramsey's Annals of Tennessee this section was at one time included in the proposed borders of the State of "Franklin" as laid out by Colonel Campbell, the originator of the idea of a state separate and apart from all other states of the union. Colonel Campbell began to agitate for the headwaters of the Tombigbee River, thence east, posed a boundary for the new state to begin at a point on the

LESSON 16 – INDIAN TRAILS AND PATHS

Holston River and "run west to the shoals of the Ohio, thence south across the Cherokee lands to the headwaters of the Tombigbee River, thence east to the top of the Appalachian mountains, where the waters divide and then north to the beginning."(Times, 1969:8)

It should be noted that the ridge along the top of the Appalachian Mountains is the Continental Divide through Lawrence County, which separates the water that drains south into Mobile Bay from the water that drains north into the Tennessee River. Along this dividing ridge, lies the High Town Path, which was a clearly marked geographic division for tribal boundaries, political entities, as well as an east-west route across North Alabama.

Another major route into the Warrior Mountains portion of Lawrence County was by way of the High Town Path also known as the Ridge Path. The path ran along the Continental Divide in Lawrence County and followed portions of the Old Corn Road, Leola Road, Cheatham Road, Ridge Road, and Byler Road.

Gaines' Trace (c1805) was apparently the first federal road in Lawrence County. The Gaines Trace ran from Melton's Bluff north of present-day Courtland, through part of Colbert County, to Russellville in Franklin County, and to Cotton Gin Port at the head of navigation on the Tombigbee River. One fork from Russellville went to Eastport, MS and on to New Orleans, Louisiana.

General George Strother Gaines, brother of Captain Edmund P. Gaines.

When reading the early history of Lawrence County, the first existing road mentioned before our county became a county and before our state became a state is the Gaines' Trace. Gaines' Trace authorized by Congress about 1805 was a government road from Melton's Bluff on the Tennessee River, through the Warrior Mountains, to Cotton Gin Port on the Tombigbee River (show map). The route divided at Russellville with the northwestern fork going to Eastport, MS. By this route, Doublehead was able to ship his cotton to New Orleans and Mobile. Gaines Trace ran through present-day Lawrence, Franklin, and Marion Counties. It was a connection of the Tennessee River to the Tombigbee River. The route was important for trade among the white and Indian settlers. Gaines Trace was authorized by Article IV of the "Wafford Settlement," a treaty with the Cherokees, which primarily ceded Cherokee lands in central Tennessee and Kentucky. The road was named and laid out by General George Strothers Gaines about 1810. "Gaines' Trace" began approximately eight miles west of Mallard Creek at Melton's Bluff near the head of Elk River Shoals and proceeded southwest where it forked. One route continued west to Eastport, Mississippi, with the other route passing through Russellville to Cotton Gin Port on the Tombigbee River. This trace was laid by Captain Edmund P. Gaines in December 1807, and passed through the Warrior Mountains in the western portion of Lawrence County.

Captain Edmund P. Gaines noted on January 14, 1808, that he had already made one survey in 1802. "Gaines' Trace" began approximately eight miles west of Mallard Creek at Melton's Bluff near the head of Elk River Shoals and proceeded southwest where it forked. One route continued west to Eastport, Mississippi, and the other fork to Cotton Gin Port, Mississippi. The earlier route, surveyed in 1802, was approximately the same period as Natchez Trace was established.

The Gaines route was described by Captain Edmund Pendleton Gaines in a letter to the Secretary of War on January 29, 1808. As requested by the Secretary of War on July 31, 1807, Captain Gaines surveyed and marked a way for a road from the head of Muscle Shoals (Melton's Bluff) to Cotton Gin Port on the Tombigbee River.

LESSON 16 – INDIAN TRAILS AND PATHS

Gaines said in his letter, "I have also explored the route,...From the head of the shoals (Brown's Ferry) to the northeast sources of Bear Creek, distance 35 miles, is as nearly level as could be wished, either for making a good road for carriages by going near a straight course; but by waving the course in conformity of the slopes of the ridges all will be crossed without ascent or decent of more than 13 ½ degrees... The route for the greater part of this distance, is on the dividing ridges, between the waters of the Tennessee and Mobile...Several Cherokees have designated different places, where they promised to settle in the course of the present year, along the way as far as Bear Creek Ridge, which they call their South boundary..."

As given in the Territorial Papers of the United States, compiled and edited by Clarence Carter, one description describes the dividing ridge south of Mt. Hope in western Lawrence County between the Bear Creek drainage, which flows to the Tennessee River, and the Sipsey River drainage, which flows to Mobile. The High Town Path, which was the Chickasaw's southern boundary, defined by the Treaty of January 10, 1786, also follows the same dividing ridge through this area.

In his letter, Captain Edmund Gaines states that the Cherokee claim the Continental Divide of Bear Creek Ridge as their south boundary. In addition, Edmund Gaines identified two routes from the Shoals that joined on the ridge near the headwaters of Bear Creek; however, the 1808 route runs basically 45° southwest of north through the Tennessee Valley from Melton's Bluff. The two other routes could be previous surveys.

It is thought that one of the other two routes run the dividing ridge in southwest Lawrence County and also became a small portion of the first legislative road in Alabama – the Byler Road. In addition, the closest route of 35 miles, from Melton's Bluff at the head of the shoals toward the northeast sources of Bear Creek, would be just south of Mt. Hope approximately some four miles. Since the headwaters of Bear Creek and the headwaters of Sipsey River lie in southwestern Lawrence County, a small portion of one of the Gaines routes probably lay along the portion of mountain ridges of the watershed divide that became the Byler Road by Act of Alabama Legislature on December 15, 1819.

Natchez Trace - In October 1801, a treaty between the U. S. and the Chickasaws gave permission to cut and open a wagon road between Nashville, Tennessee and Natchez, Mississippi. The road known as the Natchez Trace, passed through Colbert and Lauderdale Counties in North Alabama.

Colbert's ferry at the crossing of the Natchez Trace on the Tennessee River

LESSON 16 – INDIAN TRAILS AND PATHS

The Indian trail known as the **Black Warriors' Path** or Mitchell Trace led from Melton's Bluff toward the Mulberry and Sipsey Forks of the Black Warrior River, and then traversed southeast to Fort Mitchell on the Chattahoochee River in present-day Russell County, Alabama. The route continued from Cusseta near Ft. Mitchell to the Atlantic Coast at St. Augustine. The route became known as the Mitchell Trace, and connected Fort Hampton in Limestone County to Fort Mitchell in Russell County, Alabama.

The 1818 John Melish Map shows the Black Warriors' Path through Lawrence County beginning at Marathon (Melton's Bluff), proceeding east of Courtland several miles, following closely to the present-day Hillsboro Road to Fairfield Church, crossing Elam Creek and the Fish Dam Ford on the West Fork of Flint Creek passing through the Oakville Indian Mounds Park near the ceremonial mound, into Beaty Hollow south of Speake, through Poplar Log Cove, and exiting the county near Basham's Gap at Piney Grove.

The Black Warriors' Path led south through Lawrence County and passed the area of Oakville. Just north of Oakville, the trail crossed the West Fork of Flint Creek and appears to have proceeded adjacent to the large ceremonial Indian mound at the Oakville Indian Mounds Park. Remnants of the very old road are still visible on the west side of the mound.

According to William Lindsey McDonald's article on Melton's Bluff, "The renowned pioneer and soldier, David Crockett, remembered two occasions when his military unit crossed at Melton's Bluff. The first instance was in November 1813. Actually according to Crockett, he crossed the Tennessee River twice on this first occasion in order to maneuver around the local Indians. After crossing at Huntsville, they moved westward to cross the river again at Melton's Bluff. Crockett described the river at this point as being about two miles wide. The rocky bottom of the river was rough and dangerous. While fording the river, several of the horses became stuck in the rocky crevices and had to be left there while the military command moved onto their destination. Crockett's second crossing at Melton's Bluff was in October 1814. Payroll and muster records reveal that he was a third sergeant in Captain John Cowan's company at the time." According to McDonald, the above information was obtained from the book A Narrative of the Life of David Crockett.

In 1813, David Crockett helped General John Coffee's forces burn the large Creek Indian village known as Black Warrior Town after finding it deserted. Crockett and General Coffee's forces traveled along the Black Warriors' Path through present day Lawrence County to destroy the Creek town. James Richard Gillespie from Indian Tomb Hollow also served with David Crockett. Gillespie served under Captain Cowan in 1813 during the same period of time as David Crockett. Gillespie attended the muster rolls in Blount County, Tennessee on January 1, 1814.

Lawrence County's forgotten Indian trail or road, the Black Warriors' Path, from Melton's Bluff at the head of Elk River Shoals, across the Warrior Mountains, to the center of the Creek Indian Nation near the Little and Big Oakfuskee Towns, preceded Gaines' Trace. The trail or road was last known as the Mitchell Trace. Mitchell Trace probably received the name after the building of Fort Mitchell in 1811 on the Chattahoochee River in present-day Russell County, Alabama. Mitchell Trace became a post route which connected Fort Hampton, a Cherokee Indian outpost located near the forks of Elk River and the Tennessee River in present-day Limestone County, to Fort Mitchell, a Creek Indian outpost. Fort Mitchell was named after David Brady Mitchell, who was listed as Indian Agent or Governor.

The relationship of the Gaines and Mitchell Traces does not end with a common beginning point at Melton's Bluff the trails were connected on their southern ends by a trading route from Fort Mitchell to St. Stephens; therefore, an early Indian trading triangle was established in the area that became the State of Alabama (show picture of Mitchell Trace).

Along the western edge of the ceremonial mound are remnants of the Black Warriors' Path or Mitchell Trace. This trail was a major trading route utilized by Indian people. The path connected Fort Hampton near the

Black Warriors' Path just west of the crossing on the Mulberry Fork of the Warrior River near old Baltimore

LESSON 16 – INDIAN TRAILS AND PATHS

Tennessee River crossing at Elk (Chuwalee) River Shoals to Fort Mitchell near the Chattahoochee River in present day Russell County, Alabama. The Black Warriors' Path is clearly shown on the 1814 and 1818 Melish maps and shows it crossing both the West Fork of Flint Creek and Elam Creek. These crossings are still clearly visible just one mile north of the burial mound at Oakville. Remnants of the very old road are still visible on the west side of the ceremonial Indian mound at Oakville. In addition, just south of Lindsey Cemetery at the edge of the mountains, the old road bed is clearly visible as it crosses U.S. Forest Service property into Beaty Hollow and on into Poplar Log Cove. The trail crossed the Southeastern United States from Nashville, TN, to Columbus, GA, and onto St. Augustine, FL on the Atlantic Coast.

Fort Mitchell, marked a southern point along the Mitchell Trace (Black Warriors' Path) that passed through the Oakville Indian Mounds Park, and played a vital role in the final days of the Creek Indian removal during the 1830s. By 1835, many Creeks had been removed west. A detachment of 511 Creeks passed through the Oakville Indian Mounds Park along the Mitchell Trace on December 19, 1835.

The Old Mitchell Trace crosses the West Fork of Flint Creek approximately one mile north of the Oakville Indian Mounds Park. After crossing the Fish Dam Ford on West Flint, an old wagon road between Flint and Elam Creeks known as the Chickasaw Trail runs west toward Moulton. Both Black Warriors' Path and the Old Chickasaw Trail that runs from Chickasaw Island (Huntsville) to Cotton Gin Port cross Elam Creek in the same place. The Creeks arrived in Moulton on December 19, 1835. An 1813 map of Indian country in the area that became Lawrence County shows two roads beginning at Melton's Bluff which is located at the head of Elk River Shoals. Of course, the two roads shown on the map are the Gaines and Mitchell Traces. The date of the map was three years before these Indian lands were given up by the Turkey Town Treaty of 1816.

Beginning near the eastern end of Elk River Shoals on the Tennessee River at Melton's Bluff in Lawrence County, the old Black Warriors' Path lead south into the foothills of Bankhead Forest, through the forest, and into the Black Warrior River Valley. The Black Warriors' Path crossed the Warrior River just northeast of the junction of the Mulberry and Sipsey forks where it intersected another trail coming from the Tennessee River at Ditto's Landing near present-day Huntsville called Black Warrior Road. The trails joined and a few miles southwest of the road junctions and river crossing was the Indian village of Black Warrior Town. The Creek Indian town was destroyed by the military forces commanded by General Coffee and David Crockett.

Since General Coffee and Davy Crockett crossed the Tennessee River at Melton's Bluff twice during 1813, it is highly probable that Crockett and Coffee traveled the Black Warriors' Path (Mitchell Trace) to Black Warrior Town. In a letter from John Coffee to General Jackson, dated October 22, 1813, and belonging to Mr. Richard C. Sheridan, the following describes the crossing: "...I proceed to cross the river at the upper end of the Shoals, all my efforts failed to procure a pilot. I took with me one of John Melton's sons who said he knew not the road, he showed me a path that had been reputed the **Black Warriors' Path**..."

To confirm the existence of the Black Warriors' Path, one can just look at old maps showing the area known as Melton's Bluff in Lawrence County. The Black Warriors' Path or Mitchell Trace is clearly shown on the following maps listed by date: 1813, 1818, 1823, 1825, 1831, and 1842. Since the road is not shown after the 1850's, the route probably became a part of the vast Wheeler Plantation and the Town of Marathon became one of the dead towns of North Alabama. After the railroad around the Shoals was completed in 1834, Marathon at the head of Elk River Shoals died.

It does not appear accidental that the trail connected areas of cultural importance to the Indian people of the Tennessee River Valley, the Black Warrior River Valley, and the Chattahoochee River Valley. An Indian trail also ran from Ft. Mitchell to St. Stephens on the Tombigbee, thus completing a trading triangle.

Doublehead's Trace (Old Buffalo Trail) was formerly a Chickasaw trail. It ran the general route of Highway 101 and crossed the Tennessee River from Blue Water Creek to Lawrence County between Big Nance and Town Creek and went to Tuscaloosa.

Along the western edge of the present-day Black Warrior Wildlife Management Area, a trail running the Tennessee Divide was the Old Buffalo Trail, Doublehead's Trace, and later, the Byler Road. The portion of this early route that runs the divide, identified by old timers as Doublehead's Trace or the Old Buffalo Trail, ran portions of the Byler Road and High Town Path. The route followed a ridge between Bear Creek and Sipsey River for some five miles in the southwestern corner of Lawrence County.

The trail was used by Creeks and Choctaws traveling north toward the French Lick (Nashville, Tennessee area) in search of

LESSON 16 – INDIAN TRAILS AND PATHS

buffalo and later as a trade route by the Cherokees. Doublehead's Trace or Buffalo Trail ran from the French Lick (Nashville, TN) to Duck River, to Shoal Town (Blue Water-Town Creek Villages), to Town Creek, to Hatton, Old Town Creek Church, McClung Gap, then followed what is now the Byler Road to Haleyville, then to Tuscaloosa. Doublehead's Trace or the Old Buffalo Trail probably crossed the Tennessee River at Blue Water Creek near Wheeler Dam to Path Killer's Creek (Big Nance), and followed close to the route now known as State Highway 101. At one time, the route was a Chickasaw trail.

Along the western edge of the present-day Black Warrior Wildlife Management Area, a portion of the Byler Road runs the divide that was recorded by Captain Edmund Pendleton Gaines on January 29, 1808. According to the Territorial Papers, he described a route from the head of the Shoals toward Bear Creek Ridge, then south toward Cotton Gin Port. The portion from the Ridge Road to Haleyville (Flat Rock) of the early route has been identified by old timers as the Old Buffalo Trail or Doublehead's Trace. Doublehead's Trace or Old Buffalo Trail ran portions of the Byler Road and High Town Path along the ridge dividing Bear Creek and Sipsey River for some five miles in the southwestern corner of Lawrence County, then turned south toward Tuscaloosa.

Doublehead's Trace or Buffalo Trail came from the French Lick (Nashville), to Duck River, to the mouth of Blue Water Creek to Town Creek, to Hatton, Old Town Creek Church, McClung Gap, then to Byler Road, to Haleyville, and then Tuscaloosa. The trail was used by Creeks and Choctaws traveling north toward the French Lick (Nashville, Tennessee area) in search of buffalo. Buffalo were known to be abundant in middle Tennessee around the Duck River and Buffalo River Valleys. It later became a trade route used by the Cherokees. Eventually, part of the approximate route of Doublehead's Trace or Buffalo Trail became portions of the Byler Road. Doublehead's Trace or Old Buffalo Trail crossed the Big Muscle Shoals on the Tennessee River near Wheeler Dam from the east mouth of Blue Water Creek to the area between Town Creek and Big Nance Creek (Path Killer's Creek) in Lawrence County.

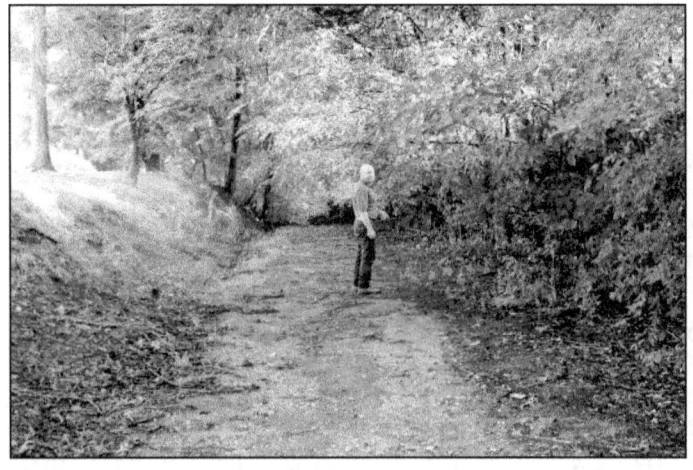
Coosa Path between Moulton and Oakville

Coosa Path - Just past the entrance of Oakville Indian Mounds Park, some 100 yards north, the Coosa Path turns west and crosses West Flint Creek toward Moulton. By December 19, 1835, this was the major road from Moulton to Somerville by way of Oakville. During this time, the Coosa Path (also known as the Moulton to Sommerville Road via Irwin's Mill) had the only known bridge across Flint Creek from Moulton to the Black Warriors' Path at Oakville; therefore, the Creek removal followed Black Warriors' Path to this old crossing then turned west to Moulton along the major road - Moulton to Somerville via Irwin's Mill (Coosa Path was also known as the Muscle Shoals Path).

Brown's Ferry Road - Trappers and Indian traders came down the Tennessee River by flatboat to the head of Elk River Shoals at Brown's Ferry. As early as 1813, travelers could travel southwest by way of the best Indian roads in Lawrence County which were known as Brown's Ferry Road. At this time, Brown's Ferry Road ran from Huntsville to Courtland and crossed the river at the Brown's Ferry which was the location of Doublehead's Village.

These early white intruders on Indian lands were allowed to remain because most had married into and were accepted in the Cherokee Nation. Ann Royall gave an account of one such individual in a letter dated January 12, 1818. Ms. Royall called the white guide Rhea and explained that he had married one of John Melton's half blood Cherokee daughters. John Melton, who was an Irishman by birth, had a large plantation in Lawrence County at the head of Elk River Shoals. Rhea had lived among the Cherokees for 15 years (1803) and John Melton had established his plantation around 1790.

Braziel Creek Trail - According to local folklore, this trail was originally an Indian path which ran from the Elk River Shoals south toward Tuscaloosa along the creek and river bottoms. In Lawrence County, the trail followed Braziel Creek to Borden Creek, to Sipsey River, and to parts south. Portions of the trail of which I write may represent the escape route of some Cherokees during removal, as well as other Southern Indians and black slaves and appears untouched by white man. According to Jim Manasco, the trail was a secret route, which now runs through Bankhead Forest's Sipsey Wilderness Area in Lawrence County, Alabama.

LESSON 16 – INDIAN TRAILS AND PATHS

The trail was strategically located between the Byler Road to the west, and the Cheatham Road to the east both of which traverse the Warrior Mountains in north-south directions. Isolated from military movements and traffic along the two major Bankhead roads and passing through the forest on a north-south course, the trail offered protection from detection over its long course from the south to its junction with the High Town or Ridge Path on the northern border of the forest.

According to folklore and Indian legend passed through some 130 years of time, arbor glyphs of snakes were drawn on beech trees along the trail by Indian people around the time of removal. According to Jim Manasco, his Indian ancestors passed through the area along the trail to settle on the Rocky Plains.

Sipsie Trail - According to early historical information concerning the Indian inhabitants of the Warrior Mountains, most of the major dividing ridges of the forest served as trails, paths, and primitive roads from one part of the country to another. The dividing ridge which separates the watersheds of Brushy Creek and Sipsey River was no different and was known in local folklore as the Sipsie Trail.

Archaeological evidence in bluff shelters near the Sipsie Trail indicates the route was used as early as the prehistoric Woodland period. One such bluff site, the McDougal shelter and mortar rock, was located not far from the dividing ridge. The McDougal Shelter lay close to the divide route and had numerous artifacts dating back to prehistoric times.

The High Town Path ran a portion of the Sipsie Trail from near the junction of the Leola Road to the Ridge Road. Local folklore indicates the north-south dividing ridge was one of many routes utilized primarily by Creek Indians in the early historic period and most likely by Creek people during late prehistoric times just prior to Desoto.

The Sipsie Trail junction with the High Town Path was on top of Wren Mountain some five miles south of Moulton. The route crossed Sipsey River in Winston County, proceed south to Lost Creek, and then paralleled Wolf Creek toward the Black Warrior River Basin near Tuscaloosa. In all probability, the route was utilized by southern Indians hunting buffalo in the Cumberland River basin during the prehistoric and historic periods. Creek and Choctaw hunters used the trail when heading north from the Warrior River Basin toward the French Lick in search of buffalo.

According to an 1830s map of the Cherokee Nation, the route ran the dividing ridge of Brushy and Sipsey to the Sipsey crossing about one mile southeast of the Sipsey and Caney Creek junction. Another 1850s map shows the route running from Pulaski, Tennessee, to the Rogersville crossing of the lower Elk River Shoals of the Tennessee River at Lamb's Ferry, then through Courtland, Moulton, and Wren in Lawrence County, to Double Springs, and then to Rocky Plains in Winston County and on to Tuscaloosa. According to local folklore, Rocky Plains was an Indian stronghold even after the 1838 removal known as the "Trail of Tears."

LESSON 16 – INDIAN TRAILS AND PATHS

KINDERGARTEN

DIBELS Reading Objective: PHONEMIC AWARENESS

Objective: After the teacher directs this lesson, Kindergarten Indian students will develop an understanding of phonemic awareness by breaking apart various terms used throughout the lesson about Indian Trails and Paths.

Objective Activity: The teacher will have the students break apart terms from the lesson and identify how many word parts are in each. Ex: s-a-c-r-e-d=6 word parts or f-oo-t=3 word part

STATE STANDARDS Reading Objective:

PG. 15 #13   Gain an awareness of others through exposure to written, spoken, and visual forms of communications
- The teacher will discuss the importance of trails/paths used by our early Indian ancestors and help the students gain a better understanding of how their trails/paths eventually became the roads we use to travel on today.
  - *How did our early Indian ancestors first travel on water? (canoe)*

STATE STANDARDS Social studies objective:

PG. 11 #1   Develop initial map and globe skills
- Show several maps out of various books to illustrate the trails/paths that have been discussed.
  - *After looking at the maps, name the longest trail/path. (High Town Path)*

PG. 15 #35   Develop an awareness of how people are the same yet different
- Discuss how our early ancestors traveled by foot on trails/paths and/or by canoe on water versus the unlimited modes of transportation used today. (Ex: airplane, vehicles, trains, boats, etc.)
  - *Name one way we travel today. (car, bus, train, plane, etc.)*
  - *Do people today still travel on trails/paths? (yes)*

Review Questions

1. How did our early Indian ancestors travel on land? (foot)
2. Name three ways the early Indians travel. (foot, canoe, horse)
3. What was the longest Indian trail/path in Lawrence County? (High Town Path)
4. What was the first federal road of Lawrence County? (Gaines' Trace)
5. What road was known as the wagon road? (Natchez Trace)

LESSON 16 – INDIAN TRAILS AND PATHS

FIRST GRADE

DIBELS Reading Objective: PHONEME SEGMENTATION FLUENCY

Objective: After the teacher directs this lesson, first grade Indian students will utilize the following reading content standards of phoneme segmentation fluency.

Objective Activity: The teacher will write terms on the board from the lesson or use other visual aids. The students will identify each letter and pronounce each sound in the word. Then they will blend the sounds together and orally read the word.

STATE STANDARDS Reading Objective:

PG. 17 #3   Exhibit phonemic awareness
- After the teacher directs the lesson the students will utilize the following reading content standards of letter naming, nonsense word fluency and phoneme segmentation. (Ex: the teacher will write terms on the board or use other visual aids and the students will pronounce each letter/sound of each word. Next, the teacher will write words on the board changing the initial letter making a nonsense word. (Ex: man-gan)
  - *How did our early Indian ancestors first travel on land? (foot)*

STATE STANDARDS Social Studies Objective:

PG. 18 #3   Extend initial ability to locate new information and to express understanding in various classroom
- Show the class "Indian Trails of the warrior Mountains" for a picture of High Town Path and any other trail or path, or location such as Indian Tomb Hollow.
  - *Name three ways the early Indians traveled. (foot, canoe, and horse)*

Review Questions

1. What is the longest path our ancestors traveled through Lawrence County? (High Town Path)
2. How did our Indian ancestors travel on water? (canoes)
3. In order for our people to travel from place to place, what was developed for easier traveling? (trails/paths)
4. Old Buffalo Trail was also called what? (Doublehead's Trace)
5. What were these paths used for? (trade and travel)

LESSON 16 – INDIAN TRAILS AND PATHS

SECOND GRADE

DIBELS Reading Objective: ORAL READING FLUENCY

Objective: After the teacher directs this lesson, second grade Indian students will demonstrate oral reading fluency by reading aloud.

Objective Activity: The teacher will orally read the lesson and a paragraph from the book, "Indian Trails of the Warrior Mountains." Next, let each student read a sentence from that paragraph. Then allow the students to retell the information in their own words.

STATE STANDARDS Reading Objective:

PG. 24 #7   Read and comprehend a variety of material
- After the directed lesson, have students read orally, and ask questions pertaining to the lesson to ensure comprehension from the student.
  - *What was the longest path of Lawrence County? (High Town Path)*

STATE STANDARDS Social Studies Objective:

PG. 22 #1   Develop map and globe skills
- Show students on a map where some of the trails and paths are located. Give them a visual of where they are.
  - *What was another name for High Town Path? (The Path or Ridge Path)*

PG. 25 #22   Compare transportation methods of families now to those used by families long ago
- Discuss how today we have roads/highways where as then they had trails and paths and we have automobiles and they had animals or walked.
  - *Which trail is about 100 yards north of Oakville? (Coosa Path)*

Review Questions

1. What was the name of the first federal road in Lawrence County? (Byler Road)
2. How did our ancestors travel from one place to another? (walked on the trails)
3. Gaines' Trace was also known as what? (Black Warriors' Path)
4. Doublehead's Trace or Old Buffalo Trail was formerly what type of Indian trail? (Chickasaw)
5. Along with the High town Path, what trail was on top of Wren Mountains some five miles south of Moulton? (The Sipsie Trail)

LESSON 16 – INDIAN TRAILS AND PATHS

THIRD GRADE

DIBELS Reading Objective: LISTENING SKILLS

Objective: After the teacher directs this lesson, third grade Indian students will gain knowledge about the different Indian trails and paths that run through Lawrence County.

Objective Activity: The teacher will ask the students a variety of questions during a remedial game. Divide the students into two teams and allow each child the chance to answer a question. Each question is worth one point. Keep score to see who wins.

STATE STANDARDS Reading Objective:

PG. 31 #1 Use a wide range of strategies to interpret, evaluate, appreciate, and construct meaning from print materials
- While the teacher is reading the lesson, the students will listen to gain knowledge of letter-sound correspondence.
  - *What was the first federal road in Lawrence County? (Gaines' Trace)*

STATE STANDARDS Social Studies Objective:

PG. 31 #1 Extend development of map and globe skills
- After the directed lesson, the teacher will show the students the "Indian Trails and Towns" map to let them know where the Indian trails and paths were located that our ancestors once traveled. (High Town Path, Gaines' Trace, etc.)
  - *Where was Black Warriors' Path located? (Melton's Bluff)*

Review Questions

1. What two Indian trails crossed at Oakville? (Black Warriors' Path and Coosa Path)
2. What do we have today that follows early Indian trails? (highways and railroad lines)
3. Were the Cherokees nomadic? (no)
4. What Indian village was located near present-day Brown's Ferry? (Doublehead's Village)
5. What path was also known as the Moulton to Sommerville Road via Irwin's Mill? (Coosa Path)

LESSON 16 – INDIAN TRAILS AND PATHS

FOURTH GRADE

SAT Reading Objective: WORD RECOGNITION

Objective: After the teacher directs this lesson, fourth grade Indian students will utilize the reading content standard of word recognition.

Objective Activity: The students will identify terms from the lesson during a remedial word game. Ask the students to identify the meaning of each word.

STATE STANDARDS Reading Objective:

PG. 40 #20   Demonstrate vocabulary growth developed through reading and listening to literature
- After the teacher directs the lesson, the students will read aloud from "Indian Trails of the Warrior Mountains." The students will answer questions about the text to show comprehension.
- Teacher will introduce new words from the text to the students.
  - *Black Warriors' Path was also known as what? (Mitchell Trace)*

STATE STANDARDS Social Studies Objective:

PG. 34 #1   Apply an understanding of intermediate directions
- Use a map of Bankhead Forest to show students different directions that the trails travel. (NE, NW, SW, etc.)
- Draw directions on the board to show where each direction is located.
  - *Name the famous part in Mississippi that Gaines' Trace connected to Melton's Bluff. (Eastport)*

PG. 34 #2   Interpret and display information and data using various graphic organizers
- The teacher will show the students a map of the Bankhead Forest and locate the individual trails. Locate the starting points, key areas, and ending points of each trail.
- Have the students draw their own map on a blank sheet of paper to help memorize the locations of the trails.
  - *Who were two famous men that traveled Black Warriors' Path? (David Crockett and General Coffee)*

Review Questions

1. The High Town Path was also known as: (The Path/Ridge Path)
2. How would you confirm the existence of an old road, path, or trail? (old maps of the area)
3. Where was Black Warriors' Path located? (Melton's Bluff)
4. Which trail is about 100 yards north of Oakville? (Coosa Path)
5. The Natchez Trace road passed through what two counties in North Alabama? (Colbert and Lauderdale)

LESSON 16 – INDIAN TRAILS AND PATHS

FIFTH GRADE

SAT Reading Objective: LISTENING SKILLS

Objective: After the teacher directs this lesson, fifth grade Indian students will gain knowledge about the Indian trails and paths located in Lawrence County.

Objective Activity: The students will play a matching game on the board in order for the teacher to check for listening and comprehension skills. (Include vocabulary terms and definitions and review question and answer.)

STATE STANDARDS Reading Objective:

PG. 46 #13 Apply strategies of a skillful listener
- When the teacher is directing the lesson, he/she should be establishing a purpose and needs to make sure the students are focusing on the speaker. Ask questions to ensure comprehension.
  - *What road is between Nashville, Tennessee and Natchez, Mississippi? (Natchez Trace)*

STATE STANDARDS Social Studies Objective:

PG. 46 #4 Describe the natural environment of North America
- Discuss with the students how our ancestors used the natural environment for trails and paths.
  - *What trail was formerly a Chickasaw Trail? (Doublehead's Trace)*

Review Questions

1. Doublehead's Trace or the Old Buffalo Trail crosses Big Muscle Shoals of the Tennessee River near what two creeks? (Blue Water, Town Creek and Big Nance)
2. Who was an Irishman by birth? (John Melton)
3. What two roads represent the most accurate route of the High Town Path through Lawrence County? (the Leola Road and Ridge Road)
4. What path was used to divide early counties in the Mississippi Territory? (High Town Path)
5. In 1813, who helped John Coffee burn the large Creek Indian village known as Black Warrior Town? (Davy Crockett)

LESSON 16 – INDIAN TRAILS AND PATHS

SIXTH GRADE

SAT Reading Objective: COMPREHENSION

Objective: After the teacher directs this lesson, sixth grade Indian students will be able to relate to the information learned from the lesson and answer various questions in order to ensure comprehension.

Objective Activity: The students will answer the review questions during a remedial game of *Jeopardy*. Divide the students into two teams and keep up with the points.

STATE STANDARDS Reading Objective:

PG. 52 #1   Interpret and construct meaning by applying appropriate strategies to materials across the curriculum.
- After the teacher directs the lesson, the students will utilize the following reading content standards: literary and informational comprehension and recognition of text element in functional materials in the text on Indian Trails and Paths. The students will answer the review questions to show their understanding of the lesson's main idea and answer.
    - *Which path crosses west Flint Creek toward Moulton? (Coosa Path)*

STATE STANDARDS Social Studies Objective:

PG. 54 #1   Extend development of map and globe skills
- Show a map of where the different trails are located, give them some everyday places they may be familiar with.
- Oakville, Speake, and East Lawrence -Black Warriors' Path
- Hatton (AL Hwy 101) and Hazlewood -Doublehead's Trace/Old Buffalo Trail
- Mt. Hope (AL Hwy. 24) and Moulton-Old Chickasaw Trail
- Moulton, Oakville, and Speake -Coosa Path
- Wren, Moulton, and R.A. Hubbard (AL Hwy 33)-Sipsie Trail
    - *Which trail was known as the dividing ridge that separates the watersheds of Brushy Creek and Sipsey River? (Sipsie Trail)*
    - *Which trail runs through the Oakville Indian Mounds Educational Center? (Black Warriors' Path)*

Review Questions

1. What trail, according to the legend, was marked with arbor glyphs on beech trees at the time of removal? (Braziel Creek Trail)
2. How early, according to archaeological evidence in bluff shelters near the Sipsie Trail, indicate that the route was used? (Prehistoric Woodland Period)
3. What trail was formerly a Chickasaw Trail? (Doublehead's Trace)
4. According to local folklore, what was an Indian stronghold even after the 1838 removal known as the Trail of Tears? (Rocky Plains)
5. Identify the early Indian path used as a geographic, tribal, and political boundary. (High Town Path)

LESSON 16 – INDIAN TRAILS AND PATHS

SEVENTH GRADE

SAT Reading Objective: LISTENING SKILLS

Objective: After the teacher directs this lesson, seventh grade Indian students will gain knowledge about the Indian trails that run through Lawrence County.

Objective Activity: The teacher will project a map of Lawrence County on the overhead projector and have individual students label the location of the seven Indian trails/paths.

STATE STANDARDS Reading Objective:

PG. 58 #11 Refine general listening behaviors
- After the teacher directs the lesson the students will utilize their listening and comprehension skills when answering the review questions on Indian trails and paths.
  - *What trail followed the Continental Divide through Lawrence County? (High Town Path)*

STATE STANDARDS Social Studies Objective:

Online Alex #6 Analyze the distribution of urban areas to determine how they are linked together
- Explain to the students how the trails and paths were very important to our Indian ancestors. Describe the different routes used by our ancestors and the significance of using the different routes. Show the location of trails/paths on "Indian Trails and Towns" map and relate to where they live.
  - *What trail was used as an escape route for Indians and slaves and ran along a creek in our county? (Braziel Creek Trail)*

Review Questions

1. What path was not only a geographic boundary but also used as a tribal and political boundary to traders and early settlers? (High Town Path)
2. Which path crosses west Flint Creek toward Moulton? (Coosa Path)
3. Which trail was known as the dividing ridge that separates the watersheds of Brushy Creek and Sipsey River? (Sipsie Trail)
4. What path became the line of the Chickasaw land claims under the Treaty of January 10, 1786? (High Town Path)
5. The High town Path was not only a geographic boundary, but what other type of boundary? (tribal and political)

LESSON 17 – INDIAN VILLAGES

Today, we are learning about the different kinds of Indian mounds located in Lawrence County which was the focus of early Cherokee villages. Raise your hand if you know the answer. What is an Indian mound? There were different kinds of Indian mounds such as burial, ceremonial, and shell. Many things were found in the mounds that tell us about the past. Some of the things found in a burial mound were skeletons, jewelry, pottery, weapons, and tools. Burial mounds were places where Indian people buried their dead. When a person died, they would bury them by covering with a layer of dirt. The next person to die would be buried on top until a huge mound was formed. Burial mounds could be found in the shapes of circles, ovals and pyramids. Burial mounds were found throughout Lawrence County and along the Tennessee River. The ceremonial mounds were used for weddings, celebrations, and religious purposes of different kinds. The most important ceremony was the Green Corn Ceremony. The festival was like our Thanksgiving and New Year rolled into one. It was a time to give thanks for a successful harvest, to settle differences, and to begin a New Year. The Cherokees of Lawrence County, Alabama lived in houses from log cabins to two-story plank houses. Many owned slaves and had plantations of cotton, corn, sugar cane, and other crops. The large Indian farms usually had lots of livestock—cattle, horses, mules, hogs, sheep, goats, and chickens.

Cherokee towns of Lawrence County

1. Mouse Town was, also known as Monee Town, located at the mouth of Fox Creek on the Tennessee River.
2. Doublehead's Village or Brown's Ferry was the location of Cherokee Chief Doublehead's home from c1790 to 1802.
3. Melton's Bluff (known later as Marathon) was owned by General Andrew Jackson from November 1816 until 1827.
4. Gourd's Settlement was located at Courtland and was named after a Cherokee soldier who fought at Horseshoe Bend under Andrew Jackson. Gourd also had an island in Elk River Shoals named after him which was called Gourd's Island.
5. Cuttyatoy's Village was located near Courtland on an Island in the Tennessee River.
6. Shoal Town (known as Town Creek-Blue Water Town) was Doublehead's home from c1802 until his death, August 9, 1807.
7. Oakville was Cherokee village located at the forks of Black Warriors' Path and Coosa Path (Old Indian Trace or Muscle Shoals Path). Show map and point out locations of each of these Indian towns.

Moneetown or Mousetown – Some three miles easterly, from the head of Elk River Shoals at the junction of Fox Creek and Tennessee River was the Cherokee Indian town of Moneetown or Mousetown. This was the first Cherokee town beginning on the east edge of present-day Lawrence County and was our county's most upstream Cherokee town on the south side of the Tennessee River. The Indian village was located between Courtland and Decatur on Fox Creek on the north side of Trinity Mountain.

According to a letter from Waco, Texas, May 9, 1882, and printed in The Moulton Advertiser on May 25, 1882, page 2, column 4, "Lawrence was the banner County in Alabama in furnishing soldiers in the Texan struggle. Had not Dr. Shackleford and the Red Rovers been captured near Goliad, just after the fall of the Alamo, there would, doubtless, be many a veteran of that gallant band now living...Lawrence County still has her representatives in that band of patriots. I noticed...Aaron Burleson. The latter will be remembered by the old people who lived between Courtland and Decatur in the year 1817. If any such are now living. He was a brother of Gen. Ed Burleson of Texan Revolutionary fame. He was engaged in the killing of some Indians at **Mousetown** on Foxe's Creek, east of Courtland in 1817, for which he fled the country, went to Missouri, thence to Texas. He has made many greasers as well as red skin bite the dust...He now lives in Bastrop, County."

In another account, the Indian village is called Moneetown. "*James Burleson settled with his family on the north side of the mountain on Fox Creek. Here near an Indian village called* **Moneetown**, *the family became involved in a feud following an altercation between a son-in-law, Martin, and the Cherokees. After three of the Indians were slain, James Burleson and his son, Edward, fled to Missouri*" (Gentry, 1962).

In personal communication on December 18, 2003, Mr. Paul Ausbon and Mr. Bill Sams, whose ancestors lived on the river at Brown's Ferry, reported that Mousetown was located at the junction of Fox Creek and the Tennessee River. Mr. Ausbon told me that he was born in 1925 and had known all his life of the Indian town that was called Mousetown by his grandparent and parents. Both men told that the Mousetown area was a favorite fishing location of their families. For years, the story of Mousetown was

LESSON 17 – INDIAN VILLAGES

passed down to Mr. Paul Ausbon. According to his grandparents, an Indian fight occurred at the old town site. They said the town was on the present-day Lawrence and Morgan County line, north of Trinity Mountain some two miles from Highway 20.

Rayford Hyatt (1993) gives the best description of the altercation between Burleson and the Cherokees as follows: *"The last Indian and white battle in present Lawrence County, of which we have found and record, occurred near Melton's Bluff (Mousetown) in 1816. This indicates that some whites had already come into the area and were leasing farms from the Cherokee Indians.*

James Saunders, in 'Early Settlers,' writing many years later from oral tradition, says the fight occurred on Foxes Creek near a village called Moneetown when James Burleson and family killed three Cherokees and fled to Missouri. The 1820 census shows Burleson still in Lawrence County. This is the related Burlesons of later Texas fame.

In the 'National Intelligenser,' Washington, D.C., September 5, 1816, is given editorially the substance of a letter, dated August 13, 1816, to Col. Winston from James Burleson. It states in effect 'that he, Burleson, and others who had settled near Melton's Bluff (Mousetown), on the south side of the Tennessee River to the number of eight men were attacked by a party of Cherokees armed with guns and warclubs, the number not known, on the night of the 11th inst. The whites resisted and three Indians were killed and one wounded. The fear of the Indians caused consternation among the settlers, and many moved away leaving promising crops.'

The 'Intelligenser' of September 10, 1816, from information at Huntsville dated August 17, 1816, enters further into details concerning the disturbance. '"It seems that a Mr. Taylor had rented a field from some Cherokees. In his absence they offered some insult to Mrs. Taylor, who escaped to the home of her father, James Burleson. Burleson, Taylor and others went to the Indian settlement, where they found a number collected. They demanded an explanation. The Indians raised a yell and said fight. An attempt was made by the whites to cut them off from their arms. This produced a conflict.'"

Map of Doublehead's Village at Browns Ferry

Doublehead's Village – Doublehead's Village was located at Brown's Ferry near the head of Elk River Shoals. *"Yet, Doublehead was without influence or position until about the year 1790, when he established a town on the Tennessee River at the head of the Muscle Shoals. An early map of the Cherokee country shows this village at a site near the south bank of Brown's Ferry below Athens. He later, in 1802, moved it to the north bank of the river near the mouth of Blue Water Creek in Lauderdale County, Alabama…Inhabitants of Doublehead's Town, originally about 40 in number, were mostly cast-offs from other Cherokee and Creek villages. This motley bunch became infamous in Tennessee history as The Ravagers of the Cumberlands."* (McDonald, 1989)

Historical records indicate that Doublehead lived in his Cherokee Indian town at Brown's Ferry from 1790 through December 1801.

LESSON 17 – INDIAN VILLAGES

According to History of Alabama by Albert James Pickett (1851), *"Dec. 1801: Emigrants flocked to the Mississippi Territory…constructing flat-boats at Knoxville, they floated down the river to the head of the Muscle Shoals, where they disembarked at the house of Double-Head, a Cherokee Chief…placing their effects upon the horses, which had been brought down by land from Knoxville, they departed on foot for the Bigby settlements."* Based on this historical note, Doublehead was still living at Brown's Ferry until 1802. The route immigrants utilized for bringing their horses to Brown's Ferry was no doubt portions of the South River Road.

In 1803, Patick Wilson traveled along the southern side to the Tennessee River and followed the same route as the South River Road. The following excerpt describes the route along the South River Road, *"The expedition continued on the Natchez Trace to present-day Alabama, here Wilson observed land controlled by the Chickamauga Cherokee, who,…were highly resistant to territorial encroachment in the Tennessee Valley… At the Muscle Shoals…the expedition left the Natchez Trace to follow the south bank of the Tennessee River. Here the party rested in a Chickamauga Cherokee town (Doublehead's Village at Brown's Ferry) administered by Tal Tsuska (Doublehead), a controversial and historically significant chief who controlled transportation routes…continuing in Cherokee territory, Wilson's party traveled north, passing through "Watts or Wills Town"… Wilson's narrative ends in Hiwasee, a Cherokee town no longer in existence"* (Hathorn and Sabino, 2001). By the time of Wilson's expedition in 1803, Doublehead had already moved from Brown's Ferry to the Shoal Town area on the north side of the river near Blue Water Creek.

Doublehead's Village at Brown's Ferry was also known for a brief period as Cox's Ferry. A man by the name of Cox, who was supposedly the son of Zecharaiah Cox, had apparently married one of the Brown Cherokee girls and briefly called the area Cox's Ferry. Some two miles west of the Indian village, the Brown's Ferry Road intersected Black Warriors' path and the South River Road.

Doublehead's Village was on the south bank of the Tennessee River at river miles 293 and 294. The town site lay between present-day Mallard Creek Campground and the old Brown's Ferry Road. Doublehead's home was thought to be on a point just downstream from the ferry location but within sight of the old river crossing. Doublehead ran a house of entertainment that catered to all kinds of needs of travelers. It is said that he was very generous to allow two older ladies, both of whom had a bunch of girls, to live in his house. Many have speculated that Doublehead's entertainment probably included many types of mischief. Doublehead had learned very rapidly about making money from his mixed-blood friends. One such business partner was Captain John D. Chisholm.

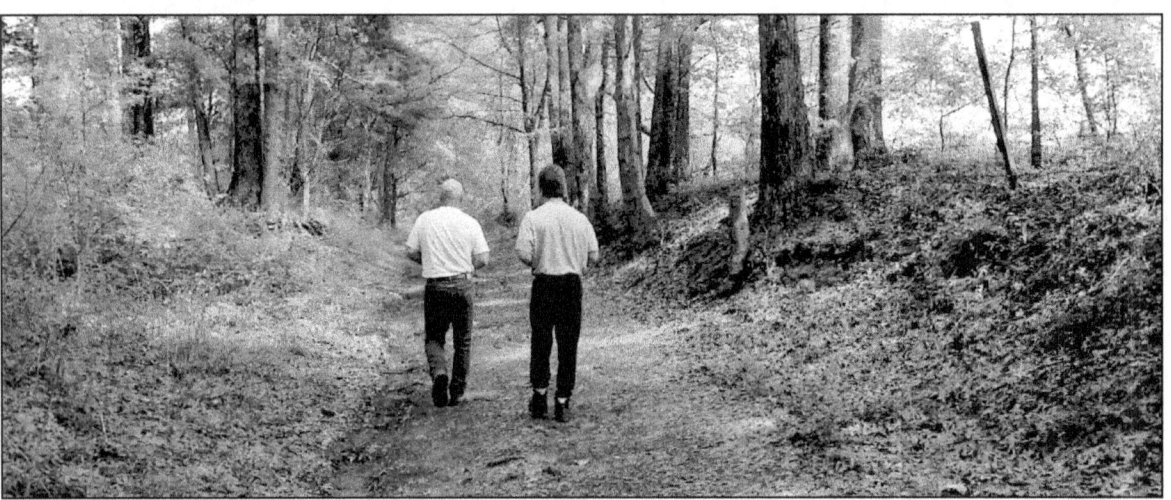

Butch Walker and Charles Borden walking the Brown's Ferry Road at Doublehead's Village

Today, you can walk over the fields along the old river bank and find plenty of evidence of a large, extensive, and historic dwelling site. Old nails are in abundance along with pieces of glassware, historic pottery, slave made bricks, and even a large area of garlic, buttercups, and other plants that indicate historic occupation. In particular, the garlic grows on a small knoll just a few hundred yards from the ferry site. We refer to this knoll as Doublehead's homesite and the plants as Doublehead's garlic. His garlic has been transplanted to the Oakville Indian Mounds Park. Remains of chert projectile points indicate prehistoric Indian occupation as early as the Archaic Period; therefore, Doublehead's village site was used for thousands of years by native people.

LESSON 17 – INDIAN VILLAGES

Melton's Bluff - The next downstream Indian village was Melton's Bluff, approximately seven miles west of Brown's Ferry. The site was also a prehistoric town located on the west side of Jack's Slough, at Tennessee River mile 288.5. The site contains a large ceremonial Indian mound covering over one acre in size and stands some 15 to 20 feet high. In addition, approximately 100 feet from the Tennessee River, a small snail mound is located between the large mound and the present river bank. During historic occupation by the Cherokee Indians, the site from the mounds west for about one mile became known as Melton's Bluff, named after an Irishman, John Melton. Melton's Bluff was a historic Cherokee Town that was purchased by General Andrew Jackson from half blood Cherokee David Melton on November 22, 1816 (McDonald, William Lindsey, 1989). At Melton's Bluff, located between Tennessee River miles 287 to 288.5, the South River Road continued west while Black Warriors' Path turned north, crossed the river, and passed Ft. Hampton, Bridgewater, Elkton, and on to the French Lick.

In <u>Letters from Alabama</u> 1817-1822 by Anne Newport Royall, is a description of a route to Melton's Bluff from Florence as follows, *"Melton's Bluff, January 8th, 1818... I was three days on the road to this place. Melton's Bluff is at the head of Mussel Shoals...I went direct to the foot of the Shoals, 70 miles from Huntsville, crossed the river, and come upon the south side of Tennessee River...three miles in width! the largest body of water that I ever saw. It was at this time very high and muddy; and the noise produced by the water washing over the rocks was tremendous... we saw a boat hung on a rock, about the middle of the stream...I took a guide, one of the pilots, and crossed the river next morning, in a ferry boat...upon leaving the ferry... I was to pass by several Indian farms... About ten o'clock we came in sight of the first Indian farm... you cross Town Creek in a canoe and swim your horses; this will cost you one dollar...I, with my horses, were safely on the other side... Rhea (my guide's name) said I had two more creeks to pass... however, these were easily forded...Rhea... had piloted boats through the Muscle Shoals, fifteen years; sometimes four at a time, at ten dollars each. He sails down one day, and walks back to the next... this land is so clear of undergrowth that you may drive a wagon any where through the woods...we passed many Indian houses in the day, and some beautiful springs. Melton's Bluff is a town, and takes its name from...John Melton...Irishman by birth...attached himself to the Cherokee Indians... Melton's Bluff... a very large plantation of cotton and maize, worked by about sixty slaves and owned by General Jackson, who bought the interest of old Melton."*

This first hand account in January 1818 of Ms. Royall confirms the existence of a road along the south bank at the Tennessee River which still has Indian houses standing. The Cherokee and Chickasaw Indians had given up the land in September 1816 approximately 15 months prior to Ms. Royall's visit to Melton's Bluff. The route of the South River Road was clearly established and had been in existence for some time.

The following portion of a story on Melton's Bluff by Rayford Hyatt (1993) gives details on the Indian village. *"The place was named for a white man, Melton, who settled there probably as a trader, married a Cherokee woman, thereby becoming a member of the Cherokee Nation. James Saunders in "Early Settlers" says his name was James Melton. Anne Royall in "Letters From Alabama" says he was John. A Cherokee Treaty of 1806 ceding lands north of the Tennessee River exempted a tract 2 by 3 miles to Moses Melton and Charles Hicks in equal shares. Oliver D. Street in a paper on "The Indians of Marshall County" says that Meltonsville of Marshall County was named for Charles Melton, an old man of Herculean frame who once lived at Melton's Bluff. Whichever he was, the others were probably his sons.*

Melton's Bluff was located at the head of the Muscle Shoals in the SE 1/4 - SE 1/4 Sec 25 T3S R7W. Most of the buildings were in a line on top of the bluff. Anne Royall in "Letters From Alabama" who stayed at the Bluff for a long period in 1818-19 says Melton got started by robbing flat boats coming down the river. It is more likely that Indians did the robbing and he traded for the slaves and goods. He also for many years furnished river pilots to boats through the Muscle Shoals for a fee with the pilots walking back to the Bluff from Florence.

In 1774, a settlement party of 15 whites and 21 slaves from South Carolina led by William Scott, were descending the Tennessee by flat boat to Natchez when they were attacked at the head of Muscle Shoals by a number of Cherokees under the Bowle. All of the white people were killed, and the slaves and goods taken. The Cherokee tribe disavowed the act of The Bowle and his followers who, fearing capture and punishment, fled to the west and located on the Arkansas River and with subsequent additions to their settlement they remained there many years.

LESSON 17 – INDIAN VILLAGES

Marathon

Town of Marathon

In later years, Melton seemed to operate in a profitable legal manner. Besides houses of entertainment and boating activities at the Bluff, he owned large cotton and corn plantations on both sides of the river. There were numerous travelers down the river. Goods came down by flatboat from the Watauga settlement bound for New Orleans. Settlers from Virginia and Carolina crossed the mountains and descended by boat, some bound for the lower Mississippi and others for the lower Tombigbee. Those bound for the latter stopped at the bluff, traveled by horseback to Cotton Gin Port, built more boats and descended. Those going on downstream sometimes had to lay over a long time at the Bluff waiting for a rise in the river to get over the Shoals.

In "Letters From Alabama," Anne Royal states that Melton had removed across the river in present Limestone County and died there about 1815 in old age. General Andrew Jackson leased his Melton Bluff plantation. It consisted of cotton lands, about 60 slaves and an overseer who lived in Melton's old log house of two stories, located a short distance from the village. General Jackson had trouble with his overseers and fugitive slaves, and was an anxious absentee landlord.

In 1818, the village stretched along the top of the bluff, consisted of two large houses of entertainment, several doctors, one hatters shop, one

202

LESSON 17 – INDIAN VILLAGES

warehouse, and several mechanics. Living there were ten permanent families. There were a lot of travelers there at this time looking at lands and waiting for the coming land sales.

Melton's Bluff village died out soon after the land sales in the fall of 1818. All lands in present Lawrence County became the property of the United States and had to be purchased from it. The first event that then occurred at Melton's Bluff was a failed attempt to set up the city of Marathon, apparently by General Andrew Jackson, General John Coffee, and other speculators. The town which was surveyed into blocks and lots by Coffee, who was then surveyor general, was almost a mile square and located at and west of Melton's bluff. A few of the 556 lots were sold with a down payment, but all were relinquished, and there is no evidence any buildings went up.

A block in the center of Marathon was set aside as a public square, so there may have been hope that it would be selected as county seat. Moulton was selected, and it and Courtland built quickly into towns, and this may have caused the downfall of Marathon. The former site of Melton's Bluff is now TVA property, and Marathon is a part of the Wheeler Plantation."

The following lesson is a shortened and edited version of "Melton's Bluff" by William Lindsey McDonald. Melton's Bluff was the site of a Cherokee Indian village established about 1770 on the Tennessee River in Lawrence County. The site is between Spring Creek and Mallard Creek.

John Melton, according to lore and legend, was a fearsome pirate at the Muscle Shoals from the early 1790s until about 1806. He made a sizable fortune preying upon often times luckless adventurers who came down the Tennessee River in their flatboats or keelboats while North Alabama was the home of the Cherokee and Chickasaw Indians.

Melton's Bluff is located across from the mouth of Elk River, a few miles upstream from Rogersville; this site is north of Wheeler Station in Lawrence County. Some of the land that was once owned by Melton is now a part of the vast General Joe Wheeler Estate. Completely isolated, it affords one of the most scenic sites along the Tennessee River.

It has been said that Melton was an Irishman who for some reason harbored a deep grudge against the early white settlers. He attached himself to the Cherokees and soon had his own followers. He took for himself a Cherokee wife and built a large log house on the bluff that bears his name.

In the Articles of Agreement made that year between Henry Dearborn, Secretary of War, and the chiefs and headmen of the Cherokee Nation, Moses Melton was granted an interest in a tract of land described in part as follows: "... and the other reserved tract, on which Moses Melton now lives, is to be considered the property of said Melton, and of Charles Hicks in equal shares."

John Melton's notorious days as a pirate came to an end following the Cherokee Treaty of 1806. It is believed, however, that Melton's final decision to quit his pirating came about when Fort Hampton was established around 1810, near the mouth of Elk River. Although federal troops were sent to the Muscle Shoals to expel the early white settlers from Doublehead's Reserve, it is probably not without coincidence that Fort Hampton was located near the north bank of the Tennessee River.

Following his earlier years of high crime on the Tennessee, Melton opened an inn or tavern at this house on the bluff. By then a much-traveled wilderness road, known as Gaines Trace, had been established. This road was part of an effort to save from extinction the American settlements on the Tombigbee River in South Alabama. In 1805, the Secretary of War appointed George S. Gaines to negotiate a treaty with the Chickasaws for the right to build this road so as to connect the Tennessee and Tombigbee Rivers. The Chickasaws resisted, but finally agreed to a horse path which was to become known as the Gaines Trace. The language in Gaines' original survey specified that this road began "at the house of Mr. Melton, on a bluff, left (or south) bank of the Tennessee River, near the head of the Muscle Shoals." This early Wilderness Road terminated at Cotton Gin Port on the Tombigbee River in Mississippi. After the establishment of Gaines Trace on the south side of the river and the building of Fort Hampton and the early roads on the north side of the river, Melton's Bluff became a much-used river crossing point. Hence, John Melton's Inn did a prosperous business until about 1816.

Early documents show a number of military crossings at Melton's Bluff during the Creek War. General John Coffee, in his report dated October 22, 1813, described one event as follows: "... I proceeded to cross the river at the upper end of the Shoals, all my

LESSON 17 – INDIAN VILLAGES

efforts failed to procure a pilot. I took with me one of John Melton's sons, who said he knew not the road, he showed me a path that had been reputed to be the **Black Warriors' Path**..."

The renowned pioneer and soldier, David Crockett, remembered two occasions when his military unit crossed at Melton's Bluff. The first instance was in November 1813. Actually, according to Crockett, they crossed the Tennessee River twice on this first occasion in order to maneuver around the local Indians. After crossing at Huntsville, they moved westward to cross the river again at Melton's Bluff. Crockett described the river at this point as being about two miles wide. The rocky bottom of the river was rough and dangerous. While fording the river several of the horses became stuck in the rocky crevices and had to be left there while the military command moved on to their destination. Crockett's second crossing at Melton Bluff was in October 1814. Payroll and muster records reveal that he was a third sergeant in Captain John Cowan's company at the time.

Early letters show that Melton gave excellent service at his inn where the travelers could find plenty of meat, coffee, tea, and the best of liquors. A gentleman who had been a guest for a week remarked to a fellow traveler that he had never fared better in any part of the country.

The most colorful accounts of Melton's Bluff can be found in Anne Royall's letters. She described Melton's house as a large mansion built probably between the years 1788 and 1793. There was an impressive courtyard that fronted the house, and a road that ran to the river. She said that one could see upriver to Brown's Ferry, about eight miles away, and about the same distance down the river from the house.

John Melton and his Cherokee wife had a number of children. One son, James, made quite a reputation for himself as a pilot or guide. This involved meeting the boats at the upper end of the Muscle Shoals and piloting them through the dangerous and often deadly passage over that part of the river. There were a number of these pilots who operated from Melton's Bluff. They would ride downriver to Colbert's Ferry where they would disembark and walk back to Melton's Bluff. James became identified with the bluff that was named for his father. In fact, a number of early historians refer to James as the Indian for whom Melton's Bluff was named.

James Melton, half blood Cherokee, worked mainly for Malcolm Gilchrist to pilot flatboats over the Muscle Shoals. Gilchrist, whose ancestors were from Scotland, settled near Melton's Bluff before Alabama became a state. He became the "Commodore Vanderbilt" of the lower Tennessee River. He owned a fleet of flatboats that plied the river from Muscle Shoals to New Orleans and made for himself quite a fortune. In fact, his earnings from boating and land speculation became so enormous that his descendants enjoyed the prestige and power of their inherited wealth for many years after his death.

One of John Melton's daughters married a white man by the name of Rhea. He was the pilot who guided Anne Royall at the Muscle Shoals:

> "I learned he was from Rockbridge County, Virginia; had piloted boats through the Muscle Shoals, fifteen years; (since 1803) sometimes four at a time, at ten dollars each. He sails down one day, and walks back the next. He never met, in all that time, with an accident! There are several of these pilots."

General Andrew Jackson in partnership with his wife's nephew, Colonel John Hutchings, purchased Melton's Bluff from a David Melton in 1816. It is believed that David was a son of the old pirate, John Melton. This deed, signed November 22, 1816, described the property as follows:

> "I David Melton of the Cherokee Nation do by these presents bargain and sell ... unto General Andrew Jackson and Captain John Hutchings all my right title and interest to the tract of land where I now live, and agree to give them possession of all the improvements laying north and east of the spring, including said spring, on said tract where I live and adjoining where I live, and the houses and ... land southeast of the spring. Possession to be given of as many Negro houses as will house the Negroes of the said Andrew and the said John ... and possession of the other houses on or before the first day of February ... For which I acknowledge to have received the consideration of sixty dollars in cash and in full of the above sale."

LESSON 17 – INDIAN VILLAGES

Jackson and Hutchings were owners of Melton Bluff at the time Anne Royall wrote her interesting letters from there in 1818. She wrote:

> "Here is a very large plantation of cotton and maize, worked by about sixty slaves, and owned by General Jackson, who bought the interest of old Melton."

In another letter written two days later she described a visit by Jackson to his Melton's Bluff plantation:

> "... I was devouring Phillip's Speeches ... in a corner, when a loud cry, 'General Jackson, General Jackson comes!' and, running to my window, I saw him walking slowly up the hill, between two gentlemen, his aids."

There is no accounting for the number of trips Jackson made to his Alabama plantation over the period of ownership from 1816 until 1827. However, as many as they may have been, these infrequent inspections of his holdings were not enough to insure stability in matters of management. One noted historian concluded that Old Hickory "... had trouble with overseers and fugitive slaves and was a rather anxious absentee landlord."

A biographer, Marquis James, listed a number of the General's trips to Alabama. One such journey occurred following the emptying of Jackson's cotton warehouses at his Hermitage plantation and his Melton's Bluff plantation in March of 1822. This occasion came about following the swelling of the Cumberland and Tennessee Rivers which allowed his boats, loaded with cotton, to commence their journeys to New Orleans. Three months later, General Jackson rode his horse from Nashville to Alabama to inspect his plantation. This same biographer, in relating the events of the 1824 national presidential election, wrote:

> "During the last weeks before the balloting began, General Jackson visited Melton's Bluff to make arrangements for the marketing of his Alabama cotton - an important detail, as the winter in Washington had been costly and the absentee planter was pressed for funds."

Jackson's political life seems to have been the major cause for his extended absences from the affairs of his cotton kingdom. By 1827 he was in financial trouble. A biographer noted:

> "The General's cotton seemed to have suffered from inattention, however, the 1827 crop being no better than average in quality. A plague decimated the stables leaving Jackson without a team to take him to Alabama to straighten out an overseer tangle."

The General and his partner soon afterwards sold their Melton Bluff plantation. Jackson was convinced that one cotton farm was enough for a busy politician to handle. It is believed that one of his mismanagement problems stemmed from the old soldier's extreme loyalty to his servants and former comrades. As an example, the General placed one of his beloved slaves, David Hutchings Smith, who had been his camp man during the Indian campaigns, as overseer of the Melton's Bluff plantation. "Old Pap" as Smith was called was as devoted to his master as his master was to him. Yet, from all indications, Old Pap was not the man for the job. After the General disposed of his Melton's Bluff Cotton farm, he tenderly placed Old Pap in the care of his ward Andrew Jackson Hutchings. David Hutchings Smith lived a long and eventful life that amounted to 108 years. His last days were at Ardoyne plantation near Florence where he is buried. A number of tales were handed down through the Coffee family about Old Pap's remembrances of the time he was overseer of "Marsa Jackson's plantation" at Melton's Bluff.

In 1818, soon after Jackson and Hutchings purchased the property of Melton, they opened up and promoted a town on that part of the plantation on the bluff facing the river. They named it for the ancient Greek city, Marathon, which we affiliate with foot races. This selection probably had something to do with Jackson's love for the racetrack. Marathon was located adjacent to John Melton's log house, later Melton's Inn.

The first mention of plans for the town was in a letter from Josiah Meigs to John Coffee, dated May 26, 1818. Jackson had employed his friend and kinsman, General John Coffee, to plan and survey his new town. Coffee laid out 658 lots.

LESSON 17 – INDIAN VILLAGES

Marathon served as the seat of justice for Lawrence County while Alabama was a territory; for a number of years it was the first and largest town in the county. People rapidly moved in from Virginia and North and South Carolina. They built their homes facing the river on the main residential road that stretched for more than a mile along the bluff.

Marathon soon became a ghost town when the county seat was moved to Moulton in 1820. The town site was included in the large tract of land purchased by Colonel Richard Jones in 1829, to become one of the largest ante-bellum plantations in the Tennessee Valley. Jones built his home not far from Melton's Bluff. Here was born his daughter Daniella Ellen, who in 1866 became the wife of the famed Confederate Cavalry General "Fighting Joe" Wheeler.

A large monument adjacent to Melton's Bluff identifies the site as the place where General Wheeler crossed the Tennessee River on October 9, 1863, following his raid down the Sequatchie Valley after the Battle of Chickamauga. Nearby is an abandoned watering hole that still bears the name "Dora Belle's Well." Not far away is a decaying log house. Down the lane, they say, is where the beloved ex-slave, Sweet Peter, and his wife once lived. The old bluff, anchored in antediluvian limestone formed near the dawn of time, is strangely silent now. Only the refreshing winds across Wheeler Lake can be heard through the overhanging limbs of old, gnarled trees. The likes of John Melton and his marauding pirates are but fading memories to the wanderer of the Twentieth Century. Yet the story of Melton's Bluff ever remains history's flamboyant account of a place on the Tennessee River called the Muscle Shoals.

Goard's (Gourd's) Settlement - The fifth downstream Indian town was a Cherokee village called Goard's Settlement which was at the present-day town of Courtland. On December 28, 1807, Captain Edmund Pendleton Gaines made this note on his survey from Melton's Bluff to Cotton Gin Port, "8th mile…. At 119 chs. Cross the path which leads from the Shoal Town, eastwardly, to the **Goard's Settlement**, *about 3 miles distance"* (Stone, James H., 1971). Based on Gaines measurements of some 8.7 miles westerly from Melton's Bluff, then easterly for three miles, Goard's settlement was in the center of present-day Courtland, Alabama. Eventually, three Indian roads intersected at Goard's settlement which were Gaines' Trace, South River Road, and Sipsie Trail which later became the Cheatham Road or portions of present day Highway 33.

Goard's Settlement was obviously named after a Cherokee Indian man called Goard. According to <u>Letters from Alabama 1817-1822</u> written by Anne Royall on January 12, 1818, page 131, is the following, *"Guide says Goard was very kind; he knew him for fifteen years. He helped subdue the Creeks, and made an excellent soldier."* Anne Royall described Goard's log house as being on the west side of Town Creek which was ten years after Gaines location; however, she wrote her letter after the fact and might have been wrong on the exact location; furthermore, Gaines was a surveyor and made precise measurements and locations.

Goard's Town was at the junction of the South River Road and the Sipsie Trail, an early Indian route from Tuscaloosa to the French Lick (Nashville, TN). Also, a prehistoric village containing an Indian mound was located at the site on the banks of Path Killer Creek which later became known as Big Nance. According to Captain Edmund Pendleton Gaines on December 27, 1807, *"we proceeded, same course…6th mile…At 116 [chaines] (west of Melton's Bluff) Path Killer's Creek, 3 chains wide from tops of banks"* (Stone, James H., 1971). In 1807, when Captain Gaines identified Path Killer Creek (named after Cherokee Chief Path Killer), he was traveling portions of the South River Road but was intent on surveying a line from Melton's Bluff on the Tennessee River to Cotton Gin Port on the Tombigbee River; therefore, he basically followed the Old Chickasaw Trail to the heart of the Chickasaw Nation.

According to a February, 1829 Lawrence County court record, *" a road from Gourd landing on the Tennessee River to intersect the road from Courtland to Lamb's Ferry at or near Gordon's fence the nearest and best way…Order, 1829, Jury of Review of a road from Courtland to Gourds."* This road either crossed or followed portions of both the Sipsie Trail and Gaines' Trace.

Cuttyatoy's Village - The fourth down stream Indian town connected by the South River Road was Cuttyatoy's Village. The village was actually on Gilchrist Island at the western end of Elk River Shoals near the south bank of the Tennessee River. According to the American Whig Review, Volume 15, Issue 87, March 1852, page 247, *"Colonel (Joseph) Brown…a participant in the battle of Talledega (November 9, 1813)…met Charles Butler… and learned from him that…Chief Cuttyatoy, was still alive…he was then living on an island in the Tennessee River, near the mouth of Elle (Elk) River, and that he had with him several Negroes … taken by him at Nickajack on the 9th of May, 1788… with ten picked men, Brown proceeded to the island, went to the head man's (Cuttyatoy) lodge and exhibited to him General (Andrew) Jackson's order, and demanded that Cutty-a-toy's Negroes be*

LESSON 17 – INDIAN VILLAGES

immediately sent over to Fort Hampton…In crossing the river, Colonel Brown and his men took up the Negroes, and Cutty-a-toy's wife behind them, to carry them over the water while the Indian men crossed on a raft (Brown's Ferry) higher up (stream)." Cuttyatoy and his men utilized the South River Road to reach Brown's Ferry. Colonel Joseph Brown and his men reached Fort Hampton that morning while Cuttyatoy and his men arrived in the afternoon.

Today, Cuttyatoy's Village is under the backwaters created by Wheeler Dam. The old Indian town site lies buried below the surface of Wheeler Lake, as most of the river villages that were located on islands of Elk River Shoals. Between the mouth of Spring Creek on the south side and Elk River on the north side of the Tennessee River, the islands of Elk River Shoals are under some twenty feet or more of water. It was between these islands of Elk River Shoals that General Joe Wheeler's cavalry crossed the Tennessee River on October 9, 1863.

Shoal Town - The final Lawrence County Indian town connected by the South River Road was the Cherokee village of Shoal Town located between Blue Water Creek and Town Creek on the Tennessee River. Shoal Town was the home of Talohuskee Benge, the half brother to Sequoyah. Later, Talohuskee's great uncle Doublehead moved to the Shoal Town area about 1802. Shoal Town was located some six miles from the eastern end of Big Muscle Shoals at the junction of Doublehead's Trace and the South River Road. Again, during Captain Edmund Pendleton Gaines survey on December 28, 1807, he notes the following, *"8th mile… at 119 chs. Cross the path (South River Road) which leads from **Shoal-Town**, eastwardly, to the Goards Settlement (Courtland), about 3 miles distance"* (Stone, James H., 1971)

1816 Peel and Swanner Map. Circle shows location of Shoal Town – Doublehead Spring

Shoal Town was considered the largest Cherokee Indian village in the Big Bend of the Tennessee River. At the location, the Blue Water Ferry crossed the river from the eastern side of the mouth of Blue Water Creek to the western side of the mouth of Path Killer's Creek. Talohuskee Benge, son of Doublehead's niece, Wurteh Watts and trader John Benge, and Doublehead lived at Shoal Town and probably operated the ferry which was common practice at large Cherokee River Towns.

*"Both the French and the English contended for the Indian trade along the western waters; the French planted a post at Muscle Shoals before 1715. Because of the increasing importance of trade with the whites the Cherokees planted villages near the Muscle Shoals area in the last quarter of the eighteenth century. There was Doublehead's village on the Tennessee and **a large settlement (Shoal Town) at the mouth of Town Creek, extending a mile along the river and far up the creek.**"* (Leftwich, Nina, 1935) The Cherokee village described above is Shoal Town which was located on Big Muscle Shoals of the Tennessee River between Big Nance (Path Killer's) Creek, Town Creek, and Blue Water Creek.

LESSON 17 – INDIAN VILLAGES

While living at Shoal Town, Doublehead requested help from the U.S. Government; however, he was no stranger to the government when asking for help, money, or handouts. This particular incident is recorded in Henry T. Malone's (1956) book <u>Cherokees of the Old South</u>:

"A scarcity of corn caused by a drought in the Cherokee Nation during the year 1804 was a crisis which Meigs faced in his typical fashion. The first request for food came from **Doublehead** *and other Cherokees in the Muscle Shoals area on the Lower Tennessee River. The Agent immediately sent them three hundred bushels of corn, for which the Indians paid $110. Meigs, however, requested and received permission from the War Department to return the money; he thought it his duty "to give the necessary relief — believing that humanity and interest combine to make it proper especially when interesting negotiations with them are now soon to be opened." Meigs' policy pleased his government. Henry Dearborn sent him the President's congratulations, urging Meigs to continue helping needy Indians: "You will embrace so favorable an opportunity for impressing the minds of the Cherokees with the fatherly concern and attention of the President to the distresses of his red children."*

Today, Doublehead's Resort is located in Lawrence County, Alabama, at the site of Shoal Town. The resort is a modern facility catering to thousands of people each year and is located on the east bank of Town Creek near where it empties into the Tennessee River. The resort area extends up the river toward Big Nance Creek and has became a popular tourist site. Along the bank of Town Creek are numerous two-story cabins which can accommodate entire families. Each cabin has a water-front dock which provides boating facilities for resort visitors. The resort also boasts a lodge, swimming facilities, horseback riding, and many other accommodations that make for a pleasurable stay. If Doublehead were alive today, he would have to be proud of the facility at his old homesite that bears his name; therefore, the legends of Doublehead live on at this beautiful recreational facility in the county his descendants still call home.

Oakville - Do you know of any mounds in Lawrence County? (There are burial and ceremonial mounds found in Oakville.) Do you know where Oakville is located? (Oakville is in Lawrence County east of Moulton.) Maybe you can visit there sometime. Do you know why a mound would be called a shell mound? (Shell mounds were found along the Tennessee River where our early Indian ancestors had piled up huge mounds of mussel shells.)

Indian villages were located near natural springs with lots of water. Mussels were a main source of food. (show mussel shell) When they ate the mussels, the shells would be thrown down and they would pile up and form a shell mound. Also found in the shell mounds were animal bones, stones, pebbles, flint chips, and broken objects. The shells were used for jewelry and tools.

Our story begins over 12,000 years ago when our Indian ancestors first entered the beautiful Tennessee Valley and settled in Oakville which is one of the most beautiful places in North Alabama. Oakville is located between the Warrior Mountains to the south and the Tennessee River to the north. For thousands of years, our ancestors lived, died, and worshipped in our area primarily because of the bountiful nurturing elements of life.

Our Indian people in Lawrence County have long sought to have a more active role in retaining the remnants of our Indian heritage, traditions, customs, and history. Today, we have the opportunity and ability through our Indian program to provide the areas and facilities where glimpses of our rich pre-historic and historic Indian past can be seen at the Oakville Indian Mounds Education Center.

The Oakville Indian Mounds have long been a site in Lawrence County deserving of protection and utilization as an educational area. Since, Lawrence County Schools' Indian Education Program was established, the Oakville Indian site has been seen as an area which would compliment and enhance our county's rich Indian heritage. Today, the Indian education program is headquartered at the Oakville site.

The Oakville site has been written about for over 100 years with historic settler burials occurring some 175 years ago on the burial mound. The burial mound was the site of Copena Indian burials some 2,000 years ago. The large ceremonial mound is estimated to have been built during the Woodland Period, which covers a time span from 1,000 BC to 1,000 AD. The Oakville area was considered a religious center and social complex of the middle Woodland Indian people with outlying villages and farms. Additional Copena mounds located nearby supports the complex social center theory.

LESSON 17 – INDIAN VILLAGES

During historic times, the area was the site of an early Cherokee town located at the junctions of the Coosa Path and Black Warriors' Path. Oakville became a settler town on the southeastern frontier of Lawrence County, Alabama. Early 1800 maps show Oakville being one of only four towns located in Lawrence County with the others being Courtland, Marathon (no longer exists), and Moulton. The Town of Oakville appeared near its peak during the middle 1800s, just prior to the Civil War.

In 1817, the first government surveys of the Oakville area identified a good stream of fresh water flowing from a huge spring. The stream ran about 1/2 mile before running into a limestone crevasse and going underground. Eventually hogs stopped up the sink, which caused the area to flood. In addition to flooding, a disease called the "bloody flux" led to the death of many Oakville residents. The Town of Oakville was abandoned around 1855.

In 1924, a Smithsonian archaeological team, who were part of pre-impoundment survey for Wilson Dam and Lake, visited the site. During the Oakville site visit, Smithsonian archaeologists identified five Indian mounds in the area. Three of the mounds were in the process of being plowed down. At that time, some three miles up stream on West Flint Creek, the Smithsonian crew excavated the Alexander Mound, which was smaller, but similar to the Oakville burial mound. Some 106 skeletons along with numerous artifacts were removed from the Alexander Mound.

Oakville is located in Lawrence County near the Jesse Owens Monument at Speake. Oakville was the birthplace of Jesse Owens, but also an important part of Indian history. Long before it was ever called Oakville; it was the site of a large Woodland Indian village. Later, tradition has it that the Cherokees had a large village at the site. There are two mounds still intact in the Oakville area. One mound is a ceremonial mound is about 1.8 acres in size and stands about 27 feet high. It is believed that a temple may have been on top at one time. Archaeologists survey from places in the same area, date the mounds around 2,000 years old. For this reason, it is considered a Woodland mound. It is the largest Woodland mound in Alabama and the second largest mound in the state by volume. Two Indian trails crossed near the big Oakville mound--Black Warriors' Path and Old Indian Trace (Coosa Path).

Ceremonial Mound at Oakville

The other mound is a burial mound. It is conical in shape and believed to hold Indian burials. These two mounds have not been excavated so no one is certain. The Indian people have been trying to protect the mounds and preserve them for some time. At one time there were at least five mounds in the area.

On top of the Indian burial mound are several false stone crypts where early settlers were buried. Some say they considered it a sacred place because the Indian burials were already there. There are black slaves in unmarked graves believed to be buried on the large ceremonial mound at Oakville.

Evidence gathered from surrounding areas indicates the Indian people here worked with copper and galena metals. Therefore, they were called Copena Indians. As time progressed, the fate of these people is unknown as to where they went. Mixed-blood marriages, warfare, and trade probably scattered the tribe throughout the Southeast.

Years later, the Town of Oakville was established in the same area as the mounds. This was a thriving town with a hotel, saloon, post office, blacksmith shop, and a few stores. It is uncertain exactly what became of the Town of Oakville. Most likely, the people living there died after an epidemic called the bloody flux contaminated the area in the 1850s. Many of the graves date in the 1850s. In 1830, Oakville was one of only four towns in Lawrence County and was incorporated in 1833. Another reason for its demise may have been the depression or crash of 1837. The merchants became broke and almost every building rotted down.

Regardless of exactly what happened, the Town of Oakville ceased to exist. The early settlers' graves have been vandalized over the years. Several of the local Indian education students worked on a summer youth project to repair these. This cemetery is called the Indian Mound Cemetery (show students a copy of the names that were on crypts).

LESSON 17 – INDIAN VILLAGES

KINDERGARTEN

DIBELS Reading Objective: INITIAL SOUND FLUENCY

OBJECTIVE: After the teacher directs this lesson, Kindergarten Indian students will develop initial sound and sound of various terms used throughout the lesson about Indian villages.

OBJECTIVE ACTIVITY: Write various terms on the board and let individual students identify the beginning sound. Also, show pictures of certain people, places, and/or things and have the students identify a word that begins with the same sound. Ex: Does the word cat, goat, or Monday begin with the same sound as Melton's Bluff?

STATE STANDARDS READING OBJECTIVE:

PG. 14 #9   Begin to use pictures and text to gain meaning from written material
- Use pictures to help students gain a better understanding of the Indian villages being discussed such as: Doublehead's Village, Melton's Bluff, and Oakville.
- While showing pictures, the teacher will ask students to give the beginning sound of each picture. Then have the class say the word in unison.
  - *Whose village was located at Brown's Ferry? (Doublehead)*

PG. 15 #13   Gain an awareness of others through exposure to written, spoken, and visual forms of communication
- While showing pictures of the different villages, the teacher should discuss them in depth with the students in order for them to gain an awareness of how and where our early ancestors lived.
  - *What is the name of the village where Andrew Jackson bought? (Melton's Bluff)*

STATE STANDARDS SOCIAL STUDIES OBJECTIVE:

PG. 11 #1   Develop initial map and globe skills
- Show different maps where villages were located.
  - *What is another name for Moneetown? (Mouse Town)*

Review Questions
1. Where is the Indian education office located? (Oakville)
2. What ceremony is the most important to the Indians? (Green Corn Ceremony)
3. Where was Melton's Bluff located? (head of the Muscle Shoals)
4. Who was a fearsome pirate? (John Melton)
5. Name a respected pioneer and soldier. (David Crockett)

LESSON 17 – INDIAN VILLAGES

FIRST GRADE

DIBELS Reading Objective: PHONICS

Objective: After the teacher directs this lesson, first grade Indian students will gain an understanding through learning about the Indian villages.

Objective Activity: The teacher will write terms on the board from the lesson or use other visual aids and the students will pronounce each sound and letter of the word. Next, the teacher will write words on the board changing the initial letter making a nonsense word. Then, the students will pronounce the word. (Ex: Man-Gan, etc.) Also some words will be broken down to their individual letters and students will pronounce each sound.

STATE STANDARDS Reading Objective:

PG. 17 #3   Exhibit phonemic awareness
- After the teacher directs the lesson, students will utilize the phonics instruction by pronouncing each sound and letter and identifying the entire word.
  - *What is another name for Moneetown? (Mouse Town)*

PG. 20 #6   Comprehend material read, heard, or viewed
- Once the teacher directs the lesson on Indian villages ask students questions to ensure comprehension on the text that was taught.
  - *Who was the Irishman that Melton's Bluff is named after? (John Melton)*

STATE STANDARDS Social Studies Objective:

PG. 18 #3   Extend initial ability to locate new information and to express understanding in various classroom activities.
- Show pictures of where villages were located and what they looked like.
  - *Where was Shoal Town located? (Tennessee River-mouth of Town Creek)*

PG. 18 #10   Relate land use in their locality to the physical features of the land
- During the lesson on Indian villages the teacher will discuss how the land was used while living near the Tennessee River.
  - *Do you know where Oakville is located? (Lawrence County)*

Review Questions

1. Whose village was located at Brown's Ferry? (Doublehead)
2. Who owned Melton's Bluff? (Andrew Jackson)
3. What is a burial mound? (a place to bury the dead)
4. What is a ceremonial mound? (a mound to have a ceremony on)
5. Where is the Indian mounds cemetery located? (Melton's Bluff or <u>Oakville</u>)

LESSON 17 – INDIAN VILLAGES

SECOND GRADE

DIBELS Reading Objective: NONSENSE WORD FLUENCY

Objective: After the teacher directs this lesson, second grade Indian students will utilize the reading content standards of nonsense word fluency.

Objective Activity: The teacher will pick terms from the text and change the first or last letter to create nonsense words. Then have some students come to the board and correct the nonsense word to ensure comprehension.

STATE STANDARDS Reading Objective:

PG. 26 #14   Exhibit expanded vocabulary and sentence awareness
- The teacher will choose new and unfamiliar words such as: village, settlement, bluff, etc., to expand the student's vocabulary and incorporate new words into daily conversation.
  - *Who owned Melton's Bluff? (John Melton)*
  - *Moneetown was also called _____ Town. (Mouse or Midget)*
  - *_____'s Village was located at Brown's Ferry. (Doublehead's)*

STATE STANDARDS Social Studies Objective:

PG. 22 #1   Develop map and globe skills
- Use map of Lawrence County to show the student the locations of Moneetown, Doublehead's Village, Melton's Bluff, Gourd's Settlement, Cuttyatoy's Village, Shoal Town, and Oakville.
- Give the students blank map of Lawrence County and have them color the different towns on the map.
  - *Moneetown, Oakville, and Melton's Bluff are located in what county? (Lawrence)*

Review Questions

1. Where is the largest ceremonial mound in Lawrence County made by Woodland people? (Oakville)
2. Which town was the fifth down stream? (Gourd's Settlement)
3. Name three types of Indian mounds. (burial, shell, and ceremonial)
4. Who was the Irishman that Melton's Bluff is named after? (John Melton)
5. Where is Shoal Town located? (Tennessee River--mouth of Town Creek)

LESSON 17 – INDIAN VILLAGES

THIRD GRADE

DIBELS Reading Objective: INTERPRETING READING MATERIALS

Objective: After the teacher directs this lesson, third grade Indian students will discuss and be able to identify the location of the Indian villages.

Objective Activity: First, the teacher will read orally from the lesson and then let each student read a paragraph. Then the students will explain what they have read in their own words. Then, students will compare early Indian villages to our homes today.

STATE STANDARDS Reading Objective:

PG. 33 #14   Develop an understanding of cultural similarities and differences noted through exposure to multicultural literature
- After the teacher directs the lesson, the students will read about early Indian villages and compare to today. (Ex: We live in house trailers, etc. today. Whereas then they lived in huts and cabins, and discuss where they were located.)
  - *Where was Mouse Town/Moneetown? (at the mouth of Fox Creek on Tennessee River)*

PG. 33 #16   Employ study strategies to gain information
- After discussion of the lesson, the teacher will ask questions to ensure comprehension.
  - *Where was Melton's Bluff located? (at the head of the Muscle Shoals)*

STATE STANDARDS Social Studies Objective:

PG. 30 #6   Compare different groups of Native Americans
- Discuss with students about the homes of our ancestors and the different types they had such as summer and winter.
  - *What two types of homes did they have? (summer and winter)*

Review Questions

1. What is another name for Melton's Bluff? (Marathon)
2. How did our ancestors form a shell mound? (they would eat mussels and throw the shells down and it would pile up and form a mound)
3. Whose village was located at Brown's Ferry? (Doublehead)
4. Moneetown was also known as what? (Mouse Town)
5. Melton's Bluff was owned by whom and was later known as what? (Andrew Jackson, Marathon)

LESSON 17 – INDIAN VILLAGES

FOURTH GRADE

SAT Reading Objective: VOCABULARY

Objective: After the teacher directs this lesson, fourth grade Indian students will be able to gain meaning of the vocabulary terms from the text. Terms: transplanted, relinquished, flamboyant, crypts, etc.

Objective Activity: The students will complete a word find puzzle. The puzzle should include the vocabulary terms discussed in the lesson and their correct definitions.

STATE STANDARDS Reading Objective:

PG. 38 #5   Interpret passages in print material
- After the teacher directs a lesson, have the students identify the vocabulary words and use each in a sentence to ensure comprehension.
- What two types of mounds are located in Oakville? (ceremonial and burial)

STATE STANDARDS Social Studies Objective:

PG. 34 #2   Interpret and display information and data using various graphic organizers
- While teaching the lesson, show pictures/maps of where some of the villages are located such as: Mousetown, Doublehead's Village, Melton's Bluff, Shoal Town, etc.
- What Indian village is located approximately seven miles west of Brown's Ferry? (Melton's Bluff)

Review Questions

1. Which Indian town was a Cherokee village located at present-day Town of Courtland? (Gourd's Settlement)
2. Who lived at Shoal Town from 1802 until his death on August 9, 1807? (Doublehead)
3. Why was the Green Corn Ceremony celebrated? (give thanks for harvest to settle differences and to begin a new year)
4. Where was Mouse Town/Moneetown located? (at the mouth of Fox Creek on the Tennessee River)
5. Who was a fearsome pirate at the Muscle Shoals from the early 1790s until about 1806? (John Melton)

LESSON 17 – INDIAN VILLAGES

FIFTH GRADE

SAT Reading Objective: VOCABULARY

Objective: After the teacher directs this lesson, fifth grade Indian students will read and be able to identify the following vocabulary terms: established, abundance, negotiate, descendants, relinquished, transplanted, flamboyant, crypt, etc.

Objective Activity: The students will recognize the five vocabulary terms during a game of Hangman. In order for the team to receive a point, the student must also correctly identify the definition.

STATE STANDARDS Reading Objective:

PG. 45 #6   Demonstrate reading improvement gained through substantial amounts of daily reading
- Have the students read aloud various sections from the text. The students should practice their reading skills and try to improve their reading ability.
- Where was Doublehead's Village located? (Brown's Ferry)

PG. 46 #13   Apply strategies of a skillful listener
- Have the students listen as the teacher reads the material from the lesson. After presenting the lesson, the teacher will question the students to check for understanding of the text.
- What was another name for Moneetown? (Mousetown)

STATE STANDARDS Social Studies Objective:

PG. 46 #6   Discuss the progression of culture of the early American people
- After the teacher directs the lesson, the teacher will discuss the impact of farming and hunters on the Indian villages. Explain the roles of the men in the villages. (get food, grow crops, etc.) Be sure the students understand the significance of farming and hunting to the Indian villages.
- Melton's Bluff was also known as what? (Marathon)

Review Questions
1. What early town was flooded and abandoned after a disease called "bloody flux?" (Oakville)
2. Oakville was a Cherokee village located at the forks of which two paths? (Black Warrior & Coosa)
3. What town was considered the largest Cherokee Indian village? (Shoal Town)
4. What town served as the county seat before it was moved to Moulton in 1820? (Marathon)
5. Where was Cuttyatoy's Village located? (Gilchrist Island)

LESSON 17 – INDIAN VILLAGES

SIXTH GRADE

SAT Reading Objective: LISTENING SKILLS

Objective: After the teacher directs this lesson, sixth grade Indian students will gain an understanding about the Indian villages and their locations in Lawrence County.

Objective Activity: The students will play a remedial matching game consisting of the terms and definitions and the review questions and answers.

STATE STANDARDS Reading Objective:

PG. 53 #12   Develop general listening behaviors for different purposes and situations
- The students will utilize their listening skills by retelling the information they have learned about Doublehead's Village, Melton's Bluff, Cuttyatoy's Village, and Oakville in their own words.
- Name five Lawrence County Cherokee villages established under the leadership of Doublehead. (Moneetown at Fox Creek, Doublehead's Village at Brown's Ferry, Melton's Bluff, Gourd's Settlement, Shoal Town)

STATE STANDARDS Social Studies Objective:

PG. 54 #1   Extend the development of map and globe skills
- Show the students the location of the Indian villages on a Lawrence County map or the Indian Trails and Towns map. Such as Moneetown or Mouse Town located from the head of Elk Rive at the junction of Fox Creek and Tennessee River. The teacher could have the students draw a map and locate some of where the Indian villages were located
- Where was Doublehead's Village located? (Brown's Ferry near the head of Elk River Shoals)

Review Questions

1. What early town is presently buried below the surface of Wheeler Lake? (Cuttyatoy's Village)
2. Shoal Town was the home of whom? (Talohuskee Benge)
3. Which town was three miles east of Elk River Shoals and was the first Cherokee town beginning on the east edge of Lawrence County? (Moneetown/Mouse Town)
4. About what year did Doublehead establish his village on the Tennessee River? (1790)
5. Which Indian town was connected by the South River Road? (Cuttyatoy's Village)

LESSON 17 – INDIAN VILLAGES

SEVENTH GRADE

SAT Reading Objective: LITERARY ELEMENTS

Objective: After the teacher directs this lesson, seventh grade Indian students will be able to construct and interpret meaning and appreciate literary elements in the lesson about Indian villages.

Objective Activity: The teacher will project a map of Lawrence County on the overhead with the Indian trails/paths already labeled. The seventh grade students will then label the seven Indian villages and discuss each.

STATE STANDARDS Reading Objective:

PG. 58 #7   Appreciate the characteristics, literary elements, and cultural influences of literary works representative of various eras
- Create a timeline using the dates that each villages was established. They will also identify the literary elements of the text related to these villages.
  - Mouse Town was also known as? (Moneetown)

STATE STANDARDS Social Studies Objective:

Online Alex #10   Describe changes in social and economic conditions in the U.S. during the twentieth and twenty-first centuries.
- Use the Indian Trials and Towns map to show the students where the seven Indian villages are located. Relate the locations to places that are familiar to the students. Ex: Doublehead's Village is near Mallard Creek Recreational Area and Doublehead's Resort is located at the site of Shoal Town.
  - Where was Cuttyatoy's Village located? (Gilchrist Island at the western end of Elk River Shoals)

Review Questions

1. What was the Indian town that became the largest Cherokee town in Lawrence County? (Shoal Town)
2. Who was known as a fearsome pirate that Melton's Bluff is named after? (John Melton)
3. Where was Doublehead's Village located? (Brown's Ferry)
4. Name a renowned pioneer and soldier: (David Crockett)
5. Name the seven Cherokee towns of Lawrence County? (Mouse Town, Doublehead's Village, Melton's Bluff, Gourd's Settlement, Cuttyatoy's Village, Shoal Town, and Oakville)

LESSON 18 – LOCAL INDIAN LEADERS

Sequoyah - Sequoyah, George Gist, was born about 1776, near Fort Loudoun, Tennessee in the village of Tuskegee. His mother, Wurteh Watts, who was a daughter to the sister of Doublehead, a full-blood Cherokee, and John Watts (Scotch). Sequoyah's father probably was Nathaniel Gist, the famous scout and soldier. Nathaniel Gist was thought to be German or Irish.

Doublehead's older sister married a Celtic man (Scotch) named John Watts. They had two famous children, John Watts, Jr. who became Chief of the Cherokee Nation and Wurteh Watts, the mother of Sequoyah.

Although Sequoyah's father was white and his mother was only half Cherokee, he had a traditional Cherokee childhood. When Sequoyah was a small boy, his mother moved them to Alabama to an Indian settlement near Willstown. Here, Sequoyah spent most of his early life, learning to trace honey bees, to shoot the bow and arrow, and to look after his mother's small farm. Sequoyah's great uncle, Doublehead and his half brothers lived in and around Lawrence County, Alabama.

Sequoyah Teaching His Alphabet

Army records show that Sequoyah fought in the Creek War of 1812 with a group of Cherokee volunteers. He, along with Junaluska, another famous Cherokee, fought with Andrew Jackson in the Battle of Horseshoe Bend. Early in life, Sequoyah was a silversmith. He wanted to sign his silver work and got Charles Hicks to show him how to write his name. This stimulated his early interest in writing an alphabet for his Cherokee people.

There are many stories about when and how Sequoyah started working and thinking about his alphabet. One of these stories is that he and some of his friends fell into a discussion about writing, after having heard the Bible translated at a white man's house. His friends said that writing was a most wonderful thing, to be able to put all the wisdom down on the talking leaves so that they would not be forgotten. Sequoyah, hearing this remark, said, "I could do this thing that the white man does." His friends laughed and said, "You are foolish, you could not even begin to do this wonderful thing. This has taken many long winters for the white man to do. It is his gift. The Great One has not given us this gift. It would be foolish for us even to try such a task." But Sequoyah did not hear their last remark. He was already turning over in his mind how he was going to put his own talk down on the talking leaves.

LESSON 18 – LOCAL INDIAN LEADERS

He first drew a picture or symbol to represent each word, but there were so many that he realized this was impossible. Then he tried to figure out a way to make a symbol for a sentence. But this too, he saw would not do because there were so many ways to make a sentence. Eventually, he began to listen for the different sounds that the Cherokee language had. These, he would record with a mark that he thought would be easy to remember. Soon, he ran out of ideas for new marks; his signs began to all look alike. For a long time, he did not know what to do. Then, while walking one day, he found a piece of old newspaper that he discovered was full of symbols, which he had never even thought of making. Thus, Sequoyah not knowing one English letter from another used a great many of our own crooked marks to represent sounds in the Cherokee language. Sequoyah encountered many problems before he completed his project. He neglected his family responsibilities and once, his angry wife burned two years of his work. Since many Indians believed that Sequoyah's strange marks meant he was in league with the devil, they burned his cabin while he was away.

In 1821, his work was completed. He had 86 characters to represent each syllable in the Cherokee language. Thus, a three-syllable word needed only three characters to write. Within a few years, almost all the young and middle-age men in the Cherokee Nation could read and write the Cherokee syllabary.

With the interest to learn to read and write in their own language, Bibles, pamphlets, and other materials were printed using Sequoyah's syllabaries. The first Indian newspaper, the Cherokee Phoenix, was published. This paper printed news in both English and Cherokee.

Sequoyah was a famous member of the Cherokee tribe. His mother, Wurteh Watts, was ½ Cherokee and ½ Celtic (Scotch). Her father was John Watts and her brother, John Watts, Jr., became chief of the Cherokee Nation. Sequoyah's father was a white man, Nathaniel Guess or Gist; but, Sequoyah, also known as George Gist, always considered himself as an Indian. Doublehead was Sequoyah's great uncle. Sequoyah was lame in one leg, probably from polio. Young Sequoyah could not go hunting or on war parties with other Cherokee men; so he became a fine silversmith and artist.

He listened to the Cherokee leaders talk of the white man's treaties. They called the papers with words on them "talking leaves" and felt they were magic. Sequoyah realized that there was no magic that the marks stood for words. Even though the Cherokee leaders laughed and thought him insane, Sequoyah promised that someday, he would be able to write down every word of the Cherokee language.

Sequoyah finally finished his work on the alphabet. Within a few years, almost all of the young Cherokee men could read and write. Newspapers, pamphlets, Bibles were printed using Sequoyah's alphabet.

Two of Sequoyah's half brothers, Robert (Bob) Benge (The Bench) and Tahlontoiskee (Talohuskee) Benge, for a while lived in or near Lawrence County. Bob Benge and Talohuskee Benge were the sons of trader John Benge (Scotch) and Wurteh Watts;

LESSON 18 – LOCAL INDIAN LEADERS

therefore, Bob Benge was ¼ Cherokee and ¾ Celtic and was the most feared warrior in the Appalachian Frontier. Doublehead first lived in Lawrence County near Brown's Ferry. Charles Hicks, half-Cherokee, first showed Sequoyah how to write his name in English. David Melton deeded the land in Lawrence County between Mallard and Spring Creeks at Melton Bluff's to General Andrew Jackson on November 22, 1816.

John Melton – John Melton was one of the early Irish people in Lawrence County who came during the 1780s with the Cherokee Indians. Melton, an Irishman, married a Cherokee woman and died at a large farm on the north side of the Tennessee River about 1815. Melton owned large farms and a great number of slaves. According to the Cotton Gin Treaty of 1806, the first cotton gin in Lawrence County was placed at Melton's Bluff by the U. S. Government. Cotton became a very important Cherokee product and the use of black slaves in the early 1800s was common among the Cherokee. Melton's Bluff, located near the head of Elk River Shoals on the Tennessee River in Lawrence County, was named after John Melton. Melton had several children by his Indian wife, most married white people. Remarkable advancement of the Cherokee came about largely through the influence of the mixed-blood or metis families. Many Celtic people coming into North Alabama in the 1700s, made friends with the Indians and married their young women. During Indian removal, mixed-blood inhabitants were allowed to remain in North Alabama because they were married to whites or were able to identify themselves with white ancestry. Due to Indian removal and intermarriage, Lawrence County's Indian people became thoroughly absorbed into the general population.

Doublehead was another important Cherokee man. Doublehead, (c1744-1807), aka Dsugweladegi or Chuqualatague, was the son of Great Eagle (Willenawah) and grandson of Moytoy. Among his siblings were Pumpkin Boy, Old Tassel, and unnamed grandmother of Sequoyah. After his sister's son, John Watts Jr. was elected chief over him, Doublehead moved into Lawrence County becoming a powerful Cherokee leader. Living at Brown's Ferry, the head of Elk River Shoals (c1790-c1802), Doublehead terrorized settlers on the Appalachian frontier until his 1794 meeting with George Washington. By the treaty on January 10, 1786, most of Lawrence County became Chickasaw land. Doublehead was permitted to stay because of his daughters, Tuskiahooto and Saleechie, marriages to Chickasaw Chief George Colbert. Learning of the wealth in cotton, Doublehead in 1802 petitioned the government for a keelboat, signed the 1805 treaty authorizing Gaines Trace, and negotiated the 1806 Cotton Gin Treaty. This treaty placed a cotton gin at Melton's Bluff and gave him a 99-year lease on Doublehead's Reserve between Elk River and Cypress Creek. In partnership with John D. Chisholm, they leased this reserve to settlers. On 9, Aug 1807, Major Ridge, Alex Saunders and John Rogers killed Doublehead, either for control of the cotton trade or for his ceding of Indian lands.

Doublehead or "Talo Tiske"-meaning two heads. What do you think that means? (two personalities) Doublehead was from a prominent family of the Cherokee. His brothers were Old Tassel, a principal chief of the Cherokee Nation, and Pumpkin Boy. Doublehead's older sister married a Fort Loudoun soldier, John Watts. Their son, John Watts, Jr. became chief of the Cherokee Nation. They had, "Wurteh" who was the mother of Sequoyah. Wurteh Watts was ½ Celtic (Scotch) and ½ Cherokee. Sequoyah's father was Nathaniel Gist (Guess), who was of uncertain European lineage, but was thought to be German or Irish. Who knows who Sequoyah was? What did he do that was important to the Cherokee? (Cherokee alphabet) Nathan Gist and Wurteh Watts became the parents of the most famous Cherokee of all, the notable Sequoyah. Wurteh Watts had earlier married trader John Benge (Scotch) and had children: Robert Benge, Talohuskee Benge, and Utana Benge.

In 1790, Doublehead established his first town on the Tennessee River at the head of Mussel Shoals. Now, I'm talking about Shoals as being the river and not the city. The town was located in Lawrence County at Brown's Ferry just east of the mouth of Mallard Creek. The town was known as Doublehead's Village or Brown's Ferry.

After moving from the area that became Lawrence County in 1802, Doublehead settled on Blue Water Creek in Lauderdale County. Today, the Blue Water Polo Club on Highway 72 is located on the Cherokee Blue Water Old Fields. The main Cherokee Town near Doublehead's home was called Shoal Town located between Blue Water Creek and Town Creek on the Tennessee River.

In the beginning, Doublehead was a village chief. After the death of Old Tassel in 1788, Doublehead became a powerful chief over the lower Tennessee River in our area. He moved into the Chickasaw Country of Lawrence County because his nephew, John Watts, Jr. (½ Celtic – ½ Cherokee), was elected Chief of the Cherokee Nation over him. Also, Doublehead's oldest two daughters, Tuskiahooto and Saleechie, married Chickasaw Chief George Colbert. Doublehead was assassinated on August 9, 1807, and is supposedly buried on a hill east of Blue Water Creek and on the north side of Highway 72 overlooking the Blue Water Oldfields (presently a Polo Club).

LESSON 18 – LOCAL INDIAN LEADERS

After living in Doublehead's Village at Browns Ferry until 1802, Cherokee Chief Doublehead migrated farther west along the Tennessee River into Lauderdale County, Alabama. Historical evidence indicates Doublehead settled for some 12 years at the head of Elk River Shoals at Brown's Ferry. Doublehead helped establish the following villages along the Tennessee River in Lawrence County: Moneetown (Mouse Town), at the mouth of Fox's Creek, Doublehead's Village at Brown's Ferry, between Fox's and Mallard Creeks; Melton's Bluff between Mallard and Spring Creeks; Gourd's Settlement at Courtland on Path Killer Creek (Big Nance); Shoal Town between Blue Water and Town Creek near present-day Wheeler Dam; and, Oakville located at junction of Old Indian Trace (Coosa Path) and Black Warriors' Path.

From the 1770s, Chief Doublehead and the Cherokee Nation inhabited and controlled the area of the Warrior Mountains and north to the present-day Tennessee State Line. By 1790, Doublehead had settled and lived in Lawrence County at Doublehead's Village at Brown's Ferry, which was at the head of Muscle Shoals. The following text tells of Doublehead's home and is found on page 62 of Volume V, "The Journal of Muscle Shoals History," and written in a speech by William B. Wood published in 1876 is the following:

> "As early as 1802, a party set out from North Carolina, who, with great difficulty, ascended the Blue Ridge, with their wagons, and descended through its gorges, into the valley of the Tennessee. Constructing flat boats at Knoxville, they floated down the Tennessee River, to the head of Muscle Shoals, where they disembarked at the house of Doublehead, a Cherokee Chief. This party; however, did not remain in this valley, the lands belonging to the Indians, their title having not yet been extinguished."

Sometime around 1802, Doublehead moved down river to the Indian village of Shoal Town between Blue Water and Town Creeks. According to William L. McDonald's "The Lore of Chief Doublehead and His Home at Muscle Shoals" found in Volume IX of the Journal of Muscle Shoals History on page 103 is the following:

> *Yet, Doublehead was without influence or position. That is, until about the year 1790, when he established his first town on the Tennessee River at the head of the Muscle Shoals. An early map of the Cherokee Country shows this village at a site near the south bank of Brown's Ferry below Athens. He later moved it to the north bank of the river near the mouth of Blue Water Creek, in Lauderdale County, Alabama.*

According to this historical information, Doublehead lived at Doublehead's Village at Browns Ferry for some 12 years at the head of Muscle Shoals on the south bank of the Tennessee River in present day Lawrence County. The Cherokee village is also shown on a 1779-1796 map of the proposed "State of Franklin" and was located between Mallard Creek and Fox Creek. Doublehead lived at Brown's Ferry prior to moving to his Blue Water home of Shoal Town in present-day Lauderdale County. Doublehead's old two-story log home and tavern was destroyed during the four-laning of Highway 72 between Athens and Florence.

Tahlonteskee (Talohuskee Benge) the great nephew of Doublehead, had his settlement of Shoal Town at the mouths of Town Creek in Lawrence County and Blue Water Creek in Lauderdale County on the banks of the Hogohegee (Tennessee) River, known as the "River of the Cherokees." The village actually lay on both sides of the river about six miles from the eastern upstream end of the Big Muscle Shoals. Actually at this point, the Blue Water Ferry crossed the river from the eastern point of Blue Water Creek to the area halfway between Town Creek and Big Nance Creek in present day Lawrence County. According to Nina Leftwich's book, Two Hundred Years at Muscle Shoals, the Cherokees had a large settlement at the mouth of Town Creek, which extended a mile along the river and far up the creek.

Doublehead was the feared war chief of the Big Bend of lower Tennessee River Cherokees known as Chickamaugans. Tahlonteskee, Talohuskee Benge, was probably the peace chief, since each Cherokee village had both a war chief and a peace chief. The Shoal Town, (Blue Water-Town Creek Village), was the final Alabama home of both men. Doublehead is supposedly buried in Butler Cemetery on Blue Water Creek in Lauderdale County, Alabama. Some say he is buried on the east side of Blue Water Creek and just north of Highway 72 on a knoll overlooking the Blue Water Old Fields now known as Blue Water Polo Club.

LESSON 18 – LOCAL INDIAN LEADERS

In 1806, Cherokee Chief Doublehead, Tahlonteskee, and other Cherokees signed the Cotton Gin Treaty, which gave up Cherokee Claims to land north of the Tennessee River except for Doublehead's Reserve. The reserve lay between Elk River (Chuwalee) and Cypress Creek (TeKeetanoeh) in present day Lauderdale County.

The signing of the Cotton Gin Treaty brought the wrath of other Cherokee leaders upon the individuals who signed the treaty giving up Cherokee Lands. Major Ridge, a powerful Cherokee leader, made known that Doublehead and others would pay with their lives for relinquishing Cherokee lands. At a meeting of Cherokee headmen in Tennessee, Doublehead paid with his life at the hand of Ridge, Alex Saunders, John Rogers, and their accomplices. Alex Saunders and John Rogers had ties to Lawrence County and probably profited from the assassination of Doublehead.

Doublehead's town site, near Center Star, was located where his nephew, Tahlonteskee (Talohuskee) Benge, had lived before moving to Arkansas in 1808. This location had the advantage of about a square mile of bottomlands that Tahlonteskee's people had cleared and made ready for farming. These "Old Fields" at the mouth of Blue Water Creek were very fertile and appealed to the very first white settlers, and, subsequently, became the enticement that made this community the first to be settled in the county.

Inhabitants of Shoal Town where Doublehead lived, originally about forty in number, were mostly cast-offs from other Cherokee and Creek villages. This motley bunch became infamous in Tennessee history as "the ravagers of the Cumberland's." However, as years passed, other and more respectable Indians, mostly Cherokees, moved in, and by the time of the arrival of the first whites, they were of the genial sort and, according to some diaries, made "mighty good neighbors."

The Shoal Town site was in the disputed reserve that was called the "Chickasaw Hunting Grounds." For over two hundred years both the Chickasaws and the Cherokees claimed these lands as their own. Thus, the settlement at the Muscle Shoals was cause for concern by the Federal Government, and especially General James Robertson, the protector of the Cumberland's. However, the Cherokee Agent, Colonel Return Jonathon Meigs, thought Doublehead's settlement was an attempt by the Cherokees to test their title to that portion of the disputed Chickasaw Hunting Grounds. Robertson was finally calmed by the assurance from Chickasaw Chief George Colbert, who operated a ferry across the Tennessee at the nearby Natchez Trace that Doublehead was at the Muscle Shoals by his permission.

George Colbert was a double son-in-law of Doublehead. Colbert, according to one traveling preacher, "indulged in more than one marital adventure simultaneously." Two of his wives, observed Methodist historian John B. M'Ferrin, were daughters of Chief Doublehead. The principal wife, Tuskiahooto, presided over the household. She raised a few eyebrows when she attended a formal dinner with her husband at the White House, dressed in the latest Washington fashion and barefooted. Old families of Colbert County remembered how this princess by birth, and principal "first lady" in marriage by her extremely good looks, refused to ride in the elegant carriage provided by her husband. Instead, she followed the carriage and driver, astride her favorite pony seated on a colorful blanket, and, as usual barefooted. The other wife was Saleechie, or sometimes "Shullechie." She was a successful businesswoman and operated an inn on the Natchez Trace near Tupelo, Mississippi. Edwin C. Thomas stayed at their inn during the year 1836 and wrote: "She was a woman well fixed up, had a good house, and gave a good fare."

Old Tassel, head chief of the Cherokees, was a well-known friend of the whites. In the year 1788, he was invited, along with his son and two others, to the headquarters of Mayor James Hubbert under a flag of truce. Hubbert quartered the unarmed Cherokee party in a vacant house. Here, while he guarded the door, they were murdered by a young man with a tomahawk, who it seems had recently lost his parents in like manner to a party of Cherokee raiders. He demanded revenge, and was handed a tomahawk by Hubbert, who even set up the scenario for the blood bath. Doublehead, upon hearing this tragic report of his brother's death, sought and found revenge against the white man.

He went on the warpath, and took his followers from Shoal Town with him. The very name of Doublehead and his raiding party brought fear and trembling to the white settlements between Muscle Shoals and Nashville, and especially in the Cumberland Mountain area between Nashville and Knoxville.

Doublehead's first "hunting party" of record was in the fall of 1791. He had with him a group of 28 men plus women and children. Together they made a horrendous "scalping excursion" up the Cumberland. General Robertson sent an expedition to "get

LESSON 18 – LOCAL INDIAN LEADERS

Doublehead" on January 16, 1792. This noble crusade, however, resulted in the death of five of Tennessee's finest young men. Doublehead killed the three sons of Colonel Valentine Sevier, the noted brother of General John Sevier, and two of their friends.

The murder of Captain William Overall and a man named Burnett in 1793, at Dripping Springs, was gruesome and gory. Doublehead, it has been recorded, dishonored Overall's body by cutting away and eating the flesh from his bones, and dancing with his scalp in the Indian villages at Lookout Mountain, Willstown, and Turnip Mountain. In May of that same year, while meeting with a delegation of Chickasaws, he apparently alluded to this act of cannibalism when he said: "We, the Cherokees, had eaten a great quantity of the white men's flesh, but have had so much of it we are tired of it, and think it too salty."

Doublehead was accompanied on many raids by his great nephew "Bench" (also known as Robert Benge), and his brother, "Pumpkin Boy." Bench was a wild sort of fellow himself. Yet, on at least one occasion he tried to hold back his Uncle Doublehead in an unmerciful crime against women and children. Pumpkin boy was a handsome warrior, well equipped with trinkets and a pair of expensive silver mounted pistols. When Pumpkin Boy was killed by Sevier's men, his brother Doublehead, fierce and sullen by nature, proposed that every settler's cabin be burned.

The saga of Doublehead's warpath covers some six years, beginning in 1788, and ending, rather abruptly, in June of 1794. Always ambitious, the eager chief had managed an appointment of importance and prestige. He became the leading delegate of a party of Cherokee chiefs visiting Philadelphia, where they met the first President of the United States, George Washington. It is said that Doublehead was the center of attention and that he was dressed in his most elaborate costume that was embroidered with a silver eagle design. Later, following what must have been a long and drawn out negotiation with Secretary of War Henry Knox, Doublehead and the other chiefs in the party of Cherokee chiefs came away with their personal annuities increased from $1,500 to $5,000 annually. This enabled the crusty old warrior to go home and live in style. Loaded with presents, he came back to Alabama by way of Charleston, and reached Doublehead's Village at Brown's Ferry in October, 1794. A lot had happened while the chiefs were in Philadelphia. On the way home he wrote Governor Blount a long letter concerning his meeting with the President. Two parts of this rather lengthy letter say something about the "new personality" of Chief Doublehead that emerges in history.

Determined now to copy the whites rather than to destroy their possessions and take their lives, he built what was then considered to be a pretentious story and a half log house in the wilderness about 1802. This structure, which later became a stagecoach inn, was nestled on the side of a hill that overlooked his expanding village in the Blue Water Creek valley below. Here he lived at peace with man, and became a well-known figure in various treaties between Indian Nations and the Federal Government.

At a meeting of head men near Hiwassee, real trouble began almost immediately afterwards when Doublehead was accosted by a fellow chief by the name of Bone Polisher. He denounced Doublehead as a traitor, referring to Doublehead's trip to Washington on January 7, 1806, with Chief Vann, Chief Taluntuskee, and Colonel Return J. Meigs. At that time, the Cherokee delegation ceded all the area between the Tennessee and Duck Rivers, except for Doublehead's Reserve. Most of this land actually belonged to the Chickasaws by the January 10, 1786 treaty.

This episode with the trader, John Rogers, gave the others time to act. Someone managed to extinguish the tavern light and instantly a pistol shot rang out from a dark corner. When the light was restored, Rogers, Ridge and Saunders had fled and Doublehead lay motionless on the floor. The ball had shattered his lower jaw and lodged in the nape of his neck.

Friends pulled the mortally wounded chief from the building, and across a field, and hid him in the loft of the schoolmaster at Hiwassee. But they left a trail of blood and it was easily followed by Major Ridge, Alex Saunders and two clansmen of Bone Polisher. When they arrived the dying warrior was lying on the attic floor in a pool of blood. Showing no mercy, not even to the dying, both Major Ridge and Alex Saunders drew their pistols with the intent to finish off their adversary. But the hand of fate that had been so busy that night again intervened, causing their pistols to misfire.

This seemed to be a cue in this dialogue of death for old Doublehead suddenly sprang to life and physically attacked Major Ridge with almost super human strength. Sam Dale wrote that he would have overpowered Ridge had Ridge's partner, Alex Saunders, not shot Doublehead again - this time through the hips and then jumped him with his tomahawk swinging! But Doublehead wrenched free and leaped again upon Major Ridge. This gave Saunders time to grab another tomahawk and drive it full force into

LESSON 18 – LOCAL INDIAN LEADERS

the skull of the dying Doublehead. As he fell to the floor again, one of Bone Polisher's tribesmen crushed the old warrior's head with a sharp spade.

At last, Doublehead was dead! He was no ordinary man, and his was no ordinary death. He died as he had lived, and it took a room full of enemies to bring it about. Ironically, Major Ridge, who played a key role in this execution, came by a similar fate some thirty years later in Oklahoma.

Cotterill, the historian, states that Colonel Meigs drove the Cherokees out of the Shoal Town (Blue Water Creek village) following Doublehead's death and that he burned the home of the old chief.

Both the lore of the land at the Muscle Shoals is filled with its own version of stories. Legends have been passed from generation to generation. One legend tells us that the friends of the old chief carefully brought his battered and lacerated body back to Blue Water Creek where they gave him a white man's burial.

Two graves have been pointed to as the possible sites of his resting place. One is at the top of the hill behind where his log house stood. The other grave is in the bottomland about where Doublehead's village once stood. Kit Butler, an ex-slave who met the stagecoaches and tended to the horses at Wayside Inn, remembered the "awesomeness of that Indian's grave upon the hill behind the house." Old Doublehead's spirit he said, "would rant and rave on that hill, especially on dark and stormy nights."

Cuttyatoy - Another important Cherokee Indian living in Lawrence County by 1813 was Chief Cuttyatoy. Cuttyatoy lived near the mouth of Spring Creek with his main home located on an island in the area. He had earlier stolen the slaves of Joseph Brown's father. In 1813, Joseph Brown was fighting at the Battle of Talledega when he learned where Cuttyatoy had his father's slaves. With Andrew Jackson's permission, Joseph Brown and 10 of Jackson's best men came to Lawrence County and took back his family's slaves. Brown became a big landowner between Columbia and Pulaski, TN. His slaves eventually killed him.

Dragging Canoe - While a young boy, this future Cherokee Chief wanted to accompany his father, Attakullakulla, and a Cherokee war party going to battle the Shawnee. Attakullakulla flatly refused the young boy permission to go, but he slipped away from home ahead of the war party and hid in a dugout canoe he knew the warriors must use. When the warriors arrived at the portage and discovered the determined lad, there was much teasing. Attakullakulla told his son that if he could carry the canoe across the portage he could go along, so the young boy grabbed one end of the canoe and started dragging it through the sand. The excited warriors shouted encouragement, saying "he is dragging the canoe," and Dragging Canoe was his name from then on.

Dragging Canoe became a leader of a group hostile Indians to the Americans and American settlements during and after the Revolutionary War. He was unusually tall for a Southeast Indian, standing well over six feet, was very broad-shouldered and excellently proportioned. His most striking feature was a pockmarked face due to a case of smallpox. Nevertheless, he was rated as one of the handsomest and strongest in the Nation. He was a great warrior, had been wounded in battle, and hated the Americans implacably. He was always dressed for battle, wearing only a breechcloth and a necklace of long bear claws.

After being driven south by white forces, Dragging Canoe and his warriors established what came to be known as the Five Lower Towns of Dragging Canoe in the east portion of the Great Bend in the Tennessee River. Two of these, Long Island Town and Crow Town, were located in Jackson County, Alabama. These towns formed a natural fortress ringed with cliffs and mountains, and on the west side had a great cave, roofed at the entrance with great horizontal layers of solid rock. Protecting this stronghold was a series of guard posts manned by fleet runners. Thus barricaded, Dragging Canoe and his braves successfully resisted the advance of white settlement on the Tennessee for a quarter of a century.

At the same time, his south flank was open, so that he could receive food, munitions, and trade goods from the English and occasional reinforcements from the friendly Creeks. Thus it was said that under his blanket, Dragging Canoe's tomahawk laughed at the white man. He died in 1792, but his stronghold continued to be effective until well into the next century.

Red Eagle - One of the most picturesque and courageous scenes of the whole war took place here in the appearance and surrender of Chief "Red Eagle," William Weatherford, who had led the Battle of Fort Mims, Calebee, and Holy Ground. "Red Eagle" had come alone, accompanied by neither warriors nor soldiers. I am sure General Jackson was greatly surprised. According to Pickett, General Jackson upon seeing "Red Eagle" ran from his marquee and exclaimed, "How dare you, sir, to ride

LESSON 18 – LOCAL INDIAN LEADERS

Charles Weatherford, Son of Red Eagle

up to my tent, after having murdered the women and children at Fort Mims?"

Weatherford replied, "General Jackson, I am not afraid of you. I fear no man, for I am a Creek Warrior. I have nothing to request in behalf of myself; you can kill me, if you desire. But I come to beg you to send for the women and children of the war party, who are now starving in the woods. Their fields and cribs have been destroyed by your people, who have driven them to the woods without an ear of corn. I hope that you will send out parties, who will safely conduct them here, in order that they may be fed. I exerted myself in vain to prevent the massacre of the women and children at Fort Mims. I am now done fighting. The "Red Sticks" are nearly all killed. If I could fight you any longer, I would most heartily do so. Send for the women and children, they never did you any harm. But kill me, if the white people want it done."

At this point, many persons present cried out, "Kill Him! Kill Him! Kill Him!" But General Jackson commanded silence, and in an emphatic manner, said, "Any man who would kill as brave a man as this would rob the dead!" Thus his life was spared and Chief "Red Eagle" took no more part in the war except to encourage his warriors to surrender. He became a resident of Monroe County where he operated a farm and gained the respect of his neighbors.

Pickett reports that some 5000 of the Indian women and children for whom "Red Eagle" pled for were fed at the various American Posts. Jackson later dictated peace terms to the Creek, who gave up 23 million acres of land in present-day Georgia and Alabama.

Talohuskee Benge (Tahlonteskee) - After the assassination of Chief Doublehead by his own people, due to the circumstances of the Cotton Gin Treaty of 1806, several Cherokees living in the Lawrence County area moved west to avoid the same fate. The following is from <u>The Cherokees</u> by Grace Steele Woodard published in 1963 and found on page 131:

> *"However, in 1808, the Compact 1802 was not needed to effect the removal of some 1,130 Chickamaugans to lands west of the Mississippi (today Dardanelle, Arkansas, in Pope County). Jefferson had merely to suggest to Tahlonteskee and other Chickamaugans that if they did not care to remain in the same country with their enemy countrymen; they could remove to Dardanelle Rock. Thus, in the Spring of 1808, Tahlonteskee-fearing assassination-notified President Jefferson that his people were ready to migrate. Following their migration, Tahlonteskee's band of Cherokees called themselves "Cherokees West" or "Old Settlers.""*

Since Tahlonteskee (Talohuskee) signed the 1806 Cotton Gin Treaty and feared the same punishment that Doublehead received for giving up land north of the Tennessee River, Tahlonteskee and his Cherokee followers agreed to move from the Shoal Town Village at the Big Muscle Shoals of the Tennessee River to the west. It is believed by some that Sequoyah, George Guess, went west after the 1816 Turkey Town Treaty in search of his half-brother, Tahlonteskee or Talohuskee Benge.

Even though some Cherokees in the Warrior Mountains area left with Tahlonteskee's (Talohuskee) group in 1808, many Cherokee people still lived in the Tennessee Valley from the river to the High Town Path in southern Lawrence County. Within the great valley of the Tennessee, cotton became the agricultural "king" for making money. With the new government cotton gin at Melton's Bluff and black slaves for farm labor, both the Chickasaws and Cherokees, who shared ownership of the river valley, became wealthy; however, the government and settlers wanted the cotton wealth of the Tennessee Valley, which was controlled by the Indians.

LESSON 18 – LOCAL INDIAN LEADERS

In 1816, with several more years of pressure, the Chickasaws and Cherokees finally relinquished their claim to the remainder of Warrior Mountains. Therefore, due to the circumstances of the Turkey Town Treaty of September 16 and 18, 1816, another contingent of Chickasaws and Cherokees moved west, from the land of the Warrior Mountains in Lawrence County, Alabama.

Tahlonteskee (Talohuskee Benge) was the great nephew of Doublehead. Talohuskee's half-brother was Sequoyah and his full brothers were Robert (Bob) Benge, and Utana (The Tail) Benge. His settlement was located at the mouths of Town Creek in Lawrence County and Blue Water Creek in Lauderdale County on the banks of the Hogohegee (Tennessee) River, known as the "River of the Cherokees." The Shoal Town village actually lay on both sides of the river about six miles from the eastern upstream end of the Big Muscle Shoals. Actually at this point, the Blue Water Ferry crossed the river from the eastern point of Blue Water Creek to the area west of the mouth of Path Killer on Big Nance Creek in present day Lawrence County. According to Nina Leftwich's book <u>Two Hundred Years at Muscle Shoals</u>, the Cherokees had a large settlement at the mouth of Town Creek, which extended a mile along the river and far up the creek.

Doublehead was the feared war chief of the lower Tennessee River Cherokees known as Chickamaugans. Tahlonteskee, was probably the peace chief, since each Cherokee village had both a war chief and a peace chief. The Blue Water and Town Creek Village was the final Alabama home of both men and was known as Shoal Town. Doublehead is supposedly buried in Butler Cemetery on Blue Water Creek in Lauderdale County, Alabama; however, many believe his grave is located under a small mound of chert stones on a knoll north of Highway 72 and east of Blue Water Creek overlooking the Blue Water Oldfields, now a polo club.

In 1806, Cherokee Chief Doublehead, Tahlonteskee, and other Cherokees signed the Cotton Gin Treaty, which gave up Cherokee claims to land north of the Tennessee River except from Doublehead's Reserve. The reserve lay between Elk River (Chuwalee) and Cypress Creek (TeKeetanoeh) in present-day Lauderdale County. The Treaty placed a Cotton Gin at Melton's Bluff in present-day Lawrence County and a blacksmith by the name of Sameul Hall to be paid one shilling of silver each day by the government.

Black Fox- (<u>Inali, Enoli, or Eunolee</u>), the Principal Chief of the Cherokee Nation, lived in Lawrence County, Alabama during the latter portion of his illustrious life. Fox's Creek in the northeastern corner of this county still bears his name. Black Fox was chosen by the Cherokee Nation to be chief of his people in 1801.

Black Fox was associated with many important Indian people and leaders in this area during his reign as chief: Doublehead; Doublehead's daughters who married George Colbert-Tuskiahooto and Saleechie; James Colbert's half blood Chickasaw sons-George Colbert-Tooteemastubbe (Ferryman) and Levi Colbert-Itawamba Mingo (Wooden Bench Chief); John Benge's sons who were half brothers to Sequoyah-Taluskee (Tahlonteskee) Benge and Robert (Bob) Benge-The Bench; John Melton's half blood Cherokee sons-Charles, David, James, and Lewis-the father of Moses; Cuttyatoy; Pathkiller; Charles Hicks; John Brown; Richard Brown, and others had their names associated with the Lawrence County area of northwest Alabama. However, after the Turkey Town Treaty of September 1816, the historical records of Indian people became somewhat clouded for this area. Nevertheless, very influential Indian people made their reputations, homes, and lifestyles in this portion of the Tennessee Valley from 1770 through 1816. These people, their exploits, and historic significance became intertwined with the life of the old Chief Black Fox.

During Black Fox's reign as chief, eight Cherokee Indian towns flourished along the banks of the River of the Cherokees (Tennessee) in this area. These Lawrence County Indian towns included Mousetown or Moneetown, Fox's Stand, Doublehead's Village at Brown's Ferry, Melton's Bluff, Cuttyatoy's Village, Gourd's Settlement (Courtland), and Shoal Town. The towns were located adjacent to the Elk River Shoals and Big Muscle Shoals at major Indian trail crossings of the river called Chake Thlocko (Big Ford or Great Crossing Place). These Indian towns benefited from the shoals that provided an abundance of food in the form of freshwater mussels.

Black Fox and Doublehead lived in Lawrence County a few miles from each other on the old Brown's Ferry Road. Black Fox lived for a while at Mousetown on the Tennessee River at the mouth of the creek that became his namesake before moving a few miles to the road junction that became his stand. By 1790, Doublehead had established a village at Brown's Ferry on the Tennessee River that became his stronghold until 1802 when he moved down the river to Shoal Town, which was located some seven miles from the eastern end of the Big Muscle Shoals between the mouths of Big Nance, Town Creek and Blue Water Creek. Shoal Town was controlled by Doublehead's nephew and Bench's brother, Taluskee Benge.

LESSON 18 – LOCAL INDIAN LEADERS

Black Fox and Doublehead were friends and signed numerous treaties with the United States government. Doublehead would sign treaties benefiting Black Fox and Black Fox would sign treaties that benefited Doublehead. John Watts, Doublehead, Black Fox and others signed the Treaty with the Cherokee on July 2, 1791. On October 20, 1803, Black Fox places his (X) between his name and Principal Chief; however, this treaty refers to "our beloved Chief Doublehead." Both Black Fox and Doublehead signed Cherokee treaties of October 25, 1805, and October 27, 1805. Also Doublehead signs the Cotton Gin Treaty of January 7, 1806, that gives the Cherokees a machine for cleaning cotton and places the gin at Melton's Bluff. The treaty also gives the old Cherokee Chief Black Fox $100.00 annually for the rest of his life. The final payment recorded for Chief Black Fox is found as follows: *"Abstract of Disbursements made by Return J. Meigs, Agent of war in Tennessee on account of the Indian Department between the 30th June & the 1st of October 1810...date of payments. July 11th, number of payments. 4. to whom made, Black Fox Cherokee King, Nature of Disbursements. Being the amount of Annual Stipend for the current year received by his proxy, Amount. $100.00."* It is probable that Black Fox was getting in bad health because he had some of his people to pick up the money, then he died the next year.

Little Turkey preceded Black Fox as the Principal Chief of the Cherokee Nation. Pathkiller succeeded Black Fox as chief of the Cherokee Nation. Doublehead's nephew, John Watts, Jr. was elected Chief of the Cherokee over him after the death of Dragging Canoe in March 1792. Chief Watts was wounded at Buchanan's Station near Nashville in September 1792 but recovered and led his army the next year against Cavett's Station near Knoxville, Tennessee. The Bench (Robert Benge) acting as an interpreter convinced the people to surrender. Soon as they had surrendered, Doublehead killed every one. The Bench wept because he had given his word and felt that his honor had been betrayed by his uncle Doublehead. The Bench was ambushed and killed in 1794 by Lieutenant Vincent Hobbs. John Watts, Jr. eventually died at Willstown in 1808. Doublehead was assassinated on August 9, 1807. Black Fox died in 1811. Path Killer died in 1828. Thus, as the great Cherokee leaders of the lower or southern faction of Cherokees died, the tribal control and leadership shifted to the upper or northern faction.

After Black Fox was elected chief in 1801, a lot of differences began between the Upper and Lower Cherokees. With the lower towns in this area having secured control of the tribal leadership, they were assured favorable distribution of annuity funds. A delegation of Upper Cherokees complained to President Thomas Jefferson that the Lower Cherokees divide all funds from annuities and land sales among those of their own neighborhood. President Jefferson explained that once the funds were turned over to the authorized representatives of the tribe that it was purely a Cherokee affair. Alexander Saunders proposed that the funds be split between the Lower and Upper Cherokees. Both Black Fox and Doublehead, who were Lower Cherokees, had serious conflicts with Major Ridge, a Cherokee Chief of an upper town. After Doublehead signed the Cotton Gin Treaty of 1806, giving up Cherokee claims to lands on the north side of the Tennessee River except for Doublehead's Reserve between Elk River and Cypress Creek, he was assassinated by Major Ridge, Alexander Saunders, and John Rogers on August 9, 1807.

In early 1808, Colonel Return J. Meigs had convinced Black Fox and Tahlonteskee to seek the Cherokee council approval for exchanging their lands for territory west of the Mississippi. At the fall council meeting of the Cherokee Nation, Black Fox made the proposal as follows, *"Tell our Great Father, the President (Thomas Jefferson), that our game has disappeared, and we wish to follow it to the West. We are his friends, and we hope he will grant our petition, which is to remove our people towards the setting sun. But we shall give up fine country, fertile in soil, abounding in water-courses, and well adapted for the residence of white people. For all this we must have a good price."* The Ridge was very upset and spoke against Black Fox in such an eloquent manner that the tribal council rejected both Fox and his proposal. Black Fox was reinstate at a later council meeting, but felt disgraced for the rest of his life. However, in the summer of 1808, Tahlonteskee took the offer from President Thomas Jefferson and some 1,131 Cherokees left the Shoal Town area to lands west of the Mississippi River. Tahlonteskee told President Thomas Jefferson that his reason for leaving was the fear of assassination as his uncle Doublehead. Jefferson was the first president to strongly advocate Indian removal.

Today, Fox's Creek is the name of a small tributary to the Tennessee River that flows into the river at the north border of Morgan and Lawrence Counties at an old Cherokee town site of Mousetown or Moneetown. Black Fox's home was located between the drainages of Fox and Mallard Creeks some two miles west of Doublehead's Village, which was on the Tennessee River at Brown's Ferry in Lawrence County, Alabama. The location of Fox's Stand was at the junctions of two Indian trails-Brown's Ferry Road and Black Warriors' Path. Black Warriors' Path continued six miles northwest to Melton's Bluff which was established by Irishman John Melton, who had married a Cherokee woman. His half blood sons became important in the local early history of Lawrence County.

LESSON 18 – LOCAL INDIAN LEADERS

From Fox's Stand, the Brown's Ferry Road continued west some eight miles to Gourd's Settlement (present-day Courtland) on Pathkiller's Creek (present-day Big Nance Creek).

According to General John Coffee's Diary -1816 is the following: "**21st Feb'y 1816.** *This morning Maj. Hutchings left us to go to meet Gen. Jackson – Mr. Bright surveys and we pass on down the river. When at Huntsville I did not pay my bill – neither did I pay it at Mr. Austin's – I paid Mrs. Austin for buiskit, candles and washing $2.00 – paid Charles Melton 3 bushels corn $1.50 – fodder, $1.00 – whiskey 75¢. Paid to Charles for Reed $2.00. Encamped all night on Big Nance Creek."* From Big Nance, Coffee continues to the mouth of Caney Creek and run a boundary line up the creek crossing Gaines Trace. Coffee continued the line to Cotton Gin Port before starting back to Melton's Bluff on March 2, 1816. This became the Chickasaw boundary in the Turkey Town Treaty of September 1816. Coffee's diary continues, "**6th March, 1816.** *This day we reached Melton's Bluff about one o'clock. Bought sundry supplies &c Viz; whiskey $1.00-whiskey, $1.371/2- 3 dinners, 75¢ - 20 lbs Bacon 9¢ $2.50 Paid for corn and fodder to Charley Melton $5.00"* It should be pointed out that Coffee specifically mentioned Charles Melton who moved east after the Turkey Town Treaty of 1816 and established an Indian town known as Meltonsville. James Melton became a keel boat guide for Malcolm Gilchrist and his family remained in Lawrence County. David Melton sold Andrew Jackson all the land at Melton's Bluff and some 60 slaves. Lewis' son Moses Melton and Charles Hicks were given by treaty a tract of land on the north side of the Tennessee River. These Melton boys were the half blood Cherokee sons of Irishman John Melton.

On December 20, 1807, John Sevier, Governor of Tennessee, writes to Black Fox concerning a report from Colonel Meigs about the Creek Indians settling on the Tennessee near Elk River. Sevier writes, *"I am informed that the Creeks have built Huts, and is living on the banks of the Tennessee; what business have they there? They have none only to be convenient to kill some of our people, and plunder our Boats as they are going down the River – You know the Creek people are Rogues, and you say steal from and rob your own people; if it be true, why don't you drive them from out of your Country? For a people who both murder & steals, aught not to be Suffered to live in any place – You are Surely able to drive away the few that comes to do Mischief, and disturb the peace of your people and ours; If their nation means to protect them in their murdering and plundering excursions, you then know where you can resort to for protection and Strength enough to do yourselves Justice – I state these circumstances to inform You how you aught to conduct towards the white people, who are your Fathers, Brothers, friends, and your good neighbors."* It should be noted that Meigs and Sevier confirm that the old Chief Black Fox was still living at the Elk River Shoals some four months after the death of his friend and cohort Doublehead.

The old Principal Chief Black Fox evidently had a son also known as Black Fox that also lived in Lawrence County, AL and his name appears on numerous Cherokee documents after the death of his father in 1811. John Coffee put the following note in his diary, "**26th July, 1816.** *Borrowed Capt. Hammond's large tent- left my old one – breakfasted with the Captain. Started on and got to Wilders where I dined, Bought corn to carry with me – bill $1.50. Went to the river – crossed at Brown's Ferry – paid ferrage &c $1.25. Hired young Wilder to go on to Col. Barnett &c. This night went to **Black Foxe's** and lay all night; bought _ bushels of corn to carry with me. Hired ____ Lancaster to carry six bushels to Major Russell's, for which I am to pay three and half dollars –bought some salt from **Fox**, hired him and McClure to carry the corn to the wagon road about two miles – paid bill at **Fox's** $6.75."* Coffee continued on to Major Russell's (Russellville) to survey Indian boundary and begin his return. Coffee's notes continue, " **1st August 1816**. *This morning we start in towards Madison County – lay all night at the Path Killer's creek near Jones'.* **2d August.** *This morning we hired Vanpelt to carry letters to Col. Brown inviting him to meet us as Campbell's Ferry on the 12th. Come to the **Black Fox'es** – bought 2 1/2 bushels corn – paid the bill $1.75 –Same day came on – crossed the Tennessee River at Brown's Ferry and came to Wilders where we lay all night."* After the Turkey Town Treaty of 1816 took the Cherokee lands in this area, the young Black Fox moved east into the Cherokee Nation. Other historical references indicate there may have been other Cherokee men with the name Black Fox after the original died 1811. Also another important note is that Colonel Richard Brown was a Cherokee leader during the Creek Indian War and negotiated the Turkey Town Treaty of September 1816 for the Cherokee Nation.

According to Chronicles of Oklahoma, volume 16, number 1, March 1938, by John P. Brown, *"Black Fox died in 1811. He was succeeded by Pathkiller, Nunna-dihi, a very honorable man who was to guide the destinies of the Cherokee through sixteen years."*

Black Fox's death was reported in the Columbia Centinel, Boston, Massachusetts on August 31, 1811. His obituary stated, *"In the Cherokee country, Black Fox, a worthy chief of the Cherokee Tribe of Indians, and a great friend of the U.S."*

LESSON 18 – LOCAL INDIAN LEADERS

According to an article titled A Description and History of Blount County from the Transactions of the Alabama Historical Society on July 9 and 10, 1855, *"Most of the first settlers of Blount as well as those of the adjoining counties, believe that lead mines existed in Blount and Jefferson Counties, and that the Indians knew their location and obtained lead from them. Perhaps, this general belief originated from the following circumstances, which occurred in 1810: An old Cherokee Chief, named Black Fox, died in the north of our county, and was buried in an old mound; and in digging his grave, the Indians found some pieces of lead ore. This trivial discovery was magnified and circulated in Madison County, and many intelligent persons in the county believed a lead mine really existed, at, or near the grave of the old Chief. This opinion became so strong, that Alexander Gilbreath, who then resided in Huntsville, was induced to visit the grave of Black Fox. His searching there, proving unsuccessful....Mr. George Fields, at that time fifty or sixty years old, informed him that the Indians knew of no lead mines nearer than those of Missouri and Illinois, and gave it as his opinion, that the lead found in the grave of Black Fox, had been brought from one of those States."* It is important to note that Blount County at one time included this area of North Alabama. According to a proclamation by David Holmes, Governor of Mississippi Territory, *"All that tract of country lying south of the River Tennessee, east of the Chickasaw boundary line, north of the high-lands that divide the waters of the Tennessee from the water of the Mobile Bay and west of the Cherokee boundary line shall form one other County to be called and known by the name of Blount, the courts of justice whereof will be held at Melton's Bluff."* Melton's Bluff is in Lawrence County some six miles northwest of Black Fox's Stand.

Black Fox was probably buried near home which was the custom of the Cherokees at that time. For example, Doublehead was killed in east Tennessee and transported back to his home overlooking Blue Water Creek where he was buried. Since Black Fox's family resided at his stand for several years after his death, they probably had his body interred nearby.

Within a few years, several magnanimous and powerful leaders of the Cherokee people of North Alabama were dead. Along with their demise, the colorful lives and exploits faded as the sunsets disappear on the rolling hills and roaring shoals of the great bend of the Hogohegee (Tennessee) River.

LESSON 18 – LOCAL INDIAN LEADERS

KINDERGARTEN

DIBELS Reading Objective: PHONICS INSTRUCTION

Objective: After the teacher directs this lesson, Kindergarten Indian students will recognize phonemes (sounds) and graphemes (letters) in the selected terms that are related to the text.

Objective Activity: The students will develop an understanding of the beginning sounds of the letters and sounds while using alphabet flashcards, pictures, and/or words written on the board. The students will identify the letters/sounds then; blend sounds together to read the selected terms. Terms: Irish, paper, river, Fox Creek, whites, etc.

STATE STANDARDS Reading Objective:

PG. 14 #6   Demonstrate an initial understanding of letter-sound relationships
- Teacher should discuss Sequoyah and the significance of the Cherokee alphabet. Then choose words such as: work, boy, picture, word, letter, etc. The teacher should write the word on the board as she says it. Ask students name each beginning letter and give the initial sound they make. Then, the students should say the word together orally.
  - ∾ What did Sequoyah write? (Cherokee alphabet)

STATE STANDARDS Social Studies Objective:

PG. 15 #34   Develop an awareness of the uniqueness of individuals
- The teacher should tell different characteristics of Doublehead, Sequoyah, and John Melton. This will help students understand more about these three men.
- Students will then describe how these three men are unique and why they were important.
  - ∾ Was John Melton an Irishman? (yes)
  - ∾ Did John Melton marry a Cherokee or Shawnee woman? (Cherokee)
  - ∾ Who was the Cherokee leader killed by three men because of cotton or land? (Doublehead)

Review Questions

1. Who was an important chief to the Cherokee of Lawrence County? (Doublehead)
2. Sequoyah was a famous member of which tribe? (Cherokee)
3. What does Doublehead or "Talo Tiske" mean? (two heads)
4. How did Dragging Canoe get his name? (by dragging his canoe)
5. What did the Cherokee call papers with words on them? (talking leaves)

LESSON 18 – LOCAL INDIAN LEADERS

FIRST GRADE

DIBELS Reading Objective: LETTER NAMING FLUENCY

Objective: After the teacher directs this lesson, first grade Indian students will gain the ability to pronounce and recognize letters while learning about the local Indian leaders.

Objective Activity: Use alphabet cards or other visual aids and present a letter to each individual student. If he/she identifies it correctly, he/she gains opportunity to participate in the activity.

STATE STANDARDS Reading Objective:

PG. 17 #4   Demonstrate understanding of letter-sound relationships
- After the teacher directs this lesson, have students play a memory card game.
- Create flashcards with words and letters to match word with that sound. Ex: river-r
- Make about 40-50 cards
- Turn cards face down and let kids turn two over. If cards do not match they will have to remember where the cards are in order to make any future pairs.
  - *Who was also known as George Gist? (Sequoyah)*

PG. 20 #6   Comprehend material read, heard, or viewed
- After the teacher directs the lesson, read to your class "Indian Trails of the Warrior Mountains" or any other text material about Doublehead. Then ask questions to ensure comprehension.
  - *How many years did it take for Sequoyah to invent the alphabet? (12 years)*

STATE STANDARDS Social Studies Objective:

PG. 18 #3   Extend initial ability to locate new information and to express understanding in various classrooms
- Show the class pictures of the different Indian leaders so they will be able to recognize them.
  - *Who was the son of Great Eagle and the grandson of Moytoy? (Doublehead)*

Review Questions

1. What did Sequoyah invent? (Cherokee alphabet)
2. Who owned large farms and a great number of slaves? (John Melton)
3. Who terrorized settlers on his frontier? (Doublehead)
4. Who burned nearly two years of Sequoyah's work on the alphabet? (his wife)
5. Who were Doublehead's brothers? (Old Tassel and Pumpkin Boy)

LESSON 18 – LOCAL INDIAN LEADERS

SECOND GRADE

DIBELS Reading Objective: TEXT COMPREHENSION

Objective: After the teacher directs this lesson, second grade Indian students will be able to relate to the information learned from the lesson and answer various questions in order to ensure comprehension.

Objective Activity: The students will play *Who wants to be a Millionaire*, and allow students to decode the answer using this format: Where was the first cotton gin located? (Doublehead's Village, Melton's Bluff, Horseshoe Bend)

STATE STANDARDS Reading Objective:

PG. 23 #1 Understand the concept of story
- After the directed lesson, let students discuss some of the leaders that they know today. Also discuss some of the leaders in the lesson, and make sure the students understand.
  - *How long did it take Sequoyah to invent the alphabet? (12 years)*

STATE STANDARDS Social Studies Objective:

PG. 25 #23 Compare occupations of family members to those of family members long ago
- Discuss with the class how the leaders of our ancestors helped with the tribe and what their job was compared to the occupations available to us today.
  - *Who assassinated Doublehead? (Major Ridge, Saunders, and Rogers)*

Review Questions

1. What future Cherokee Chief had a father named Attakullakulla? (Dragging Canoe)
2. Who was the great nephew of Doublehead? (Tahlonteskee)
3. Sequoyah was also known as whom? (George Gist)
4. What is another name of William Weatherford? (Chief Red Eagle)
5. Who was the son of Great Eagle? (Doublehead)

LESSON 18 – LOCAL INDIAN LEADERS

THIRD GRADE

DIBELS Reading Objective: COMPREHENSION

Objective: After the teacher directs this lesson, third grade Indian students will be able to recognize, and better understand our local Indian leaders.

Objective Activity: The teacher and students will read orally from the lesson about a specific leader. After discussing each one individually, have a student retell the information learned in his/her own words to ensure comprehension.

STATE STANDARDS Reading Objective:

PG. 32 #8   Read grade-level texts aloud and silently with fluency and comprehension
- Allow students to read aloud or silently so they can utilize the reading content standards of oral reading fluency and ask questions to ensure comprehension.
- *Who was known as the friend of the whites? (Old Tassel)*

PG. 33 #12   Apply strategies of a skillful listener
- While the teacher is conducting the lesson, he/she needs to make sure that the students are focusing on the speaker and are applying strategies of a skillful listener. Ask questions to check if they were listening.
- *Sequoyah was also known as whom? (George Gist)*

STATE STANDARDS Social Studies Objective:

PG. 31 #11   Describe relationships between early settlements and the natural environments
- Describe the relationships between early settlements and the natural environment that our ancestors lived in.
- *How did Dragging Canoe get his name? (from dragging a canoe)*

Review Questions

1. Where in Lawrence County did Doublehead live? (Brown's Ferry)
2. Who was a double son-in-law of Doublehead? (George Colbert)
3. What was the name of the first Indian newspaper? (The Cherokee Phoenix)
4. How long did it take Sequoyah to invent the alphabet? (12 years)
5. Who assassinated Doublehead? (Major Ridge, Saunders, Rogers)

LESSON 18 – LOCAL INDIAN LEADERS

FOURTH GRADE

SAT Reading Objective: COMPREHENSION

Objective: After the teacher directs this lesson, fourth grade Indian students will be able to interpret and demonstrate an understanding about the local Indian leaders.

Objective Activity: The teacher will divide the students into two teams. One question will be written on the board for each team. The first to get to the board and answer the question correctly will earn the point.

STATE STANDARDS Reading Objective:

PG. 39 #12 Apply strategies of a skillful listener
- After the teacher directs the lesson, have a class discussion making sure they have a clear understanding and are listening.
  - *Who invented the Cherokee alphabet? (Sequoyah)*

STATE STANDARDS Social Studies Objective:

PG. 36 #10 Describe aspects of the lives of historic Indians in Alabama
- The teacher will direct the lesson on the local Indian leaders. Explain the aspects of the leaders, for example Sequoyah is the one who invented the alphabet. Doublehead was the chief of the Cherokee nation.
  - *Who were Doublehead's brothers? (Old Tassel, Pumpkin Boy)*

Review Questions

1. Name one Celtic man in the 1700s in Lawrence County to marry an Indian woman. (John Melton)
2. What kind of trade did Sequoyah have earlier in life? (silversmith)
3. Which Cherokee leader practiced cannibalism? (Doublehead)
4. Where did Doublehead and his half brothers live? (in and around Lawrence County)
5. Who saved the lives of some 5,000 Indian women and children by surrendering and risking his own life? (Red Eagle)

LESSON 18 – LOCAL INDIAN LEADERS

FIFTH GRADE

SAT Reading Objective: COMPREHENSION

Objective: After the teacher directs this lesson, fifth grade Indian students will utilize their comprehension awareness of the local Indian leaders.

Objective Activity: The teacher will play "popcorn" and randomly call on students to answer questions from the lesson.

STATE STANDARDS Reading Objective:

PG. 44 #1   Use a wide range of strategies to interpret, evaluate, appreciate, and construct meaning from print materials
- After the teacher directs the lesson, the students will read from "Indian Trails of the Warrior Mountains" or "Warrior Mountain Folklore." The students will then discuss orally aloud one by one what they read.
- *Name three people we talked about today. (Sequoyah, Doublehead, John Melton)*

PG. 46 #13   Apply strategies of a skillful listener
- Throughout the lesson have students re-tell the information being discussed to make sure they are focusing on the speaker and applying the strategies of a skillful listener.
- *How long did it take Sequoyah to invent the Cherokee alphabet? (12 years)*

STATE STANDARDS Social Studies Objective:

PG. 46 #6   Discuss the progression of culture of the early American people.
- The teacher will lead a class discussion comparing/contrasting these local Indian leaders to the leaders of today.
- *What Cherokee leader practiced cannibalism? (Doublehead)*

Review Questions

1. Who was Doublehead's father? (Great Eagle)
2. What year was Sequoyah's alphabet completed? (1821)
3. Where is Doublehead supposedly buried? (Butler Cemetery-Lauderdale County)
4. Who was one of the early Irishmen that came into Lawrence County during the 1780s with the Cherokee Indians? (John Melton)
5. What were the names of Doublehead's two daughters and also George Colbert's wives? (Tuskiahooto and Saleechie)

LESSON 18 – LOCAL INDIAN LEADERS

SIXTH GRADE

SAT Reading Objective: LITERARY ELEMENTS

Objective: After the teacher directs this lesson, sixth grade Indian students will be able to construct and interpret meaning and appreciate literary elements in the lesson about local Indian leaders.

Objective Activity: The students will answer the review questions to show their understanding of the lesson's main idea and their recognition of other text elements.

STATE STANDARDS Reading Objective:

PG. 52 #1   Interpret and construct meaning by applying appropriate strategies to material across the curriculum
- After the teacher directs the lesson, the students will utilize the reading content standards of literary and informational comprehension and recognition of literary elements in functional materials by answering questions related to the text and identifying the main idea, setting, plot, characters, etc. from the lesson on various local Indian leaders.
    - *Who was Talohuskee's half brother that created the Cherokee alphabet? (Sequoyah)*
    - *Why did Sequoyah invent the alphabet? (so the Cherokee people could read and write)*
    - *How long did it take him? (12 years)*

STATE STANDARDS Social Studies Objective:

PG. 54 #1   Extend the development of map and globe skills
- Use Lawrence County map and/or the Indian Trails and Towns map to show students where the different Indian leaders lived or where their people were located. (Ex: Doublehead's Village, Cuttyatoy's Village, etc.)
    - *Where was Doublehead's Village located? (Brown's Ferry)*

Review Questions

1. Who was the half brother to Sequoyah who signed the 1806 Cotton Gin Treaty? (Talohuskee)
2. Who was Melton's Bluff named after? (John Melton)
3. Who was Doublehead's nephew who accompanied him on many raids? ("Bench" Robert Benge)
4. What year was the Cotton Gin Treaty signed? (1806)
5. Who was a well known friend of the whites? (Old Tassel)

LESSON 18 – LOCAL INDIAN LEADERS

SEVENTH GRADE

SAT Reading Objective: LITERARY GENRES

Objective: After the teacher directs this lesson, seventh grade Indian students will be able to identify the geographic and culturally diverse terms used in literary genres.

Objective Activity: The teacher will select vocabulary terms to review with the students. Ask them to identify the meaning of the terms in their own words. Terms: cannibalism, delegation, dialogue, accosted, crusade.

STATE STANDARDS Reading Objective:

PG. 53 #12   Develop general listening behaviors for different purposes and situations
- After the teacher directs the lesson, the students will identify the local Indian leaders and where they lived and retell the important details of each in their own words.
- *How many years did it take Sequoyah to finish the Cherokee alphabet? (12)*

STATE STANDARDS Social Studies Objective:

Online Alex #9   Identify individual and civic responsibilities of citizens
- Discuss the responsibilities of each individual leader of the various individual tribes. Have the students answer questions concerning the text to check for understanding.
- *Name the three men that killed Doublehead. (Ridge, Saunders, Rogers)*

Review Questions

1. What were the two towns in this area where Doublehead lived? (Brown's Ferry and Shoal Town)
2. What year did Doublehead establish his first town on the Tennessee River? (1790)
3. The Shoal Town site was in the disputed reserve that was called what? (Chickasaw Hunting Grounds)
4. What degree of Indian blood was Sequoyah? (1/4)
5. In 1806, what treaty was signed that gave up Cherokee claims to land north of the Tennessee River except for Doublehead's Reserve? (Cotton Gin Treaty)

LESSON 19 –INDIAN BATTLES

Creek Indian War - The Creek Indian War in Alabama became a part of the American-English War of 1812. The citizens of the still young United States were hemmed in on the Atlantic coast from New England all the way to Georgia. The English and other native Indian people claimed much of the land that the Americans wanted for westward expansion.

In the north, the Americans and the English fought vicious land and sea battles. In Alabama, the soil and the rivers were stained with American and Indian blood. Even though all of the Indian land in Alabama was in danger of being lost, only the hostile Creeks chose to go to war. The war party thought the English were strong enough to help them win the conflict with the Americans.

The first skirmish of the Creek Indian War was at Burnt Corn Creek. The Red Stick Creeks won. Next, was Ft. Mims, also an Indian victory under the leadership of Red Eagle, William Weatherford. After the battle at Ft. Mims, the Americans realized that more settlers in the Indian Territory and on the borders would be in danger if they did not have protection.

Andrew Jackson - The Governor of Tennessee assembled an army of volunteers led by Andrew Jackson, and sent them to Alabama to begin a war of extermination of Creek people – men, women, and children (genocide). The Cherokees, newly trying to develop friendly relationships with the white man and long in conflict with the Creek Indians, began to discuss joining forces with Andrew Jackson. Later, on November 22, 1816, Andrew Jackson became the first white landowner in Lawrence County, Alabama. He established the Town of Marathon in Lawrence County at Melton's Bluff on the Tennessee, between Spring Creek and Mallard Creek.

Chief Junaluska had convinced the Cherokee to remain neutral and not join with Tecumseh's Creek forces. Now, with the challenge from the Tennessee Legislature along with payment for support of their causes, it was hard for the Cherokee to remain neutral. Junaluska recruited some 800 Cherokee warriors to go to the aid of Andrew Jackson in an advance down the Coosa River. Upon their arrival with Andrew Jackson, Junaluska was made captain of the Cherokee men.

The decisive battle of the Creek and Indian War was fought on March 26, 1814. It took place near the Creek village on Horseshoe Bend of the Tallapoosa River, near present-day Alexander City.

Albert James Pickett describes the setting of the battle thusly, "At six o'clock in the morning to the battle, General Coffee with his 700 mounted men and 600 friendly Indians; was detached from the main army and ordered to cross the river three miles below and occupy positions on the south side and along the top of the Horseshoe to prevent the escape of the enemy in the direction where Jackson's main army should attack the breastworks across the heel of the Horseshoe. The Cherokee Indians were assigned positions along the margin of the river while the 700 mounted men were held in reserve on higher ground further back. The enemy Creeks had many canoes tied along the opposite bank across from the Indians' position, to be used for escape in case of emergency. The stage is set for the remarkable action reputed to have been conceived and carried into execution by Junaluska and his comrades. As General Jackson's main army opened fire on the breastworks, the roar of the cannon and rattle of the musketry so aroused the Creeks that they could not be retained inactive on the riverbank. Junaluska become so animated that all fear of danger and death was destroyed in him and he craved to be at the center of action; that after obtaining permission from his superior officer (Colonel Morgan) he, with one assistant, swam the river, cut loose some of the canoes, tied them together and carried them to the other side. They were at once filled with Cherokees. Other boats were brought over, and the entire Cherokee force, together with some of the white troops, ferried over. His surprise attack in their rear (of the Red Sticks under command of Chief Menawa) so divided the attention and efforts of the enemy that the main army under Jackson was enabled to take the breast works by storm and led to a completely victorious outcome of the engagement.

This section came from the book History of Alabama, Vol. II.: A short time after the Battle of the Horseshoe, Jackson had built a fort at the site of old Fort Toulouse and named it Fort Jackson. Now, many of the "Red Sticks" began to come in and surrender to General Jackson.

After the Creek Indian War was over in 1814, the Creek land in Lawrence County and areas to the south was declared public land. Land-hungry whites rushed in to claim the Creek land. During the war between the Creek Indians and the white settlers, two major battles that may be familiar to you: The Battle of Fort Mims and the Battle of Horseshoe Bend. The fight at Horseshoe Bend was the final battle for the Creeks. The 1,000 mighty Creek warriors could not win against General Jackson and his 3,300 soldiers. After the Battle of Horseshoe Bend, most of the Creek land was taken from them. In 1835 and 1836, with some of their chiefs in

LESSON 19 – INDIAN BATTLES

Map of the Battle of Horseshoe Bend

LESSON 19 – INDIAN BATTLES

chains, some 14,000 Creeks were forced to move to Oklahoma. Two groups of Creeks came through Lawrence County during removal.

Lawrence County has several things in common with Creek people: (1) Creek land in Lawrence County lay from the High Town Path to the south. (2) Moulton is named after Lt. Michael Moulton who was killed during the Battle of Horseshoe Bend. (3) Andrew Jackson who defeated the Creeks became the first white landowner in Lawrence County, Alabama. (4) The High Town Path, the Creek Nation's northern border, ran across southern Lawrence County. (5) A major Creek trading path, Black Warriors' Path, ran across eastern Lawrence County from Piney Grove, through Oakville, and then to Melton's Bluff on the Tennessee River.

During Indian removal two large groups of Creek people were moved through Lawrence County. On December 19, 1835, 511 Creeks came through Lawrence County and were in Moulton on December 19, 1835. Again, in September 1836, 2000 Creeks with all their belongings were marched through our county to Tuscumbia landing. From Tuscumbia, many were moved west by boat and others marched over land driving their livestock.

Battle of Indian Tomb Hollow - The following is a shortened version of the "Battle of Indian Tomb Hollow" which occurred in Lawrence County. The story was published in The Moulton Democrat on November 7, 14, and 21, 1856, some twenty years before Custer's "Battle of Little Big Horn" in 1876. According to the story, the battle occurred in 1776, some 100 years before the "Battle of Little Big Horn."

The author says the story was told to him by one long connected to the Chickasaw Tribe. The final fight is thought to have occurred in the upper portion of the southwest fork of Indian Tomb Hollow within sight and sound of the waterfalls. Now, begins a shortened version of the "Battle of Indian Tomb Hollow."

But never having met with a history of the following scenes and trials of the Chickasaws, in their warfare with their neighbors the Creeks, and having often visited the spots where the following scenes were enacted, and heard the incidents related by one long connected with the tribe, I have been induced to give them publicity.

It was a beautiful day in that loveliest of months, October, the deep old forest had begun to present the first indications of the approaching change of the seasons. The bright scarlet hue of the sumac, the golden leaf of the sassafras, the poplar's dull yellow contrasted beautifully, and blended agreeably with the many tints of green of the old wood. This hill is the last of a series of undulations, that gives to the old wood to the east a wavy appearance, whilst to our left, or farthest west, it becomes level and of a low swampy character, made so by the springs, four in number, that gush forth from the base of these hills, and empty their bright waters into the small creek bounding the western border of this flat.

Early, on a bright October morning, eighty years ago (1776), our story opens. The sun had scarce marked a hand's breadth on the horizon, as two Chickasaw warriors approached the largest of the four springs we have spoken of, and leaning their rifles against the black walnut trees, from amidst whose roots the bright waters flowed, drank from the gushing fount ere proceeding to make their frugal morning meal; their simple repast consisting of a handful of parched Indian corn, and a small piece of dried venison; being finished they sat for some time in perfect silence, when the elder of the two warriors arising and taking his rifle said, "The leaf of the sumac is red, and ere its fall, Ittaloknah, the pride of our tribe, must be again in the wigwam of her father.

Then, let us fly with the speed of the deer, for when yonder's rising sun shall have set and rose again, the warriors of the Chickasaws will await us in council."

The Chickasaw, a powerful and brave nation, in the time of which we write, inhabited all of the northern part of the State of Mississippi, reaching from west of the Mississippi River to the meandering creek in Franklin County, Alabama, known as Caney Creek. Such were the boundaries of the nation, yet claiming farther east than this.

Some three days previous to the opening of our story, at the close of a warm sultry day, with the prospect of a stormy night ahead, there sat at the door of a wigwam, situated near the eastern boundary of the Chickasaw Nation, a warrior of this tribe engaged in assisting an Indian youth in fashioning his bow. The youth seemingly some fifteen years of age, stood eagerly watching his aged companion, and ever and anon addressing some question to him. The warrior was a perfect type of his race. Remarkably tall and

LESSON 19 – INDIAN BATTLES

of perfect form for strength and endurance; he was now passed the meridian of life, and marked with the scars of many and various hard fought battles; yet that eagle eye and those sinewy limbs, spoke forth that age had not yet quenched the fire of his youth, nor destroyed the power that made him ever a brave of renown, and a chief of importance with his tribe. Such was Eagle Eye.

As the sun went down behind a dark and heavy mass of clouds, and the first burst of heaven's artillery was heard in the west, and aged squaw (White Lily) appeared at the door of the wigwam and spoke to the warrior, who now left his work, and began to gaze intently towards the east, as if eagerly watching for someone. The squaw, like the warrior, had passed the meridian of life, yet the remnants of great beauty were plainly to be seen in her features; and a close observer, tho' dressed as an Indian, and an Indian in every action and movement, tell that the blood of the white man coursed through her veins. When an infant, captured by a party of Chickasaws from a company of French emigrants ascending the Mississippi, she alone escaped death. Taken to the Chickasaw village at Pontotoc, she was placed under the charge of an aged squaw, and being but two years of age, and reared as an Indian child, she soon forgot her parents, and grew in feelings and acts, as well as looks, a perfect Indian. She had, when about twenty years of age, blessed the wigwam of the Eagle Eye as his bride. They were the parents of but one child - a daughter - whom they called Ittaloknah or Magnolia. She, like the beautiful tree of her native mountains, possessed that grace and perfection of form and fairness of skin that made her sobriquet perfectly appropriate.

"It is Ponioc," said the warrior, as an Indian youth, apparently some twelve years of age, emerged from the brush, and came running towards the group with a countenance bespeaking alarm.

"What makes Ponioc seem as the fleeing fawn, when the panther follows fast on his trail?" said the old warrior to the breathless boy, who had now reached them and stood exhausted by his fright and rapid gait.

"The Creek warrior bears away the light of our wigwam and Ponioc mourns for her he loves," spoke the youth in broken accents.

"What! My child! My Magnolia!" cried the alarmed mother seizing the boy by the arm.

"Yes, Ittaloknah is a captive. I met Kokomah, who bleeding from his wounds, told me to haste to the wigwam of the Eagle Eye and tell the tiding while he returned to the trail.

The nine Chickasaw warriors pursued the Creeks on a Southeastward course for some time, when they separated into parties of two, one however having been detailed to go back to the tribe and inform the council should the eight not return in time to meet them at Tulumah or the four springs, agreeing among themselves to search that day, and if no signs were seen, all to return to the council save two who were to keep up the search until the war party from the council should reach Tulumah, and then report their success, and accompany the party in the invasion of the Creek Nation.

Let us again go back to the time of Ittaloknah's leaving her parents wigwam. Taking Kokomah, she went in the direction of the creek, east of the wigwam, for the purpose of fishing. Having a description of the maiden sufficient for our purpose, let us describe her companion - Kokomah, or Wild cat, as he was called by his tribe, was about thirty years of age, not exceeding four feet in height, with a breadth of chest and length of arm indeed remarkable.

Like most dwarfs, his features bore the appearance of greater age than really belonged to him. With all the cunning instincts of his race, he had even apparently the instincts of the animal combined with it. Taken by Eagle Eye and by him reared, and treated with contempt by all save the inmates of this wigwam and the Panther, he seemed to hate all save these few, and for them his affections knew no bounds.

Ponioc, who was near by, hearing the cry of Magnolia, was making to her, when he was met by Kokomah, who, having revived, was hastening to the wigwam to give the alarm, but sending Ponioc, he returned, and crossing the stream he was soon on the trail of his assaulters. Coming in sight of them he found that three more warriors had been added to their number.

Pursing their course still southeast, they did not stop with the fall of night, but continued on their way, until the long uninterrupted march overcame with fatigue, Magnolia; and they were reluctantly forced to stop. It was near midnight when they halted at the place chosen for their rest within a small gorge or hollow of the mountain, where firmly securing their prisoners, the two warriors

LESSON 19 – INDIAN BATTLES

made preparations for their night watch.

With the same serpent like motion, Kokomah approached the captives, and with his knife severed the bonds that bound the Panther's hands. The Panther, severing the bands that held his feet confined, rushed into the combat; calling to Wild Cat to ascertain his position, and finding him beneath, with his arms pinioned around the Creek warrior, who was striving manfully to relieve an arm, but in vain, the knife of the Panther soon put an end to the combat. Relieving Magnolia, upon consultation they determined to remain in their present position until day. The two Chickasaws now took their post of watch, while the Indian maiden slept.

With the first rays of light the Chickasaws were on their way back to their nation; and with what difference in feeling, from those experienced on the previous night, as they passed over the same trail they were now retracing! Leaving the mountains, they now entered the beautiful valley of land running across the now County of Lawrence in Alabama. When the sun was some two or three hours above the horizon, they met, near Tulamah a party of Chickasaws under the lead of Eagle Eye, who were fast following the trail made by the Creeks and their prisoners the night previous.

The meeting was indeed a joyous one; and as neither party had as yet made their morning meal, they were in the act of going to a small spring nearby, when with the whoop of a set of fiends, a party of Creeks fired upon them from the surrounding trees and brush.

A party of Creeks, some sixty in number, being out in search of the six warriors, who we have seen slain, and finding the bodies of Topeka and his companion, had followed the trail of the returning Chickasaws, and had succeeded in making a near approach to the party, unperceived; so much were they engaged with the returned captives. Darting to some cover the Chickasaws, began to battle for life. With the first fire, several of their number having fallen, and the assailing party being more numerous, the odds were greatly against them. Three of the Creek warriors seeing Magnolia, and knowing her to be the cause of the loss of their braves, determined upon her recapture. Gradually advancing to her rear, which reaching, they rushed upon her, one seizing her in his arms, bore her shrieking for aid, farther into that part of the woods occupied by his party; her cry caused her friends to rush to her rescue and in so doing, exposed themselves to the fire of their enemy. This so much weakened their force, that they were compelled to retire, leaving Magnolia again a captive in the hands of their foemen. Returning, towards evening, from the pursuit, they buried their few slain, and scalped their slain enemies, proceeded with their captive homeward. The retiring Chickasaws, collecting their forces found that they had lost twenty of their number.

The place which the Creeks had chosen for their halting place was a large natural amphitheater. Entering it from the north, the sides rose quite abruptly, and gradually enlarging from the mouth, where it was about fifty paces in width for some distance, when having reached the width of two hundred paces, it gradually closed again, and ended in a perpendicular ledge of rock some forty feet in height, over which passed a stream of limpid water. Some six or eight feet from the base of this ledge of rock, on one side it shelved off into a cave of considerable length but shallow. The Chickasaw warriors now approached the point around which the Creeks had passed and disposing their forces so as to open deadly fire upon the unsuspecting Creeks. This was soon done, and pouring a well-aimed fire of rifle ball and arrows upon them with a whoop rushed upon their astonished enemies.

The fight was fast drawing to a close; there now remained only ten Creek warriors to combat, not now for victory, or even life, but to die with as many slain around them as possible; those few were fast falling beneath the Chickasaw knives, for this now was the only instrument of death used by either party.

Magnolia upon the onset of the battle was led into the cave at the head of the gorge, where, unconfined, she was a witness of the terrible conflict. She saw the onslaught of the Creeks upon her father, and also saw him fall; but as the combat thickened around him; she was unable to tell whether he had arisen, and was yet leading the now victorious Chickasaws, or lay a corpse amidst the heap of slain, she saw around the spot where he had fallen. The battle fast receding down the gorge, she determined to allay her anxiety by going to the spot where she had seen her father fall; reaching which, she beheld his lifeless body, with his life blood clotting the grass at their feet with a wild shriek she cast herself upon the inanimate clay.

A Creek warrior, stunned by a blow from her father's rifle, recovering from it and hearing the battle passing away, was arising from the ground to make good his escape, and hearing the cry of the maiden, and seeing who it was, determined, with a fiendish purpose, to be yet avenged for the loss of his companions.

LESSON 19 – INDIAN BATTLES

With the bound of the deer, the Panther sped to her relief. The Creek encumbered by his burden, saw he must fall a prey to his rapidly advancing foe; with a fiendish yell, he raised his knife high above his head; and buried it to the hilt in the bosom of the Indian Maiden; and with wild quivering limbs she sank from the embrace of her murderer. The Panther saw the hellish deed, and it lent speed to his already rapid steps; and ere he reached the summit of the hill, the death of Magnolia was revenged by the knife of her lover.

Returning to Magnolia, who yet lived, but was fast sinking into death, he heard from her why she screamed, and the attack of her murderer. "Bury me with my father, down in the gorge there, where my lovely namesake will bloom in springtime o'er my grave, and where the spirit of Magnolia may wander in the bright light of the summer morn;" sighed the dying maiden."

The white man ere long began to be seen in the country and the red man was fast failing before him. In autumn's sad time of each year, for a long while, an Indian might be seen wending his way to "Indian Tomb Hollow," - Grief had marked his sad features and wan countenance. With the taciturnity of his race, he bore them without a murmur, and when at length he felt his days numbered, he wended his way to the spot of all others most dear to him, and there upon the grave of her he loved so well in life, he breathed his last. The "pale face" now soon occupied the land far and wide - not satisfied with his treatment to the red man during life - his bones were not sacred in death. The grave of Eagle Eye and Magnolia was torn open, and the bones were left to molder in the winds of winter and the dews of summer.

Read, before students arrive, "Ittaloknah" (The Battle of Indian Tomb Hollow). Condense as you like, tell students story or use play to tell story.

Cherokee War - In 1763, the war, known as the French and Indian War, between the French and British ended with the British victorious in controlling most of the eastern North America. In addition to ending the war, a Proclamation Line of 1763 was established to protect the Indians west of the Appalachians and to halt encroachment on their lands. The Proclamation Line did not prevent settlers from invading Indian lands west of the line.

Eventually, the Cherokee were forced into making land cessions west of the Appalachians. In 1768, 1770, 1772, and 1773, treaties were made between the government and the Cherokee Indians. The Cherokee were pressured to give up land claims in South Carolina, Georgia, Virginia, West Virginia, Kentucky, and Tennessee. The Treaty of Sycamore Shoals, in 1775, took Cherokee lands through the middle of Kentucky and Tennessee.

Dragging Canoe

Now, with the door to settlement opened, settlers poured into the area north of the Little Tennessee River to the heart of the once powerful Cherokee Nation. As the settlers moved in from the north and east, the Cherokees began moving south and west. By the 1750s, Cherokees were occupying eastern Alabama. By 1770, the Cherokees were firmly established in the area of the Warrior Mountains to the Muscle Shoals.

The Cherokee decline and loss of lands continued after the Revolutionary War partly because of their alliance with the British. The Middle, Valley, and Overhill Towns of the Cherokee were practically destroyed by military movements lead against the Cherokees by men such as Colonel William Christian and Colonel John Sevier. Eventually in 1780, the armies of John Sevier and Arthur Campbell destroyed the Overhill Towns including the Cherokee Capital of Chota. By this time, a thriving population of Cherokees was occupying the lower Tennessee Valley.

Many of the Cherokee moved south under the leadership of Dragging Canoe, son of Oconostota. The Cherokees under Dragging Canoe settled from Chattanooga to the south and west in five villages referred to as the "Five Lower Towns on the Tennessee"— Running Water, Nickajack, Long Island Village, Crow Town, and Lookout Mountain Town.

LESSON 19 – INDIAN BATTLES

Cherokee Chief Doublehead migrated farther southwest along the Tennessee River into North Alabama. Historical evidence indicates Doublehead settled for some 12 years at the head of Elk River Shoals at Doublehead's Village on the south bank of the Tennessee River at Brown's Ferry. Doublehead helped establish the following villages along the Tennessee River in Lawrence County: Moneetown at Fox's Creek, Doublehead's Village at Brown's Ferry, between Fox and Mallard Creeks; Melton's Bluff between Mallard and Spring Creek; Cuttyatoy's Village on an island in the mouth of Spring Creek. Gourd's Settlement; Courtland on Big Nance Creek; Shoal Town at the Blue Water/Town Creek Village just one mile west of present-day Wheeler Dam; and, Oakville at the junction of Black Warriors' Path and the Coosa Path.

In east Tennessee, by the 1780s, the Cherokee were a defeated people trying to survive in a country controlled by a newly established government of the United States. Devastated by war, disease, and land hungry American settlers, their days east of the Mississippi River were numbered.

By the beginning of the 1800s, the once flourishing towns along the Little Tennessee River were practically abandoned by the Cherokee people. By 1817, even the lands along the Great Mussel Shoals were taken by the Turkey Town Treaty. Then, in 1830, the Indian Removal Act spelled doom for many Cherokee. Two years after the Treaty of New Echota in 1836, the Army of Winfield Scott attempted to remove all the Cherokee remaining east of the Mississippi. The remnants of the Cherokee and mixed bloods that remained in the east were a scattered and defeated people living in a state of denial of their aboriginal beginnings, but in their hearts, holding to their beliefs and staying in the land they loved-- "Warrior Mountains."

LESSON 19 – INDIAN BATTLES

KINDERGARTEN

DIBELS Reading Objective: COMPREHENSION

Objective: After the teacher directs this lesson, Kindergarten Indian students will gain knowledge on the material taught about Indian battles.

Objective Activity: The students will develop an understanding of initial sounds while using alphabet flashcards, pictures, objects, or the board. Then, the students will pronounce the initial letter of various terms found in this lesson.

STATE STANDARDS Reading Objective:

PG. 14 #9   Begin to use pictures and text to gain meaning from written material
- Show pictures of Indian Tomb Hollow while explaining the battle to the students in order to help them connect the battle to the actual place it occurred.
  - *Which tribe of Indians won the battle? (Chickasaws)*

PG. 15 #13   Gain an awareness of others through exposure to written spoken and visual forms of communication
- The teacher will help the students gain an understanding of why the Battle of Indian Tomb Hollow occurred in Lawrence County over 200 years ago, which was with the Chickasaws and Creeks.
- Began Oct 1776
- Chickasaw Chief Eagle Eye
- His wife, White Lily
- His daughter, Magnolia (Ittaloknah)
- Creeks took Eagle Eye's daughter Magnolia
- Creeks and Chickasaw fight
- Eagle Eye was killed and Magnolia was stabbed by Creek warrior in chest
- Buried at Indian Tomb Hollow
  - *Name the two tribes that fought in the Battle of Indian Tomb Hollow. (Chickasaw and Creek)*

STATE STANDARDS Social Studies Objective:

PG. 11 #1   Develop initial map and globe skills
- Show students Lawrence County on the map.
- Show map of Indian Tomb Hollow in "Indian Trails of Warrior Mountains."
  - *In what county did this battle occur? (Lawrence County)*

PG. 12 #11   Discover characters and events from literature that demonstrate the impact of one person's behavior upon another
- Explain how the actions of the Creeks caused problems for the Chickasaws and resulted in a horrible battle with the two tribes which took the lives of many warriors, Eagle Eye's, and Magnolia's.
  - *How did Magnolia die? (knife wound in the chest)*

Review Questions

1. What county do you live in? (Lawrence)
2. Where was the first skirmish battle of the Creek Indian War? (Burnt Corn Creek)
3. When was the Creek Indian War fought? (1813 and 1814)
4. When was the Creek War over? (1814)
5. Who fought in the French and Indian War? (French and British)

LESSON 19 – INDIAN BATTLES

FIRST GRADE

DIBELS Reading Objective: NONSENSE WORD FLUENCY

Objective: After the teacher directs this lesson, first grade Indian students will develop an awareness of the Indian battles the various tribes fought using nonsense word fluency.

Objective Activity: The teacher will write terms on the board from the lesson and the students will pronounce each sound and letter of the word. Next, the teacher will change the initial letter making a nonsense word. Then, the students will pronounce the word. (Ex: Man-Gan, etc.)

STATE STANDARDS Reading Objective:

PG. 20 #6   Comprehend material read, heard, or viewed
- After discussing the Creek Indian War, the students will use comprehension skills to answer teacher generated questions such as… What was the tribe that fought in the war?
  - *What state was the Creek Indian War fought? (Alabama)*

STATE STANDARDS Social Studies Objective:

PG. 18 #3   Extend initial ability to locate new information and to express understanding in various classroom
- Locate Alabama on a state map to show students where the Creek Indian War took place.
- Locate Fort Mims in the book to show battle site in Creek Indian War.
- Also locate Horseshoe Bend and Lawrence County.
- Show on a map, the direction "west" because the war sent the Creeks west with the Indian Removal.
  - *The battle of <u>Horseshoe</u> Bend was the last battle or fight for the Creeks in what state? (Alabama)*

PG. 19 #13   Exhibit an awareness of the ways personal actions benefit or harm the local environment
- When discussing Andrew Jackson, make sure the students are aware of the harmful and cruel things that led to the removal of the Creek Indians.
  - *Who was the General that the Creeks lost to in the Battle of Horseshoe Bend? (Andrew Jackson)*

Review Questions
1. What is another name for the Indian maiden, Magnolia, in the Battle of Indian Tomb Hollow? (Ittaloknah)
2. Where was the first skirmish of the Creek Indian War? (Burnt Corn Creek)
3. Who is Moulton named after? (Lt. Michael Moulton)
4. How did Magnolia die? (knife in chest)
5. Marathon is located on what river? (Tennessee)

LESSON 19 – INDIAN BATTLES

SECOND GRADE

DIBELS Reading Objective: VOCABULARY

Objective: After the teacher directs this lesson, second grade Indian students will utilize the reading content standards of vocabulary. Terms: vicious, extermination, assembled, neutral, disposing, aboriginal

Objective Activity: The students will play a remedial game consisting of matching the vocabulary term to the correct definition.

STATE STANDARDS Reading Objective:

PG. 26 #14   Exhibit expanded vocabulary and sentence awareness
- While the teacher directs the lesson he/she will allow students to participate in reading the lesson to be sure they understand and expand their vocabulary. Once the lesson is completed, the teacher can write words on board to make sure the students recognize them.
  - *Who won the first battle of the Creek Indian War? (Creeks)*
  - *Was General Andrew Jackson for or against the Creeks? (against)*

STATE STANDARDS Social Studies Objective:

PG. 25 #26   Describe the contributions of significant individuals who have affected our lives
- After teaching the lesson, have the class orally discuss the contributions of Andrew Jackson to Lawrence County.
  - *What was the name of the town Andrew Jackson founded? (Marathon)*

Review Questions

1. Who was the Indian maiden who was killed at the Battle of Indian Tomb Hollow? (Magnolia)
2. Where was the first and last skirmish of the Creek Indian War? (Burnt Corn Creek and Horseshoe Bend)
3. Marathon is located on what river and was founded by whom? (Tennessee, Andrew Jackson)
4. Who was killed by a knife wound to the chest? (Magnolia)
5. Who was called Ittaloknah in the Battle of Indian Tomb Hollow? (Magnolia)

LESSON 19 – INDIAN BATTLES

THIRD GRADE

DIBELS Reading Objective: WORD RECOGNITION

Objective: After the teacher directs this lesson, third grade Indian students will identify key terms found throughout the lesson.

Objective Activity: The teacher will write various sentences on the board with blanks that individual students will fill in with the correct term. (Allow the students to have a word bank)

STATE STANDARDS Reading Objective:

PG. 32 #3   Demonstrate literal understanding of print material
- The teacher will draw a timeline to show the dates of the different Indian battles. As each battle is presented, the teacher can present the high points of each battle such as: who was involved, who was victorious, dates and location, etc.
- *Where was the first battle of the Creek Indian War? (Burnt Corn Creek)*

STATE STANDARDS Social Studies Objective:

PG. 29 #1   Extend development of map and globe skills
- The teacher will locate the sites of the different battles on an Alabama state map.
- The students will use a blank state map to label the various locations of the Indian battles.
- *Where was the town of Marathon located? (Melton's Bluff)*

Review Questions

1. The French and Indian War was also known as: (Cherokee War)
2. What was Magnolia's Indian name? (Ittaloknah)
3. Was General Jackson for or against the Creeks? (against)
4. Who won the first and last battles of the Creek Indian War? (Creeks, Andrew Jackson with help from the Cherokees)
5. Who founded the town of Marathon? (Andrew Jackson)

LESSON 19 – INDIAN BATTLES

FOURTH GRADE

SAT Reading Objective: LITERARY ELEMENTS

Objective: After the teacher directs this lesson, fourth grade Indian students will identify the elements: characters, setting, main idea, etc.

Objective Activity: After reading selected paragraphs, the students will identify several literary elements from lesson to show their understanding of the lesson's main idea, plot, theme, etc. (Ex: Who fought in the battle? Where did it occur? Why did the battle take place?)

STATE STANDARDS Reading Objective:

PG. 39 #11 Read materials encountered in daily lives
- After the teacher directs the lesson, the students will read about the different battles in "Indian Trails of the Warrior Mountains" and then the class will have an open discussion on the setting, characters, main idea, etc.
  - During what month or season did this battle begin? (October/fall)
  - Who was the leader of the Creeks during the Battle of Fort Mims? (Red Eagle or William Weatherford)

STATE STANDARDS Social Studies Objective:

PG. 34 #2 Interpret and display information and data using various graphic organizers
- As the teacher directs the lesson, he/she will draw a timeline on the board of the Indian battles and show the students where the battles took place and when they happened.
  - What year did the French and Indian War (The Cherokee War) end? (1763)

Review Questions

1. What was the first skirmish of the Creek-Indian War? (Burnt Corn Creek)
2. The French and Indian War was also known as: (Cherokee War)
3. Where was the town of Marathon located? (Melton's Bluff)
4. Who won the first battle and the second battle of the Creek Indian War? (Creeks)
5. Magnolia was what type of Indian? (Chickasaw)

LESSON 19 –INDIAN BATTLES

FIFTH GRADE

SAT Reading Objective: LITERARY ELEMENTS

Objective: After the teacher directs this lesson, fifth grade Indian students will utilize the following reading content standard of literary elements to discuss Indian battles.

Objective Activity: Create a story using the information from the lesson. Ask the students to identify where the battles took place, why they occurred, who fought in the battles, and who won, etc.

STATE STANDARDS Reading Objective:

PG. 45 #7   Use literary analysis
- ∾ Name one battle we discussed. (The Creek Indian War)

PG. 46 #13   Apply strategies of a skillful listener
- After the teacher directs the lesson, the students will read aloud about Indian battles in the "Warrior Mountain Folklore" or "Indian Trails of the Warrior Mountains." When the students are finished, they will orally discuss what they read.
  - ∾ Who was the General of the Army that defeated the Creeks in the Creek and Indian War? (Andrew Jackson)

STATE STANDARDS Social Studies Objective:

PG. 47 #7   Analyze the different cultures of Native American groups by geographic regions
- The students will discuss the conflicts that were taught to them in the lesson and what brought the conflicts on.
  - ∾ Who fought against each other in the French and Indian War? (French and British)
  - ∾ Why did this battle occur? (for control of eastern North America)

Review Questions

1. What were the two tribes fighting each other in the Battle of Indian Tomb Hollow? (Chickasaw and Creek)
2. When did the Cherokee war end? (1763)
3. Where did the final battle of the Creek-Indian War take place? (Near Creek village on Horseshoe Bend of the Tallapoosa River near present-day Alexander City)
4. When was the Battle of Horseshoe Bend in the Creek Indian War fought? (March 26, 1814)
5. Where was the first skirmish of the Creek Indian War and won by whom? (Burnt Corn Creek, Creeks)

LESSON 19 – INDIAN BATTLES

SIXTH GRADE

SAT Reading Objective: PHONETIC PRINCIPLES

Objective: After the teacher directs this lesson, sixth grade Indian students will be able to recognize, understand, and apply various terms discussed in the lesson about the different Indian battles.

Objective Activity: The teacher will allow the students to look up any challenging terms in the dictionary and tell the class the definition of the term and how it should be pronounced.

STATE STANDARDS Reading Objective:

PG. 52 #4   Demonstrate reading improvement gained through substantial amounts of daily reading
- After the teacher directs the lesson the students will have an open discussion about what they learned in class and the teacher will ask them questions that they will answer appropriately.
  - *Where was the first skirmish of the Creek and Indian War? (Burnt Corn Creek)*

STATE STANDARDS Social Studies Objective:

PG. 54 #1   Extend the development of map and globe skills
- As the teacher directs the lesson she/he will show the students an Alabama map and show the students where all the battles took place.
  - *Who won the battle at Burnt Corn Creek? (Red Stick Creeks)*

Review Questions
1. When was the Cherokee war? (1763)
2. What Chickasaw maiden was killed by a knife would to the chest? (Magnolia)
3. Who founded the town of Marathon and what river was it located near? (Andrew Jackson, Tennessee River)
4. Where did the final battle of the Creek and Indian War take place? (near Creek village on Horseshoe Bend of the Tallapoosa River near present-day Alexander City)
5. When was the Battle of Horseshoe Bend of the Creek-Indian War? (March 26, 1814)

LESSON 19 – INDIAN BATTLES

SEVENTH GRADE

SAT Reading Objective: VOCABULARY

Objective: After the teacher directs this lesson, seventh grade Indian students will recognize and have an understanding of various vocabulary terms used throughout the lesson. (Terms: sobriquet, meandering, seizing, reluctantly, amphitheater, encroachment, aboriginal)

Objective Activity: The class will play a remedial game such as *Jeopardy* using the vocabulary terms and review questions from the lesson.

STATE STANDARDS Reading Objective:

PG. 58 #11   Refine general listening behaviors
- After the teacher directs this lesson, the students will utilize the following reading content standards.
  - *Where did the first skirmish of the Creek-Indian War take place? (Burnt Corn Creek)*

STATE STANDARDS Social Studies Objective:

Online Alex #11   Describe examples of conflict in societies
- Students will read the text about the different Indian battles and discuss the importance of the battle to each individual location.
  - *What year did the French and Indian War end? (1763)*

Review Questions

1. The Battle of Fort Mims was an Indian victory under the leadership of whom? (Red Eagle, William Weatherford)
2. Who fought at the Battle of Indian Tomb Hollow? (Creek and Chickasaw)
3. What year did the Indian Removal Act occur and who was responsible for it? (1830, Andrew Jackson)
4. Who was the Indian maiden who was killed at the Battle of Indian Tomb Hollow and how was she killed? (Magnolia, knife wound to the chest)
5. Which chief convinced the Cherokees not to join forces with Tecumseh's Creek and to remain neutral? (Chief Junaluska)

LESSON 20 – INDIAN TREATIES

Our Indian people utilized the Warrior Mountains for years before the coming of the white man. Shortly before the first settlers arrived in the Warrior Mountains, many treaties had taken the last remnants of the native lands.

The Cherokee people of Lawrence County and North Alabama were unfairly treated through agreements with the United States. Between 1750-1819, the United States forced or bribed the Cherokees into making twenty-five treaties which took their land. Before the end of the 1830s, the United States had taken all Cherokee lands east of the Mississippi River which consisted of over 50,000 square miles.

Treaty of Sycamore Shoals of March 17, 1775 – The Treaty of Sycamore Shoals involved the ceding of Indian lands in Kentucky and middle Tennessee. These lands were sold to the Transylvania Company.

Treaty of Hopewell of November 28, 1785 – The Treaty of Hopewell set up the boundary line between Indian people and the citizens of the United States.

Chickasaw Boundary Treaty of January 10, 1786 – The Chickasaw Boundary Treaty recognized the High Town or Ridge Path along the Continental Divide in Lawrence County as the Chickasaw's southern boundary and Creeks northern boundary. This early boundary between the Creeks and Chickasaws lay primarily along the present-day Leola Road and Ridge Road of Lawrence County's portion of the Warrior Mountains.

The backbone of North Alabama or divide was also the boundary line between the Cherokees and Creeks. The boundary line lay along the divide with Chickasaw claims extending eastward to a north-south line drawn between The Path and Hobb's Island or Chickasaw Old Fields just south of present-day Huntsville, Alabama. The north-south line lay along the Huntsville Meridian and formed the eastern boundary of the Chickasaw Nation until the Turkey Town Treaty of 1816. After the December 1801, Treaty from Ditto Landing or Hobbs Island, the Chickasaw boundary crossed present-day Madison County about 45 degrees toward the northwest to the Tennessee State Line. Prior to 1801, the Chickasaws owned the land from their eastern boundary at the mouth of Flint River to the North and South to the Tennessee Divide.

First Treaty of Tellico of October 2, 1798 - Cherokees ceded land north of Little Tennessee River forcing more Cherokee people to migrate south and west into Alabama.

The 1800s - During the early part of the 1800s some 20,000 Cherokees were living on 43,000 square miles with half of the land in Tennessee, and the rest divided equally between Alabama and Georgia.

Georgia Compact of 1802 - The United States paid Georgia $1,250,000.00 for their western lands and agreed to obtain land title from the Cherokees.

Wafford Settlement of October 25 and 27, 1805 - The Cherokees ceded in two treaties a large tract of land in central Tennessee and Kentucky with the United States paying $15,600.00 plus an annuity of $3,000.00. Article IV authorized construction of Gaines' Trace through Lawrence County, Alabama. This treaty was signed by Doublehead.

Cotton Gin Treaty of January 7, 1806 - The Cotton Gin Treaty was between the Cherokee Indians (Doublehead) and the U.S. Government. The treaty identified the tract of land that Moses Melton, the half-blood Indian son of John Melton, lived on and declared the land to be the equally shared property of Melton and Charles Hicks in equal shares. Charles Hicks was noted in Cherokee history as being the first person to show Sequoyah how to write his name in English. In addition, Doublehead and his great nephew, Tahlonteeskee (Talohuskee the Overthrower) controlled the Lawrence County area. Talohuskee was the half brother to Sequoyah.

The treaty gave up Cherokee claims to Indian land north of the Tennessee River, except for Doublehead's Reserve, and placed a cotton gin at Melton's Bluff. Doublehead was killed because of the terms of this treaty. Doublehead's Reserve lay between Elk River (Chu wa lee) and Cypress Creek (Te Kee ta no-eh) in present day Lauderdale County. The Cotton Gin Treaty with the Cherokees did not relinquish the Chickasaw claims to the area; therefore, Ft. Hampton was established to remove squatters from Chickasaw land, located primarily in the area of Limestone County known as the Simms Settlement. Fort Hampton was the only fort built in the United States to remove white settlers from Indian lands.

LESSON 20 – INDIAN TREATIES

The Cherokees ceded a large part of land north of the Tennessee River, which consisted of nearly 7,000 square miles in Tennessee and Alabama, for $10,000.00, a gristmill and cotton gin, and $100.00/year for Black Fox. The cotton gin was placed at Melton's Bluff. The cotton gin was noted by Anne Royall on January 14, 1818, at Melton's Bluff.

Supplemental Treaty to Cotton Gin Treaty of September 11, 1807 - This treaty extended and defined the cession boundaries as Elk River to the west and the Tennessee River and Tennessee Ridge to the south and north. It also gave the Cherokees hunting rights until white settlement and $2,000.00 in expenses.

Treaty of Ft. Jackson of August 9, 1814 - The majority of the new frontier in Lawrence County that now makes up Bankhead Forest was taken from the Creeks at the Treaty of Fort Jackson in 1814. The Creeks did not receive monetary compensation for their vastly large tracts of land from Bankhead Forest to the south near Montgomery, Alabama. This large tract was taken after Jackson's defeat of the Red Stick Creeks at the Battle of Horseshoe Bend. The 1814 cession of land was from the High Town Path or Continental Divide in Lawrence County and extended south for nearly 200 miles.

The Creeks ceded Lawrence County land south of the High Town Path which lies along the Leola and Ridge Roads. The first white settlement near Haleyville was made by Richard McMahon in 1815.

Boundary Treaty of March 22, 1816 - This treaty clarified the Cherokee - Creek Boundary between the Coosa and Tennessee Rivers by recognizing Cherokee land claims South of Tennessee.

Turkey Town Treaty of September 14, 1816 - The Turkey Town Treaty gave up Cherokee and Chickasaw land in the Lawrence County portion of the Warrior Mountains. Both tribes had legitimate claims to the land.

According to the terms of the Turkey Town Treaty, the last Indian lands of the Warrior Mountains were bought from the Chickasaws and Cherokees on September 16 and 18, 1816, respectively. The Chickasaws were paid $125,000.00 with the Cherokees being paid $60,000.00 for land that now makes up Colbert, Franklin, Lawrence, and Morgan Counties.

The Cherokees ceded all claims south of the Tennessee River and west from Chickasaw Island in the Tennessee to the junction of Wills Creek and Coosa River at Gadsden. The cession of 3,500 square miles included Franklin, Lawrence, and Cotaco (Morgan) Counties in North Alabama. The Cherokees received $60,000.00, including $5,000.00 for improvements.

The Chickasaws and Cherokees had overlapping land claims with the Cherokees claiming land west to Natchez Trace some 10 to 15 miles west of Caney Creek in Colbert County. The Chickasaws claimed land east to the old official Chickasaw boundary, which runs from the Chickasaw Old fields (Hobbs Island) south to the High Town Path then west along the High Town Path to Flat Rock in present-day Franklin County. From Hobbs Island, the original boundary of the Chickasaw ran north across Madison County from the mouth of Flint River and up the river to the north; however, in December 1801, the boundary traversed northwest 45° across Madison County from Chickasaw Island.

The Cherokee Chief Doublehead and the Cherokees farmed and controlled the Tennessee Valley to Natchez Trace by agreement with George Colbert. Two of Chief Doublehead's daughters married Chickasaw Chief George Colbert. It was thought that by agreement of Colbert and Doublehead, the Cherokee people were allowed to remain within the Chickasaw Territory including lands west of Caney Creek in present-day Colbert County, Alabama.

The Turkey Town Treaty signed by the Cherokees on September 16, 1816, ceded Colbert, Franklin, Lawrence, and Morgan Counties; however, the U.S. Government established the Chickasaw's new eastern boundary from Franklin County's Flat Rock to Caney Creek in Colbert County until 1832. The High Town Path was recognized as the southern boundary of the cessions for both the Chickasaw and Cherokee, until the Turkey Town Treaty of 1816. The 1816 treaty identified the new cession boundary as a straight line drawn from Flat Rock in Franklin County to Ten Islands on the Coosa River. Previous treaties recognized the Continental Divide along which ran the High Town or Ridge Path.

LESSON 20 – INDIAN TREATIES

Reserve Treaty of July 8, 1817 - The Cherokees ceded in Alabama reserves of one square mile family blocks between the Tennessee and Flint Rivers. These "reserves" were Cherokee Indians and mixed-bloods that had accepted reservations under previous treaties and were thus citizens of the United States.

Technically reserves had given up their rights as Cherokee citizens and became individual landowners and citizens of the United States.

Indian Removal Act of May 28, 1830 - Congress passed this act authorizing the exchange of lands in the west for those lands east of the Mississippi River held by Indian tribes. President Andrew Jackson was intent on seeing all Indian people removed from the eastern United States.

Treaty of New Echota of December 29, 1835 - The Treaty of New Echota was signed by a small number of Cherokees. The U.S. Congress ratified the treaty on May 23, 1836. The treaty ceded the entire Cherokee territory east of the Mississippi River.

Cherokees on the Trail of Tears – The Rise and Fall

Trail of Tears of 1838 - The Cherokee people were given two years to move at which time the forced removal known as the "Trail of Tears" began in the spring of 1838. The forced march began in October 1838 and ended in March 1839.

An estimated 4,000 Cherokees died on the forced march to the west. Many of the Cherokees from the east passed through Lawrence County during 1838 by railroad. By the time of the "Trail of Tears" in 1838, much of the land of the Warrior Mountains had already been claimed by Celtic/Cherokee mix-bloods who denied their heritage in order to remain in the "Warrior Mountains," the land they loved.

Conclusion - Many of Lawrence County's Indian people were already mixed with Celtic settlers (Irish, Scotch, and Welsh) and stayed in the hill country of the Warrior Mountains. They denied their ancestry and basically lived much of their lives in fear of being sent west. Full bloods claimed to be Black Irish or Black Dutch, thus denying their rightful Indian blood. After being fully assimilated into the general population years later, these Celtic/Cherokee mixed-blood descendants began reclaiming their Indian heritage in the land of the "Warrior Mountains."

LESSON 20 – INDIAN TREATIES

KINDERGARTEN

DIBELS Reading Objective: VOCABULARY / LETTER NAMING

Objective: After the teacher directs this lesson, Kindergarten Indian students will utilize the following reading content standards: initial sound and letter naming fluency. Verbally identify the key terms presented in the lesson.

Objective Activity: The students will develop an understanding of letter naming fluency while identifying the letters that make up the selected vocabulary terms.

STATE STANDARDS Reading Objective:

PG. 32 #17   Exhibit expanded vocabulary and sentence awareness.
- After the lesson, the teacher can write terms on the board and have students give the meaning of each term.
  - *What tribe of Indians had to leave their homes and walk the "Trail of Tears?" (Cherokee)*

STATE STANDARDS Social Studies Objective:

PG. 11 #1   Develop initial map and globe skills
- The teacher will show the students the direction the Cherokees marched on the state map (west or left of Alabama)
- Show Lawrence County on Alabama map.
- Show Oklahoma on state map.
  - *Where did the Cherokee live before they had to move? (Lawrence County)*
  - *What state did they move to? (Oklahoma)*

PG. 12 #11   Discover characters and events from literature that demonstrate the impact of one person's behavior upon another
- Explain how Andrew Jackson's actions hurt the Cherokee and the impact this had on all the Cherokees. (took home away from them, a lot died before reaching Oklahoma, had to deny who they were and lie, etc.)
  - *Name the man who made them leave. (Andrew Jackson)*

Review Questions

1. What direction did our ancestors travel during removal? (west)
2. The Cotton Gin Treaty was between which two groups? (Cherokee Indians and U.S. Government)
3. How many Cherokees died on the Trail of Tears? (estimated 4,000)
4. The backbone of North Alabama was divided by which tribes? (Cherokee and Creeks)
5. When did the "Trail of Tears" begin? (fall of 1838)

LESSON 20 – INDIAN TREATIES

FIRST GRADE

DIBELS Reading Objective: TEXT COMPREHENSION

Objective: After the teacher directs this lesson, first grade Indian students will use prior knowledge and their comprehension skills to relate and gain an understanding about the various Indian treaties.

Objective Activity: The teacher will write terms on the board from the lesson and the students will pronounce each sound and letter of the word. Next, the teacher will write sentences on the board and allow the students to fill in the blank with the correct term.

STATE STANDARDS Reading Objective:

PG. 17 #3   Exhibit phonemic awareness
- Have the students to clap out the syllables in various words from the lesson such as: cotton-2 syllables, treaty-2 syllable, Indians-3 syllables, etc.
- *Where was the Cotton Gin placed? (Melton's Bluff)*

PG. 20 #6   Comprehend material read, heard, or viewed
- During the lesson about the cotton Gin Treaty of January 7, 1806, between the Cherokee Indians and the U.S. Government, the teacher will check for understanding by asking several comprehension questions. He/she will also use pictures to help students connect with text.
- *What tribe of Indians was a part of the Cotton Gin Treaty? (Cherokee)*

STATE STANDARDS Social Studies Objective:

PG. 18 #3   Extend an initial ability to locate new information and to express understanding in various classroom
- Locate the Tennessee River which runs through Alabama and Tennessee. Locate the direction north to show the land that the Cherokee had to give up their claims to. Locate Melton's Bluff to show where the Cotton Gin was located. Locate Doublehead's Reserve, which is in Lauderdale County.
- *What river did we discuss in this lesson? (Tennessee)*

Review Questions

1. Who forced the Cherokee removal? (Andrew Jackson)
2. What year was the Cotton Gin Treaty signed? (1806)
3. Who signed the Cotton Gin Treaty? (Doublehead)
4. Full blooded Indians claimed to be: (Black Dutch/Black Irish)
5. Celtic people were what? (Irish, Scotch and Welsh)

LESSON 20 – INDIAN TREATIES

SECOND GRADE

DIBELS Reading Objective: LISTENING AND COMMUNICATING

Objective: After the teacher directs this lesson, the first grade Indian students will utilize their listening skills by identifying and orally communicating various key terms from the text. Terms: treaties, utilized, remnants, ceded, compensation.

Objective Activity: The teacher will allow students to retell the information discussed about specific treaties and give their opinion on the issue.

STATE STANDARDS Reading Objective:

PG. 25 #13   Demonstrate appropriate listening and communicating behavior
- Discuss Indian treaties with the class and explain how it relates to our ancestors.
  - *Was Franklin County affected by the Turkey Town Treaty? (yes)*

STATE STANDARDS Social Studies Objective:

PG. 22 #1   Develop map and globe skills
- After the teacher instructs the students on the Trail of Tears, the students will locate various things on the United States map such as: Mississippi River, Tennessee River, Oklahoma, etc.
- The teacher will also locate the intermediate directions (northwest, southeast, etc.) on the map.
- The children will draw a map of the path the "Trail of Tears" traveled.
- Students will locate Franklin, Lawrence, and Morgan Counties on the Alabama map to show what areas were ceded in the Turkey Town Treaty of September 14, 1816.
  - *Did the "Trail of Tears" begin in the spring or summer of 1838? (spring)*

Review Questions

1. What was the forced removal of Indians known as? (Trail of Tears)
2. How many years did they give our Cherokee ancestors to move? (two)
3. Where did the Cherokee live before they had to move? (Lawrence County)
4. The United States forced the Cherokees into making how many treaties which took their land? (25)
5. When did the Trail of Tears end? (spring of 1839)

LESSON 20 – INDIAN TREATIES

THIRD GRADE

DIBELS Reading Objective: ORAL READING FLUENCY

Objective: After the teacher directs this lesson, third grade Indian students will utilize the following reading content standard: oral reading fluency.

Objective Activity: First, the teacher will orally read sentences from the text. Next, allow individual students to read sentences from selected paragraphs. Then, the students will echo read (repeat teacher) sentences from the text.

STATE STANDARDS Reading Objective:

PG. 32 #3   Identifying sequence of events
- While discussing the lesson, the teacher will draw a time line on the board having the students to identify five of the treaties by asking appropriate questions pertaining to the lesson.
  - *What treaty was between the Cherokee Indians and the U.S. Government? (Cotton Gin Treaty)*

STATE STANDARDS Social Studies Objective:

PG. 29 #1   Extend their development of map and globe skills
- Locate various rivers, paths, areas, and directions on the U.S. map, Alabama map, and/or Lawrence County map.
  - *The Chickasaw Boundary Treaty of January 10, 1786, recognized what path? (High Town, Ridge Path)*

Review Questions

1. The Turkey Town Treaty was signed in what year? (1816)
2. What state did our ancestors move to during the Trail of Tears? (Oklahoma)
3. How much did the United States pay Georgia for their western lands? ($1,250,000.00)
4. Who was Sequoyah's half brother? (Talohuskee)
5. The Cotton Gin Treaty gave up Cherokee claims and placed a cotton gin where? (Melton's Bluff)

LESSON 20 – INDIAN TREATIES

FOURTH GRADE

SAT Reading Objective: LISTENING SKILLS

Objective: While the teacher directs this lesson, fourth grade Indian students will utilize their listening skills.

Objective Activity: The students will retell the information presented during the lesson in their own words to insure their listening and comprehension skills.

STATE STANDARDS Reading Objective:

PG. 38 #4   Identifying sequence of events
- Draw a timeline on the board. Label the timeline with the names and dates of each treaty. Under each treaty, ask the students to add the important details such as: who was involved, what area was affected, where it took place, etc.
- *What treaty was between the Cherokee Indians and the U.S. Government? (Cotton Gin Treaty)*

STATE STANDARDS Social Studies Objective:

PG. 34 #2   Interpret and display information and data using various graphic organizers
- Show the students a map of Alabama. Locate what areas were involved in each treaty. Discuss the boundaries of each treaty and ask questions for understanding of the text.
- *What counties were involved in the Turkey Town Treaty? (Colbert, Franklin, Lawrence, and Morgan)*

Review Questions

1. What year was the Cotton Gin Treaty? (1806)
2. Which treaty was signed by Doublehead? (Wafford Settlement)
3. The Chickasaw Boundary Treaty of January 10, 1786, recognized what path? (High town Path/Ridge Path)
4. Why was Doublehead killed? (because of the terms of the Cotton Gin Treaty)
5. What was the only fort built in the United States to remove white settlers from Indian lands? (Fort Hampton)

LESSON 20 – INDIAN TREATIES

FIFTH GRADE

SAT Reading Objective: GENRES

Objective: After the teacher directs this lesson, fifth grade Indian students will gain knowledge about the various genres encountered in our daily lives.

Objective Activity: All the students will identify the key terms and important details about the Indian treaties to insure their understanding of the lesson.

STATE STANDARDS Reading Objective:

PG. 46 #12   Read a variety of materials and genres encountered in daily lives
- After the teacher directs the lesson, the students will read aloud from "Indian Trails of the Warrior Mountains" from a pre-selected passage on treaties.
  - *What treaty recognized the High Town Path? (Chickasaw Boundary Treaty of January 10, 1786)*

STATE STANDARDS Social Studies Objective:

PG. 41 #9   Describe the impact of the early European exploration and settlement on Native American cultures
- Discuss in detail the different tribes of Indians that signed treaties and gave their land to the white men.
  - *Which treaty was between the Cherokee Indians and the U.S. Government? (Cotton Gin Treaty)*

Review Questions

1. What law did Andrew Jackson have passed on May 28, 1830? (Indian Removal Act)
2. What counties were involved in the Turkey Town Treaty? (Colbert, Franklin, Lawrence, and Morgan)
3. Who did Doublehead and the Cherokees have an agreement with over land? (George Colbert)
4. What were reserves? (people who had given up their rights and became individual landowners and citizens of the U.S.)
5. The Indian Removal Act did what to our ancestors land? (exchanged lands in the west for lands east of the Mississippi)

LESSON 20 – INDIAN TREATIES

SIXTH GRADE

SAT Reading Objective: VOCABULARY

Objective: After the teacher reviews the previous lessons, sixth grade Indian students will be able to recognize and identify different culturally diverse geographical terms and vocabulary terms listed from the lesson. (Terms: treaty, Continental Divide, boundary, migrate, Cotton Gin)

Objective Activity: The teacher will write various sentences on the board. The students will fill in the blank with the correct vocabulary term. (Allow a word bank if needed)

STATE STANDARDS Reading Objective:

PG. 53 #12   Develop general listening behaviors for different purposes and situations
- The students will utilize their listening skills by drawing a timeline on the board and labeling each treaty with the names and dates. Allow the students to verbally identify the significant details or write them under each treaty.
  - *When was the Cotton Gin Treaty that was between the Cherokee Indians and U.S. Government? (January 7, 1806)*

STATE STANDARDS Social Studies Objective:

PG. 54 #1   Extend the development of map and globe skills
- Locate on the Lawrence County map the different counties that were involved in the various treaties.
  - *What tribes were involved in the Turkey Town Treaty? (Cherokee and Chickasaw)*

Review Questions

1. The Treaty of January 10, 1786 gave most of Lawrence County to which tribe? (Chickasaw)
2. What law did Andrew Jackson have passed on May 28, 1830? (Indian Removal Act)
3. What tribe of Indians had to leave their homes and walk the Trail of Tears? (Cherokee)
4. Which treaty took away the majority of land from the Creeks? (Fort Jackson)
5. The first white settlement near Haleyville was made by whom? (Richard McMahon)

LESSON 20 – INDIAN TREATIES

SEVENTH GRADE

SAT Reading Objective: COMPREHENSION

Objective: After the teacher directs this lesson, seventh grade Indian students will utilize their comprehension skills and prior knowledge in order to gain an understanding of all the Indian treaties.

Objective Activity: The students will play *Who wants to be a Millionaire* to insure comprehension of the text. (Ex: the Treaty of _____ _____ of August 9, 1814, took away the majority of land from the Creeks.

STATE STANDARDS Reading Objective:

PG. 58 #11   Refine general listening behaviors
- After the teacher directs this lesson, have the students read from "Indian Trails of the Warrior Mountains." Read about the different areas affected by each treaty. Ask questions to check for understanding and comprehension of the material from the text.
  - *What tribes were involved in the Turkey Town Treaty? (Cherokee and Chickasaw)*

STATE STANDARDS Social Studies Objective:

Online Alex #10   Describe changes in social and economic conditions in the United States during the 20th and 21st centuries
- After the teacher directs the lesson, the students will read aloud from "Warrior Mountain Folklore" on page 14 about Indian treaties of the Warrior Mountains and compare/contrast then and now.
  - *What year was the Cotton Gin Treaty signed? (1806)*

Review Questions

1. What treaty ceded all Indian land east of the Mississippi? (Treaty of New Echota)
2. The Cotton Gin Treaty was between the U.S. Government and which Indian tribe? (Cherokee)
3. There were 25 treaties forced upon whom? (Cherokees)
4. How much were the Cherokee paid for their land? ($60,000.00)
5. Which two tribes had overlapping land claims? (Cherokee and Chickasaw)

LESSON 21 – INDIAN REMOVAL

At the time of removal, many Lawrence County Indians were already mixed with white settlers and stayed in the hill country of the Warrior Mountains. They denied their ancestry and basically lived much of their lives in fear of being sent west. Full blooded Indians claimed to be Black Irish or Black Dutch and denied their Indian blood. Many years later, the descendants of these mixed-blood Indians still live in Lawrence County. Those descendants are you--students in this Indian education class. You are eligible to attend these classes because your parents, or grandparents have reclaimed their Indian heritage. There seems to be a renewed pride in our Indian heritage and so the Cherokee culture will go on here in the old homeland.

1808 Removal - In 1806, Cherokee Chief Doublehead, his great nephew Tahlonteskee (Talohuskee Benge), and other Cherokees signed the Cotton Gin Treaty which gave up Cherokee claims to land north of the Tennessee River except for Doublehead's Reserve. The reserve lay between Elk River (Chuwalee) and Cypress Creek (TeKeetanoeh) in present day Lauderdale County.

The signing of the Cotton Gin Treaty brought the wrath of other Cherokee leaders upon the individuals who signed the treaty giving up Cherokee Lands. Major Ridge, a powerful Cherokee leader, made known that Doublehead and others would pay with their lives for relinquishing Cherokee lands. At a meeting of Cherokee headmen in Tennessee, Doublehead paid with his life at the hand of Ridge, Alex Saunders, John Rogers, and their accomplices. Alex Saunders and John Rogers had ties to Lawrence County and probably profited from the assassination of Doublehead.

After the assassination of Chief Doublehead by his own people, due to the circumstances of the Cotton Gin Treaty of 1806, several Cherokees living in the Lawrence County area moved west to avoid the same fate. The following is from "The Cherokees" by Grace Steele Woodard published in 1963 and found on page 131:

> "However, in 1808, the Compact 1802 was not needed to effect the removal of some 1,130 Chickamaugans to lands west of the Mississippi (today Dardaneele, Arkansas, in Pope County). Jefferson had merely to suggest to Tahlonteskee and other Chickamaugans that if they did not care to remain in the same country with their enemy countrymen, they could remove to Dardanelle Rock. Thus, in the Spring of 1808, Tahlonteskee-fearing assassination-notified President Jefferson that his people were ready to migrate. Following their migration Tahlonteskee's band of Cherokees called themselves "Cherokees West" or "Old Settlers."

Even though some Cherokees in the Warrior Mountains area left with Tahlonteskee's group in 1808, many Cherokee people still lived in the Tennessee Valley from the river to the High Town Path in southern Lawrence County. Within the great valley of the Tennessee, cotton became the agricultural "king" for making money. With the new government cotton gin at Melton's Bluff and black slaves for farm labor, both the Chickasaws and Cherokees, who shared ownership of the river valley, became wealthy; however, the government and settlers wanted the cotton wealth of the Tennessee Valley which was controlled by Indian people.

1816 Removal - In 1816, with several more years of pressure, the Chickasaws and Cherokees finally relinquished their claim to the remainder of Warrior Mountains. Therefore, due to the circumstances of the Turkey Town Treaty of September 16 and 18,

LESSON 21 – INDIAN REMOVAL

1816, another contingent of Chickasaws and Cherokees moved west, from the land of the Warrior Mountains in Lawrence County, Alabama. The first documented removal from Melton's Bluff in Lawrence County is found in the following excerpt given in the book Letters from Alabama 1817-1822 by Anne Royall on pages 134 and 135 with the Letter XXIV dated January 14, 1818:

> "Melton's Bluff is a town, and takes its name from a person by the name of John Melton, a white man ceased two years since, at an advanced age...
> You recollect Rhea whom I have mentioned: he married one of Melton's daughters-a most amiable woman, and very lame. When the Cherokee Indians abandoned this territory last fall, some of them went up the river to the Cherokee nation, there to remain, till boats were provided for their removal to the west, by the government; others went directly down the river to Arkansas-of whom Rhea's wife was one.
>
> The order for their departure was sudden and unexpected. Rhea, at that time was absent from home, but returned on the same day and learning what had happened, was almost frantic jumped into a canoe, and soon overtook the boats. He flew to his wife, and clasped her in his arms. Neither spoke a word, but both wept bitterly. In a few moments, he resumed his canoe and returned to the Bluff, and she went on. They had no children.
>
> Whether Rhea was prohibited by the treaty from accompanying his wife, or whether he was under a prior engagement, none here are able to inform me-but certain it is, he is now married to a white woman."

Rhea had moved to Melton's Bluff about 1803 and had married one of John Melton's half-blood Cherokee daughters. According to Royall, he had guided as many as four boats at a time, ten dollars each, through the Elk River Shoals, Big Mussel Shoals, and Little Mussel Shoals for some 15 years. Also, at this time, James Melton, Rhea's half-blood Cherokee brother-in-law, was a river boat guide that piloted boats through the Shoals for Malcolm Gilchrist, one of the early settlers of the Courtland area.

Shortly, after the Turkey Town Treaty was signed, several Cherokees left Melton's Bluff in Lawrence County for lands in the west during the Fall of 1816. In addition, Andrew Jackson did not wait until the dust of the 1816 removal had settled to begin staking his claims to Indian lands and property in Lawrence County as early as November 22, 1816.

1818 Removal - After Jackson had acquired Melton's Bluff which he named Marathon, another group of Cherokees were facing removal. On January 20, 1818, while at Melton's Bluff, Anne Royall observed some 300 Cherokees camped just two miles east of the Bluff in Lawrence County. These Cherokees were in the process of moving west of the Mississippi River. The following writing was found in Letter XXX dated January 20, 1818 and on pages 154 and 155 of the Letters from Alabama 1817-1822:

> "Hearing eleven boats had arrived about two miles from hence, and had haulted up the river, we set off, as I said before, in a little canoe, to see the Indians, which are on their way to their destination beyond the Mississippi. Government, agreeably to their contract, having completed the boats, the news of the arrival of the Indians had been received with much interest; but being unable to proceed by water, we quit the canoe, and proceeded by land in our wet shoes and hose.
>
> We arrive at the Indian camps about eleven o'clock. There were several encampments at the distance of three hundred yards from each other, containing three hundred Indians. The camps were nothing but some forks of wood driven into the ground, and a stick laid across them, on which hung a pot in which they were boiling meat; I took it to be venison. Around these fires were seated, some on the ground, some on logs, and some on chairs, females of all ages; and all employed, except the old women. There were some very old gray-haired women, and several children at each camp. The children were very pretty; but the grown females were not."

This group of Cherokees was probably waiting for a rise in the river in order to pass through the Elk River Shoals safely. Keelboats and flatboats waited at the head of Brown's Island until the water conditions permitted safe passage. At Brown's Island, the river channel divided as it passed around either side. Before the channels rejoined on the island's downstream end, rapids on both sides of the island created dangerous situations for boats. At the upstream end of Brown's Island was Brown's Ferry which Ms. Royall said was visible eight miles upstream from Melton's Bluff. At Brown's Ferry, the head of Elk River Shoals, Doublehead lived on a slight hill just west of the ferry and south of the river until 1802.

LESSON 21 –INDIAN REMOVAL

Indian Removal Act of May 28, 1830 - On May 28, 1830, Congress passed an act authorizing the exchange of lands in the west for those lands east of the Mississippi River held by Indian tribes. President Andrew Jackson was intent on seeing all Indian people removed from the eastern United States.

It should be noted that Jackson later lost the respect of the Cherokee when he ordered their removal from Georgia and Alabama. Jackson had the Indian Removal Act passed in 1830, which later led to the removal of southeastern Indians. After the discovery of gold in Georgia, the greed of the white men created a greater desire for Indian land. In 1828, the Georgia Legislature passed a law that no Indian must deal with gold in any way and they were under the law of Georgia.

Georgia assumed authority over the Cherokee Nation's capital at Echota, Georgia. It was then moved to Wills Valley (present day Fort Payne, Alabama). Later, it was moved to Red Clay, Tennessee. Chief John Ross hired a famous Philadelphia lawyer to represent the Cherokee cause before the Supreme Court of the United States. The court ruled this law was illegal and ordered President Jackson to remove the white intruders. President Jackson refused the order. Chief Junaluska upon hearing this said he would have killed him that day at the Battle of Horseshoe Bend if he had known of his attitude. There was a report that Chief Junaluska prevented Jackson from being stabbed by a captured Creek Warrior. This made Jackson's attitude even more bitter for Junaluska to understand.

Treaty of New Echota of December 29, 1835 - The Cherokees gave up all Indian land claims east of the Mississippi River and were forced into removal during 1838-1839.

On December 29, 1835, the Treaty of New Echota was signed by a small number of Cherokees. The U. S. Congress ratified the treaty on May 23, 1836. The treaty ceded the entire Cherokee territory east of the Mississippi River. Most of the members of the signing party of Cherokees were eventually assassinated by Cherokees of the northern faction under the leadership of John Ross. Stand Watie of the southern faction was one of the lone survivors in the signing of the Treaty of New Echota. Stand Watie was also the last Confederate general to surrender at the close of the Civil War.

Treaty of New Echota 1835 - On December 29, 1835, the Treaty of New Echota was signed by a small number of Cherokees. The United States Congress gave formal approval to the treaty on May 23, 1836. The treaty took the entire Cherokee territory east of the Mississippi River. The Cherokee people were given two years to move. At this time, the "Trail of Tears" began. It was the spring of 1838. The forced march began in October 1838 and lasted until March 1839, five months.

Trail of Tears from October 1838 until March 1839 - The Cherokee people were given two years to move at which time the forced removal known as the "Trail of Tears" began in the spring of 1838. The forced march began in October 1838 and ended in March 1839. During the spring and summer of 1838, General Winfield Scott under orders of President Andrew Jackson began placing Cherokees in stockades for removal to the west.

An estimated 4,000 Cherokees died on the forced march to the west. Many of the Cherokees from the east passed through Lawrence County during 1838 by railroad. By the time of the "Trail of Tears" in 1838, much of the land of the Warrior Mountains had already been claimed by Cherokee mix-bloods who denied their heritage in order to remain in the land they loved which was the "Warrior Mountains."

The March West - In Georgia and Alabama, Cherokee Indians were forced off their farms and herded into newly built stockades (like an animal pen) which are east of us. Fort Payne, was built to house Cherokees prior to their forced march to the west. In the stockades, the Indians were overcrowded and many were very sick. Close to 2,000 Cherokees died there, before they even left on the long march west.

Many were weak and underfed at the start of the journey. Many were also poorly clothed and barefoot. None were prepared for November's raging snowstorms and icy winds. Sickness and death were everywhere, but the march went on. One of the soldiers wrote, "the exiles (Indians)...had to sleep in the wagons and on the ground without fire. And I have known as many as 22 of them to die in one night of pneumonia due to ill treatment, cold, and exposure."

A traveler who passed the struggling Cherokees reported seeing a Cherokee mother carrying her child, who was close to death. He wrote that when the child died, the mother would have to stop in a strange land and bury her baby in the cold ground. The

LESSON 21 –INDIAN REMOVAL

traveler was deeply troubled. He said, "I turned from the sight with feelings which language cannot express. And wept like childhood then." The Cherokees also wept.

Broken Promises - Treaties signed between the Cherokees and the United States Government had been broken before. It was always the government that broke these treaties. This time was no different. The United States promised the Cherokees they could keep some of their land, but in the end that promise was also broken.

A newspaper, entitled "The American History Herald," December 12, 1838, published an article about the Trail of Tears. The author wrote, "And so, the Cherokees struggle west on their Trail of Tears. Some white Americans watch in sorrow. Most seem untroubled by this tragedy. Yet, the ghosts of this disgrace may haunt America for many years to come. What do you think? Who would like to share your opinion of the Cherokee Removal, Trail of Tears, or Broken Promises? (Discuss lesson with students and let them tell their opinions). Have you been told that your ancestors were on the Trail of Tears? Explain how you would feel if we were forced from our homes today.

Conclusion - Many of Lawrence County's Indian people were already mixed with Celtic settlers and stayed in the hill country of the Warrior Mountains. They denied their ancestry and basically lived much of their lives in fear of being sent west. Full bloods claimed to be Black Irish or Black Dutch in denying the rightful Indian blood.

After the Civil Rights Act of 1968 and after being assimilated into the general population, our Cherokee mixed-blood descendants began reclaiming their heritage in the land of the "Warrior Mountains."

LESSON 21 – INDIAN REMOVAL

KINDERGARTEN

<u>DIBELS</u> Reading Objective: ALL DIBELS SKILLS

Objective: After the teacher directs the lesson, Kindergarten Indian students will utilize the following reading content standards: initial sound and lettering naming.

Objective Activity: The students will develop an understanding of letter naming and initial sounds by identifying the beginning sound and individual letters that makeup the selected terms from the lesson. (terms: <u>w</u>arrior, <u>I</u>ndians, <u>r</u>emoval, <u>l</u>eader, <u>t</u>reaty)

<u>STATE STANDARDS</u> Reading objective:

PG. 14 #6   Demonstrate an initial understanding of letter sound relationships
- While discussing the "March West", the teacher will choose a few words from the lesson, sound out each letter, and say the word aloud with the students. (Ex: west, wept, etc.)
- *What direction did the Cherokee travel? (west)*

PG. 14 #9   Begin to use pictures and text to gain meaning from written material
- Show pictures of a stockade to the students to show them what they had to stay in after their farms were taken away. Show pictures of the Cherokee Indians on the march. (all of them walking together, some having to stop and bury their loved ones, etc.)
- *Name the other state, that the Cherokee Indians were forced to move. (Georgia)*

<u>STATE STANDARDS</u> Social Studies Objective:

PG. 11 #1   Develop initial map and globe skills
- Show direction (west) their ancestors traveled after leaving Lawrence County on state map.
- Show Georgia and Alabama on state map.
- Show Fort Payne on Alabama map.
- *What fort was built in order to give the Cherokee a place to stay before they started the march west? (Fort Payne)*

PG. 12 #7   Exhibit behaviors that are partial responsible civic life in the school setting resulting in harmonious and socially satisfying relationships with others
- Let the children give their opinions about the situation. Ask them if they thought it was fair that their ancestors were treated the way they were. Did they think it was right that Andrew Jackson took their homes from them and made them move far away and didn't help them and didn't care if they died or got sick? Ask them if they would want someone to ever do that to them and their family or would they ever do that to anybody else.
- *Were Andrew Jackson's actions good or bad for your ancestors? (bad)*

<u>Review Questions</u>

1. How long did the Trail of Tears last? (five months)
2. What does assassination mean? (to kill)
3. What year did the Indian Removal Act pass? (1830)
4. When was the Treaty of New Echota signed? (1835)
5. Who signed the Cotton Gin Treaty? (Chief Doublehead and his great nephew)

LESSON 21 – INDIAN REMOVAL

FIRST GRADE

DIBELS Reading Objective: ALL DIBELS SKILLS

Objective: After the teacher directs this lesson, first grade Indian students will utilize the following reading content standards of letter naming, initial sound fluency, and nonsense word fluency.

Objective Activity: The teacher will write terms on the board from the lesson and the students will pronounce each sound and letter of the word. Next, the teacher will write the words on the board changing the initial letter making a nonsense word. Then, the students will pronounce the word. (Ex: Man-Gan, etc.)

STATE STANDARDS Reading Objective:

PG. 17 #3   Exhibit phonemic awareness
- Choose several vocabulary words from the lesson to define with students. Play a rhyming game with them using the vocabulary words in order for them to exhibit phonemic awareness. (Ex: Write vocabulary words on board such as gin, kill, and money. Then, ask the students replace the first letter of each word to make rhyming words (Ex: gin-pin-tin, kill-dill-hill, money-honey)
    - Why did the Lawrence County Indians, during the time of removal, deny their ancestry? (fear of being sent out west)

PG. 21 #16   Demonstrate appropriate listening and speaking behaviors
- Have a class discussion with students which should include a review of the Cotton Gin Treaty, details about the assassination (killing) of Chief Doublehead, and the importance of cotton (made them wealthy) to the Indians during this time. Also, make sure to ask teacher generated questions throughout discussion to check for understanding and/or comprehension of the material discussed.
    - What treaty gave up Cherokee land? (Cotton Gin Treaty)

STATE STANDARDS Social Studies Objective:

PG. 17 #2   Extend initial ability to display information in graphic form
- Locate Elk River and Cypress Creek in Lauderdale County on state map to show students where Doublehead lived and the only place the Cherokee's didn't lose claim.
    - The Cherokees lived in the _____ Valley? (Tennessee)

PG. 18 #3   Extend initial ability to locate new information and to express understanding in various classrooms
- Show location of Tennessee Valley (from Tennessee River to High Town Path.
    - Who was Chief of the Cherokee when the Cotton Gin Treaty was signed in 1806? (Black Fox)

Review Questions
1. Approximately how many Cherokees died on the Trail of Tears? (4,000)
2. Who killed Doublehead? (Ridge, Saunders, Rogers)
3. What was the Trail of Tears? (The removal of our Indian ancestors from here to Oklahoma)
4. What year was it ok to say you were Indian? (1968)
5. What mountain did our ancestors live in? (Warrior Mountain)

LESSON 21 – INDIAN REMOVAL

SECOND GRADE

DIBELS Reading Objective: ALL DIBELS SKILLS

Objective: After the teacher directs the lesson, second grade Indian students will utilize the reading content standards of oral reading fluency and nonsense word fluency.

Objective Activity: The teacher will orally read from the lesson and then let each student read a sentence from that paragraph. Then, the students will retell what they have read in their own words. The teacher will monitor students for oral reading fluency.

STATE STANDARDS Reading Objective:

PG. 24 #7   Read and comprehend a variety of material
- After the teacher directs the lesson on the "Trail of Tears" the students will read from "Indian Trails of the Warrior Mountains" about the "Trail of Tears." Then, the teacher will ask the students a few preselected questions from the text. Also, the teacher can show pictures from the text of the trail and the direction that was traveled by our ancestors.
  - *What president wanted the Cherokees removed? (Andrew Jackson)*

STATE STANDARDS Social Studies Objective:

PG. 22 #1   Develop map and globe skills
- The teacher will use an Alabama map to show where the trail started and then continue on a U.S. map to show where the trail stopped. at. The teacher can also show the students where the Warrior Mountains are located on the Lawrence County map.
  - *Where did the "Trail of Tears" end? (Oklahoma)*

Review Questions

1. Who was responsible for the Indian removal? (Andrew Jackson)
2. How long did the Trail of Tears last? (5 months)
3. What fort was built in order to give the Cherokee a place to stay before they started the March west? (Fort Payne)
4. Who signed the Cotton Gin Treaty and in what year was it signed? (Chief Doublehead, 1806)
5. The Warrior Mountains were home to what people? (Cherokee ancestors)

LESSON 21 – INDIAN REMOVAL

THIRD GRADE

DIBLES Reading Objective: ALL DIBLES SKILLS

Objective: After the teacher directs the lesson, third grade Indian students will utilize the reading content standards of oral reading fluency.

Objective Activity: First, the teacher will orally read paragraphs from the lesson and let each student read a sentence from those selected paragraphs. Then, the students will explain what they have read. Students will review questions and explain the answers in their own words.

STATE STANDARDS Reading Objective:

PG. 32 #8 Read grade-level texts aloud and silently with fluency and comprehension
- During the directed lesson, the teacher will have the students read any text material pertaining to the lesson. While they are reading the material make sure they are reading with fluency. Then ask questions to ensure comprehension.
  - *When did the Trail of Tears begin and end? (October 1838-March 1839)*

STATE STANDARDS Social Studies Objective:

PG. 29 #1 Extend their development of map and globe skills
- While conducting the lesson, the teacher will show a map/picture of where the Indians were forced to move. (Oklahoma)
  - *Where were our ancestors forced to move? (Oklahoma)*

Review Questions

1. After what act did the Indian mixed-blood descendants begin claiming their heritage? (Civil Rights Act of 1968)
2. What president wanted the Cherokees removed? (Andrew Jackson)
3. When did the Trail of Tears begin and end? (October 1838-March 1839)
4. Where were our ancestors forced to move? (Oklahoma)
5. The Cherokees lived in what valley? (Tennessee)

LESSON 21 – INDIAN REMOVAL

FOURTH GRADE

SAT Reading Objective: ALL SAT SKILLS

Objective: After the teacher directs this lesson, fourth grade Indian students will develop an understanding of the Indian removal.

Objective Activity: After reading selected paragraphs, the students will identify several vocabulary terms from the lesson, then the students will write a summary of the material learned from the paragraphs and create an illustration of their writing.

STATE STANDARDS Reading Objective:

PG. 38 #4   Demonstrate literal understanding of print material
- After the teacher directs the lesson the students will be able to identify important details. For example, the teacher will allow the students play the game *Jeopardy* for the students to identify important details from the lesson and learn to follow directions.
  - *Name one chief we talked about today? (Doublehead)*

STATE STANDARDS Social Studies Objective:

PG. 34 #2   Interpret and display information and data using various graphic organizers
- As the teacher directs the lesson, he/she will draw a timeline on the board to show the students the sequence of events.
  - *What was the Treaty of 1835 called? (Treaty of the New Echota)*

Review Questions

1. President Andrew Jackson had what act passed in 1830? (Indian Removal Act)
2. What three men killed Doublehead? (Ridge, Saunders, Rogers)
3. Which treaty took the entire Cherokee territory east of the Mississippi River? (Treaty of New Echota)
4. What did our ancestors claim to be while denying their Indian heritage? (Black Dutch or Black Irish)
5. Which president began placing Cherokees in stockades for removal to the west? (Andrew Jackson)

LESSON 21 – INDIAN REMOVAL

FIFTH GRADE

<u>SAT</u> Reading Objective: ALL SAT SKILLS

Objective: After the teacher directs the lesson, fifth grade Indian students will utilize their listening skills by identifying the important details from the lesson.

Objective Activity: The teacher will check the students listening behaviors by asking questions during a game of *Jeopardy*. (Treaties: Treaty of New Echota, The March West, Indian Removal Act, etc.)

<u>STATE STANDARDS</u> Reading Objective:

PG. 45 #5   Interpret passages in print material
- After the teacher directs the lesson, have a group discussion and ask questions to ensure comprehension.
  - *What did our ancestors claim to be by denying their heritage? (Black Dutch or Black Irish)*

<u>STATE STANDARDS</u> Social Studies Objective:

PG. 47 #9   Describe the impact of the early European exploration an settlement on Native American cultures
- Discuss with the students how the removal sometimes separated the family.
  - *The Cherokee people were given how many years to move during the Trail of Tears? (two)*

Review Questions

1. What place was built for the Cherokee removal? (Fort Payne)
2. President Andrew Jackson had what act passed in 1830? (Indian Removal Act)
3. The Cherokee people were given how many years to move during the Trail of Tears? (two)
4. Who was Melton's Bluff named after? (John Melton)
5. What became the agriculture king for making money? (cotton)

LESSON 21 – INDIAN REMOVAL

SIXTH GRADE

<u>SAT</u> Reading Objective: ALL SAT SKILLS

Objective: After the teacher directs this lesson, sixth grade Indian students will read and gain an understanding of the material learned from the lesson.

Objective Activity: After the teacher reviews the lesson, the students will read selected paragraphs and answer questions concerning the Indian removal.

<u>STATE STANDARDS</u> Reading Objective:

PG. 57 #2   Read with ease textual, functional, and recreational materials encountered in daily life
- After the teacher directs the lesson, the students will read aloud from "The Trails of the Warrior Mountains" about the Trail of Tears and then have a group discussion.
  - *Approximately how many people died on the Trail of Tears? (4,000)*

<u>STATE STANDARDS</u> Social Studies Objective:

PG. 54 #1   Extend the development of map and globe skills
- As the teacher directs the lesson, he/she will show the students a map of Alabama and the United States to show the students the path of the Trail of Tears.
  - *When was the Treaty o f New Echota signed? (1835)*

Review Questions

1. What did our ancestors claim to be by denying their heritage? (Black Dutch and Black Irish)
2. What place was built for the Cherokee removal? (Fort Payne)
3. Why did the Lawrence County Indians, during the time of removal, deny their ancestry? (fear of being sent out west)
4. What bluff was named after John Melton? (Melton's Bluff)
5. When was the Treaty of New Echota signed? (1835)

LESSON 21 – INDIAN REMOVAL

SEVENTH GRADE

<u>SAT</u> Reading Objective: ALL SAT SKILLS

Objective: After the teacher directs this lesson, seventh grade Indian students will recognize and identify selected vocabulary terms from the lesson. (Terms: relinquish, descendents, assassination, wrath, stockade)

Objective Activity: The teacher will divide the students into two teams and play a remedial game using the vocabulary terms and review questions from the lesson. The teacher will ask a question and which ever team writes the correct answer on the board the fastest will get a point.

<u>STATE STANDARDS</u> Reading Objective:

PG. 52 #1   Construct, interpret, and evaluate meaning by applying appropriate strategies to materials across the curriculum
- After the teacher directs the lesson, the class will have a group discussion and then the teacher should ask questions to ensure comprehension on the text.
  - In what year was the Treaty of New Echota signed? *(December 29, 1835)*

<u>STATE STANDARDS</u> Social Studies Objective:

Online Alex #10   Describe changes in social and economic conditions in the United States during the 20th and 21st centuries
- Discuss with the students how the economy has changed over time, yet, still the same.
  - How did the Cherokees and Chickasaws become rich? *(cotton gin at Melton's Bluff and slaves for labor)*

Review Questions

1. When did the Trail of Tears begin and end? (March 1838-October 1839)
2. How did the Cherokees and Chickasaws become rich? (cotton gin at Melton's Bluff and slaves for labor)
3. In what year was the Treaty of New Echota signed? (December 29, 1835)
4. Ridge, Saunders, and Rogers killed what famous Indian chief? (Doublehead)
5. Fort Payne was built for what reason? (A place for the Cherokees to stay before their march west.)

LESSON 22 – TRADITIONAL CULTURAL PROPERTIES

For thousands of years, inhabitants of the Moulton Valley have looked south to see a beautiful range of mountains rising from the flat middle plain in the heartland of Lawrence County, Alabama. This east-west mountain range has represented many things to modern man, but probably was more important and sacred to our red ancestors than any of our European immigrants.

By the time of Desoto's visit to our state in 1540, our Muscogee people recognized the range of mountains as a tribal and geographic boundary along the Continental Divide. The High Town Path or Ridge Path is a prehistoric east-west Indian trail that lies along the divide. The divide begins separating the Atlantic's coastal waters from those of the Mississippi drainage in Maine and continues through the upper Tombigbee watershed in the western portion of Alabama and into Northern Mississippi.

Black Warrior - Probably the most accurate and appropriate name for the Lawrence County portion of this vast chain of mountains is derived from the Muscogee people who lived along the forest streams hundreds of years before white people came to our county. The Creek word "taskagu" or "taska," and the Choctaw word "tashka" refer to the English translation of "warrior" with the Muscogee word "lusa" meaning "black." We know from reading Alabama history, Desoto encountered a giant of a man known as "Chief Tuscaloosa" or the Black Warrior; therefore, the name was here long before the first European settlers claimed the land in the southern portion of our county.

Mountains - In early days, the stream forming south from the mountains of Lawrence County also became known as the Tuscaloosa River. On a French map dated March 1733, Baron De Crenay, Commandant of the Post of Mobile, identified the southern drainage from our mountains as the Tuscaloosa River. On other early maps, the main river, which drains south, was also called the Tuscaloosa. Later in 1814, a map of Alabama identified the river draining south from our county as the Black Warrior River.

John Bull - In 1829, a frontiersman and famous rifle maker by the name of John Bull, engraved two of his masterpieces from the Warrior Mountains. According to information provided by Mr. Dan Wallace, the exceptional rifle is inscribed on a silver platelet in the stock, "John Bull for David Smith, Warrior Mountain." The inscription on the silver cheek piece is as the following:

"Ann"
this gun is named Charlotte,
from hills and mountains came,
made to delight the heart of man,
with Joy, the labouring Swain,
and from the sportsmen of the day
Victorious bear the prife,
Away"

John Bull Rifle made for David Smith

According to Old Land Records of Lawrence County, Alabama by Margaret Cowart, David Smith entered 79.92 acres of land in Section 36 of Township 7 South and Range 7 West, near Indian Tomb Hollow on September 12, 1818, and 79.92 acres on September 28, 1818, in Section 35. He married Charlotte Ann Havens, who was the daughter of James Havens. According to the Havens family legend provided by Spencer Waters, James Havens was buried next to his Indian friends on the side of the Warrior Mountains where the magnolia blooms in the spring. It is highly probable that James Havens was buried in the Indian Tomb Hollow Cemetery,

Warrior Mountains - In his 1899 book, Early Settlers of Alabama, Colonel Edmonds Saunders refers to Lawrence County's southern highlands as the "Warrior Mountains." Later in 1918, when the government began organizing our mountains into a national forest the area was called the Black Warrior. Today, the State Wildlife Management Area is still known as the Black Warrior.

LESSON 22 –TRADITIONAL CULTURAL PROPERTIES

It is a shame that our forest had a name that could be traced back for over 400 years and has been changed to honor a white politician. However, with the Indian pride that has grown strong in Lawrence County, our mountains will never take second place. These mountains will always remain the Sacred Land of our ancestors, and be known as the "WARRIOR MOUNTAINS."

Indian Tomb Hollow - Indian Tomb Hollow is located primarily in Section 2 of Township 8 South, Range 7 West in on the northern edge of William B. Bankhead National Forest. In the distant hollows of Indian Tomb, the wood hen can be heard as the evening sun sinks behind the bluffs. Three gracious waterfalls of the southwest fork echo eternal sounds that formed the sandstone canyon containing vertical walls reaching to the sky. Looking down the canyon toward the northeast sandstone bluffs on either side of the canyon causes one to be in awe of the area because of its beauty.

Early settlers and Indian mixed-bloods settled to the north and west of the hollow's southwestern fork. Several folks lived for a while in the old High House located on a small knoll at the southern mouth of Indian Tomb. Families of the Warrior Mountains would enter the hollow from Chestnut Ridge, Beulah, and High House Hill not only to view and enjoy the beauty of the area, but to dig roots, herbs, and hunt. It was in this same tradition that I, Butch Walker, was first introduced to the mysterious but beautiful Indian Tomb Hollow.

The late, Mr. G. H. Melson told me of experiences he had as a small boy in Indian Tomb Hollow and was a wealth of information concerning an Indian fight occurring near the mouth of the famous canyon. He tells of his father working on the old plantation and passing down stories through many generations about our Indian people of the area, the black slave cemetery, and the early settlers who called the area home.

Over many years, the Gillespie family has traditionally been drawn to Indian Tomb. Not only does the family consider the area a sacred Indian burial site, but their ancestor, James Richard Gillespie, a veteran of the Creek Indian War, is buried in the Gillespie or Indian Tomb Hollow Cemetery. In addition, Gillespie Spring and Gillespie Creek, which runs through Indian Tomb Hollow, are named after the Gillespie Family of Lawrence County.

My family (Rickey Butch Walker) also has strong ties to Indian Tomb Hollow. My great, great, great grandmother, Mary E. Welborn (Granny Naylor) Segars Naylor, is buried at Beulah, on the western edge of Indian Tomb. My grandfather, Authur Wilburn, lived as a young boy in the hollow and carried me many times to this sacred place. Many of my family are buried within sight of this mysterious place.

According to William Lindsey McDonald's article on Melton's Bluff, "The renowned pioneer and soldier, David Crockett, remembered two occasions when his military unit crossed at Melton's Bluff. The first instance was in October 1813. Actually according to Crockett, he crossed the Tennessee River twice on this first occasion in order to maneuver around the local Indians. After crossing at Huntsville, they moved westward to cross the river again at Melton's Bluff. Crockett described the river at this point as being about two miles wide. The rocky bottom of the river was rough and dangerous. While fording the river, several of the horses became stuck in the rocky crevices and had to be left there while the military command moved onto their destination. Crockett's second crossing at Melton's Bluff was in October 1814. Payroll and muster records reveal that he was a third sergeant in Captain John Cowan's company at the time." According to McDonald, the above information was obtained from the book <u>A Narrative of the Life of David Crockett</u>.

In 1813, David Crockett helped General John Coffee's forces burn the large Creek Indian village known as Black Warrior Town after finding it deserted. Crockett and General Coffee's forces traveled along the Black Warriors' Path through present day Lawrence County to destroy the Creek town. James Richard Gillespie, who eventually settled and was buried in Indian Tomb Hollow also served with David Crockett. Gillespie served under Captain Cowan in 1813 during the same period of time as David Crockett. Gillespie attended the muster rolls in Blount County, Tennessee on January 1, 1814.

The ancient beech trees of Indian Tomb are a record of family traditions, which has spanned hundreds of years of time. From early Indian drawings (known as arborglyphs) and settler names, the beeches of Indian Tomb bear record of visitation. The markings also indicate much of the time spent in Indian Tomb was recorded in the numerous beech carvings located throughout the canyon. In addition, the Indian marker tree in Indian Tomb Hollow is a symbol considered sacred by the descendants of those who once roamed the beautiful valley.

LESSON 22 –TRADITIONAL CULTURAL PROPERTIES

A story called the "Battle of Indian Tomb Hollow" or "Ittaloknak" was originally printed in The Moulton Democrat on November 7, 14, 21, 1856. The articles are a beautiful love story that describes a fierce fight in Indian Tomb between the Creek and Chickasaw inhabitants of the Warrior Mountains.

Treasures can be found in Indian Tomb Hollow for all who enter her solitude. The treasures lie not in the destruction of her timber nor the looting of her artifacts, but in beautiful waterfalls, sheer rock walls, virgin timber, and the mysterious closeness of GOD. Four waterfalls lie just beyond a clear-cut with the first waterfall's branch being the southwest boundary of the clear-cut. The other three waterfalls are upstream at the end of the canyon. In three different areas along the way, Gillespie Creek flows under huge boulders and has a splendor that only GOD could create. Let's hope that man does not destroy the rest of GOD's handiwork in Indian Tomb Hollow.

In 2001, the U.S Forest Service set aside Indian Tomb Hollow as a traditional cultural property to be protected from future logging operations.

Kinlock Rock Shelter

Kinlock - Kinlock Rock Shelter is located in Section 31 of Township 8 South and Range 9 West. The shelter is one of the largest of its kind with an overhang of sandstone rock some 250 feet wide, 30 to 100 feet deep, and 30 to 150 feet high. The Indian shelter is a premier petroglyph site of prehistoric Indian occupation. The sacred Indian shelter is still actively used by American Indians for ceremonies. Kinlock Bluff Shelter has been deemed eligible to be nominated to the National Register of Historic Places.

You don't need to travel far from your home to experience the beauty of nature. Our county offers many beautiful sites to behold. One that's rich with Indian history is Kinlock. Kinlock Falls is probably the best known waterfall or cascading waterfall in Bankhead. Water flows over Kinlock for the entire year, but the waterfall is most beautiful during the spring creating a white cascade among the green leaves. Kinlock Falls is located on Hubbard Creek.

Also, within walking distance, is the Kinlock Rock Shelter. After you cross the bridge, take a left at a gate near Kinlock Spring and walk about a quarter of a mile. Take a right at the old logging trail and follow this down to the shelter. Keep on the trail. Be sure to have a partner if you go there because it is a steep climb down. Kinlock is considered a sacred place to many Indian people so always treat it with respect. It was believed to be used for vision quests.

Teachers may read from Walking Sipsey pages 1, 2, and 3, "The Sacred Fire." This explains some of the feelings of Terra Manasco about the Kinlock Rock Shelter. Also, teachers may read pages 43 through 46 from High Town Path about Kinlock.

Sipsey Wilderness - Sipsey Wilderness is found in the southwestern portion of Lawrence County. Many people enjoy the beauty of Lawrence County's greatest resource, the Sipsey Wilderness Area of Bankhead Forest that lies in the heart of the Warrior Mountains. Sipsey River Picnic Grounds are located on Sipsey River near the Cranal Road, the south border of the wilderness. Many people not only hike in the wilderness, but also drive along Highway 33 and the Cranal Road to enjoy the fall colors and splendors of the Sipsey Wilderness.

LESSON 22 – TRADITIONAL CULTURAL PROPERTIES

Needle's Eye or Windows in King Cove

Sightseeing, hiking, canoeing, and horseback riding are only a few of the many outdoor recreational activities available to Lawrence County residents, as well as visitors from all over the southeastern United States. The Sipsey Wilderness is the place for those who want to get away from modern conveniences without the sound of traffic, telephones, and TV's, but instead listening to the songs of warblers, the hammering beaks of woodpeckers, the hoot of the great horned owl, the howl of a lone coyote, and the sound of water running over rocks and boulders in the many streams flowing through this portion of the Warrior Mountains. Avid outdoorsmen cherish the stimulating sounds, sights, and smells that only Mother Nature can provide to those who visit the Sipsey Wilderness.

Ship Rock - Ship Rock is located in the Sipsey Wilderness Area in Section 27 of Township 8 South and Range 9 West. The large rock is located some 200 yards east of the forks of Hubbard and Thompson Creeks in the heart of the Sipsey Wilderness. The site is known as Ship Rock, Herron Point, Boat Rock, Needle's Eye, or the Windows. The following text is a descriptive but symbolic version of the Ship Rock of Sipsey.

Ship Rock is a monument in time and a symbol of persistence before the age of the great reptilian dinosaurs, the age of the gigantic mammals, and the age of the red man who once inhabited her great-forested seas. No time, force, or age is her master, for God is her pilot and only he knows her true destiny. As God spins the eternal swirl of the universe, Ship Rock holds steady while dragging the Warrior Mountains along with the rest of the world.

Narrows Ridge - Narrows Ridge is located in Bankhead Forest in Section 21 of Township 8 South and Range 8 West. While walking south on a ridge from the Northwest Road, suddenly a high narrow strip of land emerges between two beautiful old growth hardwood valleys. The valley to the east was the Borden Creek Canyon and the valley to the west was the Flanagin Creek Canyon. The old settler road along the top of the ridge continued along the slender natural bridge of sandstone rock connecting the two mountaintop ridges, which divided the beautiful creek bottoms. To either side of the old road were the edges of bluffs, which rose some 40 to 60 feet above the two hardwood valleys.

The narrow ridge runs in a north-south direction for approximately 100 yards narrowing to as little as some 12 feet wide. The unique and beautiful ridge is known to most local people as the "Narrows Ridge." Narrows Ridge is now in the Sipsey Addition to the Wilderness Area, which will provide protection for the beautiful hardwood valleys on either side of this natural bridge ridge.

King Cove - King Cove is located Township 8 South, Range 9 West in Sections 22 and 27 of the southwestern portion of Lawrence County. King cove lies adjacent to the forks of Hubbard and Thompson Creeks, which is the beginning of Sipsey River in the western portion of Bankhead Forest. The King Cove extends up Thompson Creek to the forks of Tedford and Mattox (Thompson). Ship Rock is found at the southern end of King Cove and is just east of the forks of Hubbard and Thompson.

King Cove shows evidence of early Indian habitation. Mortar Rock, located to the north across the creek from Ship Rock, contains five mortar holes and a huge nutting stone used by early Indian people. Local folklore tells of numerous arrowheads and spear points picked up in the old creek bottom fields.

The canyon area of King Cove was not heavily settled but farmland lies adjacent to the creek bottoms. Most of the early settler homes were located on the ridges above the cove but still make up the early King Cove Community of the Warrior Mountains.

Parker Cove - Parker Cove is located in Section 30 of township 7 South and Range 7 West and is named from the Parker family who settled the cove long ago. Parker Cove forms the headwater streams of Elam Creek on the north-central edge of Bankhead Forest. The cove still contains three old log houses that were used over 100 years ago. When going south on Highway 33, the

LESSON 22 –TRADITIONAL CULTURAL PROPERTIES

main entrance to Parker Cove is along the first steep winding road turning east off of Wren Mountain. The deep cove is visible east of the Wren Mountain portion of the Wilderness Parkway, which runs through the center of the Warrior Mountain.

Borden or Blankenship Cove - The lower portion of Blankenship Cove is still an active cattle-farming site and is located primarily in Section 2 of Township 8 South and Range 8 West on the upper portion of Borden Creek. The Cove was originally called Borden Cove, settled by the family of Christopher Borden. The upper portion of Blankenship Cove extends through the northeast part of Sections 34 and 35 of Township 7 South and Range 8 West. Some of the Borden Family originally settled along portions of the cove adjacent to Borden Creek. The cove was owned by Glenn Whisnant, who bought the property from the heirs of his Granddaddy Willis Blankenship. Two areas of the Blankenship Cove were known as the upper place and the lower place. Willis Blankenship lived on the lower place. David Borden earlier had his home near the Borden Spring in the beautiful cove.

Bee Branch Canyon - Bee Branch of the Sipsey Wilderness Area is located primarily in Section 26 of Township 8 South, Range 9 West. Bee Branch is a deep canyon located east of Sipsey River. The area is probably the most primeval site in the Warrior Mountains. Most of the canyon was protected by the U.S. Forest Service as early as 1919.

Bee Branch is a forked canyon with seasonal and beautiful waterfalls in each fork. The Bee Branch Falls plunge from some 50 feet above the canyon floor. Both forks are virtually box canyons forming a small creek that flows into Sipsey River. The eastern fork of the canyon features the largest yellow poplar in the Southeastern United States. The whole canyon is a botanical garden of a virgin gorge in the Warrior Mountains.

Tar Springs Hollow - Located in the upper portion of Capsey Creek, once known as Capp's Creek, is a place not found elsewhere in William B. Bankhead National Forest. The creek begins at Cave Springs on Highway 41 and on the Leola Road at Basham Shelter and Spring. The area, not noted for the two-headwater springs, is unique because of the two mineral springs downstream in the middle of the big hollow. This unusual site found on Capsey Creek is known as Tar Springs Hollow. The road from Poplar Log Cove into Tar Springs Hollow was originally an Indian Trail and called the Double Springs Road or Trail.

Capsey Creek is a tributary to Brushy Creek, which empties its waters into Sipsey River on Smith Lake. The Tar Springs Hollow on Capsey Creek contains two mineral tar springs which are located about one-quarter mile apart in the southwest ¼ of Section 26, Township 8 South, and Range 6 West.

Glyphs - Our Indian ancestors did not have a written language until Sequoyah invented the Cherokee alphabet in 1821. How then did the Cherokees keep records of the things that happened? (response) One method was picture writing.

Arborglyphs, petroglyphs, and pictographs were all forms of picture writing. Arbor meaning tree, glyph meaning drawing--tree drawing (show example in book High Town Path). The American beech tree was commonly used for arborglyphs because carvings would remain on the bark for hundreds of years. Beech trees were also known as boundary trees because they marked tribal boundaries. The Warrior Mountains (Bankhead Forest) contains many beech trees with Indian drawings.

Petro means rock and glyph means drawing. Petroglyphs, meaning rock drawings, are pictures that have been carved or scratched onto hard surfaces such as rocks, shell, or copper. These symbols can be found in Kinlock Bluff Shelter in our county (show picture in the book Walking Sipsey).

Pictographs are pictures that have been painted on hard surfaces or animal skins. These have been found all over the United States and date back hundreds of years. Animal skins were used by some tribes to draw pictographs. Since animal skins were used to make blankets and clothing, Indian people would draw pictures on their personal belongings. Examples include their names, battles that were fought, deaths, hunger, brave deeds, or anything they wanted told about their everyday lives.

Warrior Mountain Wildlife - How many of you have ever been to the Warrior Mountains (Bankhead Forest)? What did you see? (trees, paved roads, rock roads, mountains, and animals) What kinds of animals did you see? (deer, rabbits, squirrels, chipmunks, beavers, bats, snakes, turkeys - show animal pictures as they are discussed)

LESSON 22 – TRADITIONAL CULTURAL PROPERTIES

We are going to talk about some other animals and plants that once lived in the Warrior Mountains before the 1900s. These animals have since been eliminated. It is very sad to learn that there were certain animals that our Indian ancestors depended upon, no longer live in our forest and are now gone.

Animals - One of the animals that had been eliminated in the Warrior Mountain was the whitetail deer (show picture). By the early 1900s there were no more whitetail deer. These deer had to be brought into the forest again from the north. Again in 1990, more whitetail deer from South Alabama were restocked in the forest. Just think what our forest would be like if deer had not been brought in after the first deer were eliminated.

How do you think the first deer were eliminated? (too many hunters were killing too many deer, finally, there were no more deer until they were brought in from another place)

Other animals that once lived in the Warrior Mountains were the elk, bear, panther and three kinds of wolves – gray timber, red, and black wolves. The last of these animals were seen in the early 1900s. Trade between Europeans and Alabama Indians was based largely on the barter of animal skins (furs and hides). An Indian could swap about 30 deer hides for a rifle. All of the commercialized fur trade led to the elimination of these animals in the Warrior Mountains.

Hunting parties, an important part of wilderness life, provided a means of obtaining meat for hungry families, hides and furs which could be traded for goods, and the thrill of the hunt along with the fellowship of friends and neighbors. However, unregulated hunting practices began taking their toll on the native wildlife. Between 1890 and 1910, big game species, which were eliminated from the Warrior Mountains by over hunting probably, included the whitetail deer, black bear, timber wolf, and eastern cougar.

Whitetail Deer - After the last original Warrior Mountains whitetail deer was killed, the herd was restocked with a northern subspecies of deer during the 1920s. Again in the 1990s, deer from South Alabama were restocked in the Black Warrior Wildlife Management Area.

Mr. Rayford Hyatt, past conservation officer of Bankhead, relates an interesting story about the last native deer to be killed in the forest. According to Mr. Hyatt, the last pure bloodline deer was a small racked buck that was hunted for two or three days before it was eventually killed. The deer was killed by James M. Flanagin on Hagood Creek in early 1909. Mr. Amos Spillers, a Cherokee Indian descendant and one of the first conservation officers of Bankhead, had the antlers of the last known native Bankhead whitetail deer, which were seen by many people.

Wolves - The last known timber wolf of Bankhead was killed during snowy weather in the Hurricane Creek area in 1910 by Cherokee descendant William Straud Riddle according to Mr. Hyatt. The wolf had killed several sheep owned by a Mr. Sewell who lived south of Grayson. After hunting and tracking the wolf in the snow nearly all day, the hunt was ended without success. As Mr. Riddle started home toward the western side of Sipsey River, he found fresh wolf tracks in the snow. After tracking the animal a short distance, he saw the wolf standing next to a huge hollow log where it had denned. Once the wolf was shot and killed, it was taken home and was placed in a standing position before it became stiff. Many people came to see the carcass before it was finally discarded.

At one time three species of wolves inhabited Lawrence County, they were known as the Red Wolf, Black Wolf, and Grey Wolf. In the early days of this county, all three wolf scalps could be used in the payment of taxes. Notice in the following law:

ACTS OF ALABAMA 1835 SESSION. ACT NO. 123 Pages 119, 120

"After passage of this Act, it shall be lawful for Tax Collectors of Franklin and Lawrence Counties to receive all wolf scalps in payment of any county tax due from any person in the county, on prior affidavit made before an acting Justice of the Peace that the wolves were killed in Franklin or Lawrence County, as the case may be - Scalps received at the following rate; all scalps under one year $1.00; all scalps one year and upward $1.50. Tax Collector of each county to return affidavits with scalps to the County Treasurer as money for any county tax due from them as tax collectors - no money to be paid out for scalps; only receive scalps in payment of taxes."

LESSON 22 – TRADITIONAL CULTURAL PROPERTIES

Bear and Panther - The black bear and eastern cougar were eliminated from Bankhead as a breeding population in the early 1900s. Specific information about the demise of the last bear and cougar in Bankhead is unknown, however, many mountaineers tell stories of encounters their grandparents had with bears and panthers during the early 1800s. Reports of bears and cougars still persist to this very day; however, no known population of either exist in the Warrior Mountains.

It is estimated that some 30 wild eastern cougars still roam the swamps of southern Florida and ranks as the most endangered animal in the Southeastern United States. Today, beautiful captive eastern cougars can be seen in Lawrence County at the Animal House Zoological Park at Hatton.

Elk - The eastern elk migrated the Appalachian Mountains into Alabama in the early 1800s. The elk were rapidly eliminated by Indian and early settler hunters. The eastern elk were killed out in the state of Tennessee by 1870. No known record exists on the demise of eastern elk in the Warrior Mountains of Lawrence County.

Birds - The passenger pigeons, which are now extinct, were once beautiful birds in the Warrior Mountains. The last passenger pigeons seen here was in 1893. Eight birds were killed before the flock (with over 300 birds) flew away, never to return here.

Another bird which was once native to the Warrior Mountains was the ivory-billed woodpecker. These woodpeckers have not lived in Alabama since about 1906 and are almost extinct due to habitat destruction and needless killings.

Passenger Pigeon - Passenger pigeons were beautiful birds that once filled the skies and woodlands of the Warrior Mountains. Old-timers have passed down stories of passenger pigeons, which were extremely abundant and roosted in mature hardwoods in flocks containing thousands of birds. The passenger pigeons, much larger but similar to an oversize mourning dove, would use the same roosts for years. One such roost existing in the northern portion of Bankhead was near the forks of Thompson and West Flint Creeks, which was at the site of the old Jake Alexander Place (now Dallas Yeager's farm). Other places in surrounding areas immortalized the name of the passenger pigeon by being named "Pigeon Roost."

The pigeons were smoked out at night while on the roost by huge bond fires. They were also shot and killed at their nesting sites. Eventually, this beautiful wilderness bird was eliminated from Bankhead Forest with its last verified flock appearance in Alabama in 1893. Eight birds were killed before this flock containing some three hundred birds flew away never to return to our state. The last known passenger pigeon died while in captivity on September 1, 1914, at the Cincinnati Zoological Garden. This wilderness bird that once fed on the giant chestnut, oak, and beech in Bankhead Forest is now extinct.

Ivory-billed Woodpecker - The ivory-billed woodpecker, another large bird once native to the Warrior Mountains, is on the verge of extinction due to habitat destruction as well as needless killings. The last known ivory-billed woodpecker in Alabama died about 1906. The bird met its fate at the hands of a hunter who probably never considered his kill would be the last of the species reported from our state.

The ivory-billed woodpecker's form was mystic and immortalized by prehistoric Alabama Indians who engraved its image on stone plates, handles of axes, and other ornaments of the Mississippian culture. If our early ancestors who used rifles had cared that much for this bird of mystery, our children today may have been blest not only by sight of the bird but also by the sound of its hammering beak in the hills and hollows of the Warrior Mountains.

Carolina Parakeet – In January 1818, Anne Royall describes flocks of Carolina parakeets in Lawrence County. The Carolina parakeets were probably the most colorful and beautiful birds to inhabit our country. Anne Royall noted they were beautiful birds with yellow and green plumage. They loved very ripe fruit and corn. When one bird was wounded, the others would hover over it making the whole flock easy prey for hunters. Eventually, all the Carolina parakeets were wiped out and never seen here again. They are now extinct.

Plants - The American chestnut was the largest nut producing tree in North America. It was killed by the chestnut blight in the 1930s. The American Indians utilized vast quantities of the American Chestnut. Old growth timber only exists in a few places in the Warrior Mountains. Trees over 100 years old are considered old growth. Most old growth timber at one time was replaced with pines.

LESSON 22 – TRADITIONAL CULTURAL PROPERTIES

Protection of TCPs - Our ancestors used the natural resources without destroying them. They developed a balanced way of life in harmony with nature. Our Indian people practiced conservation of soil, water, plant, and animal life. This allowed them to live in the same region for century after century with no ill effects. To our Indian people, the land was sacred. All forms of life were equal because each plant and animal was a link in the life cycle chain. To upset this balance could destroy life as it was meant to be. Because of their reverence for the earth, Indians lived in harmony with nature. They felt they had the right to take what they needed but no more. Our society no longer has the same respect for land that it once did.

Raise your hand to give an example of how our environment is being abused? (1)Littering; (2)Pollution-factories, cars, garbage; (3)Clear cutting; (4)Wildfires; (5)Oil spills. Our main focus today is on clear cutting. What exactly do you think clear cutting means as far as the Warrior Mountains is concerned? Why should it bother you as an Indian person? Clear cutting is the process of destroying acres upon acres of timber with the use of heavy equipment such as bulldozers. When an area is set to be clear cut, nothing is left standing. Several thousand acres of old growth hardwood timber in our own community has been destroyed by clear cutting. Much of the clear cutting in the Warrior Mountains has been done by the U. S. Forest Service. In 2005, it is hoped that the U.S. Forest Service has taken new steps that will protect our public lands from the ravages of clear cutting.

There are many historical sites in the Bankhead National Forest. Much of our heritage lies within the beautiful mountainous areas. Do we want it to be destroyed? How many of you have been through the Bankhead Forest in the last year? You can't help but see the destruction that has taken place over the years. Maybe the healing processes of this public land of ours can begin to recover to its former old growth state.

You need to realize that not all the land being clear cut is on public lands. Many private landowners chose to sell their timber for money. They are concerned with money in their pocket now. Clear cutting affects the entire environment. Many of the old growth hardwood trees are homes to many animals. What if you went home one day and your house was flattened by a bulldozer?

You would feel confused, hurt, and lost. As these old trees are being destroyed many are replaced with pine plantations. The reason is they grow faster and could be cut again sooner. Some of the trees like the beech tree which was used for Indian markings are hundreds of years old. That means it will take hundreds of years to reach this size again, but the markings are lost forever.

LESSON 22 – TRADITIONAL CULTURAL PROPERTIES

KINDERGARTEN

DIBELS Reading Objective: ALL DIBELS SKILLS

Objective: After the teacher directs this lesson, Kindergarten Indian students will develop initial sound fluency by matching the letter to the sound of words found within the text.

Objective Activity: Ask student to identify the letter that matches the beginning sounds of selected words. Example: warrior, area, forest, etc.

STATE STANDARDS Reading Objective:

PG. 14 #9 Begin to use pictures and text to gain meaning from written material
- Throughout the lesson show numerous pictures of the plants, animals, and places that are a part of the Warrior Mountains. (Ex: tree in Indian Tomb Hollow Kinlock Rock Shelter, Sipsey River, Ship Rock, turkeys, whitetail deer, black bear, Eastern cougar and elk, Carolina parakeet, ivory-billed woodpecker, American chestnut tree, etc.
  - *What's the name of the place located in Bankhead that has the tree shaped like a goal post or long horns? (Indian Tomb Hollow)*
  - *What's the name of the rock shaped like a ship? (Ship Rock)*
  - *What kind of deer used to live there? (whitetail deer)*

PG. 15 #14 Demonstrate an interest in an enjoyment of literature in a variety of forms, contexts, and media
- After discussing the Warrior Mountains and showing a variety of pictures, let the students draw a picture of what they think the mountains look like. (have them include rivers or waterfalls, animals, plant, etc.)
  - *Name one of the birds that used to live in Bankhead. (passenger pigeons, ivory-billed woodpecker, and Carolina parakeet)*

STATE STANDARDS Social Studies Objective:

PG. 11 #1 Develop initial map and globe skills
- Locate Lawrence County on map. Show them where Bankhead is versus where they live on county map.
- Show map of Bankhead and mark locations of different places like Sipsey, Kinlock, etc.
  - *What county in Alabama is Bankhead located? (Lawrence County)*
  - *Is this National Forest located near you? (yes)*

Review Questions
1. What important animal to our Indian ancestors still lives in the Bankhead Forest? (deer)
2. Who was John Bull? (a frontiersman and famous rifle maker)
3. Name one way our early ancestors kept records of things that happened: (picture writing)
4. Who helped General John Coffee's force burn Black Warrior Town? (David Crockett)
5. What type of tree was the Indian marker tree? (beech)

LESSON 22 – TRADITIONAL CULTURAL PROPERTIES

FIRST GRADE

DIBELS Reading Objective: ALL DIBELS SKILLS

Objective: After the teacher directs this lesson, first grade Indian students will develop and understanding of the traditional cultural properties, nonsense word fluency, and phonemic awareness.

Objective Activity: Take words from the text and write them on the board changing the first letter of each word to a nonsense word. Then orally say the word and ask the students if the words sound right. Finally, have the students relate the word to the lesson and explain what the letter and sound should be. (Ex: land-mand, gun-zun, hear-cear)

STATE STANDARDS Reading Objective:

PG. 17 #4 Demonstrate understanding of letter-sound relationships
- Throughout the lesson the teacher will choose several vocabulary words such as: arbor, petro, picto, glyph, etc. to display on the board. The students will sound out each letter then blend the letter-sounds together to form words. The teacher will then discuss the definition of each word. Arbor-tree, petro-rock, picto-pictures, glyph-drawing.
  - ∾ _____ is another word for drawing. (glyph)

PG. 20 #6 Comprehend material read, heard, or viewed
- During a teacher directed lesson about our Indian ancestor's traditional cultural properties, the teacher will describe in detail about the various forms of Cherokee writing in order to create mental pictures of the text. Also show pictures and examples of arborglyphs, petroglyphs, and pictographs. (Beech tree-"Warrior Mountain Folklore" and Kinlock Rock Bluff Shelter in "Indian Trails of the Warrior Mountains" in order for the students to gain a better understanding of material in lesson.
  - ∾ Where can you find an arborglyph in Bankhead? (trees)

STATE STANDARDS Social Studies Objective:

PG. 17 #3 Describe the impact of cultural changes on the locality over time
- Using the general locations map on the back of "Warrior Mountains Folklore" show the students the location of various areas in Bankhead that contain various arborglyphs, petroglyphs, and other drawings.
- Locate Lawrence County on map to show where Bankhead Forest is located.
- A cultural impact that has changed our community over time is the invention of the Cherokee alphabet in 1821 by Sequoyah. Before this time, our Indian ancestors did not have a written language. Since then, our alphabet has improved tremendously into the one we all know and use today.
  - ∾ Sequoyah invented the Cherokee _____. (alphabet or dictionary)
  - ∾ What county do we live in? (Lawrence)

Review Questions

1. What does it mean when you cut all of the trees down with heavy equipment? (clear cutting)
2. What, in Indian Tomb Hollow, is a symbol considered sacred by the descendant of that area? (Indian marker tree)
3. What is a petroglyph? (rock drawing)
4. What is a pictograph? (pictures painted on hard surfaces or animal skins)
5. What is an animal that doesn't live in Bankhead anymore? (Carolina parakeet, passenger pigeon, ivory-billed woodpecker)

LESSON 22 –TRADITIONAL CULTURAL PROPERTIES

SECOND GRADE

DIBELS Reading Objective: ALL DIBELS SKILLS

Objective: After the teacher directs this lesson, second grade Indian students will relate information learned from an orally read text accompanied by a remedial game.

Objective Activity: The teacher and the students will read text from the lesson. Then, the teacher will ask comprehension questions that come directly from the orally read text. Play the game, Who Wants to be a Millionaire, and allow students to decode the answer using this format. Place students on teams and allow one point for that team if they answer correctly. What is another name for Warrior Mountains? (Bankhead Forest)

STATE STANDARDS Reading Objective:

PG. 24 #7   Read and comprehend a variety of material
- The teacher will direct the lesson showing them the book Alabama Canyon or any other text material. Making sure they have an understanding of where they are located.
- *What is another name for the Warrior Mountains? (Bankhead National Forest)*

PG. 25 #10   Read orally with accuracy, fluency, and comprehension
- Students will orally read the section of the lesson about Indian Tomb Hollow. The teacher will encourage the students to read loudly and to properly pronounce their words. The teacher will help the students to read the text clearly and to understand what they have read.
- *Where is the Indian Tomb Hollow located? (Bankhead National Fores)*

STATE STANDARDS Social Studies Objective:

PG. 22 #2   Develop the ability to interpret and display information in graphic form
- While the teacher directs the lesson he/she will show the student Indian Trails of the Warrior Mountains, having the students locate the "Big Tree." Then, the teacher will make sure the students understand why it is called the "Big Tree."
- *What is a tree drawing called? (arborglyph)*

PG. 24 #11   Identify ways people affect the land
- The teacher will have an open discussion with the class and ask questions to ensure the students understand why the livestock was so important to our ancestors.
- *Explain what a pictograph is. (picture drawn or painted on animal skins)*

Review Questions

1. What animal is extinct from the Warrior Mountains? (Carolina parakeet)
2. Petroglyphs, meaning rock drawings, are pictures that have been carved or scratched onto hard surfaces such as: (rocks, shell, or copper)
3. Where did the name "Black Warrior" come from? (Muscogee)
4. Identify the early Indian name for the Black Warrior River. (Tuscaloosa River)
5. Who was the famous rifle maker who made two masterpieces from the Warrior Mountains? (John Bull)

LESSON 22 – TRADITIONAL CULTURAL PROPERTIES

THIRD GRADE

DIBELS Reading Objective: ALL DIBLES SKILLS

Objective: After the teacher directs the lesson, third grade Indian students will able to interpret and gain meaning from the terms in the text. (Ex: traditional, frontier, engraved)

Objective Activity: The teacher will orally read each term to the students. Discuss terms with the students then, tell students to orally say the word and tell the teacher the meaning of the term.

STATE STANDARDS Reading Objective:

PG. 32 #8   Read grade level texts aloud silently with fluency and comprehension
- After the teacher directs the lesson, the students will read from "Indian Trails of the Warrior Mountains" about Indian Tomb Hollow, the Warrior Mountains, Kinlock, Sipsey, and Ship Rock.
- *Identify the rock shelter still used today for ceremonies. (Kinlock Rock Shelter)*

PG. 33 #11   Read materials encountered in daily lives
- The teacher will allow the students to read "Alabama Canyons" to see Kinlock and "Walking Sipsey" about the Sipsey River.
- *Explain the outdoor activities available to visitors of the Sipsey Wilderness Area of Bankhead Forest. (picnicking, hiking, canoeing, horseback riding, etc.)*

STATE STANDARDS Social Studies Objective:

PG. 30 #4   Describe the natural environment of North America (Physical Geography)
- The teacher will show the students pictures of the various places of the Warrior Mountains and ask the students to describe the regions.
- *Explain the difference between an arborglyph and petroglyph. (arborglyph-tree drawing, petroglyph-rock drawing)*

Review Questions

1. What is a symbol considered sacred to descendants of Indian ancestors? (Indian marker tree)
2. The name Warrior Mountains, that has since been renamed after a white politician, can be traced back how many years? (400)
3. Identify the large rock located in the heart of the Sipsey Wilderness. (Ship Rock)
4. What area on Capsey Creek contains two mineral tar springs? (Tar Springs Hollow)
5. What extinct animal was once used as a way of paying taxes? (wolf-red, black and gray)

LESSON 22 – TRADITIONAL CULTURAL PROPERTIES

FOURTH GRADE

SAT Reading Objective: ALL SAT SKILLS

Objective: After the teacher directs this lesson, fourth grade Indian students will gain reading vocabulary knowledge of three out of the six terms found in traditional cultural properties. (Terms: mountains, frontiersman, inscription, etc.)

Objective Activity: Have students read paragraphs from the lesson and select words which they are not familiar. The teacher will explain unfamiliar words to the students and have them repeat words aloud. Students will write word and definition.

STATE STANDARDS Reading Objective:

PG. 37 #1   Using a wide range of strategies to interpret, evaluate, appreciate, and construct meaning from print materials
- Have the students locate information in reference sources such as an encyclopedia, internet, etc. in order to gain a better understanding of material discussed in lesson. (Ex: find pictures of extinct animals/plants in Warrior Mountains)
- If encyclopedia or internet isn't available in classroom, teachers should already have copies of pictures printed to show students.
    - *What's the name of the woodpecker now extinct in the Warrior Mountains? (Ivory-billed woodpecker)*

STATE STANDARDS Social Studies Objective:

PG. 34 #1   Extend the development of map and globe skills
- Locate Bankhead National Forest on the map.
- Locate Lawrence County.
- Mark two different locations on the map of Bankhead Forest such as Indian Tomb Hollow and Kinlock and have the students use the scale on the map to measure distances between the two places.
    - *Name the tree that is now extinct in Warrior Mountains. (American Chestnut)*

PG. 35 #5   Describe the natural environment of Alabama including significant geographical features
- Describe how the Warrior Mountains located in Lawrence County is a significant geographical feature of Alabama. Also, show pictures of the various places, animals, plants, rivers, waterfalls, etc. and explain how these mountains are now the Bankhead National Forest. (Use "Alabama Canyon's book)
    - *What is the name of the National Forest in Lawrence County that is also called the Warrior Mountains? (Bankhead National Forest)*

Review Questions
1. What is an arborglyph? (tree drawing)
2. Bankhead National Forest is also known as what mountains in what county? (Black Warrior, Lawrence)
3. What year did Indian Tomb Hollow become a cultural property? (2001)
4. What giant of a man did Desoto encounter who was also known as Black Warrior? (Chief Tuscaloosa)
5. Name at least two geographical locations within the Bankhead National Forest. (Kinlock and Indian Tomb Hollow)

LESSON 22 – TRADITIONAL CULTURAL PROPERTIES

FIFTH GRADE

SAT Reading Objective: ALL SAT SKILLS

Objective: After directed lesson, fifth grade students will gain understanding and be able to identify terms from the traditional cultural properties.

Objective Activity: The teacher will review the lesson and play *Wheel of Fortune* or *Hangman* with students. Give clues from the text that means the same as the terms.

STATE STANDARDS Reading Objective:

PG. 46 #12   Read a variety of materials and genres encountered in daily lives
- After the teacher directs the lesson, the students will read from "Indian Trails of the Warrior Mountain" and "Alabama Canyons" about things taught from the lesson. (Ex: Black Warrior, Indian Tomb Hollow, Kinlock)
  - *What's the name of the woodpecker now extinct in the Warrior Mountains? (ivory-billed woodpecker)*

PG. 46 #13   Apply strategies of a skillful listener
- The students will listen to other students and be able to answer the teacher's questions after the lesson.
  - *What is an arborglyph? (tree drawing)*

STATE STANDARDS Social Studies Objective:

PG. 46 #4   Describe the natural environment of North America
- After the teacher directs the lesson, the teacher will discuss with the students the wildlife, mountains, and the different places in the mountains. The teacher will show pictures, books, and allow the students to tell if they have been to any of these places.
  - *What is another name for Warrior Mountains? (Bankhead National Forest)*

Review Questions

1. What are symbols found on rocks at Kinlock Rock Shelter called? (petroglyphs)
2. In 2001, Indian Tomb Hollow became protected from what by the U.S. forest Service? (future log operations)
3. What shelter, in the Bankhead Forest, is one of the largest of its kind? (Kinlock Rock Shelter)
4. What are other names the Ship Rock site is known for? (Herron Point, Boart Rock, Needles Eye, and the Windows)
5. What deep canyon is located east of Sipsey River and is probably the most primeval site in the Warrior Mountains? (Bee Branch Canyon)

LESSON 22 –TRADITIONAL CULTURAL PROPERTIES

SIXTH GRADE

<u>SAT</u> Reading Objective: ALL SAT SKILLS

Objective: After the teacher directs the lesson, the students will gain an understanding of different informational materials from the text on Traditional Cultural Properties.

Objective Activity: The teacher will draw a timeline on the board discussing the different events and properties such as: Battle of Indian Tomb Hollow-Nov 7, 14, 21 of 1856 and John Bull-1829-two rifle masterpieces in Warrior Mountains, 1910-last known timber wolf of Bankhead and etc. Next, students will discuss each event and the teacher will write the details under each event.

<u>STATE STANDARDS</u> Reading Objective:

PG. 52 #2   Read with ease textural, functional, and recreational materials encountered in daily life
- After the teacher directs the lesson, the students will utilize the following reading content standards: literary and informational comprehension and recognition of text elements in functional materials in the text in aboriginal places of the Warrior Mountains, Indian Tomb Hollow, and Kinlock, etc. The students will answer the review questions to show their understanding of the lesson's main idea and their answer.
  - *What is the premier petroglyph site in Lawrence County? (Kinlock Rock Shelter)*

<u>STATE STANDARDS</u> Social Studies Objective:

PG. 54 #1   Extend the development of map and globe skills
- While the teacher directs the lesson, he/she will show maps or pictures of the different locations and review the material to be sure the students comprehend the material heard and seen.
  - *Chestnut Ridge, High House Hill, and Beulah make up the high ground around this sacred canyon known as _____ _____ _____. (Indian Tomb Hollow)*

Review Questions

1. Where are Indian Tomb Hollow, Sipsey River, and Bee Branch Canyon located? (Warrior Mountains)
2. What Creek is Kinlock Falls located? (Hubbard Creek)
3. What two animals were eliminated from Bankhead as a breeding population in the early 1900s? (black bear, eastern cougar)
4. What tree was the largest nut producing tree in North America, killed by blight in the 1930s? (American Chestnut)
5. How old does a tree have to be to be considered old growth? (100 years)

LESSON 22 – TRADITIONAL CULTURAL PROPERTIES

SEVENTH GRADE

<u>SAT</u> Reading Objective: ALL SAT SKILLS

Objective: After the teacher directs this lesson, the students will respond and apply basic principles of how information is properly presented and viewed, heard, or read materials from the text on traditional cultural properties.

Objective Activity: Each student can read aloud from the lesson. Next, play a remedial game, such as, *Jeopardy, Wheel of fortune*, etc., and ask questions concerning the lesson during the game to ensure comprehension.

<u>STATE STANDARDS</u> Reading Objective:

PG. 59 #15   Respond with understanding and empathy to information read, viewed, and heard
- After the teacher directs the lesson, discuss with the class the traditional cultural properties making sure the class has an understanding of the lesson. (Ex: The Warrior Mountains was also known as Black Warrior)
  - *Warrior Mountains is also known as? (Bankhead National Forest)*

<u>STATE STANDARDS</u> Social Studies Objective:

Online Alex #10   Describe changes in social and economic conditions
- After the teacher directs the lesson have the students read aloud on traditional cultural properties.
  - *Where is Kinlock Falls located (Hubbard Creek in Bankhead Forest)*

Review Questions
1. What is the best known waterfall in the Bankhead Forest? (Kinlock Falls)
2. Later in 1814, a map of Alabama identified what river draining south for Lawrence County? (Black Warrior River)
3. Colonel Edmonds Saunders refers to Lawrence County's southern highland as what? (Warrior Mountains)
4. What shelter in the Bankhead Forest has been deemed eligible to be nominated to the National Register of Historic Places? (Kinlock Bluff Shelter)
5. What cove, in the Bankhead Forest, still contains three old log houses that were used over 100 years ago? (Parker Cove)

LESSON 23 – STATE RECOGNIZED INDIAN TRIBES OF ALABAMA

Map of State Recognized Indian Tribes

There are nine Indian tribes in the State of Alabama that have enrolled several thousand Indians. These represent about 13% of the 165,416 persons in Alabama who disclosed that they were of Indian ancestry in the Federal Census of 1980. Most of those with Indian ancestry in Alabama are descendants of the Cherokee, Choctaw, and Creek tribes who were the aboriginal inhabitants of the State. While the majority of the members of these tribes were removed to Indian Territory in the 1830s, a significant Indian minority remained in the State, including Cherokees in North Alabama, Creeks in South Alabama, as well as a sizeable community of Choctaws in Southwest Alabama (Alabama Indian Affairs Commission, 1988). As of February 2006, Alabama has officially nine Indian tribes with only the Poarch Band of Creek Indians being recognized by the Federal government. In addition to the Poarch Band of Creek Indians, the other state recognized tribes are as follows: Echota Cherokee Tribe of Alabama; Cherokee Tribe of Northeast Alabama; Machis Lower Creek Indian Tribe; Star Clan of Muscogee Creeks; Cher-o-Creek Intra Tribal Indians; MOWA Band of Choctaw Indians; Piqua Shawnee Tribe; and, United Cherokee Ani-Yun-Wiya Nation.

Poarch Band of Creek Indians –
The Poarch Band of Creek Indians descended from the original Creek Nation, which avoided removal and remained in South Alabama. The Creek Nation originally occupied a territory covering nearly all of Georgia and Alabama. The War of 1812 divided the Creek Nation between an Upper party hostile to the United States and a group of Upper and Lower Creeks friendly to the government. The Treaty of Ft. Jackson compelled the Creek Nation to cede much of the territory of those friendly Creeks to the United States including the present site of Poarch. Those Creeks who had actively fought with the United States were permitted a reservation of one square mile. Several Creek families including the Gibsons, Manacs, Colberts, and Weatherfords, secured reservations immediately after the treaty. Congress in 1836 passed an act allowing Lynn McGhee and the others to set aside 640 acres as reservations under the 1814 Treaty of Fort Jackson. The United States continued to protect the Poarch settlement after the removal of the main Creek body to Oklahoma in 1836.

Today, there are nearly 2,200 members of the Poarch Band of Creek Indians, with over 1,500 living in the vicinity of Poarch, Alabama in rural Escambia County. The Poarch Band of Creek Indians is bound by kinship. A leader, that helped to improve the social and economic situation of the Poarch Creeks was Calvin W. McGhee, who pressed for settlement of a land claims case. Also, Eddie L. Tullis, Tribal Chairman as of 1987, led the Poarch Creek Indians in their petitioning the U.S. Government to be federally recognized.

 The Echota Cherokee Tribe of Alabama – During the 1990 U.S. Census, 6.7% of Lawrence Countians were listed as American Indian. In the 2000 U.S. Census, 5.8% of Lawrence Countians indicated they were American Indian. The vast majority of Lawrence County's Indian people are members of the Echota Cherokee Tribe of Alabama. Many of the Lawrence County Echota Cherokees are descended from Cherokee Chief Doublehead and his followers.

LESSON 23 – STATE RECOGNIZED INDIAN TRIBES OF ALABAMA

The United Cherokee Tribe of Alabama was organized on June 14, 1978, at Daleville, Alabama. B. J. Faulkner was elected principal chief, and Thomas McCloski was elected vice-principal chief. A council of nine people was formed, and the Secretary and Treasurer positions were filled. In 1978, Chief Faulkner opposed the development plans for an industrial park near Northport that would disturb a 1,000-year-old Indian village site and burial ground. In January of 1980, he sought the reburial of 3,000 Indians along the route to be flooded by the Tennessee - Tombigbee Waterway. In 1980, disenchanted members of the United Cherokee Tribe of Alabama formed a new tribe called Echota Cherokee Tribe, Inc.

Joseph "Two Eagles" Stewart was elected principal chief, and Letter of Incorporation was filed in Shelby County and their seal was registered. The tribe filed for and received non-profit status and clans were organized over the State. A newsletter, "Smoke Signals," was mailed to members. Regular monthly meetings were held at the Alabaster Community Center. The governing body of the tribe, consisting of tribal council members, elected officers, principal chief and vice-principal chief, was set in to serve a four-year term. (Cromer, 1984)

The Echota Cherokee Tribe is the largest and one of the most active tribes in Alabama today. The tribe has several thousand members in Alabama and other states. The tribe is affiliated with several Indian education programs in Madison County, DeKalb County, Jackson County, and Lawrence County.

The tribe has a land fund established for the purpose of purchasing land to build a Cherokee meeting ground and museum. Tribal members are active in voter registration drives around the state. The tribe, represented by the principal chief, is a member of the Alabama Indian Affairs Commission and the National Congress of American Indian (Cromer, 1984). Explain Echota is a tribe we are affiliated with (show shield or picture of symbol of the Cherokee). The vast majority of Lawrence County Indian students are members of the Echota Cherokee Tribe of Alabama.

Cherokee Tribe of Northeast Alabama - The Jackson County Cherokees formed a Tribal Council on May 5, 1981, at North Sand Mountain High School, Higdon, Alabama. Dr. H.L. "Lindy" Martin presided over the meeting which elected the following council members: Jaynn Kushner, Ceil Hicks, Bill Williams, Joe Hunkapiller, Marland Mountain, David Cornally and David Rooks.

The presence of the Cherokee in Jackson County was almost unknown for years even though the tribe had been under the leadership of Chief John Justice, William Keep, James McCony, and Claud Thornhill.

According to Dr. Martin, the Cherokees of Jackson, Alabama, are the descendants of the Cherokee Indians who were led by Chief Dragging Canoe. The Indians had come into Alabama in the early 1780s and settled in an area, which had traditionally been tribal hunting territory. They established five major towns and several smaller villages.

Dr. Martin resigned as chairman of the Jackson County Cherokees in the fall of 1982. In 1983, the tribe changed its name to Cherokees of Northeast Alabama, Inc. Travis Staggs became chairman, and David Rooks became vice-chairman. In 1984, Jaynn Kushner became representative to Alabama Indian Affairs Commission (Cromer, 1984).

Cher-o-Creek Intra Tribal Indians - This group was originally known as The Cherokees of Southeast Alabama In 1982 in Houston County, a group of Cherokee Indians organized into a tribe under the leadership of their elected Chief Deal Wambles. In 1984, the tribe began efforts to establish Indian education classes in their county school system, where tribal members are taught Indian beadwork, dances, and leatherwork.

In 1984, the Tribe held their first Pow-Wow, which drew members and guests from Houston and Dale Counties. The tribal government is made up of an executive committee, the principal chief, the vice-principal chief, the administrative chief, the tribal council, the medicine man, the beloved woman, and the war chief (Cromer, 1984).

Star Clan of Lower Muscogee Creek Indians - *The Yufala "Star" Clan: A Modern Day Tribe with Traditional Values* The Star Clan of Lower Muscogee Creek Indians takes its name from both the Muscogee word "Y'ufala" (Eagle), and the Star, which if found within the Tribal symbol. In the early 1970s, the Tribe chose to relocate its headquarters in the Western sphere of their traditional area of influence. Under the leadership of

LESSON 23 – STATE RECOGNIZED INDIAN TRIBES OF ALABAMA

Chief Larry Johnson, the Tribe moved to Pike County, Alabama.

In 1978, Larry Johnson retired from the office of Chief, and returned to his hometown of Panama City, Florida. It was in October of 1978 that Tommy Davenport was appointed Chief of the Star Clan. During his time in office, he was instrumental in helping to create the Alabama Indian Affairs Commission. He also served on the Commission from its inception. He was Chairman of the Alabama Indian Affairs commission at the time of his death in 1991. At that time, it was the consensus of the Tribe to elect his wife, Erma Lis Davenport, as Chief of the Yufala "Star" Clan. She presently serves in that capacity, continuing the pioneering work that her husband began almost 30 years ago.

Ma-Chis Lower Creek Indian Tribe - In 1985, almost 900 Lower Creeks of Coffee County organized into a tribe under the rules and guidelines of the Alabama Indian Affairs Commission. They were the first tribe in the state to organize under the criteria set forth by the A.I.A.C.

Mrs. Penny Wright was elected as leader of the group, the state's only "female chief." In July of 1985, Governor George Wallace appointed Dr. Johnny Wright, a high school principal from Pike County and member of the Ma-Chis tribe to represent the tribe on the A.I.A.C. Dr. Wright brought to the Board a wealth of expertise in administrative and educational experience. He serves as principal of Pike County High School.

Chief Penny Wright was cited by <u>Women's Day</u> magazine in their fall, 1985 issue, as the only female Indian chief in the United States. Since then, another woman, Chief Mankiller of the Western Cherokee nation has been elected to lead the Cherokees of Oklahoma.

MOWA Band of Choctaw Indians - The MOWA Choctaws of Mobile and Washington Counties, Alabama, get their name from a combination of the two counties where most of these Choctaws reside. They rekindled their great council fire in Washington County in December 1981 after blending in with the general population for some 160 years.

The MOWA Band of Choctaw Indians was duly incorporated in 1979 with its tribal office located in McIntosh and purchased 160 acres of land in south Washington County in 1983. There are five officers and fourteen members of the tribe's commission who voluntarily assist the operations of tribal affairs.

Today, there are nearly 6,000 members of the MOWA Band of Choctaw Indians, over 2,500 of whom live in the vicinity of McIntosh, Alabama. All the members are descendants of the original Choctaw Nation who are bound together by a complex network of multigenerational kinship.

Piqua Shawnee Tribe - Early historical records show that the Shawnee were inhabitants of Lawrence County and North Alabama. They were forced from the Tennessee Valley by the combined efforts of the Chickasaw and Cherokee. Most historians label Shawnee people as nomadic because they have found evidence of Shawnee people moving about in North America, settling in various places and often retaining small family units for long periods of time.

North Alabama has long been the home of many Shawnee people. In fact, some historians state that perhaps the Shawnee people have inhabited Alabama for a longer period of time than any other geographic region. Some archaeologist set the date of 1685 as the first evidence of Shawnee settlement in Alabama. However, oral tradition states that Shawnees have been here much longer than that. Ancient burial sites that use methods common to the Shawnee have been located in several sections of the state.

Now, in the 21st century, there are many descendants who still call Alabama home. Many of their family stories are varied. Some avoided walking the Trail of Tears. Some families escaped into the Cumberland Mountains, others hid in swamps or less traveled places. A careful study of southeastern history will reveal that not all settlers agreed with Andrew Jackson's removal policy. While many people did not escape the removal, some did. After the turmoil subsided some families returned. Many families chose to live in outlying rural areas where there was little government scrutiny and their neighbors weren't too curious. While a lot was lost, family histories and ways were passed down.

LESSON 23 –STATE RECOGNIZED INDIAN TRIBES OF ALABAMA

It is out of that background that current Piquas live and work to preserve their unique heritage. The tribe consists of several family groups that are interrelated with the majority of Piquas living in Alabama.

United Cherokee Ani-Yun-Wiya Nation - The United Cherokee were recognized by the State of Alabama on July 10, 2001. The United Cherokees are descendants of the Cherokees are descendants of the Cherokees in Northeast Alabama around the Guntersville area. The original Cherokee villages and settlements in the area included Willstown, Creek Path, Gunters, Red Hill, Wasasa Village, Turkey Town, Litafatchee, Brown's Village, and Meltonsville. Gina Williamson from Guntersville serves as the tribal chief and serves on the Alabama Indian Affairs Commission.

LESSON 23 – STATE RECOGNIZED INDIAN TRIBES OF ALABAMA

KINDERGARTEN

<u>DIBELS</u> Reading Objective: ALL DIBELS SKILLS

Objective: After the teacher directs this lesson, Kindergarten Indian students will use initial sound and letter naming fluency.

Objective Activity: The students will develop an understanding of the beginning sounds of a specific letter while using flash cards, pictures, or words written on the board. Then, the students will pronounce the letters. The teacher will identify additional words from the lesson for students to pronounce.

<u>STATE STANDARDS</u> Reading Objective:

PG. 14 #6 Demonstrate an initial understanding of letter sound relationships
- Choose a few words from the lesson. Write them on board, pronounce each letter with students then, have them say the word aloud. (Ex: Echota tribe-name of our tribe)
- *What is the name of our tribe? (Echota Cherokee Tribe)*

PG. 14 #9 Begin to use pictures and text to gain meaning from written material
- Show pictures of Echota Cherokee symbol (let them color their own after lesson)
- *What is the bird in the middle of our tribe's symbol? (eagle/Phoenix)*

PG. 15 #15 Use appropriate listening and speaking behaviors
- Continue to ask questions throughout lesson and afterwards to make sure students listened and understand/comprehend material discussed.
- *Is our tribe the largest or smallest in Alabama? (largest)*

PG. 15 #17 Exhibit expanded vocabulary and sentence awareness
- Have class discussion on why the eagle/Phoenix is the bird in the symbol while they are coloring.
- *Why is the eagle/Phoenix on our symbol? (Cherokee considered sacred)*

<u>STATE STANDARDS</u> Social Studies Objective:

PG. 11 #1 Develop initial map and globe skills
- Locate Madison County, Dekalb County, and Jackson County on Alabama map. Explain how those three counties are the only others that have privilege to have Indian education.
- *Are there other counties in Alabama that have Indian education? (yes)*

<u>Review Questions</u>
1. What is the largest tribe in Alabama? (Echota Cherokee Tribe)
2. How many Indian tribes are in the State of Alabama? (nine)
3. Where was the United Cherokee Tribes of Alabama organized? (Daleville, Alabama)
4. What year was the Echota Cherokee Tribe formed? (1980)
5. Who formed a tribal council? (The Jackson County Cherokee)

LESSON 23 – STATE RECOGNIZED INDIAN TRIBES OF ALABAMA

FIRST GRADE

DIBELS Reading Objective: ALL DIBELS SKILLS

Objective: After the teacher directs this lesson, first grade Indian students will utilize the following reading content standards of letter naming, nonsense word fluency, and phoneme segmentation.

Objective Activity: The teacher will write terms on the board from the lesson and the students will pronounce each sound and letter of the word. Next, the teacher will write words on the board changing the initial letter making a nonsense word. Then, the students will pronounce the word. (Ex: Man-Gan, etc.) The teacher will help students segment and pronounce the parts of selected words.

STATE STANDARDS Reading Objective:

PG. 20 #6   Comprehend material read, heard, or viewed
- Show various pictures of Choctaw Indians so the students will have a better understanding of the lesson and also ask teacher generated questions to check for comprehension.
  - How many members are in the MOWA Band of Choctaw? (10,000 or 6,000)

PG. 21 #16   Demonstrate appropriate listening and speaking behaviors
- During group discussion, review the nine Indian tribes of Alabama and the information previously discussed about the Echota Cherokee Tribe. After review introduce the MOWA Band of Choctaw Indians to the students.
  - Today, how many tribes are located in Alabama? (9 or 17)

STATE STANDARDS Social Studies Objective:

PG. 18 #3   Extend initial ability to locate new information and to express understanding in various classroom
- State map-show Mobile, Washington, and Lawrence Counties.
  - Did the MOWA Choctaw get their name from one or two counties? (two)

Review Questions

1. A majority of Lawrence County Indian students are members of what tribe? (Echota Cherokee Tribe)
2. Many of Lawrence county Echota Cherokees are descended from what chief? (chief Doublehead)
3. What year was the Echota Cherokee Tribe formed? (1980)
4. Were Shawnee people nomadic? (yes)
5. What is the Echota Cherokees newsletter called? (Smoke Signals)

LESSON 23 – STATE RECOGNIZED INDIAN TRIBES OF ALABAMA

SECOND GRADE

DIBELS Reading Objective: ALL DIBELS SKILLS

Objective: After the teacher directs this lesson, second grade Indian students will utilize the reading content standards of oral reading fluency and nonsense word fluency.

Objective Activity: The teacher will orally read from the lesson, "State Recognized Indian Tribes of Alabama." Then students will have an open answers and questions session. Teacher will make nonsense words for students to say aloud, by choosing words from the lesson and changing the first or last letter in the term. Then, the students will decide if the words are nonsense words or real words.

STATE STANDARDS Reading Objective:

PG. 25 #10   Read orally with accuracy, fluency, and comprehension
- While the teacher directs the lesson, the students will read aloud from the lesson and the teacher will ask questions to the students to check comprehension skills.
  - *What is the name of our tribe? (Echota Cherokee Tribe)*

STATE STANDARDS Social Studies Objective:

PG. 22 #1   Develop map and globe skills
- While the teacher directs the lesson he/she will show the children a map of Alabama and show the children Madison County, Dekalb County, Jackson County, and Lawrence County. The teacher will explain to the kids that the Echota Cherokee Tribe is affiliated with several Indian education programs. Then the teacher will get a globe and show the students the U.S. and Alabama.
  - *What county do we live in? (Lawrence)*
  - *What state do we live in? (Alabama)*

Review Questions
1. How many modern tribes are in the state of Alabama? (9)
2. The Shawnee inhabited what state for a longer period of time than any other geographic region? (Alabama)
3. The Poarch Band of Creek Indians are bound by what? (kinship)
4. How many members are in the MOWA Band of Choctaw? (10,000 or 6,000)
5. What bird is in the center of our tribe's symbol? (eagle/Phoenix)

LESSON 23 – STATE RECOGNIZED INDIAN TRIBES OF ALABAMA

THIRD GRADE

DIBELS Reading Objective: ALL DIBLES SKILLS

Objective: After the teacher directs the lesson, third grade Indian students will utilize the reading content standards of oral reading fluency.

Objective Activity: The teacher will orally read from the lesson and let each student read a paragraph. Then the students will explain what they have read in their own words.

STATE STANDARDS Reading Objective:

PG. 32 #3   Demonstrate literal understanding of printed material (Identifying sequence of events)
- While the teacher directs the lesson, the teacher will draw a time line on the board and show the students when the tribes were organized. The students will learn how to draw a time line also. (Ex: their birthday-started school-year graduate)
  - *The Jackson County Cherokees formed a tribal council when? (May 5, 1981)*

STATE STANDARDS Social Studies Objective:

PG. 30 #5   Relate the elements of geography to the time of the early Native Americans (Uses of geography. Ex: location of settlements)
- As the teacher directs the lesson, he/she will discuss the locations of the settlements of the tribes of Alabama. Also, the teacher will show the students on an Alabama map where the tribes are located.
  - *How many tribes are in Alabama? (nine)*

Review Questions

1. The Echota Cherokee Tribe was formed in what year? (1980)
2. The Echota Cherokee Tribe is the largest and the most active tribe in what state? (Alabama)
3. Most Alabamians claiming Indian ancestry are descendants of what three tribes? (Cherokee, Choctaw, and Creek)
4. The Shawnee were inhabitants of what county? (Lawrence)
5. Which tribe of Indians got their name from an eagle and a star? (Star Clan of Lower Muscogee Creek)

LESSON 23 – STATE RECOGNIZED INDIAN TRIBES OF ALABAMA

FOURTH GRADE

SAT Reading Objective: ALL SAT SKILLS

Objective: After the teacher directs this lesson, fourth grade Indian students will be able to gain meaning of vocabulary words from the text.

Objective Activity: The Indian students will participate in a word game such as *Hangman, Jeopardy, Wheel of Fortune,* etc…by identifying and recognizing important terms found in this lesson.

STATE STANDARDS Reading Objective:

PG. 38 #6   Demonstrate reading improvement gained through substantial amounts of daily reading
- After the teacher directs a lesson, have students read text from Indian Trails of the Warrior Mountains or any other text material.
  - *Which tribe is the largest and one of the most active tribes in Alabama? (Echota Cherokee Tribe)*

STATE STANDARDS Social Studies Objective:

PG. 34 #2   Interpret and display information and data using various graphic organizations
- After the lesson, show pictures of maps of where the tribes are located.
  - *Which tribe is located near Mobile and Washington counties? (MOWA Band of Choctaw Indians)*

Review Questions

1. Who was the elected principal chief when the Echota Cherokee Tribe was formed in 1980? (B.J. Faulkner)
2. In January 1980, Chief Faulkner sought the reburial of 3,000 Indians along the route to be flooded by what? (Tennessee-Tombigbee Waterway)
3. Who formed a tribal council on May 5, 1981? (The Jackson County Cherokee)
4. Chief Faulkner opposed plans for an industrial park near Northport that would disturb what? (1,000 year old Indian village site and burial ground)
5. What tribe was organized on June 14, 1978, at Daleville, AL? (The United Cherokee Tribe of Alabama)

LESSON 23 – STATE RECOGNIZED INDIAN TRIBES OF ALABAMA

FIFTH GRADE

<u>SAT</u> Reading Objective: ALL SAT SKILLS

Objective: After the teacher directs this lesson, fifth grade Indian students will be able to gain meaning of the vocabulary words from the text. (Terms: ancestry, Echota, tribe, chief, hostile, etc.)

Objective Activity: Write the vocabulary and definitions on the board and let individuals match the terms to the correct definition. You could also have several fill-in-the-blank questions.

<u>STATE STANDARDS</u> Reading Objective:

PG. 45 #6   Demonstrate reading improvement gained through substantial amounts of daily reading
- After the teacher directs a lesson, have students read text material. While the students are reading, the teacher should correct the student if they make any mistakes.
  - *Cher-o-creek Intra Tribal Indians was originally known as what? (The Cherokees of Southeast Alabama)*

<u>STATE STANDARDS</u> Social Studies Objective:

PG. 46 #7   Analyze the different cultures of Native American groups by geographic regions
- After the lesson, have an open discussion about the different tribes.
  - *The Poarch Band of Creek Indians descended form what nation? (Creek Nation)*

Review Questions

1. How long is the term of an elected governing body of the Echota Cherokee Tribe? (4 years)
2. During the 1990 U.S. Census, what percentage of Lawrence Countians were listed as American Indian? (6.7%)
3. Who was the state's only female chief? (Mrs. Penny Wright)
4. The Poarch Band of Creeks Indians descended from the original Creek Nation, which avoided removal and remained where? (South Alabama)
5. Who was the elected principal chief when the Echota Cherokee Tribe was formed in 1980? (B.J. Faulkner)

LESSON 23 –STATE RECOGNIZED INDIAN TRIBES OF ALABAMA

SIXTH GRADE

<u>SAT</u> Reading Objective: ALL SAT SKILLS

Objective: After the teacher directs this lesson, sixth grade Indian students will be able to recognize, understand, and apply different terms discussed in the lesson.

Objective Activity: The teacher will allow the students to look up any challenging words in the dictionary and tell the class what the terms mean and how it should be pronounced. (Ex: reservation, registration, commission, turmoil, etc.)

<u>STATE STANDARDS</u> Reading Objective:

PG. 52 #4   Demonstrate reading improvement gained through substantial amounts of daily reading
- After the teacher directs a lesson, the students will have an open discussion about what they learned in class and the teacher will ask them questions that they will answer appropriately.
- *The Shawnee were inhabitants of what county? (Lawrence County)*

<u>STATE STANDARDS</u> Social Studies Objective:

PG. 54 #1   Extend the development of map and globe skills
- After the directed lesson, the teacher will show pictures or maps of the different tribes of Alabama and where they were located.
- *The Star Clan of lower Muscogee Creek Indians takes its name from what word? ("Y'ufala" (Eagle) and the star)*

Review Questions

1. What is the name of the newsletter published by the Echota Cherokee Tribe? (Smoke Signals)
2. The Echota Cherokee Tribe is affiliated with several Indian education programs such as: (Madison Co., Dekalb Co., Jackson Co., and Lawrence Co.)
3. Which tribe in Alabama, is recognized by the federal government? (Poarch Band of Creek)
4. What tribe is located near Mobile and Washington counties? (MOWA Band of Choctaw)
5. What group was recognized by the State of Alabama on July 10, 2001? (The United Cherokee)

LESSON 23 – STATE RECOGNIZED INDIAN TRIBES OF ALABAMA

SEVENTH GRADE

<u>SAT</u> Reading Objective: ALL SAT SKILLS

Objective: After the teacher directs this lesson, seventh grade Indian students will gain an understanding of various terms encountered in the lesson about state recognized tribes of Alabama.

Objective Activity: Allow the students to participate in a word game such as *Hangman*. Ask then to identify the word and then discuss the definition of the word.

<u>STATE STANDARDS</u> Reading Objective:

PG. 57 #2   Read with ease textual, functional, and recreational materials encountered in daily life
- After the teacher directs the lesson, the students will read aloud from the lesson and then have a group discussion concerning the state tribes of Alabama.
  - *What year did Larry Johnson retire from duty of office? (1978)*

<u>STATE STANDARDS</u> Social Studies Objective:

Online Alex #10   Describe changes in social and economic conditions in the United States during the 20th and 21st century
- Have students read from text or any other material based on state recognized tribes of Alabama.
  - *The Poarch Band of Indians descended from what nation? (Creek)*

Review Questions

1. Out of the nine state tribes of Alabama, which one is federally recognized? (Poarch Band of Creek)
2. Name some of the state recognized tribes in Alabama: (Echota Cherokee Tribe of Alabama, Cherokee Tribe of Northeast Alabama, Machis Lower Creek Indian Tribe, Star Clan of Muscogee Creeks, Cher-o-Creek Intra Tribal Indians, MOWA Band of Choctaw Indian, Piqua Shawnee Tribe, and United Cherokee Ani-Yun-Wiya Nation)
3. In 1980, disenchanted members of the United Cherokee Tribe of Alabama formed what new tribe? (Echota Cherokee Tribe)
4. What was the name of the first tribe in the state to organize under the criteria set forth by the Alabama Indian Affairs Commission? (Ma-Chis Lower Indian Tribe)
5. The Star Clan of lower Muscogee Creek Indians takes its name from what word? ("Y'ufala" (Eagle) and the star)

LESSON 24 –REVIEW

After the teacher directs this lesson, Kindergarten Indian students will utilize the following reading content standards: initial sound and letter naming fluency.

The students will develop an understanding of the beginning sounds of a specific letter while using flashcards, pictures, objects, or board. Then the students will pronounce the initial letter after the teacher gives a series of words found in previous lessons.

REVIEW POST-TEST

Play a trivia game using history questions from previous lessons for the post-test. Cut up questions, roll them up and place in a trivia box. Have students take turns selecting a question from the box and try to answer it. If they get it correct, they can take a turn shooting the ball in the net, baseball game trivia, moving a turn on the game board, or whatever game you choose. If they do not know the answer, the teacher should tell them to make sure everyone knows the correct answer. Make sure it's a fun way to review, while making it competitive.

LESSON 25 – Post-Test

Briefly go over questions and answers covering all lessons on the post-test before handing out the test. Administer test-Teacher reads each question and allows time for students to mark their answers. Complete all test grading and data sheets for Indian students. Turn in all materials to the Oakville Indian Mounds Education Center.

ADMINISTER POST-TEST

Appendix 1

Reading and Social Studies Individual Performance Reports for Grades Kindergarten Through Seventh

Appendix 1: Reading and Social Studies Individual Performance Reports

Kindergarten
Indian education program
Reading/Social Studies

Name _____ School _____

Instructor _____ / _____ Date _____
                   1st Semester   2nd Semester

Date	Present-Absent √ / A	Skill	Topic-Reading/Social Studies	Standard Assessment-DIBELS	State Standards-Reading/Social Studies
		1	Pre-Test Introduction	Phonemic Awareness	Reading: Pictures/text for meaning, listening/speaking behaviors Social Studies: Map skills
		2	Family History and Ancestry	Initial Sound Fluency	Reading: Pictures and text to gain meaning Social Studies: Awareness of individuals (same/different)
		3	Echota Cherokee Tribe of Alabama	Phonics Instruction	Reading: Letter sound/pictures and text to gain meaning/literature Social Studies: Map skills, different cultures
		4	Periods of Prehistoric Indians	Comprehension	Reading: Pictures/text for meaning, vocabulary/sentence awareness Social Studies: Information graphics, natural resources, people
		5	Lifestyles of Early Indian People	Vocabulary/Letter Naming	Reading: Listening and speaking behaviors, vocabulary/sentence Social Studies: Environments, physical structures
		6	Early Survival Needs	Phonemic Awareness	Reading: Stories, letter sounds, pictures and text meaning Social Studies: Care of environment, lives in other places
		7	Regalia	Initial Sound Fluency	Reading: Letter sounds relationship, text to gain meaning Social Studies: Human and natural resources
		8	Ceremonial Activities	Phonics Instruction	Reading: Literature in forms, listening and speaking behavior Social Studies: New information and behaviors in the classroom
		9	Tennessee River	Comprehension	Reading: Vocabulary/sentence, Story concept, pictures/text to gain meaning Social Studies: Map skills, human and natural resources, people
		10	European Contact	Vocabulary/Letter Naming	Reading: Letter sounds, vocabulary and sentence awareness Social Studies: Display information in graphic, characters and events
		11	Mid-Test Five Tribes of Lawrence County	Phonemic Awareness	Reading: Pictures and text to gain meaning, variety of literature Social Studies: Map skills, uniqueness of individuals, people
		12	Creek Tribe	Initial Sound Fluency	Reading: Letter sounds, forms of communication Social Studies: Map skills, uniqueness of individuals
		13	Chickasaw Tribe	Phonics Instruction	Reading: Text to gain meaning, Social Studies: Map skills, different cultures
		14	Cherokee Tribe	Comprehension	Reading: Communication, text to gain meaning, forms of literature Social Studies: Map skills, uniqueness of individuals
		15	Seven Clans of the Cherokee	Vocabulary/Letter Naming	Reading: Pictures and text to gain meaning Social Studies: Uniqueness of individuals, different cultures
		16	Indian Trails and Paths	Phonemic Awareness	Reading: Forms of communications Social Studies: Map skills, people (same and different)
		17	Indian Villages	Initial Sound Fluency	Reading: Pictures and text to gain meaning, communication Social Studies: Map skills
		18	Local Indian Leaders	Phonics Instruction	Reading: Letter sound relationships Social Studies: Uniqueness of individuals
		19	Indian Battles	Comprehension	Reading: Pictures and text to gain meaning, communication Social Studies: Map skills, impact of behavior
		20	Indian Treaties	Vocabulary/Letter Naming	Reading: Vocabulary/sentence awareness Social Studies: Map skills, impact of behavior
		21	Indian Removal	All DIBELS Skills	Reading: Letter sounds, pictures and text to gain meaning Social Studies: Map skills, relationship behaviors
		22	Traditional Cultural Properties	All DIBELS Skills	Reading: Pictures and text to gain meaning, forms of literature Social Studies: Map skills
		23	State Recognized Tribes of Alabama	All DIBELS Skills	Reading: Letter sounds, text to gain meaning, listening/speaking behaviors Social Studies: Map skills
		24	Review	All DIBELS Skills	
		25	Post-Test		

Our signatures certify that we taught these areas on the dates indicated.

_____ / _____
1st Semester Signatures

Our signatures certify that we taught these areas on the dates indicated.

_____ / _____
2nd Semester Signatures

Appendix 1: Reading and Social Studies Individual Performance Reports
First Grade
Indian Education Program
Reading/Social Studies

Name_____ School_____

Instructor_____/_____ Date_____
                  1st Semester   2nd Semester

Date	Present-Absent √ / A	Skill	Topic-Reading/Social Studies	Standard Assessment-DIBELS	State Standards-Reading/Social Studies
		1	Pre-Test Introduction	Phoneme Segmentation Fluency	Reading: Phonemic awareness Social Studies: Feature of communities
		2	Family History and Ancestry	Phonics	Reading: Letter sounds Social Studies: Locate new information
		3	Echota Cherokee Tribe of Alabama	Letter Naming Fluency	Reading: Letter sound relationships Social Studies: Locate new information
		4	Periods of Prehistoric Indians	Nonsense Word Fluency	Reading: Phonemic awareness, comprehend material Social Studies: Locate new information, cultural changes
		5	Lifestyles of Early Indian People	Text Comprehension	Reading: Reflections in literature, forms of self-expressions Social Studies: Land features
		6	Early Survival Needs	Phoneme Segmentation Fluency	Reading: Phonemic awareness Social Studies: Features of communities, land features
		7	Regalia	Phonics	Reading: Phonemic awareness, listening and speaking behaviors Social Studies: Cultures in literature
		8	Ceremonial Activities	Letter Naming Fluency	Reading: Letter sounds Social Studies: Cultures in literature
		9	Tennessee River	Nonsense Word Fluency	Reading: Phonemic awareness Social Studies: Locate new information, compare transportation
		10	European Contact	Text Comprehension	Reading: Comprehend material, listening and speaking behaviors Social Studies: Benefit or harm of environment
		11	Mid-Test Five Tribes of Lawrence County	Phoneme Segmentation Fluency	Reading: Phonemic awareness Social Studies: Locate new information
		12	Creek Tribe	Phonics	Reading: Letter sounds, comprehend material read Social Studies: Cultures from literature
		13	Chickasaw Tribe	Letter Naming Fluency	Reading: Letter sound relationships Social Studies: Map skills, understanding different cultures
		14	Cherokee Tribe	Nonsense Word Fluency	Reading: Letter sounds, comprehend material Social Studies: Locate new information
		15	Seven Clans of the Cherokee	Text Comprehension	Reading: Comprehend material read, cultures in literature Social Studies: Locate new information
		16	Indian Trails and Paths	Phoneme Segmentation Fluency	Reading: Phonemic awareness Social Studies: Locate new information
		17	Indian Villages	Phonics	Reading: Phonemic awareness, comprehend material Social Studies: Locate new information, land use and features
		18	Local Indian Leaders	Letter Naming Fluency	Reading: Letter sound relationships, comprehend material read Social Studies: Locate new information
		19	Indian Battles	Nonsense Word Fluency	Reading: Letter sounds, comprehend material read Social Studies: Locate new information, environment benefit/harm
		20	Indian Treaties	Text Comprehension	Reading: Phonemic awareness, comprehend material Social Studies: Locate new information
		21	Indian Removal	All DIBELS Skills	Reading: Phonemic awareness, comprehend material read, listen/speak Social Studies: Display and locate new information
		22	Traditional Cultural Properties	All DIBELS Skills	Reading: Letter sound relationships, comprehend material read Social Studies: Impact of cultural changes
		23	State Recognized Tribes of Alabama	All DIBELS Skills	Reading: Comprehend material read, listening/speaking behaviors Social Studies: Locate new information
		24	Review	All DIBELS Skills	
		25	Post-Test		

Our signatures certify that we taught these areas on the dates indicated.   Our signatures certify that we taught these areas on the dates indicated.

_____/_____   _____/_____
1st Semester Signatures   2nd Semester Signatures

Appendix 1: Reading and Social Studies Individual Performance Reports
Second Grade
Indian Education Program
Reading/Social Studies

Name_____   School_____

Instructor_____/_____   Date_____
                  1st Semester   2nd Semester

Date	Present-Absent √ / A	Skill	Topic-Reading/Social Studies	Standard Assessment- DIBELS	State Standards- Reading/Social Studies
		1	Pre-Test Introduction	Oral Reading Fluency	Reading: Listening and communicating behaviors Social Studies: Examination of family histories
		2	Family History and Ancestry	Nonsense Word Fluency	Reading: Blend sounds, vocabulary and sentence awareness Social Studies: Locate new information
		3	Echota Cherokee Tribe of Alabama	Text Comprehension	Reading: Oral reading for comprehension Social Studies: Family history, map skills
		4	Periods of Prehistoric Indians	Vocabulary	Reading: Blend sounds, vocabulary and sentence awareness Social Studies: Interpret/display information, transportation methods
		5	Lifestyles of Early Indian People	Listening and Communicating	Reading: Oral reading, listening and communicating behaviors Social Studies: Family history, family occupations
		6	Early Survival Needs	Oral Reading Fluency	Reading: Listening and communicating behaviors Social Studies: Interpret/display information, geographic concepts
		7	Regalia	Nonsense Word Fluency	Reading: Oral reading for accuracy/fluency/comprehension Social Studies: Interpret/display information
		8	Ceremonial Activities	Text Comprehension	Reading: Listening and communicating behaviors Social Studies: Major events, interpret/display information
		9	Tennessee River	Vocabulary	Reading: Comprehensive reading Social Studies: Transportation methods, map skills
		10	European Contact	Listening and Communicating	Reading: Comprehensive reading, oral reading Social Studies: Interpret/display information, individual contributions
		11	Mid-Test Five Tribes of Lawrence County	Oral Reading Fluency	Reading: Blend sounds, Listening and communicating behaviors Social Studies: Locate new information
		12	Creek Tribe	Nonsense Word Fluency	Reading: Blend sounds to form words Social Studies: Interpret/display information, map skills
		13	Chickasaw Tribe	Text Comprehension	Reading: Comprehensive reading Social Studies: Map skills, major events
		14	Cherokee Tribe	Vocabulary	Reading: Story conception, oral reading comprehension Social Studies: Locate new information
		15	Seven Clans of the Cherokee	Listening and Communicating	Reading: Comprehensive reading, listing and communicating behaviors Social Studies: Locate new information
		16	Indian Trails and Paths	Oral Reading Fluency	Reading: Comprehensive reading Social Studies: Transportation methods, map skills
		17	Indian Villages	Nonsense Word Fluency	Reading: Vocabulary/ sentence awareness Social Studies: Map skills
		18	Local Indian Leaders	Text Comprehension	Reading: Story conception Social Studies: Family occupations
		19	Indian Battles	Vocabulary	Reading: Vocabulary and sentence awareness Social Studies: Individual contributions
		20	Indian Treaties	Listening and Communicating	Reading: Listening and communicating behaviors Social Studies: Map skills
		21	Indian Removal	All DIBELS Skills	Reading: Comprehensive reading Social Studies: Map skills
		22	Traditional Cultural Properties	All DIBELS Skills	Reading: Comprehensive reading, Oral reading Social Studies: Interpret/display information, people affect on land
		23	State Recognized Tribes of Alabama	All DIBELS Skills	Reading: Oral reading for comprehension Social Studies: Map skills
		24	Review	All DIBELS Skills	
		25	Post-Test		

Our signatures certify that we taught these areas on the dates indicated.   Our signatures certify that we taught these areas on the dates indicated.

_____/_____   _____/_____
1st Semester Signatures   2nd Semester Signatures

Appendix 1: Reading and Social Studies Individual Performance Reports

Third Grade
Indian Education Program
Reading/Social Studies

Name _____ School _____

Instructor _____/_____ Date _____
                      1st Semester   2nd Semester

Date	Present-Absent √ / A	Skill	Topic-Reading/Social Studies	Standard Assessment-DIBELS	State Standards-Reading/Social Studies
		1	Pre-Test Introduction	Listening Skills	Reading: Listening skills/retelling Social Studies: Map skills
		2	Family History and Ancestry	Interpreting Reading Materials	Reading: Listening skills, cultural similarities Social Studies: Natural environment of North America
		3	Echota Cherokee Tribe of Alabama	Comprehension	Reading: Reading for fluency and comprehension Social Studies: Environment and society
		4	Periods of Prehistoric Indians	Word Recognition	Reading: Comprehensive reading, culture in literature Social Studies: Native American groups in culture
		5	Lifestyles of Early Indian People	Oral Reading Fluency	Reading: Comprehensive reading, monitored reading Social Studies: Comparison of Native Americans
		6	Early Survival Needs	Listening Skills	Reading: Comprehensive reading Social Studies: Comparison of Native Americans
		7	Regalia	Interpreting Reading Materials	Reading: Interpret meaning from print material Social Studies: Comparison of Native Americans
		8	Ceremonial Activities	Comprehension	Reading: Listening skills Social Studies: Comparisons of Native Americans
		9	Tennessee River	Word Recognition	Reading: Interpret meaning from print material Social Studies: Natural environment, Native American geography
		10	European Contact	Oral Reading Fluency	Reading: Reading for fluency and comprehension Social Studies: Land use, early settlement and natural environment
		11	Mid-Test Five Tribes of Lawrence County	Listening Skills	Reading: Literal understanding of print material Social Studies: Map skills
		12	Creek Tribe	Interpreting Reading Materials	Reading: Understand cultural similarities and differences Social Studies: Map skills, comparison of Native American groups
		13	Chickasaw Tribe	Comprehension	Reading: Understand print material Social Studies: Map skills
		14	Cherokee Tribe	Word Recognition	Reading: Interpret meaning from print materials Social Studies: Map skills
		15	Seven Clans of the Cherokee	Oral Reading Fluency	Reading: Culture in literature Social Studies: Comparison of Native American groups
		16	Indian Trails and Paths	Listening Skills	Reading: Meaning from printed material Social Studies: Map skills
		17	Indian Villages	Interpreting Reading Materials	Reading: Culture in literature, strategies to gain information Social Studies: Compare groups of Native Americans
		18	Local Indian Leaders	Comprehension	Reading: Comprehensive reading, listening skills Social Studies: Early settlements and natural environments
		19	Indian Battles	Word Recognition	Reading: Literal understanding of print material Social Studies: Map skills
		20	Indian Treaties	Oral Reading Fluency	Reading: Sequence of events Social Studies: Forms of governing
		21	Indian Removal	All DIBELS Skills	Reading: Comprehensive reading Social Studies: Map skills
		22	Traditional Cultural Properties	All DIBELS Skills	Reading: Comprehensive reading, daily life materials Social Studies: Natural environment of North America
		23	State Recognized Tribes of Alabama	All DIBELS Skills	Reading: Literal understanding of printed material Social Studies: Geography of Native Americans
		24	Review	All DIBELS Skills	
		25	Post-Test		

Our signatures certify that we taught these areas on the dates indicated.   Our signatures certify that we taught these areas on the dates indicated.

_____/_____   _____/_____
1st Semester Signatures   2nd Semester Signatures

Appendix 1: Reading and Social Studies Individual Performance Reports
Fourth Grade
Indian Education Program
Reading/Social Studies

Name_____   School_____

Instructor_____/_____   Date_____
                1st Semester   2nd Semester

Date	Present-Absent √ / A	Skill	Topic-Reading/Social Studies	Standard Assessment-SAT	State Standards- Reading/Social Studies
		1	Pre-Test Introduction	Word Recognition	Reading: Reading for vocabulary growth Social Studies: Natural environment of Alabama
		2	Family History and Ancestry	Vocabulary	Reading: Understand printed material Social Studies: Lives of historic Indians of Alabama
		3	Echota Cherokee Tribe of Alabama	Comprehension	Reading: Understand printed material Social Studies: Map skills
		4	Periods of Prehistoric Indians	Literary Elements	Reading: Meaning from print materials, culture, vocabulary growth in literature Social Studies: Map skills, characteristics of prehistoric Indians
		5	Lifestyles of Early Indian People	Listening Skills	Reading: Reading encountered in daily lives Social Studies: Natural environment of Alabama
		6	Early Survival Needs	Word Recognition	Reading: Reading encountered in daily lives Social Studies: European contact with historic Indians of Alabama
		7	Regalia	Vocabulary	Reading: Reading for vocabulary growth Social Studies: Contributions by Alabama's early inhabitants
		8	Ceremonial Activities	Comprehension	Reading: Cultural similarities and differences in literature Social Studies: Lives of historic Indians of Alabama
		9	Tennessee River	Literary Elements	Reading: Reading encountered in daily lives, listening skills Social Studies: Interpret and display information and data
		10	European Contact	Listening Skills	Reading: Reading encountered in daily lives, cultural (same/diff) Social Studies: European contact on Native Americans
		11	Mid-Test Five Tribes of Lawrence County	Word Recognition	Reading: Understand printed material, reading in daily lives Social Studies: Lives of historic Indians of Alabama
		12	Creek Tribe	Vocabulary	Reading: Reading encountered in daily lives Social Studies: Interpret and display information and data
		13	Chickasaw Tribe	Comprehension	Reading: Reading encountered in daily lives Social Studies: European contact of historic Indians of Alabama
		14	Cherokee Tribe	Literary Elements	Reading: Interpret passages in print material, literary analysis Social Studies: Information and data, European contact of Indians
		15	Seven Clans of the Cherokee	Listening Skills	Reading: Understand printed material Social Studies: Lives of historic Indians of Alabama
		16	Indian Trails and Paths	Word Recognition	Reading: Vocabulary growth in literature Social Studies: Intermediate directions, information and data
		17	Indian Villages	Vocabulary	Reading: Interpret passages in print material Social Studies: Interpret and display information and data
		18	Local Indian Leaders	Comprehension	Reading: Listening skills Social Studies: Lives of historic Indians of Alabama
		19	Indian Battles	Literary Elements	Reading: Understand printed material, reading in daily lives Social Studies: Interpret and display information and data
		20	Indian Treaties	Listening Skills	Reading: Sequence of events Social Studies: Interpret and display information and data
		21	Indian Removal	All SAT Skills	Reading: Understand printed material Social Studies: Interpret and display information and data
		22	Traditional Cultural Properties	All SAT Skills	Reading: Meaning from printed materials, Reading in daily lives Social Studies: Map skills, natural environment of Alabama
		23	State Recognized Tribes of Alabama	All SAT Skills	Reading: Improvement through daily reading Social Studies: Interpret and display information and data
		24	Review	All SAT Skills	
		25	Post-Test		

Our signatures certify that we taught these areas on the dates indicated.   Our signatures certify that we taught these areas on the dates indicated.

_____/_____   _____/_____
1st Semester Signatures   2nd Semester Signatures

Appendix 1: Reading and Social Studies Individual Performance Reports
Fifth Grade
Indian Education Program
Reading/Social Studies

Name_____   School_____

Instructor_____/_____   Date_____
               1st Semester   2nd Semester

Date	Present-Absent √ / A	Skill	Topic-Reading/Social Studies	Standard Assessment-SAT	State Standards-Reading/Social Studies
		1	Pre-Test Introduction	Listening Skills	Reading: Listening skills Social Studies: Natural environment of North Alabama
		2	Family History and Ancestry	Vocabulary	Reading: Interpret meaning from print material Social Studies: Different cultures of Native American groups
		3	Echota Cherokee Tribe of Alabama	Comprehension	Reading: Interpret passages in print material Social Studies: Different cultures of Native American groups
		4	Periods of Prehistoric Indians	Literary Elements	Reading: Use literary analysis Social Studies: Progression of early American people
		5	Lifestyles of Early Indian People	Genres	Reading: Variety of materials/genres, listening skills Social Studies: Progression of the early American people
		6	Early Survival Needs	Listening Skills	Reading: Listening skills Social Studies: Natural environment of North America
		7	Regalia	Vocabulary	Reading: Interpret meaning from print material Social Studies: Impact of early European exploration
		8	Ceremonial Activities	Comprehension	Reading: Interpret meaning from print material Social Studies: Impact of early Europeans
		9	Tennessee River	Literary Elements	Reading: Interpret passages in print material Social Studies: Natural environment of North America
		10	European Contact	Genres	Reading: Read materials/genres from daily lives Social Studies: Impact of early European exploration
		11	Mid-Test Five Tribes of Lawrence County	Listening Skills	Reading: Listening skills Social Studies: Different cultures of Native American groups
		12	Creek Tribe	Vocabulary	Reading: Interpret meaning from print material Social Studies: culture progression of early American people
		13	Chickasaw Tribe	Comprehension	Reading: Read materials/genres in daily lives, listening skills Social Studies: Progression of early American people
		14	Cherokee Tribe	Literary Elements	Reading: Use literary analysis, listening skills Social Studies: Progression of early American people
		15	Seven Clans of the Cherokee	Genres	Reading: Read materials/genres in daily lives Social Studies: Different cultures of Native American groups
		16	Indian Trails and Paths	Listening Skills	Reading: Listening skills Social Studies: Natural environment of North America
		17	Indian Villages	Vocabulary	Reading: Improvement through daily reading, listening skills Social Studies: Progression of early American people
		18	Local Indian Leaders	Comprehension	Reading: Interpret meaning from print material, listening skills Social Studies: Different cultures of Native American groups
		19	Indian Battles	Literary Elements	Reading: Use literary analysis, listening skills Social Studies: Different cultures of native American groups
		20	Indian Treaties	Genres	Reading: Variety of materials/genres encountered in daily lives Social Studies: Impact of early Europeans
		21	Indian Removal	All SAT Skills	Reading: Interpret passages in print material Social Studies: Impact of early European exploration
		22	Traditional Cultural Properties	All SAT Skills	Reading: Variety of materials/genres in daily lives, listening skills Social Studies: Natural environment of North America
		23	State Recognized Tribes of Alabama	All SAT Skills	Reading: Improvement through daily reading Social Studies: Different cultures of Native American groups
		24	Review	All SAT Skills	
		25	Post-Test		

Our signatures certify that we taught these areas on the dates indicated.   Our signatures certify that we taught these areas on the dates indicated.

_____/_____   _____/_____
1st Semester Signatures   2nd Semester Signatures

Appendix 1: Reading and Social Studies Individual Performance Reports
Sixth Grade
Indian Education Program
Reading/Social Studies

Name _____ School _____

Instructor _____ / _____ Date _____
              1st Semester   2nd Semester

Date	Present-Absent √ / A	Skill	Topic-Reading/Social Studies	Standard Assessment-SAT	State Standards-Reading/Social Studies
		1	Pre-Test Introduction	Comprehension	Reading: Materials encountered in daily life Social Studies: Map skills
		2	Family History and Ancestry	Listening Skills	Reading: Listening behaviors Social Studies: Map skills
		3	Echota Cherokee Tribe of Alabama	Literary Elements	Reading: Interpret and construct meaning in curriculum Social Studies: Map skills
		4	Periods of Prehistoric Indians	Phonetic Principles	Reading: Improvement gained through daily reading Social Studies: Map skills
		5	Lifestyles of Early Indian People	Vocabulary	Reading: Listening behaviors Social Studies: Map skills
		6	Early Survival Needs	Comprehension	Reading: Interpret and construct meaning in curriculum Social Studies: Map skills
		7	Regalia	Listening Skills	Reading: Listening behaviors Social Studies: Map skills
		8	Ceremonial Activities	Literary Elements	Reading: Interpret and construct meaning in curriculum Social Studies: map skills
		9	Tennessee River	Phonetic Principles	Reading: Improvement gained through daily reading Social Studies: Map skills
		10	European Contact	Vocabulary	Reading: Linguistic and cultural diversity Social Studies: Major changes in America
		11	Mid-Test Five Tribes of Lawrence County	Comprehension	Reading: Listening behaviors Social Studies: Major changes in America
		12	Creek Tribe	Listening Skills	Reading: Listening behaviors Social Studies: Major changes in America
		13	Chickasaw Tribe	Literary Elements	Reading: Interpret and construct meaning in curriculum Social Studies: Map skills
		14	Cherokee Tribe	Phonetic Principles	Reading: Improvement gained through daily reading Social Studies: Major changes in America
		15	Seven Clans of the Cherokee	Vocabulary	Reading: Listening behaviors Social Studies: Map skills
		16	Indian Trails and Paths	Comprehension	Reading: Interpret and construct meaning in curriculum Social Studies: Map skills
		17	Indian Villages	Listening Skills	Reading: Listening behaviors Social Studies: Map skills
		18	Local Indian Leaders	Literary Elements	Reading: Interpret and construct meaning in curriculum Social Studies: Map skills
		19	Indian Battles	Phonetic Principles	Reading: Improvement gained through daily reading Social Studies: Map skills
		20	Indian Treaties	Vocabulary	Reading: Listening behaviors Social Studies: Map skills
		21	Indian Removal	All SAT Skills	Reading: Read materials encountered in daily life Social Studies: Map skills
		22	Traditional Cultural Properties	All SAT Skills	Reading: Read materials encountered in daily life Social Studies: Map skills
		23	State Recognized Tribes of Alabama	All SAT Skills	Reading: Improvement through daily reading Social Studies: Map skills
		24	Review	All SAT Skills	
		25	Post-Test		

Our signatures certify that we taught these areas on the dates indicated.   Our signatures certify that we taught these areas on the dates indicated.

_____ / _____   _____ / _____
1st Semester Signatures   2nd Semester Signatures

Appendix 1: Reading and Social Studies Individual Performance Reports
Seventh Grade
Indian Education Program
Reading/Social Studies

Name_____ School_____

Instructor_____/_____ Date_____
                 1st Semester   2nd Semester

Date	Present-Absent √ / A	Skill	Topic-Reading/Social Studies	Standard Assessment-SAT	State Standards-Reading/Social Studies
		1	Pre-Test Introduction	Listening Skills	Reading: Listening behaviors Social Studies: Organization of economic systems
		2	Family History and Ancestry	Literary Elements	Reading: Influences of literary works Social Studies: Organization of economic systems
		3	Echota Cherokee Tribe of Alabama	Literary Genres	Reading: Various forms of literature Social Studies: Conflict of groups using past/current events
		4	Periods of Prehistoric Indians	Vocabulary	Reading: Listening behaviors Social Studies: Individual and civic responsibilities
		5	Lifestyles of Early Indian People	Comprehension	Reading: Listening behaviors Social Studies: Changes in social and economic conditions
		6	Early Survival Needs	Listening Skills	Reading: Listening behaviors Social Studies: Changes in social and economic conditions
		7	Regalia	Literary Elements	Reading: Influence in literary works Social Studies: World in spatial terms using maps
		8	Ceremonial Activities	Literary Genres	Reading: Various forms of literature, listening behaviors Social Studies: Changes in social/economic conditions
		9	Tennessee River	Vocabulary	Reading: Listening behaviors Social Studies: Factors that contribute to change
		10	European Contact	Comprehension	Reading: Listening behaviors Social Studies: Changes in social/economic conditions
		11	Mid-Test Five Tribes of Lawrence County	Listening Skills	Reading: Listening behaviors Social Studies: Changes in social/economic conditions
		12	Creek Tribe	Literary Elements	Reading: Influences of literary works Social Studies: Individual and civic responsibilities of citizens
		13	Chickasaw Tribe	Literary Genres	Reading: Listening behaviors Social Studies: Conflict of groups using past/current events
		14	Cherokee Tribe	Vocabulary	Reading: Interpret meaning in materials for curriculum Social Studies: Individual and civic responsibilities of citizens
		15	Seven Clans of the Cherokee	Comprehension	Reading: Listening behaviors Social Studies: Individual and civic responsibilities of citizens
		16	Indian Trails and Paths	Listening Skills	Reading: Listening behaviors Social Studies: Distribution and linking of urban areas
		17	Indian Villages	Literary Elements	Reading: Influences of literary works Social Studies: Differences in rights, privileges, duties, and responsibilities
		18	Local Indian Leaders	Literary Genres	Reading: Various forms of literature Social Studies: Individual and civic responsibilities of citizens
		19	Indian Battles	Vocabulary	Reading: Listening behaviors Social Studies: Conflict in societies
		20	Indian Treaties	Comprehension	Reading: Listening behaviors Social Studies: Changes in social and economic conditions
		21	Indian Removal	All SAT Skills	Reading: Construct, interpret, and evaluate meaning Social Studies: Changes in social and economic conditions
		22	Traditional Cultural Properties	All SAT Skills	Reading: Understand information read, viewed, and heard Social Studies: Changes in social and economic conditions
		23	State Recognized Tribes of Alabama	All SAT Skills	Reading: Read materials encountered in daily life Social Studies: Changes in social and economic conditions
		24	Review	All SAT Skills	
		25	Post-Test		

Our signatures certify that we taught these areas on the dates indicated.   Our signatures certify that we taught these areas on the dates indicated.

_____/_____   _____/_____
1st Semester Signatures   2nd Semester Signatures

Appendix 2

Alabama Course of Study (August 2004 Edition)

State Standards in reading and Social Studies for Grades Kindergarten through Seventh that relate to the lessons.

Page numbers are the actual page in the Alabama Course of Study August 2004 edition.

Appendix 2: Alabama Course of Study (2004 Edition)

Kindergarten Alabama Course of Study (Aug 04)

READING

Page 13

#1   Exhibit an awareness of the concept of story.
- Associating written words with a story
- Relating personal experience to picture text
- Identifying with characters or events in a story
- Beginning to recognize elements of a story

Page 14

#6   Demonstrate an initial understanding of letter-sound relationships.
- Understanding the letter-sound correspondence
- Identifying consonant sounds

#9   Begin to use pictures and text to gain meaning from written material.
- Connecting text, message heard, or material viewed to prior knowledge and experiences
- Tracking (pointing to individual words) in a familiar story to locate a specific word
- Recalling information
  - Examples: characters, character traits, setting, details, main idea, beginning and ending of stories
- Retelling a story
- Predicting words and phrases in a story using pictures and other context clues
- Creating mental images while reading
- Answering teacher-and peer-generated questions

Page 15

#13   Gain an awareness of others through exposure to written, spoken, and visual forms of communication.
- Examples: videos, author studies, children's literature, educational television, stage drama, student publications

#14   Demonstrate an interest in and enjoyment of literature in a variety of forms, contexts, and media.
- Participating in reading activities in all content areas
  - Examples: big books, predictable books, author studies, informational books
- Participating in arts education activities
  - Examples: live drama, drawing, music, puppetry
- Participating in listening activities
  - Examples: interactive videos, listening stations
- Attending with interest to works of literature presented orally
  - Examples: stories, poems, drama
- Participating in discussions of stories read, heard, or viewed

#15   Use appropriate listening and speaking behaviors.
- Showing an interest in what others have to say
- Looking at speaker/audience
- Responding appropriately to material read, heard, or viewed
- Using grammar, expression, and words appropriate to audience
- Generating questions
- Following directions

Appendix 2: Alabama Course of Study (2004 Edition)

Kindergarten Alabama Course of Study (Aug 04)

#17   Exhibit expanded vocabulary and sentence awareness.
- Exploring reading and writing through interactions with language
  - Examples: engaging in shared reading and writing, participating in group discussions, asking questions for clarification, participating in read-alouds, retelling or dramatizing stories
- Using new vocabulary in speaking and writing
- Recognizing when simple sentences fail to make sense

SOCIAL STUDIES

Page 11

#1   Develop initial map and globe skills.
- Location: Describe self in spatial relationship to other people and objects in the room.
  - Example: locating the teacher's desk on a map of the classroom, drawing a circle-time picture showing seating of students
- Direction: Give and follow verbal instructions related to classroom positions (front, back)
  - Example: taking turns in front of the line when traveling through the school
- Distance: Estimate distance using non-standard measures
  - Example: measuring length of classroom using book lengths
- Scale: compare the differences in size between a person/object and a representation of same

#3   Develop initial ability to display information in graphic form.
- Graphs
  - Example: making a pictograph of the methods of transportation used in getting to and from school
- Maps
  - Example: making a map of the playground as a treasure map for locating hidden treasure
- Globes
  - Example: observing different sizes of globes, noting features such as land forms and water
- Time lines
  - Example: recording events on time lines such as holidays, projects, programs, daily news, yesterday, today, tomorrow
- Models
  - Example: constructing homes and school using large blocks and props

Page 12

#4   Locate new information and express understanding of the new information in various classroom.
- Examples: Projects—creating a variety of table-top models of houses from around the world, designing local neighborhoods using large appliance boxes, constructing animal homes utilizing various resources

  Research Resources—pictures, posters, charts, storybooks, fact books, trade books, songs, music, maps and globes, cooperative planning, media center use, computer and technological tools, guest speakers, field trips

#7   Exhibit behaviors that are part of responsible civic life in the school setting resulting in harmonious and socially satisfying relationships with others.
- Sharing
- Considering the rights, ideas, and feelings of others
- Using good manners
- Taking turns
- Doing chores
- Following rules and laws
- Accepting consequences

Appendix 2: Alabama Course of Study (2004 Edition)

Kindergarten Alabama Course of Study (Aug 04)

#10   Exhibit personal responsibility for the care of the physical environment.
- Examples: classroom supplies, personal property, school campus, property of others, use of biodegradable products, gardening, anti-litter projects

#11   Discover characters and events from literature that demonstrate the impact of one person's behavior upon another.
- Consequences of helping others
- Consequences of hurting others
  - Example: *Rainbow Fish* by Marcus Pfister

Page 13

#16   Increase awareness of various environments.
- Home
- School
- Neighborhood
- Farm
  - Example: *Little House* by Virginia Lee Burton and *Rooster's Off To See The World* by Eric Carle

Page 14

#20   Demonstrate the ability to construct models of physical structures in the immediate environment.
- Examples: three-dimensional floor map, table-top models

#25   Describe ways that people in various group settings satisfy wants and needs.
- Trading
- Purchasing
- Savings
  - Example: short drams of a customer buying merchandise in a store

#26   Identify human-made and natural resources.
- Energy
- Water
- Trees
- Soil
- Books

#28   Begin to compare different forms of communication from the past and the present in different times.
- Example: Pony Express, telegraph, sending letters by ship, telephone, E-mail

Page 15

#34   Develop an awareness of the uniqueness of individuals.
- Examples: characteristics, basic emotions, capabilities

#35   Develop an awareness of how people are the same and yet different.
- Example: *It Takes A Village* by Fletcher Cowen

#36   Build an understanding of different cultures through the exploration of holidays, customs, and traditions.
- Examples: singing Irish folksongs – "Michael Finnegan," reading *My Home Country: Ireland Is My Home* by Gini Holland

#37   Develop an awareness of the lives of children in other places.
- Examples: *Gilberto and the Wind* by Marie Hall Ets

Appendix 2: Alabama Course of Study (2004 Edition)

First Grade Alabama Course of Study (Aug 04)

READING

Page 17

#3 Exhibit phonemic awareness.
- Counting the number of sounds in words
- Using songs, poems, word-sound games, and verbal rhythmic activities
- Manipulating the sounds of the English language
    - Examples: rhyming, blending, substituting, deleting, reversing

#4 Demonstrate understanding of letter-sound relationships.
- Using decoding skills
- Blending sounds to form words
    - Examples: vowel sounds, consonant cluster, consonant digraphs

Page 20

#6 Comprehend material read, heard, or viewed.
- Connecting text, message heard, or material viewed to prior knowledge and experiences
- Recalling information
    - Examples: characters; character traits; setting; details; main idea; beginning, middle, and end of stories; topic
- Retelling a story
- Predicting words and phrases in a story using pictures sand other context clues
- Monitoring their reading by rereading, predicting, self-correcting, and seeking help if needed
- Creating mental images while reading
- Answering teacher-and peer-generated questions in written or spoken form
- Recognizing high-frequency words

#10 Recognize values, beliefs, and interests reflected in literature and other materials from various cultures.

Page 21

#13 Connect knowledge learned in the language arts program to life situations.
- Examples: comparing characters or events in a story to people or events in real life, making lists

#16 Demonstrate appropriate listening and speaking behaviors.
- Focusing on the listening task
    - Examples: conversation, instruction, group discussion, read-alouds
- Establishing eye contact with the speaker or audience
- Interpreting nonverbal communication of the speaker or audience
    - Example: facial expressions
- Asking appropriate questions to gain and to clarify information
- Attending to works of literature presented orally

Page 22

#24 Exhibit increased participation in self-expression in a variety of forms.
- Sharing experiences, facts, and information
    - Examples: discussion of class work at learning centers, collaboration on projects, cooperative learning
- Retelling stories
- Creating own stories
    - Examples: narratives of personal stories, story endings, word processing
- Dramatizing

Appendix 2: Alabama Course of Study (2004 Edition)

First Grade Alabama Course of Study (Aug 04)

SOCIAL STUDIES

Page 17

#2   Extend initial ability to display information in graphic form.
- Globes
- Maps
- Charts
  - Example: *Seasons of Arnold's Apple Tree* by Gail Gibbons
- Graphs
  - Example: graphing over time the number of books read
- Time lines
  - Example: constructing time lines of classroom activities, school holidays, community activities, current events
- Models
  - Example: examining several types of scaled models such as cars, homes, or communities

Page 18

#3   Extend initial ability to locate new information and to express understanding in various classroom.
- Example: imitating activities encountered in reading about other times and other places
- Research Resources: computer and technological use, storybooks, songs and music, student-generated books, field trips, guest speakers, interviews, picture, poster, fact and fiction books, maps and globes, cooperative learning, use of writing portfolios

#9   Compare features of communities.
- Rural
- Urban
- Natural
- Human-made
  - Example: lakes

#10   Relate land use in their locality to the physical features of the land.
- Example: physical features—water resources, soil, vegetation
  land use—residential areas, commercial areas, recreational areas, industrial sites, transportation systems, agricultural areas

#11   Describe the impact of cultural changes on the locality over time.
- Examples: new neighborhoods, shopping malls, highways

Page 19

#13   Exhibit an awareness of the ways personal actions benefit or harm the local environment.
- Examples: recycling, littering, volunteering

#20   Exhibit an appreciation of the way life in a locality is enriched by the world community.
- Example: goods and services, literature, music, art

#21   Compare transportation today and to transportation in the past.

Page 20

#29   Become acquainted with various cultures encountered in stories from literature.
- Examples of aspects of culture: beliefs, customs, ceremonies, traditions, social practices, moral teachings, *Raven: A Trickster Tale From the Pacific Northwest by* Gerald McDermott

Appendix 2: Alabama Course of Study (2004 Edition)

Second Grade Alabama Course of Study (Aug 04)

READING

Page 23

#1   Understand the concept of story.
- Relating personal experiences to text
- Identifying with characters or events in a story
- Recognizing elements of a story

#2   Demonstrate the ability to use decoding skills to blend sounds and form words.
- Recognizing and correcting word-recognition errors
  - Examples: substituting, reversing, deleting, omitting
- Using knowledge of print-sound correspondence to decode unknown words

Page 24

#7   Read and comprehend a variety of material.
- Selecting recreational reading material
- Reading and interpreting textual material
  - Examples: classroom text, maps, graphs, atlases, encyclopedias
- Recognizing words in the environment
- Using predictable text
- Reading and interpreting functional materials
  - Examples: maps, schedules, recipes, instructions, directions, manuals, diagrams

Page 25

#10   Read orally with accuracy, fluency, and comprehension.
- Making self-corrections
- Reading with expression
- Applying mental operations involved in comprehension
  - Examples: make inferences, relate to prior experience, recognize cause and effect, and draw conclusions

#13   Demonstrate appropriate listening and communicating behaviors.
- Focusing on the listening task
  - Examples: conversation, classroom instruction, group discussion, rhymes, read-alouds
- Establishing eye contact with the speaker and/or audience
- Interpreting the nonverbal communication of the speaker and/or audience
  - Example: facial expressions
- Asking appropriate questions to gain and to clarify information
- Using appropriate oral language behaviors
  - Example: adjusting tone and volume of voice in storytelling
- Attending with interest to works of literature presented orally

Page 26

#14   Exhibit expanded vocabulary and sentence awareness.
- Participating in shared reading and writing
  - Examples: choral reading, big books, journals, language experience
- Responding to questions
  - Examples: elements of a story, fact and fantasy, appropriate conclusion, simple sequence of events
- Engaging in word-study activities
  - Examples: synonyms, antonyms, homonyms, multiple-meaning words, concept mapping and webbing, context clues, affixes, root words, analogies
- Incorporating new vocabulary as a part of daily spoken and written language

Appendix 2: Alabama Course of Study (2004 Edition)

Second Grade Alabama Course of Study (Aug 04)

SOCIAL STUDIES

<u>Page 23</u>

#3   Develop the ability to locate new information and to express understanding of this information in various classroom projects.
        Example: imitating activities from other times and other places encountered in talks with grandparents and other "old-timers"
        Research Resources: cooperative learning groups, computer programs and technological use, speakers, field trips, writing portfolios, topics, pictures, poster, charts, fact and fiction books, songs and music, interviews

<u>Page 23</u>

#10   Identify ways the natural environment affects occupational opportunities.
        Examples: landforms, soil, water sources, climate, plant, animals

#11   Identify ways people affect the land.
        Examples: *Letting Swift River Go* by Jane Yolen

<u>Page 25</u>

#21   Develop a sense of history through the examination of family histories.
        Examples: family tree, location of family origin, migration of family to present location, family photos or letters, family adventures, family legends, Grandparents Day, interviews, *Long Way to a New Land* by Joan Sandin, *Watch the Stars Come Out* by Riki Levinson, *Home Place* by Crescent Dragonwagon

#27   Recognize individuals of various cultures who have contributed significantly to the arts and humanities.
        Examples: Leonard Berstein, Aaron Copland, Duke Ellington, George Gershwin, Lois Lenski, Robert McClosky, Beverly Sills, Phyllis Wheatley, Mother Teresa, Princess Diana

#28   Recognize similarities and differences among family culture and the cultures of appropriate literary characters
        Examples: *Keeping Quilt* by Patricia Polacco

Appendix 2: Alabama Course of Study (2004 Edition)

Third Grade Alabama Course of Study (Aug 04)

READING

Page 31

#1   Use a wide range of strategies to interpret, evaluate, appreciate, and construct meaning from print materials.
- Using knowledge of letter-sound correspondence
- Using structural analysis
  - Examples: roots, prefixes, suffixes
- Applying prior knowledge and experiences
- Using knowledge of word meaning
- Applying knowledge of sentence structure and context
- Previewing and predicting
- Locating information in reference sources

Page 32

#3   Demonstrate literal understanding of print material.
- Identifying important details
- Identifying sequence of events
- Following directions

#8   Read grade-level texts aloud and silently with fluency and comprehension.

#10   Monitor own reading.
- Self-questioning
- Rereading
- Using context clues
- Adjusting speed
- Accessing prior knowledge and experience

Page 33

#11   Read materials encountered in daily lives.
- Textual
  - Example: classroom texts
- Functional
  - Examples: directions, schedules
- Recreational
  - Examples: classic literature, writing by self and peers, trade books

#12   Apply strategies of a skillful listener.
- Focusing on the identified purposes
- Focusing on the speaker
- Attending to the listening task
- Assigning meaning to messages received

#14   Develop an understanding of cultural similarities and differences noted through exposure to multicultural literature.
    Examples: clothing, food, games

#15   Identify ways fictional characters and events reflect real experiences.
    Example: relating hardships faced by pioneers in literature to hardships

Appendix 2: Alabama Course of Study (2004 Edition)

Third Grade Alabama Course of Study (Aug 04)

#16   Employ study strategies to gain information.
- Previewing
- Predicting
- Questioning
- Following directions
- Sequencing
- Locating
- Taking notes
- Using graphic organizers

SOCIAL STUDIES

Page 29

#1   Extend their development of map and globe skills.
- Symbols: Associate symbols with features of thematic maps.
    - Examples: locating different Naïve American groups on a map of the United States using a colored dot system, creating a map of the United States using graphics to identify different types of land cover and vegetation
- Features: Demonstrate a working knowledge of maps and globes in classroom activities.
    - Hemispheres
    - Prime Meridian
    - International Date Line
    - North Pole
    - South Pole
    - Equator
    - Tropic of Capricorn
    - Tropic of Cancer
    - Arctic Circle
    - Antarctic Circle
    - Mountain ranges
    - Compass rose
    - Latitude
    - Longitude
    - Continents
    - Oceans
    - River systems
- Location: Demonstrate an understanding of simple grid systems created for and applied to various maps.
    - Example: establishing the absolute location of early American cities
- Direction: Apply understanding of compass reading in selected activities.
    - Example: acting out orienteering with and without a compass such as the movement of Native Americans, voyages of Europeans
- Scale: Become aware of relationships between time and distance.
    - Examples: discussing and recording the time it takes to travel from one world region to another, *From Sea to Shining Sea* by Amy Cohn

Page 30

#4   Describe the natural environment of North America.
- River systems
- Physical geography
    - Land forms
    - Natural regions
- Natural resources
    - Native wildlife
    - Vegetation

Appendix 2: Alabama Course of Study (2004 Edition)

Third Grade Alabama Course of Study (Aug 04)

#5 Relate the elements of geography to the time of the early Native Americans.
- The world in spatial terms
  - Example: student-generated maps or models showing landforms and bodies of water in a selected Native American community
- Places and regions
  - Examples: a three-dimensional model of a Native American village, field trip to a Native American site, listings of common characteristics shared by selected Native American communities
- Environment and society
  - Example: stories about Native Americans that describe adaptations to the environment such as clothing, crops, building materials
- Human systems
  - Example: group discussions about types of transportation used by Native Americans
- Physical systems
  - Examples: oceans, rivers, climates
- Uses of geography
  - Example: location of settlements

#6 Compare different groups of Native Americans.
- Food
- Shelter
- Clothing

Page 31

#7 Relate the movement of various Native American groups to features of the natural environment.
- Examples: mountains, deserts, rivers, plains, woodlands

#9 Compare cultural aspects of selected Native American groups.
- Examples: tribal identity, art, religion, folklore, customs, traditions, political structure, *The Legend of the Bluebonnet* by Tomie DePaola, *The Popcorn Book* by Tomie DePaola

#11 Describe relationships between early settlements and the natural environment.
- Choice of settlement sites
- Basic needs of settlers
- Occupations of settlers
- Clearing land
- Use of natural resources
  - Examples: hunting, farming, fishing, mining

#12 Identify the formation of various forms of governing
- Examples: religious principles, English Common Law, Mayflower Compact

#13 Describe land use by Native American and European settlements.
- Examples: *Wagon Wheels* by Barbara Brenner, *Little House in the Big Woods* by Laura Ingalls

#15 Compare the lives of Europeans and Africans during the exploration and settlement of America.
- Locations
- Cultures
- Economic systems
- Political systems

#16 Describe natural features.
- Physical characteristics
- Natural resources
- Interdependency

Appendix 2: Alabama Course of Study (2004 Edition)

Fourth Grade Alabama Course of Study (Aug 04)

READING

Page 37

#1 Using a wide range of strategies to interpret, evaluate, appreciate, and construct meaning from print materials.
- Applying prior knowledge and experiences
- Using knowledge of word meaning
- Applying knowledge of sentence structure and context\
- Previewing and predicting
- Using structural analysis of words
  Examples: roots, prefixes, suffixes
- Locating information in reference sources

#2 Apply knowledge of text features to gain meaning.
- Titles
- Headings
- Graphic aids
- Glossary
- Boldface print
- Index
- Table of contents

Page 38

#4 Demonstrate literal understanding of print material.
- Identifying important details
- Identifying sequence of events
- Following directions

#5 Interpret passages in print material.
- Identifying main idea
- Drawing conclusions
- Determining cause and effect
- Identifying fact and opinion
- Detecting bias
- Identifying author's purpose

#6 Demonstrate reading improvement gained through substantial amounts of daily reading.

#7 Use literary analysis.
- Identifying and analyzing literary elements
  - Theme
  - Character
  - Setting
  - Plot, including problem and solution
  - Point of view
- Identifying figurative language

Appendix 2: Alabama Course of Study (2004 Edition)

Fourth Grade Alabama Course of Study (Aug 04)

Page 39

#11   Read materials encountered in daily lives.
- Textual
    - Example: classroom texts
- Functional
    - Examples: directions, schedules
- Recreational
    - Examples: writing by self and peers, trade books

#12   Apply strategies of a skillful listener.
- Establishing purposes
- Focusing on the listening task
- Discriminating among received messages
- Assigning meaning to messages received
- Using self-monitoring techniques to assess effectiveness

#13   Exhibit increased independence in selecting appropriate print and nonprint media for a variety of purposes.
- Pleasure
    - Examples: short stories, videos, poetry, trade books
- Information
    - Examples: newspapers, magazines, television, computers, nonfiction, Internet

#15   Describe cultural similarities and differences through exposure to multicultural literature.
- Examples: school life, holidays, housing

Page 40

#20   Demonstrate vocabulary growth developed through reading and listening to literature.
- Increasing vocabulary in listening, speaking, reading, and writing
- Improving sentence and paragraph structure in writing
- Improving spelling and mechanics in writing
- Improving grammar and usage in speaking and writing

SOCIAL STUDIES

Page 34

#1   Extend the development of map and globe skills.
- Features: Extend knowledge of symbolic systems through work with various thematic maps of Alabama
    - Examples of natural characteristics: weather/climate maps, physical-relief maps, land-cover maps
    - Examples of human characteristics: transportation maps, political boundary maps, economic development maps, land-use maps
- Location: Apply an understanding of intermediate directions (NE, SE, NW, SW) in various classroom activities.
    - Examples: locating major cities and their home county in Alabama; giving directions about how to move from one location to another;
    Locating major cities in regions of the United States such as Washington, D.C., Atlanta, GA, Sacramento, CA, Denver, CO; Oklahoma City, OK, New York City, NY, Phoenix, AZ, Detroit, MI
- Direction: Demonstrate orientation skills by following and giving specific verbal instructions.
    - Examples: describe the location of Montgomery relative to other major cities using an Alabama map; describe the location of Alabama relative to other states and countries using a world map or globe
- Distance: Use a scale to measure distances between places.
    - Compare distances between places using a scale and mileage markers.
- Scale: Understand variations in a scale.
    - Examples: examine a variety of maps using different scales, draw representations of the classroom using various proportions

Appendix 2: Alabama Course of Study (2004 Edition)

Fourth Grade Alabama Course of Study (Aug 04)

#2   Interpret and display information and data using various graphic organizers.
- Maps
- Globes
- Charts
- Graphs
- Illustrations
- Tables
- Time lines

Page 35

#4   Comprehend the geographic link between Alabama and regions of the United States.
- Land regions
- River systems

#5   Describe the natural environment of Alabama including significant geographical features.
- Mountains
- Valleys
- Bodies of water
- Landform regions
  - Highland Rim
  - Cumberland Plateau
  - Ridge and Valley
  - Piedmont
  - Coastal Plain

#7   Identify the major characteristics of prehistoric Indian: Paleo, Archaic, Woodland, and Mississippian.
- Approximate times of existence
- Culture
- Government
- Economy
  - Hunting
  - Farming
  - Trading

#8   Assess the impact of European contact on native American populations in Alabama.
- Epidemics
- Reorganization of tribes

#9   Describe historic Indians of Alabama after European contact.
- Name and location during selected time periods
  - Choctaw
  - Cherokee

      Examples: *Dancing Drum: A Cherokee Legend* by Terri Cohlene
  - Chickasaw
  - Creek (Muskogee)
- Culture

      Examples: folklore, games, dance, music
- Government
- Economy
- Significant personalities

Appendix 2: Alabama Course of Study (2004 Edition)

Fourth Grade Alabama Course of Study (Aug 04)

<u>Page 36</u>

#10   Describe aspects of the lives of historic Indians of Alabama.
                Example: projects reflecting cultural aspects of historic Indians

#11   Explain lasting contributions made by Alabama's earliest inhabitants.
                Examples: place names, food, folk traditions, recreation

Appendix 2: Alabama Course of Study (2004 Edition)

Fifth Grade Alabama Course of Study (Aug 04)

READING

Page 44

#1   Use a wide range of strategies to interpret, evaluate, appreciate, and construct meaning from print materials.
- Applying prior knowledge and experiences
- Using knowledge of word meaning
- Applying knowledge of sentence structure and context
- Previewing and predicting
- Using structural analysis of words
  - Examples: roots, prefixes, suffixes
- Locating information in reference sources

#2   Use text features to gain meaning.
- Titles
- Headings
- Graphic aids
- Glossary
- Boldfaced print
- Index
- Table of contents

Page 45

#5   Interpret passages in print material.
- Identifying main idea
- Drawing conclusions
- Determining cause and effect
- Distinguishing fact from opinion
- Detecting bias
- Summarizing passages
- Identifying author's purpose

#6   Demonstrate reading improvement gained through substantial amounts of daily reading.

#7   Use literary analysis.
- Identifying and analyzing literary elements
  - Theme
  - Character
  - Setting
  - Plot, including problem and solution
  - Point of view
- Identifying and understanding figurative language

#9   Recognize the features of a variety of genres.

Page 46

#12   Read a variety of materials and genres encountered in daily lives.
- Textual
  - Examples: classroom texts, encyclopedias
- Functional
  - Examples: directions, schedules
- Recreational
  - Examples: literature, writing by self and peers

Appendix 2: Alabama Course of Study (2004 Edition)

Fifth Grade Alabama Course of Study (Aug 04)

#13   Apply strategies of a skillful listener.
- Establishing purpose
- Focusing on the listening task
- Discriminating among received messages
- Assigning meaning to messages received
- Using self-monitoring techniques to assess effectiveness

SOCIAL STUDIES

Page 46

#4   Describe the natural environment of North America.
- River systems
- Physical geography
  - Land forms
  - Natural regions
  - Native wildlife and vegetation
- Natural resources

#6   Discuss the progression of culture of the early American people.
- Big game hunters
- Hunters – Gatherers
- Farmers

#7   Analyze the different cultures of Native American groups by geographic regions.
- Impact of the environment
  - Examples: natural resources, society
- Conflict and cooperation
  - Examples: cultural differences, hunting rights, *Women in American Indian Society* by Rayna Green
- Government
  - Examples: intra-tribal, inter-tribal, *The Native Americans – An Illustrated History* by Michael Regan
- Economy
  - Examples: occupations, trading patterns, tools, weapons
- Religion
  - Examples: legends, *The Women Who Fell From the Sky: The Iroquois' Story* by John Bierhorst

Page 47

#9   Describe the impact of the early European exploration and settlement on Native American cultures.
- Cultural significance
  - Examples: new foods, religion, breakup of families, languages, diseases, medicines, clothing
- Conflict and cooperation
  - Examples: weapons, trade items, shelters, "Columbian Exchange"

#10   Analyze the English settlement of North America.
- Reasons
  - Examples: religious freedom, trade and profit, adventure
- Success of settlements
  - Examples: economic, political, social
- Interaction with native Americans
  - Examples: crops, trade, land use
- Interaction among colonies
  - Examples: religion, land, trade, boundaries
- Interaction with other nations
  - Examples: land, hunting rights

Appendix 2: Alabama Course of Study (2004 Edition)

Sixth Grade Alabama Course of Study (Aug 04)

READING

Page 52

#1   Interpret and construct meaning by applying appropriate strategies to materials across the curriculum.
         Examples: making initial predictions about text meaning, using prior knowledge, stetting purposes for reading, interpreting author's meaning, using monitoring g strategies, correcting or confirming author's message, determining cause and effect, noting sequence of events, identifying main idea and supporting details

#2   Read with ease textual, functional, and recreational materials encountered in daily life.
         Examples: textbooks, trade books, magazines, newspapers, computer materials, written correspondence, school rules

#4   Demonstrate reading improvement gained through substantial amounts of daily reading.

#5   Recognize various forms of literature according to characteristics.
         Examples: poetry, short stories, novels, plays, folktales, myths

Page 53

#7   Recognize the characteristics and cultural influences of works of literature representative of various eras.
         Examples: books and plays; presentations; class, school, and/or community productions; movies; television productions

#10   Recognize linguistic and cultural diversity.
- Geographic
- Ethnic

#12   Develop general listening behaviors for different purposes and situations.
         Examples: comprehending messages, understanding literal meaning of words, remembering significant details accurately, remembering directions or sequences, paraphrasing spoken messages

Appendix 2: Alabama Course of Study (2004 Edition)

Sixth Grade Alabama Course of Study (Aug 04)

SOCIAL STUDIES

Page 54

#1 Extend the development of map and globe skills.
- Features: Locate major geographic features associated with American's history.
    - Examples: ocean currents, prevailing winds, large forests, major rivers, significant mountain ranges
- Relative location: Use cardinal and intermediate directions to describe the relative location of selected places in North America.
    - Examples: Maine in the northeastern United States, Mexico to the south of the United States, the Atlantic Ocean on the eastern border of Georgia
- Absolute location: Use a grid system to describe the absolute location of selected places encountered during the study of America's history.
    - Latitude and longitude
    - Example: comparing climates of places in America with countries of the origin of early settlers
    - Equator
    - Tropics of Cancer and Capricorn
    - Arctic and Antarctic Circles
    - Prime Meridian, International Date Line relative to North American and the world
- Directions: Extend orientation skills by following and giving specific cardinal directions and verbal instructions.
    - Example: describing proposed trade and exploration routes through the eyes of the explorers
- Scale: Compare differences found on a variety of scales.
    - Example: comparing a local area map with a map of a larger area such as Jamestown with the 13 colonies or with the North American continent

Page 55

#4 Review major changes in America from 1870 to 1900.
- Industrialization
    - Examples: labor, railroads, monopolies and mergers, "robber barons", Horatio Alger, Rockefeller, Carnegie
- Urbanization
    - Examples: immigration, "The Melting Pot," *How the Other Half Lives* by Jacob Riis, Jane Addams
- Cultural Changes
    - Examples: women's suffrage movement, expanding educational system, emerging writers and artists, establishment of unions, Tuskegee Institute and Booker T. Washington
- Communication and Technology
    - Examples: Pony Express, Samuel F. B. Morse, Bell and the telephone, Trans-Atlantic cable

#5 Explain why the phrase "end of the Frontier" is descriptive of America in the early 1900s.
- Examples: continental expansion complete, purchase of Alaskan territory, absorption of Indian culture

Appendix 2: Alabama Course of Study (2004 Edition)

Seventh Grade Alabama Course of Study (Aug 04)

READING

Page 57

#1   Construct, interpret, and evaluate meaning by applying appropriate strategies to materials across the curriculum.
         Examples: setting purposes for reading, interpreting author's meaning, using monitoring strategies, correcting or confirming author's message, distinguishing fact from opinion, determining cause and effect, noting sequence of events, identifying main idea and supporting details

#2   Read with ease textual, functional, and recreational materials encountered in daily life.
         Examples: textbooks, trade books, magazines, newspapers, computer materials, written correspondence, school and community rules and laws, directions

#5   Recognize various forms of literature according to characteristics.
         Examples: poetry, short stories, novels, plays, folktales, myths, nonfiction

Page 58

#7   Appreciate the characteristics, literary elements, and cultural influences of literary works representative of various eras.
         Examples: reading books and plays, listening to presentations, participating in productions, viewing movie and television productions

#9   Demonstrate respect for linguistic and cultural diversity in literature.
- Geographic
- Ethnic

#11   Refine general listening behaviors.
- Identifying main idea and summarizing
- Understanding contextual meaning of words used
- Listening for implications of significant details
- Understanding relationships among idea
- Connecting spoken message to prior experiences

Page 59

#15   Respond with understanding and empathy to information read, viewed, and heard.
         Examples: large – and small – group discussions, student journals

Page 60

#22   Know and apply principles of grammar and usage in writing, speaking, and presenting and apply mechanics in writing.
- Capitalization
  - Proper nouns and adjectives
  - Regions of country
  - Titles of people, books, and works of art
  - First word in quotations
- Punctuation
  - Comma(s) with appositives, with introductory elements, and before coordinate conjunction in compound sentence
  - Colon to introduce a list
  - Quotation marks and commas with direct quotations
  - Semicolon between independent clauses with no conjunction
  - Apostrophe for possession and contractions

Appendix 2: Alabama Course of Study (2004 Edition)

Seventh Grade Alabama Course of Study (Aug 04)

- Grammar, usage, and spelling
    - Adverb and adjective forms
    - Noun and verb forms
    - Appropriate tenses including present, past, future, and perfect tenses
    - Subject-verb agreement including intervening phrase
    - Pronoun-antecedent agreement
    - Pronoun case
    - Special usage problems
  Examples: double negatives, homonym confusion
    - Parts of speech
    - Developing compound and complex sentences
    - Avoiding redundancy, fragments, run-ons, and on-and-on sentences

SOCIAL STUDIES

#6   Describe how people organize economic systems for the production, and consumption of goods and services to address the basic economic questions of which goods and services will be produced, how they will be produces, and who will consume them.
- Using economic concepts to explain historical and current developments and issues in global, national, or local contexts
  Example: increase in oil prices resulting from supply and demand
- Analyzing the distribution of urban areas to determine how they are linked together
  Example: using distribution maps to examine population flows among cities, suburbs, and small towns

#9   Identify individual and civic responsibilities of citizens of the United States.
  Examples:
    - individual-respect for right of others, self-discipline, negotiation, compromise;
    - civic-respect for the law, patriotism, participation in the political process
- Describing differences in rights, privileges, duties, and responsibilities between citizens and noncitizens
- Explaining how United States citizenship is acquired
- Interpreting an immigration map
- Identifying character traits that are beneficial to individuals and to the republic of the United States
  Examples: honesty, courage, compassion, civility

#10   Describe changes in social and economic conditions in the United States during the twentieth and twenty-first centuries.
  Examples: classroom texts
    - social-family values, peer pressures, educational opportunities;
    - economic-career opportunities, disposable income
- Describing the impact of print and electronic media and the Internet on the American way of life
  Examples: fashion trends, consumer spending, increased debt, speed of communication, changes in language and social skills

#11   Describe examples of conflict, cooperation, and interdependence of groups, societies, and notions, using past and current events.
- Tracing the political and social impact of the modern Civil Rights Movement from 1954 to the present, including Alabama's role

Appendix 3

Reading and Social Studies Teacher-made Pre/Mid/Post Tests for Grades Kindergarten Through Seventh Based on the Lessons Taught

Name _____   Date _____   Kindergarten

Kindergarten   Phonemic Awareness, Initial Sound Fluency, Phonics Instructions, Comprehension, Vocabulary, Letter Naming

_____ 1. **What race of people were Echota Cherokees?** (Lesson 1)
   a. Indians   b. pilgrims   c. Chinese

_____ 2. **How many clans make up the Echota Cherokee Tribe?** (Lesson 2)
   a. five   b. three   c. seven

_____ 3. **Echota Cherokee Indian students in Lawrence County are members of which clan?** (Lesson 3)
   a. Deer   b. Blue   c. Wolf

_____ 4. **What did the Paleo people live in?** (Lesson 4)
   a. caves   b. log house   c. tipi

_____ 5. **Who owned the home and was responsible for the children in early Indian time?** (Lesson 5)
   a. men   b. uncle   c. women

_____ 6. **What did men and women wear in the winter?** (Lesson 6)
   a. skirt   b. pants   c. leggings

_____ 7. **The Cherokee Indian clothes were made from what animal?** (Lesson 7)
   a. bear   b. deer   c. buffalo

_____ 8. **What was the most important musical instrument to the Cherokee Indians?** (Lesson 8)
   a. drum   b. horn   c. flute

_____ 9. **How did our Indian ancestors travel on water?** (Lesson 9)
   a. wade   b. swim   c. dugout

_____ 10. **What did our ancestors trade?** (Lesson 10)
   a. skins   b. guns   c. money

_____ 11. **What did Sequoyah invent?** (Lesson 11)
   a. Cherokee alphabet   b. gun   c. shoes

_____ 12. **What was the first thing the Cherokees did each morning?** (Lesson 12)
   a. eat   b. hunt   c. bathe

_____ 13. **Who raised the Chickasaw children?** (Lesson 13)
   a. brother   b. mother   c. father

_____ 14. **What was the Cherokees favorite game?** (Lesson 14)
   a. stickball   b. running   c. swimming

Name_____ Date_____ Kindergarten

_____15. **What clan are you a member of?** (Lesson 15)
      a. blue   b. black   c. bird

_____16. **How did our early Indian ancestors travel on land?** (Lesson 16)
      a. train   b. wagon   c. foot

_____17. **Where is the Indian education office located?** (Lesson 17)
      a. Courtland   b. Moulton   c. Oakville

_____18. **Who was an important chief to the Cherokee of Lawrence County?** (Lesson 18)
      a. Doublehead   b. John Ross   c. hunter

_____19. **What county do you live in?** (Lesson 19)
      a. Lawrence County   b. Morgan County   c. Colbert County

_____20. **What direction did our ancestors travel during removal?** (Lesson 20)
      a. west   b. south   c. east

_____21. **How long did the Trail of Tears last?** (Lesson 21)
      a. 5 weeks   b. 5 years   c. 5 months

_____22. **What important animal to our Indian ancestors still lives in the Bankhead Forest?** (Lesson 22)
      a. mountain lion   b. deer   c. elk

_____23. **What is the largest tribe in Alabama?** (Lesson 23)
      a. Echota Cherokee Tribe   b. Star Clan of Lower Muscogee   c. Cherokee Tribe of NE AL

_____24. **What number was sacred to the early Indians?** (Lesson 3)
      a. two   b. seven   c. four

_____25. **What weapon do we still use today to hunt deer that early Indians used?** (Lesson 4)
      a. gun   b. spear   c. bow and arrow

Name _____ Date _____ First Grade

First Grade Phonemic Segmentation Fluency, Phonics, Letter Naming Fluency, Nonsense Work Fluency, Text Comprehension

_____ 1. **What Indian tribe do most of you or your parents belong?** (Lesson 2)

a. Northeast Cherokee
b. Echota Cherokee
c. Eastern Band Cherokee
d. Western Band Cherokee

_____ 2. **What is an ancestor?** (Lesson 2)

a. friend
b. grandparent
c. brother
d. neighbor

_____ 3. **What river in Lawrence County did our Cherokee ancestors live?** (Lessons 3)

a. Mississippi
b. Tennessee
c. Cumberland
d. Sipsey

_____ 4. **Name one ice age animal:** (Lesson 4)

a. deer
b. bear
c. rabbit
d. mammoth

_____ 5. **What is another name for Bankhead National Forest?** (Lesson 5)

a. Smokey Mountains
b. Appalachian Mountains
c. Warrior Mountains
d. Rocky Mountains

_____ 6. **What are the names of the homes of our Cherokee ancestors?** (Lesson 6)

a. teepee and hut
b. log and shingle
c. fall and spring
d. summer and winter

_____ 7. **What type of fruit makes the color purple?** (Lesson 7)

a. berry
b. apple
c. orange
d. watermelon

_____ 8. **What did our early Cherokee wear as a symbol while they were dancing during a ceremony?** (Lesson 8)

a. hats
b. robes
c. masks
d. shoes

_____ 9. **Our early ancestors used what type of material to make their hunting points?** (Lesson 9)

a. wood
b. flint
c. metal
d. shells

_____ 10. **Who was the first Spanish explorer in Alabama?** (Lesson 10)

a. Hernando Desoto
b. Bob Benge
c. John Colbert
d. Pounce De Leon

_____ 11. **Where in Lawrence County did Andrew Jackson own land?** (Lesson 11)

a. Town Creek
b. Doublehead's Village
c. Melton's Bluff
d. Moulton

_____ 12. **What were two things sacred to the Creeks?** (Lesson 12)

a. water and fire
b. soil and trees
c. corn and potatoes
d. wood and rock

Name _____ Date _____ First Grade

_____ 13. **Who disciplined the boys?** (Lesson 13)

a. mother's brother
b. father
c. sister
d. grandparents

_____ 14. **What were the stories/myths called?** (Lesson 14)

a. books
b. legends
c. conversations
d. maps

_____ 15. **What ceremony was like our Thanksgiving?** (Lesson 15)

a. New Spring Ceremony
b. Christmas
c. Valentines Day
d. Green Corn Ceremony

_____ 16. **What is the longest path our ancestors traveled through Lawrence County?** (Lesson 16)

a. Black Warriors' Path
b. High Town Path
c. Coosa Path
d. Muscle Shoals Path

_____ 17. **Whose village was located at Brown's Ferry?** (Lesson 17)

a. Bob Benge
b. John Colbert
c. Doublehead
d. John Melton

_____ 18. **What did Sequoyah invent?** (Lesson 18)

a. alphabet
b. gun
c. bow
d. language

_____ 19. **What is another name for the Indian maiden, Magnolia, in the Battle of Indian Tomb Hollow?** (Lesson 19)

a. Tuskiahooto
b. Hogoheegee
c. Chake Thlocko
d. Ittaloknah

_____ 20. **Who forced Cherokee removal?** (Lesson 20)

a. Doublehead
b. Andrew Jackson
c. John Melton
d. John Coffee

_____ 21. **Approximately how many Cherokees died on the Trail of Tears?** (Lesson 21)

a. 1,000
b. 2,000
c. 3,000
d. 4,000

_____ 22. **What does it mean when you cut all of the trees down with heavy equipment?** (Lesson 22)

a. land clearing
b. cutting field
c. clear cutting
d. tree removal

_____ 23. **A majority of Lawrence County Indian students are members of what tribe?** (Lesson 23)

a. Cherokee Tribe of NE Alabama
b. Echota Cherokee Tribe
c. Star Clan of Lower Muscogee
d. Poarch Band of Creek

_____ 24. **What are the characteristics of Celtic people?** (Lesson 2)

a. dark hair, dark eyes, dark skin
b. black skin, black eyes, black hair
c. light skin, blue eyes, freckles, red hair
d. red skin, black eyes, red hair

_____ 25. **Where did the Paleo people live?** (Lesson 4)

a. tipi
b. log cabin
c. house
d. cave

Name_____ Date_____ Second Grade

Second Grade   Oral Reading Fluency, Nonsense Word Fluency, Text Comprehension, Vocabulary, Listening and Communicating

_____1. **What is the name of the tribe that most of our Indian students are members?** (Lesson 2)
a. Southeast Cherokee
b. Echota Cherokee
c. Northeast Cherokee
d. Eastern Cherokee

_____2. **What Alabama County had the highest Indian population in 1990?** (Lesson 3)
a. Winston
b. Morgan
c. Franklin
d. Lawrence

_____3. **What are two of the four prehistoric time periods?** (Lesson 4)
a. Paleo & Tennessean
b. Mississippi & Historic
c. Archaic & Woodland
d. Paleo and Historic

_____4. **The elders of the village took responsibility for care and instruction of who?** (Lesson 5)
a. girls
b. boys
c. men
d. women

_____5. **What tool did early Indians use to sew leather clothes?** (Lesson 6)
a. wood needle
b. steel needle
c. bone needle
d. fiber needle

_____6. **What were leggings made from?** (Lesson 7)
a. rabbit skin
b. buckskin
c. bear skin
d. squirrel skin

_____7. **What were rattles made from?** (Lesson 8)
a. pottery
b. rocks
c. mussel shells
d. turtle shells

_____8. **What was the Indian name of the Tennessee River?** (Lesson 9)
a. Warrior River
b. Tombigbee River
c. Sipsey River
d. Hogohegee River

_____9. **How many deerskins could an Indian trade for a rifle?** (Lesson 10)
a. 10
b. 15
c. 30
d. 45

_____10. **The word "Alabama" comes from the Indian word meaning what?** (Lesson 11)
a. Thicket Clearers
b. Forest Land
c. Roll Tide
d. River Valley

_____11. **How many towns was the Creek tribe divided into?** (Lesson 12)
a. 1
b. 2
c. 3
d. 4

_____12. **What kind of house did the Chickasaws build in Lawrence County?** (Lesson 13)
a. lean to
b. log cabins
c. stone house
d. tipi

_____13. **No tribal function was considered complete without the presence and assistance of what person?** (Lesson 14)
a. hunter
b. dancer
c. storyteller
d. medicine man

_____14. **Name three of seven Cherokee clans.** (Lesson 15)
a. fish, blue, bird
b. bird, blue, deer
c. bird, bear, deer
d. deer, wild potato, bear

_____15. **What was the name of the first federal road in Lawrence County?** (Lesson 16)
a. Mitchell Trace
b. Buffalo Trace
c. Byler Road
d. Gaines Trace

Name _____ Date _____ Second Grade

_____ 16. **Where is the largest ceremonial mound in Lawrence County made by Woodland people?** (Lesson 17)
a. Moulton
b. Oakville
c. Courtland
d. Caddo

_____ 17. **What future Cherokee Chief had a father Attakullakulla?** (Lesson 18)
a. Dragging Canoe
b. Cuttyatoy
c. Doublehead
d. Red Eagle
e.

_____ 18. **Who was the Indian maiden who was killed at the Battle of Indian Tomb Hollow?** (Lesson 19)
a. White Lily
b. Saleechie
c. Magnolia
d. Tuskiahooto

_____ 19. **What was the forced removal of Indians known as?** (Lesson 20)
a. Sorrow Road
b. Trail of Removal
c. Tears Path
d. Trail of Tears

_____ 20. **Who was responsible for the Indian Removal?** (Lesson 21)
a. George Washington
b. George Colbert
c. John Melton
d. Andrew Jackson

_____ 21. **What animal is extinct from the Warrior Mountains?** (Lesson 22)
a. Whitetail Deer
b. Carolina Parakeet
c. Cotton Tail Rabbit
d. Wild Turkey

_____ 22. **How many modern tribes are in the state of Alabama?** (Lesson 23)
a. 1
b. 2
c. 4
d. 9

_____ 23. **What state do you live in?** (Lesson 14)
a. Georgia
b. Tennessee
c. Alabama
d. Mississippi
e.

_____ 24. **Who was the most feared red-headed Cherokee warrior?** (Lesson 2)
a. Bob Benge
b. Pumpkin Boy
c. Sequoyah
d. Doublehead

_____ 25. **Where did the Cherokees & Chickasaws get their first cloth?** (Lesson 7)
a. Europeans
b. Dutch
c. French
d. English

Name _____   Date _____   Third Grade

Third Grade   Listening Skills, Interpreting Reading Materials, Comprehension, Word Recognition, Oral Reading Fluency

_____ 1. **What is the name of a Celtic group?** (Lesson 2)
a. Dutch
b. French
c. Irish
d. German

_____ 2. **What tribe represents most of Lawrence County Indian people?** (Lesson 3)
a. Eastern Cherokee
b. Northeast Cherokee
c. Western Cherokee
d. Echota Cherokee

_____ 3. **What animal did Archaic people domesticate?** (Lesson 4)
a. dog
b. cow
c. deer
d. cat

_____ 4. **What custom was considered important to the Woodland Indians?** (Lesson 4)
a. engagement
b. burial
c. marriage
d. making canoes

_____ 5. **What were fish hooks made from?** (Lesson 5)
a. deer bones
b. rabbit bones
c. flint rock
d. mussel shells

_____ 6. **What object was used by our early Indian ancestors to cook food?** (Lesson 6)
a. clay pots
b. large mussel shells
c. metal pots
d. wooden bowls

_____ 7. **Why did Indian people wear tattoos?** (Lesson 7)
a. to be chiefs
b. friends had one
c. designate honor
d. to be brave

_____ 8. **What the most sacred possession of a tribe?** (Lesson 8)
a. cane flute
b. ceremonial pipe
c. wooden whistle
d. drum

_____ 9. **The dugout canoe is made from what type of wood?** (Lesson 9)
a. poplar
b. oak
c. birch
d. maple

_____ 10. **Who was the first European to discover the Tennessee River?** (Lesson 10)
a. Sequoyah
b. Desoto
c. Columbus
d. Doublehead

_____ 11. **What tribe placed their baby's head against a wooden cradle board to make it flat?** (Lesson 11)
a. Creek
b. Cherokee
c. Choctaw
d. Shawnee

_____ 12. **If Creeks divided their town into red and white, what did the colors stand for?** (Lesson 12)
a. war and peace
b. north and south
c. eating and hunting
d. good and bad

_____ 13. **Who became the wealthiest man in the Chickasaw nation?** (Lesson 13)
a. Chief Tishamingo
b. Chief Tuscumbia
c. Doublehead
d. George Colbert

_____ 14. **Name one of the seven directions of the Cherokee.** (Lesson 14)
a. up
b. out
c. in
d. around

_____ 15. **What is one of the clans of the Cherokee Tribe?** (Lesson 15)
a. bear
b. wild potato
c. beaver
d. wild bean

_____ 16. **What two Indian trails crossed at Oakville?** (Lesson 16)
a. High Town Path/Coosa Path
b. Black Warriors' Path/Coosa Path
c. Sipsey Trail/Mitchell Trace
d. Black Warriors' Path/High Town Path

Name _____ Date _____ Third Grade

_____ 17. **What is another name for Melton's Bluff?** (Lesson 17)
a. Marathon
b. Moneetown
c. Moulton
d. Mousetown

18. **Where in Lawrence County did Doublehead live?** (Lesson 18)
a. Moulton
b. Melton's bluff
c. Brown's Ferry
d. Oakville

_____ 19. **The French and Indian War was also known as:** (Lesson 19)
a. Cherokee War
b. Battle of Indian Tomb Hollow
c. Creek Indian War
d. Battle of Fort Mims

_____ 20. **The Turkey Town Treaty was signed in what year?** (Lesson 20)
a. 1776
b. 1801
c. 1806
d. 1816

_____ 21. **After what act did the Indian mixed-blood descendants begin claiming their heritage?** (Lesson 21)
a. Heritage Rights Act of 1990
b. Civil Rights Act of 1968
c. Descendants Act of 1950
d. Indian Removal Act of 1830

_____ 22. **What is a symbol considered sacred to descendants of Indian ancestors?** (Lesson 22)
a. Indian marker tree
b. Buffalo nickel
c. waterfall
d. bluff shelter

_____ 23. **The Echota Cherokee Tribe was formed in what year?** (Lesson 23)
a. 1950
b. 1960
c. 1970
d. 1980

_____ 24. **Why did Indians have a Green Corn Ceremony?** (Lesson 8)
a. harvest corn
b. plant corn
c. give thanks for harvest
d. eat corn

_____ 25. **What portion of the animal was used to tan its hide?** (Lesson 7)
a. brains
b. meat
c. stomach
d. heart

Name _____ Date _____ Fourth Grade

Fourth Grade   Word Recognition, Vocabulary, Comprehension, Literary Elements, Listening Skills

_____ 1. **When did Lawrence County Schools' Indian Education Program start?** (Lesson 2)
a. 1986
b. 1990
c. 1992
d. 1976

_____ 2. **What tribe are most Lawrence County Indian students a member?** (Lesson 2)
a. Echota Cherokee Tribe
b. Northeast Cherokee Tribe
c. Eastern Cherokee Tribe
d. Western Cherokee Tribe

_____ 3. **What year was the Echota Cherokee Tribe formed?** (Lesson 3)
a. 1980
b. 1970
c. 1990
d. 1960

_____ 4. **What period of early Indians were farmers, gatherers, and hunters?** (Lesson 4)
a. Archaic
b. Mississippian
c. Paleo
d. Woodland

_____ 5. **What river played an important role in providing things our ancestors in Lawrence County needed to survive** (Lesson 5)
a. Mississippi River
b. Tennessee River
c. Alabama River
d. Tombigbee River

_____ 6. **What was used to heat water in early Indian times?** (Lesson 6)
a. shells
b. stove
c. stones
d. sand

_____ 7. **Who was a famous Cherokee silversmith?** (Lesson 7)
a. John Melton
b. Doublehead
c. Sequoyah
d. George Colbert

_____ 8. **What was one game Cherokee Indians played as a team?** (Lesson 8)
a. swimming
b. stickball
c. hunting
d. chunkey

_____ 9. **In the Shoals, our Indian ancestors depended on what as a seasonal source of meat for their diet:** (Lesson 9)
a. raccoons
b. beavers
c. frogs
d. mussels

_____ 10. **What does Métis mean?** (Lesson 10)
a. English speaking
b. Indian speaking
c. Mixed Native American
d. mixed people

_____ 11. **Who was the first legal white landowner in Lawrence County?** (Lesson 11)
a. Andrew Jackson
b. John Melton
c. Alex Saunders
d. Doublehead

_____ 12. **Creeks fought the Chickasaws in Lawrence County at what battle?** (Lesson 12)
a. Battle of Horseshoe Bend
b. Battle of Indian Tomb Hollow
c. Battle of Fort Mims
d. Battle of Burnt Corn Creek

_____ 13. **What Alabama County is named after a Chickasaw chief?** (Lesson 13)
a. Franklin
b. Morgan
c. Lawrence
d. Colbert

_____ 14. **Where was the Cherokee capital in Georgia?** (Lesson 14)
a. Chota
b. New Echota
c. Red Clay
d. Etowah

_____ 15. **What is placed in the center of the council house that kindles seven kinds of wood?** (Lesson 15)
a. sacred fire
b. sacred chief
c. sacred bowl
d. sacred pipe

_____ 16. **The High Town Path was also known as:** (Lesson 16)
a. Coosa Path
b. Chickasaw Path
c. Black Warriors' Path
d. Ridge Path

Name_____   Date_____   Fourth Grade

_____ 17. **Which Indian town was a Cherokee village located at present-day Town of Courtland?** (Lesson 17)
a. Shoal Town
b. Doublehead's Village
c. Goard's Settlement
d. Cuttyatoy's Village

_____ 18. **Name one Celtic man in the 1700s in Lawrence County to marry an Indian woman?** (Lesson 18)
a. John Walker
b. John Melton
c. John Ross
d. John Colbert

_____ 19. **Where was the first skirmish of the Creek Indian War?** (Lesson 5)
a. Holy Ground
b. Indian Tomb
c. Fort Mims
d. Burnt Corn Creek

_____ 20. **What year was the Cotton Gin Treaty?** (Lesson 20)
a. 1806
b. 1910
c. 1800
d. 1810

_____ 21. **President Andrew Jackson had what act passed in 1830?** (Lesson 21)
a. Civil Rights Act
b. Cherokee Friendship Act
c. Indian Removal Act
d. Treaty Act

_____ 22. **What is an arbor glyph?** (Lesson 22)
a. tree drawing
b. rock drawing
c. cave drawing
d. skin drawing

_____ 23. **Who was the elected principal chief when the Echota Cherokee Tribe was formed in 1980?** (Lesson 23)
a. Eddie Tullis
b. Joseph Stewart
c. Larry Johnson
d. Penny Wright

_____ 24. **What is another name of the Hogohegee?** (Lesson 9)
a. Tennessee River
b. Sipsey River
c. Flint River
d. Paint Rock River

_____ 25. **The early historic Cherokee Indians lived in what type of homes?** (Lesson 17)
a. plank
b. tipi
c. log
d. rock

Name_____ Date_____ Fifth Grade

Fifth Grade   Listening Skills, Vocabulary, Comprehension, Literary Elements, Genres

_____ 1. **What is the name of your tribe?** (Lesson 1)
a. Western Cherokee
b. Echota Cherokee
c. Eastern Cherokee
d. Northeast Cherokee

_____ 2. **Which county in Alabama has the largest population of Indian people according to the 1990 Census?** (Lesson 2)
a. Lawrence
b. Lauderdale
c. Colbert
d. Morgan

_____ 3. **Name one of the seven directions of the Cherokee.** (Lesson 3)
a. under
b. southeast
c. up
d. northwest

_____ 4. **What is one characteristic of the Mississippian people?** (Lesson 4)
a. cave dwellers
b. permanent towns
c. atlatl
d. first pottery

_____ 5. **What were found in the shoals that were food supply to early Indians?** (Lesson 5)
a. freshwater clams
b. freshwater crayfish
c. freshwater mussels
d. freshwater shells

_____ 6. **What was the favorite hunting weapon of Mississippian Indians?** (Lesson 6)
a. bow and arrow
b. blow gun
c. atlatl
d. tomahawk

_____ 7. **What were things our Indian ancestors used to make paint?** (Lesson 7)
a. moss, chalk, bark
b. leaves, bark, wood
c. ink, stain, bark
d. sand rocks, berries, plants

_____ 8. **Why did Indians have a Green Corn Ceremony?** (Lesson 8)
a. harvest corn
b. plant corn
c. give thanks for harvest
d. eat corn

_____ 9. **Who first introduced horses into Alabama as a new mode of travel?** (Lesson 9)
a. Europeans
b. Indians
c. pilgrims
d. Mexicans

_____ 10. **What was the worst of the new world diseases brought in by invading Europeans?** (Lesson 10)
a. flu
b. mumps
c. small pox
d. whooping cough

_____ 11. **Name the five tribes of Lawrence County.** (Lesson 11)
a. Yuchi, Creek, Shawnee, Chickasaw, Cheroke
b. Choctaw, Creek, Yuchi, Shawnee, Chickasaw
c. Yuchi, Shawnee, Chickasaw, Creek, Apache
d. Creek, Shawnee, Natchez, Yuchi, Cherokee

_____ 12. **What was the final battle for the Creeks?** (Lesson 12)
a. Battle of Burnt Corn Creek
b. Battle of Horseshoe Bend
c. Battle of Indian Tomb Hollow
d. Battle of Fort Mims

_____ 13. **What Chickasaw married Cherokee Chief Doublehead's daughters Tuskiahooto and Saleechie?** (Lesson 14)
a. George Gist
b. William Weatherford
c. John Melton
d. George Colbert

_____ 14. **All Cherokee towns had a community building where local government was run, known as what?** (Lesson 13)
a. council house
b. summer house
c. smoke house
d. government building

_____ 15. **What clan was known as the twister clan?** (Lesson 15)
a. Wolf
b. Deer
c. Long Hair
d. Wild Potato

_____ 16. **Doublehead's Trace or the Old Buffalo Trail crosses Big Mussel Shoals of the Tennessee River near what two creeks?** (Lesson 16)
a. Flint/Fox
b. Blue Water/Big Nance
c. Spring/Mallard
d. Fox/Mallard

Name _____ Date _____ Fifth Grade

_____ 17. **What early town was flooded and abandoned after a disease called "bloody flux?"** (Lesson 17)
a. Town Creek
b. Moulton
c. Courtland
d. Oakville

_____ 18. **Who was Doublehead's father?** (Lesson 18)
a. Old Tassel
b. Sequoyah
c. Great Eagle
d. Moytoy

_____ 19. **What were the two tribes fighting each other in the Battle of Indian Tomb Hollow?** (Lesson 19)
a. Choctaw/Cherokee
b. Cheroke/Creek
c. Chickasaw/Choctaw
d. Creek/Chickasaw

_____ 20. **What law did Andrew Jackson have passed on May 28,1830?** (Lesson 20)
a. Cotton Gin Treaty
b. Treaty of Ft. Jackson
c. Indian Removal Act
d. Treaty of New Echota

_____ 21. **What place was built for Cherokee removal?** (Lesson 21)
a. Fort Payne
b. Melton's Bluff
c. Fort Hampton
d. Doublehead's Village

_____ 22. **What are symbols found on rocks at Kinlock Rock Shelte called?** (Lesson 22)
a. pictograph
b. petroglyphs
c. arbor glyphs
d. cave drawings

_____ 23. **How long is the term of an elected governing body of the Echota Cherokee Tribe?** (Lesson 23)
a. 1 year
b. 2 years
c. 3 years
d. 4 years

Name _____   Date _____   Sixth Grade

Sixth Grade   Comprehension, Listening Skills, Literary Elements, Phonetic Principles, Vocabulary

_____ 1. **Today, what tribe has thousands of members in Alabama?** (Lesson 2)
a. Northeast Cherokee
b. Echota Cherokee Tribe
c. MOWA Choctaw
d. Poarch Band of Creek

_____ 2. **Since what law was it made legal to be Indian in Alabama?** (Lesson 2)
a. Indian Removal Act of 1830
b. Cotton Gin Treaty of 1806
c. Civil Rights Act of 1968
d. Wafford Settlement of 1805

_____ 3. **The Echota Cherokee is recognized by:** (Lesson 3)
a. City
b. Federal
c. County
d. State

_____ 4. **What style of projectile point was most prevalent during the Mississippian period?** (Lesson 4)
a. Clovis point
b. Triangle point
c. Big Sandy point
d. Flint Creek point

_____ 5. **Kinlock in the Bankhead Forest is known as a:** (Lesson 5)
a. seasonal shelter
b. cave shelter
c. bluff shelter
d. permanent shelter

_____ 6. **In most early Indian tribes, who provided for the spiritual needs of the people?** (Lesson 6)
a. pipe keeper
b. chief
c. storyteller
d. medicine man

_____ 7. **What was our early Indians ancestor money called?** (Lesson 7)
a. trade beads
b. skins and hides
c. wampum
d. barter

_____ 8. **During the game of stickball, everyone awaits the signal from who before the game can start?** (Lesson 8)
a. medicine man
b. peace chief
c. tribal elder
d. war chief

_____ 9. **What is the largest river that flows through Alabama and forms the north border of Lawrence County?** (Lesson 9)
a. Coosa River
b. Sipsey River
c. Mississippi River
d. Tennessee River

_____ 10. **How many miles did our Indian ancestor walk on the Trail of Tears?** (Lesson 10)
a. 200 miles
b. 500 miles
c. 650 miles
d. 800 miles

_____ 11. **What tribe divided their town into red and white?** (Lesson 11)
a. Creeks
b. Cherokee
c. Shawnee
d. Chickasaw

_____ 12. **What was the name of the head chief of the upper and lower Creeks, who had authority over all town chiefs?** (Lesson 12)
a. shaman
b. chief of Nation
c. micco
d. medicine man

_____ 13. **What Celtic man had three Chickasaw wives who had sons that became important in Chickasaw history?** (Lesson 13)
a. George Colbert
b. James Colbert
c. Levi Colbert
d. John Colbert

_____ 14. **The people of the Cherokee Nation lived in mostly what three states?** (Lesson 14)
a. AL, KY, TN
b. AL, GA, MS
c. TN, AL, MS
d. GA, TN, AL

_____ 15. **What was the flat ground by the river and the council house designated for ceremonies called?** (Lesson 15)
a. circle ground
b. holy ground
c. square ground
d. river ground

Name _____ Date _____ Sixth Grade

_____ 16. **What trail, according to legend, was marked with arbor glyphs on beech trees at the time of removal?** (Lesson 16)
a. Doublehead's Trace
b. Mitchell Trace
c. High Town Path
d. Braziel Creek Trail

_____ 17. **What early town is presently buried below the surface of Wheeler Lake?** (Lesson 17)
a. Cuttyatoy's Village
b. Shoal Town
c. Doublehead's Village
d. Melton's Bluff

_____ 18. **Who was the half brother to Sequoyah who signed the 1806 Cotton Gin Treaty?** (Lesson 18)
a. Cuttyatoy
b. Talohuskee Benge
c. John Melton
d. Old Tassel

_____ 19. **When was the Cherokee war?** (Lesson 19)
a. 1765
b. 1800
c. 1863
d. 1763

_____ 20. **The Treaty of January 10, 1786 gave most of Lawrence County to which tribe?** (Lesson 20)
a. Chickasaw
b. Cherokee
c. Choctaw
d. Creek

_____ 21. **What did our ancestors claim to be by denying their heritage?** (Lesson 21)
a. Black Dutch/Black Irish
b. Irish/Indian
c. English/Indian
d. English/French

_____ 22. **Where is Indian Tomb Hollow, Sipsey River, and Bee Branch Canyon located?** (Lesson 22)
a. Blue Ridge Mountains
b. Warrior Mountains
c. Smokey Mountains
d. Rocky Mountains

_____ 23. **What is the name of the newsletter published by the Echota Cherokee Tribe?** (Lesson 23)
a. Tribal Times
b. War and Peace
c. Cherokee Daily
d. Smoke Signals

_____ 24. **How much did the U.S. pay the Cherokee's for Georgia?** (Lesson 20)
a. $1,250,000.00
b. $125,000.00
c. $1,250.00
d. $125.00

_____ 25. **Sequoyah was also known as:** (Lesson 18)
a. George Colbert
b. John Melton
c. George Gist
d. John Walker

Name_____ Date_____ Seventh Grade

Seventh Grade   Listening Skills, Literary Elements, Literary Genres, Vocabulary, Comprehension

_____ 1. **What year was the Indian Education Program started:** (Lesson 1)
a. 1986
b. 1996
c. 1976
d. 1966

_____ 2. **What is the combination of Lawrence County student's of mixed ancestry?** (Lesson 2)
a. Indian/English
b. Indian/German
c. Indian/Celtic
d. Indian/French

_____ 3. **Where was the Cherokee capital in Georgia?** (Lesson 3)
a. Doublehead's Village
b. Chota
c. New Echota
d. Red Clay

_____ 4. **Name the four prehistoric periods in order from oldest:** (Lesson 4)
a. Archaic, Mississippian, Paleo, Woodland
b. Archaic, Paleo, Mississippian, Woodland
c. Paleo, Archaic, Woodland, Mississippian
d. Mississippian, Woodland, Archaic, Paleo

_____ 5. **How did our Indian ancestors make glue?** (Lesson 5)
a. scrapping hides
b. cooked animal brains
c. boiling meat
d. boiled deer hooves

_____ 6. **Early Indian people used what to prepare boys for hunting and sometimes to settle arguments instead of war?** (Lesson 6)
a. games
b. ceremonies
c. court
d. pow-wow

_____ 7. **Name two reasons our Indian ancestors cut their hair:** (Lesson 7)
a. beauty and wealth
b. fashion and disease
c. cleanliness and custom
d. power and health

_____ 8. **What did our Indian ancestors believe the beat of the drum would do?** (Lesson 8)
a. carry their prayers to heaven
b. heal their heart
c. attract animals
d. scare their enemies

_____ 9. **What place in N. Alabama was known by its Indian name of "Chake Thlocko" meaning Great Crossing Place or Big Ford?** (Lesson 9)
a. Courtland
b. Shoals
c. Brown's Ferry
d. Town Creek

_____ 10. **What race did the Celtic Indians claim to be in order to stay in Alabama?** (Lesson 10)
a. Black Dutch
b. Black English
c. Irish Indians
d. Dutch Indians

_____ 11. **What did Sequoyah refer to as talking leaves?** (Lesson 11)
a. Cherokee alphabet
b. syllabary
c. telegraph
d. newspaper

_____ 12. **What year did the Creek-Indian War end?** (Lesson 12)
a. 1812
b. 1810
c. 1814
d. 1816

_____ 13. **Who owned Lawrence County by the Boundary Treaty of January 10, 1786?** (Lesson 13)
a. Cherokee Nation
b. Chickasaw Nation
c. Creek Nation
d. Choctaw Nation

_____ 14. **What Chickasaw allowed the Cherokees to live in Lawrence County?** (Lesson 14)
a. George Gist
b. George Melton
c. Gorge Washington
d. George Colbert

Name _____   Date _____   Seventh Grade

_____ 15. **When was the Green Corn Ceremony?** (Lesson 15)
a. August
b. December
c. Every seventh year
d. October

_____ 16. **What path was not only a geographic boundary but also used as a tribal and political boundary to traders and early settlers?** (Lesson 16)
a. Black Warriors' Path
b. Coosa Path
c. High Town Path
d. Old Buffalo Path

_____ 17. **What was the Indian town that became the largest Cherokee town in Lawrence County?** (Lesson 17)
a. Monee Town
b. Melton's Bluff
c. Shoal Town
d. Doublehead's Village

_____ 18. **What were the two towns in this area where Doublehead lived?** (Lesson 18)
a. Gourd's Settlement/Shoal Town
b. Brown's Ferry/Shoal Town
c. Melton's Bluff/Shoal Town
d. Cuttyatoy Village/Shoal Town

_____ 19. **The Battle of Fort Mims was an Indian victory under the leadership of whom?** (Lesson 19)
a. Red Eagle
b. Doublehead
c. Junaluska
d. Andrew Jackson

_____ 20. **What treaty ceded all Indian land east of the Mississippi?** (Lesson 20)
a. Cotton Gin Treaty
b. Turkey Town Treaty
c. Chickasaw Boundary Treaty
d. Treaty of New Echota

_____ 21. **When did the Trail of Tears begin and end?** (Lesson 21)
a. October 1838-March 1839
b. November 1838-February 1839
c. March 1838-October 1839
d. September 1838-February 1839

_____ 22. **What is the best known waterfall in the Bankhead Forest?** (Lesson 22)
a. Hurricane Creek Falls
b. Bee Branch Falls
c. Kinlock Falls
d. King Cove Falls

_____ 23. **Out of the nine state tribes of Alabama, which one is federally recognized?** (Lesson 23)
a. Machis Creek
b. Poarch Band of Creek
c. Echota Cherokee Tribe
d. MOWA Choctaw

_____ 24. **What treaty gave the Lawrence County area to the Chickasaws on January 10, 1786?** (Lesson 20)
a. Treaty of Fort Jackson
b. Cotton Gin Treaty
c. Chickasaw Boundary Treaty
d. Turkey Town Treaty

_____ 25. **According to the Turkey Town Treaty of 1816, the Chickasaw were paid 125,000 and what were the Cherokee paid?** (Lesson 20)
a. $600,000.00
b. $60,000.00
c. $6,000.00
d. $600.00

Appendix 4

Activities and Crafts

Appendix 4: Activities and Crafts

Activities

Oral Reading
Teacher Reading
Identify Time Line
Ask Questions (Who? What? Where? When? Why?)
Debate
Make up a Treaty
Hangman
Jeopardy/Who wants to be a Millionaire
Basketball
Classroom Discussion
Pictionary
Draw what if's on the board
List categories on board (students fill in)
Computer
Music
Video
Act out
Hands-on
Discussion
Pair up or group discussion
Peer tutoring
Crossword puzzles
Scavenger hunt
Demonstrate tools and weapons
Sticker games
Word search
Charades
Hand puppets
Matching board game (vocabulary)
Dye material using things from nature (berries, boiled leaves and flower petals, etc.)

Crafts

Fingerweaving
Dreamcatchers
Key chains
Baskets
Bracelets
Necklace
Model Magic pots and bowls
Headbands with feather
Village out of popsicle
Key chains
Trail on the floor
Paint faces
Mask
Turtle shell rattles
Paper dolls
Bell anklets
Coloring
Draw on board
Fossils with playdough
Draw map
Vests (paperbag) with symbols
Frybread (2 c. flour, 1-1½ cups water, 1 tbsp. baking powder, 1 tsp salt-rub oil on ball of dough and fry in electric skillet *sprinkle with powdered sugar)

Appendix 5

Lesson Activities

Appendix 5: Lesson Activities

Activities Lesson 1 – *Introduction & Pre-Test*
Kindergarten – 3rd grade
- Complete a getting to know you sheet
- Let students pick out Indian name for themselves
- Color sheet of Indian picture

Grades 4-7
- Start Family Tree (tell students to identify their grandparents and great-grandparents and percent of Indian blood)
- Let each student make up an Indian name
- Build Railroad using popsicle sticks

Activities Lesson 2 – *Family History & Ancestry*
Kindergarten – 3rd grade
- Draw family tree and have students identify their parents and grandparents
- Identify things that are sacred to you
- Echota Cherokee color sheet

Grades 4-7
- Color and cut out paper doll handout
- Finish family tree
- Tell story why you chose your Indian name

Activities Lesson 3 – *Echota Cherokee Tribe of Alabma*
Kindergarten – 3rd grade
- Color Indian symbol & glue to construction paper – teacher will laminate
- Play "Who Wants to be a Millionaire" – using questions from text
- Identify 7 directions and list the color and meaning of each direction

Grades 4-7
- Start making quilt out of Indian symbols
- Draw the Cherokee symbols used in the alphabet developed by Sequoyah
- Let students pick their governing body by having an election for chief, vice chief, and clan leaders

Activies Lesson 4 – *Periods of Prehistoric Indians*
Kindergarten – 3rd grade
- Make coloring book of the prehistoric periods
- Color sheet with demonstration of tools from different prehistoric periods
- Draw houses used during each period

Grades 4-7
- Finish symbol quilt (put together with yarn)
- Start clay pots
- Make prehistoric booklet of the four periods

Activities Lesson 5 – *Lifestyles of Early Indian People*
Kindergarten – 3rd grade
- Color summer & winter home
- Buffalo color sheet which identifies uses of each part
- Make cornhusk doll

Grades 4-7
- Finish clay pot
- Go outside and play stickball – describe two styles – one with pole in center and one like football field
- Start dream catcher

Appendix 5: Lesson Activities

Activities Lesson 6 - *Early Survival Needs*
Kindergarten – 3rd grade
- Color sheet of different Indian foods
- Color deer sheet showing different parts of the deer/buffalo
- Make canoe out of clay – continue the following lesson

Grades 4-7
- Demonstrate tools/weapons outside – spear, atlatl, rabbit sticks, stone ax
- Finish dream catcher
- Identify items in fire making kit and demonstrate

Activities Lesson 7 - *Regalia*
Kindergarten – 3rd grade
- Make bead bracelets/anklets
- Coloring sheet of moccasins
- Finish & color the clay canoe

Grades 4-7
- Start basket weaving
- Make seed bead necklace
- Draw different Indian tattoos/symbols

Activities Lesson 8 – *Ceremonial Activities*
Kindergarten – 3rd grade
- Have students demonstrate the Friendship Dance
- Make a tambourine, drum, or rattle
- Play stickball around a pole
- Play bean game – one side black and one side white

Grades 4-7
- Finish basket weaving
- Make flutes out of paper towel holders
- Show students how to play chunkey
- Have a ceremony in classroom (make a fake fire out of paper, put in middle of classroom, & dance around with music playing)

Activities Lesson 9 – *Tennessee River*
Kindergarten – 3rd grade
- Make pinch clay pot – continue in next lesson
- Use large pieces of paper/allow students to draw various resources Indian people would use from the Tennessee River
- Look at a map of Lawrence County and have students identify the Tennessee River and surrounding counties

Grades 4-7
- Map Search – identify important details on Lawrence County map – Warrior Mountains, Tennessee River, surrounding counties, Indian towns.
- Identify all the Shoals that make up this area – Elk River Shoals, Big Muscle Shoals, Little Muscle Shoals, Colbert Shoals, Bee Tree Shoals, & Waterloo Shoals
- Make canoes out of model magic
- Write about modes of early travel
- Begin finger weaving

Appendix 5: Lesson Activities

Activities Lesson 10 – *European Contact*
Kindergarten – 3rd grade
- Bear claw necklaces
- Color picture of Desoto
- Make skin vest out of paper bags & draw Indian symbols
- Finish clay pot – paint & color

Grades 4-7
- Finish finger weaving
- Begin making small bead bracelets with beadloom
- Let students play Oregon Trail on computer to show effect of diseases – smallpox & measles
- Worksheet on Trail of Tears – cut out, glue on construction paper, write their feelings & display

Activities Lesson 11 – *Five Tribes of Lawrence County/Mid-Test*
Kindergarten – 3rd grade
- Make news letter of weekly activities and place on construction paper; arrange in order of lessons.
- Identify the 5 tribes of Lawrence County – when, where they moved
- Allow students to write their names using the Cherokee Alphabet – found at www.languages-of-the-world.us/yournamein/cherokee.php

Grades 4-7
- Finish bead bracelets on bead loom
- Review game for mid-test (basketball, hangman, etc)
- Trivia on Tribes
- Make leather bookmark – list 5 tribes in Lawrence County, AL

Activities Lesson 12 – *Creek Tribe*
Kindergarten – 3rd grade
- Divide class into red & white towns, then use quiz games from lesson
- Start making basket and continue to next lesson
- Color sheet of corn, cut out, and past on construction paper

Grades 4-7
- Start clay gorget (let dry for a week)
- Review game dividing class into red and white towns against each other
- Start coloring map of Alabama & label the Creek territories

Activities Lesson 13 – *Chickasaw Tribe*
Kindergarten – 3rd grade
- Demonstrate Black Drink ceremony; cut out paper leaves & allow students to mash them into water
- Make mask using paper plates and yarn for hair and then color
- Finish basket & color

Grades 4-7
- Label Alabama map with Chickasaw territories
- Chickasaw Play with characters acting out their role
- Finish gorget (let students take home)

Activities Lesson 14 – *Cherokee Tribe*
Kindergarten – 3rd grade
- Allow students to makeup myths about Cherokee
- Draw seven sided council house
- Draw Lawrence County map and identify Cherokee villages on Tennessee River

Appendix 5: Lesson Activities

Grades 4-7
- Finish Alabama map by labeling the Cherokee territory
- Write legend or story about Cherokee ancestors
- Color sheet of Cherokee stickball

Activities Lesson 15 – *Seven Clans of the Cherokee*
Kindergarten – 3rd grade
- Make puppets of 7 clans – pictures of wolf, deer, bird, etc.
- Draw the 7 directions of Cherokee and identify color
- Color sheet of seven clans of the Cherokee

Grades 4-7
- Make a pin wheel out of the 7 clans handout and glue on popsicle stick
- Color & label 7 clans handout
- Identify the Cherokee clans in the Cherokee language using website www.languages-of-the-world.us/yournamein/cherokee.php

Activities Lesson 16 – *Indian Trails & Paths*
Kindergarten – 3rd grade
- Crayon rubbing – place paper over leaf and color print
- Make trails & path on floor using bulletin board paper with trails identified
- Moccasin Trail worksheet - color

Grades 4-7
- Draw a Lawrence County map of trials & paths (label longest path, 1st road, etc)
- Put trails & path on floor & let students walk them
- Make flat boat out of popsicle sticks

Activities Lesson 17 – *Indian Villages*
Kindergarten – 3rd grade
- Draw & color Indian village – use large bulletin board paper - council house, huts, farms
- Color sheet of Indian mound
- Make paper cabin using small milk boxes

Grades 4-7
- Make village out of popsicle sticks – council house, huts, corn cribs
- Make Andrew Jackson historic farm out of shoebox or poster board – house, barn, fields of cotton or corn
- Place and identify Lawrence County Cherokee villages along the Tennessee River on bulletin board paper

Activities Lesson 18 – *Local Indian Leaders*
Kindergarten – 3rd grade
- Finger weaving – continue to next lesson
- Trivia Game – using information from text about various leaders – Doublehead, Black Fox, Pathkiller
- Worksheet – write story using Indian symbols

Grades 4-7
- Re-create the Cherokee Village of Shoal Town showing Bluewater, Big Nance, & Town Creeks.
- Worksheet – Indian crossword puzzle
- Write a story involving the local Cherokee Indian leaders and decorate border with Cherokee alphabet symbols

Appendix 5: Lesson Activities

Activities Lesson 19 – *Indian Battles*
Kindergarten – 3rd grade
- Play Hangman using information on Indian battles
- War painting – face painting
- Finish finger weaving

Grades 4-7
- Make an Indian war club
- Start timeline of the different battles (when, who & where each battle took place)
- Play jeopardy using information on Indian battles

Activities Lesson 20 – *Indian Treaties*
Kindergarten – 3rd grade
- Create treaties between two groups of students – Cherokees & Creeks
- Matching game using information on treaties
- Color sheet on Trail of Tears

Grades 4-7
- Finish timeline by listing different treaties under the correct date in which they took place
- Matching trivia game - which treaty did what
- Let students construct their own treaty (crumble paper, shade to look worn, then let them write with black ink)

Activities Lesson 21 – *Indian Removal*
Kindergarten – 3rd grade
- Make a map using shaving cream
- Make a Cherokee Removal map using sidewalk chalk on bulletin board paper
- Color Trail of Tears –"The Long Journey" coloring sheet

Grades 4-7
- Draw removal routes on Alabama maps on bulletin board paper
- Play Trivia on Indian Removal
- Class make a chart of different treaties with names and dates

Activities Lesson 22 – *Traditional Cultural Properties*
Kindergarten – 3rd grade
- Draw extinct animals from Bankhead National Forest and describe your feelings about their loss
- Draw Indian marker tree and describe importance
- Identify Indian things you would find in Bankhead National Forest- bluff shelters, artifacts, marker trees

Grades 4-7
- Construct mountains out of cardboard and playdough, etc.
- Draw on map the different cultural properties - Kinlock, Indian Tomb Hollow, and High Town Path
- Make a chart of extinct plants and animals and date they went extinct
- Make dirt shirts

Activities Lesson 23 – *State Recognized Indian Tribes of Alabama*
Kindergarten – 3rd grade
- Paint Echota Symbol on plates
- Start dream catcher – continue to next lesson
- Make headband with feathers

Grades 4-7
- Play Jeopardy on State recognized tribes
- Draw map of Alabama and locate state recognized tribes
- List role of the Alabama Indian Affairs Commission

Appendix 5: Lesson Activities

Activities Lesson 24 – *Review Post-Test*
Kindergarten – 3rd grade
- Review lessons using games
- Finish dream catcher

Grades 4-7
- Review lessons using games

Activities Lesson 25 – *Post-Test*
Kindergarten – 3rd grade
- Post Test

Grades 4-7
- Post Test

Appendix 6

End of the Year Performance Report

LAWRENCE COUNTY SCHOOLS INDIAN EDUCATION PROGRAM
End of Year Performance Report

Year: _____

School: _____ Grade: _____

Instructor: _____

Student Name (first & last)	Pre-Test Scores	Mid-Test Scores	Pre-Mid Gain	Post-Test Scores	Pre-Post Gain	Days Enrolled	Days In Class
Totals Pre & Post Test							
Range Pre & Post Test							
Average Pre & Post Test							
Total Days In Class							

Appendix 7

Check List for Instructor Improvement Plan

Date _____

Instructors _____

_____

School _____

Check List for Instructor Improvement Plan

Time class started _____ Grade _____ Number of students _____

Time class ended _____

- ☐ Class started on time
- ☐ Greeting
- ☐ Roll call/assessment form
- ☐ Last week's lesson
- ☐ Review test questions
- ☐ Transition to the week's lesson
- ☐ Social Studies Lesson
- ☐ Reading objective
- ☐ Standardized assessment-Dibels/SAT
- ☐ State standards
- ☐ Summary and review
- ☐ Transition to next week's lesson
- ☐ Review test question (last, present, and next week's lesson)
- ☐ Hands-on activity
- ☐ Class dismissed on time

- ☐ Both Instructors actively involved with the class
- ☐ All students engaged in paying attention
- ☐ Both Instructors share equal loads
- ☐ Instructors knowledgeable about the lesson
- ☐ Both Instructors arrive to school on time and leave on time
- ☐ Students disciplined and respectful
- ☐ Varied lesson presentations
- ☐ Hands-on, visuals, and auditory
- ☐ Board use, flip charts
- ☐ All students participating in class activities
- ☐ Students enjoying class
- ☐ Craft relates to lesson
- ☐ Clean classroom environment
- ☐ Bulletin boards current
- ☐ Display of student's work
- ☐ Positive reinforcement
- ☐ Higher order questions

_____   _____
Observer Signature   Date

Index

A

Alexander Mound 209
Alibamos 127, 138
Anigatogewi, ... 170
Anigilohi 170
Anikawi 170
Anisahoni 170
Anitsiskwa 170
Aniwayah 170
Aniwodi 170
Apalachees 138
Archaic 33, 36, 37, 38, 53, 65, 101, 200
Atlanta 181, 182
Attakullakulla 224

B

Bankhead National Forest ... 52, 181, 182, 187, 188, 254, 277, 278, 279, 280, 281, 282, 283
Battle of Fort Mims 138, 224, 238
Battle of Horseshoe Bend .. 138, 139, 218, 238, 240, 254, 266
Battle of Indian Tomb Hollow 138, 240, 243, 278
Battleground Mountain 182
Bean, Mrs. William 51
Bee Tree Shoals 36, 101, 102
Benge, John 11, 207, 219, 220, 226
Benge, Robert 11, 220, 223, 227
Benge, Tahlontoiskee (Talohuskee) 219
Benge, Utana (The Tail) 226
Bering Strait 34, 35
Beringa 34, 35
Bevill, Tom 1
Big Muscle Shoals 53, 101, 102, 103, 207, 225, 226
Big Mussel Shoals 36
Bird Clan 22, 170
Black Dutch 1, 13, 115, 117, 255, 264, 267
Black Fox 226, 227, 228, 229, 254
Black Irish 1, 13, 115, 117, 255, 264, 267
Black Warrior Town 186, 187, 277
Black Warriors' Path .. 139, 182, 185, 186, 187, 188, 198, 200, 201, 204, 209, 221, 227, 240, 244, 277
Blankenship, Willis 280
Blue Clan 12, 22, 170
Boaz 183
Bone Polisher 223, 224
Borden, Christopher 280
Borden, David 280
Breed Town 12, 115
Brown, Joseph 207, 224
Brown, Richard 226, 228
Brown's Ferry Road 181, 188, 200, 226, 228
Browns Ferry 220, 221, 227
Brown's Village 182, 295
Burnett 223
Butler, Kit 224
Byler Road 181, 182, 184, 185, 187, 188, 189

C

Campbell, Arthur 243
Celtic 11, 13, 22, 24, 51, 78, 92, 115, 116, 117, 126, 148, 149, 180, 181, 218, 219, 220, 255, 267
Charles Town 11, 181
Charleston 181, 223
Chattanooga 181, 243
Cheatham Road 181, 182, 184, 189, 206
Cher-o-Creek Intra Tribal Indians 160, 292, 293
Cherokee 1, 11, 12, 13, 22, 23, 24, 39, 40, 50, 51, 52, 53, 62, 63, 64, 65, 66, 67, 77, 78, 79, 80, 89, 90, 91, 101, 103, 104, 115, 116, 117, 126, 127, 128, 137, 148, 149, 158, 159, 160, 169, 171, 180, 181, 182, 183, 184, 185, 186, 188, 189, 198, 199, 200, 201, 203, 204, 206, 207, 208, 209, 218, 219, 220, 221, 222, 223, 224, 225, 226, 227, 228, 229, 238, 243, 244, 253, 254, 255, 264, 265, 266, 267, 280, 281, 292, 293, 294
Cherokee Country 182
Cherokee County 22
Cherokee Tribe of Northeast Alabama 292, 293
Cherokees of Northeast Alabama 160
Chickamaugans 221, 225, 226, 264
Chickasaw 11, 12, 13, 24, 50, 63, 115, 116, 126, 127, 138, 148, 149, 158, 159, 180, 181, 182, 183, 185, 187, 188, 201, 203, 206, 220, 222, 223, 225, 226, 228, 229, 240, 241, 242, 253, 254, 264, 278, 294
Chickasaw Island 183, 187, 254
Choctaw 126, 128, 160, 187, 189, 276, 292
Chota 22, 39, 243
Christian, William 243
Chuqualatague 220
Coffee, John 186, 187, 203, 205, 228, 277
Colbert County 102, 103, 148, 149, 184, 222, 254
Colbert Shoals 36, 101, 102, 103
Colbert, George 11, 63, 148, 149, 159, 220, 222, 226, 254
Colbert, James Logan 12, 115, 149
Colbert, Levi 11, 148, 149, 226
Coosa 50, 182
Coosa Path 188, 198, 209, 221, 244
Copena 33, 208, 209
Copper Town 182, 183
Cornally, David 293
Cotton Gin Port ... 116, 184, 187, 188, 202, 203, 206, 228
Courtland 1, 181, 184, 186, 188, 189, 198, 203, 206, 207, 209, 221, 226, 228, 244, 265
Cowan, John 186, 204, 277
Creek 1, 11, 13, 24, 50, 114, 115, 116, 126, 127, 137, 138, 139, 148, 160, 180, 181, 182, 183, 186, 187, 189, 206, 224, 225, 228, 238, 240, 241, 242, 243, 253, 254, 266, 276, 277, 278, 292, 294
Crenay, Baron De 276
Crockett, David 186, 187, 204, 277
Cullman County 182
Cuttyatoy 198, 206, 207, 224, 226, 244

D

Dale Counties 293
Daleville 23, 293
Davenport, Erma Lis 294
Davenport, Tommy 294
Deer Clan 22, 170
DeKalb County 24, 293
Desoto, Hernando 33, 104, 114, 189, 276
Doublehead 50, 53, 63, 116, 128, 138, 149, 159, 181, 184, 187, 188, 198, 199, 200, 203, 207, 208, 218, 219, 220, 221, 222, 223, 224, 225, 226, 227, 228, 229, 244, 253, 254, 264, 265, 292
Doublehead's Resort 208
Doublehead's Trace 181, 182, 187, 188, 207
Dragging Canoe 224, 227, 243, 293
Dsugweladegi 220

E

Eagle Eye 241, 242, 243
Eastport 184
Echota Cherokee .. 1, 2, 11, 12, 22, 23, 24, 160, 292, 293
Elk River Shoals 36, 53, 101, 102, 103, 180, 184, 186, 187, 188, 189, 198, 199, 206, 207, 220, 221, 226, 228, 244, 265
Elyton 182
Etowah County 182

F

Falkville 24
Faulkner, B. J. 23, 293
Flanagin, James M. 281
Flat Rock 182, 183, 188, 254
Fort Mitchell 181, 186, 187
Franklin County 182, 183, 184, 240, 254
French Lick 187
Ft. Hampton 181, 201, 253

G

Gadsden 181, 183, 254
Gaines Trace 116, 181, 184, 186, 203, 206, 220, 228
Gaines, Edmund Pendleton 184, 188, 206, 207
Gaines, George Strothers 184
Gillespie, James Richard 186, 277
Gist, Nathaniel 218, 220
Great Eagle (Willenawah) 220
Great Mussel Shoals 101
Guntersville 114

H

Haleyville 182, 188, 254
Hallmark, Charlotte Stewart 1
Havens, Charlotte Ann 276
Havens, James 276
Hicks, Ceil 293
Hicks, Charles 128, 201, 203, 218, 220, 226, 228, 253
High Shoals 182
High Town 181, 182
High Town Path. 137, 138, 139, 181, 182, 183, 184, 185, 187, 188, 189, 225, 240, 253, 254, 264, 276
High Town Trail 182
Hillsboro 1, 186
Houston County 293
Hubbert, James 222
Hughes, Mary 51
Hunkapiller, Joe 293
Huntsville ... 101, 181, 186, 187, 188, 199, 201, 204, 228, 229, 253, 277
Hyatt, Rayford 199, 201, 281

I

Indian Tomb Hollow 186, 240, 243, 276, 277, 278
Ittaloknah 240, 241, 243

J

Jackson County 24, 224, 293
Jackson, Andrew 116, 117, 126, 138, 139, 158, 198, 201, 202, 203, 204, 205, 218, 220, 224, 228, 238, 240, 255, 265, 266, 294
Jasper Road 182
Jefferson, Thomas 117, 227
Jesus Christ 37
Johnson, Larry 294
Junaluska 218, 238, 266
Justice, John 293

K

Keep, William 293
King Cove 279
Kinlock Bluff Shelter 278, 280
Kinlock Falls 278
Kinlock Rock Shelter 278
Koasatis 138
Kokomah 241, 242
Kushner, Jaynn 293

L

Lauderdale County 128, 199, 220, 221, 222, 226, 253, 264
Lawrence County 1, 11, 12, 13, 22, 24, 33, 34, 35, 36, 37, 38, 50, 51, 52, 53, 62, 63, 64, 65, 78, 101, 102, 103, 115, 116, 117, 126, 127, 128, 137, 138, 139, 148, 149, 158, 159, 180, 181, 182, 183, 184, 185, 186, 187, 188, 189, 198, 199, 203, 206, 207, 208, 209, 218, 219, 220, 221, 222, 224, 225, 226, 227, 228, 229, 238, 240, 244, 253, 254, 255, 264, 265, 266, 267, 276, 277, 278, 279, 281, 282, 292, 293, 294
Leola Road 181, 182, 184, 189, 253, 280
Limestone County 181, 186, 202, 253
Little Muscle Shoals 101, 102, 103
Little Mussel Shoals 36, 265
Little Turkey 227
Long Hair Clan 22
Lookout Mountain 181, 223

M

Machis Lower Creek 292
Madison County 24, 228, 229, 253, 254, 293
Magnolia 241, 242, 243
Manasco, Jim 189
Marathon 126, 186, 187, 198, 203, 205, 206, 209, 238, 265
Marshall County 183, 201
Martin, Dr. H.L. "Lindy" 293
McCloski, Thomas 23, 293
McCony, James 293
McGhee, Calvin W. 292
McGillivary, Alexander 11
McIntoshville 12, 115
Meigs, Josiah 205
Meigs, Return Jonathon 208, 222, 223, 224, 227, 228
Melson, G. H. 277
Melton, John 12, 115, 187, 188, 201, 203, 204, 205, 206, 220, 226, 227, 228, 253, 265
Melton, Moses 128, 201, 203, 228, 253
Melton. David 126, 201, 204, 220, 228
Melton's Bluff 12, 115, 117, 126, 128, 180, 181, 182, 183, 184, 185, 186, 187, 198, 201, 203, 204, 205, 206, 220, 221, 225, 226, 227, 228, 229, 238, 240, 244, 253, 254, 264, 265, 277
Memphis 181
Menawa 238
Mississippian 33, 38, 39, 40, 282
Mitchell Trace 181, 186, 187
Mitchell, David Brady 186
Mobile 181, 183, 184, 185, 229
Mobile Bay 181, 183, 184, 229
Montgomery 127, 254
Moulton 139
Moulton, Michael 138, 139, 240
Mountain, Marland 293
MOWA Band of Choctaw 292
MOWA Choctaws 294
Moytoy 220
Muscle Shoals 184
Mussel Shoals .. 33, 36, 53, 102, 103, 127, 182, 188, 201, 220, 221, 226, 243, 244, 265

N

Nashville 127, 182, 185, 187, 188, 205, 206, 222, 227
Natchez 185
Natchez Trace 184, 185, 200, 222, 254
Naylor, Mary E. Welborn Segars 277
New Echota 1, 12, 22, 158, 244, 255, 266
New Orleans 116, 184, 202, 204, 205

O

Oakville 1, 37, 38, 159, 186, 187, 188, 198, 200, 208, 209, 221, 240, 244
Oakville Indian Mounds 2, 186, 187
Oconostota 243
Old Buffalo Trail 182, 187, 188
Old Corn Road 181, 182, 184
Old Indian Trace 198, 209, 221
Old Tassel 220, 222
Overall, William 223

P

Paint Clan 22
Paleo 33, 34, 35, 36, 37, 53
Pathkiller 226, 227, 228
Pickett, Albert James 238
Piqua Shawnee 292
Poarch Band of Creek 292
Ponioc 241
Prucha, Francis P. 116
Pumpkin Boy 220, 223

R

Red Clay 158, 266
Red Eagle 224, 225, 238
Red Paint Clan 170
Riddle, William Straud 281
Ridge Path 184
Ridge Road 181, 182, 184, 188, 189, 253
Robertson, James 222
Rodgers, John 223
Rogers, John 128, 220, 222, 227, 264
Rooks, David 293
Russell County 181, 185, 186, 187
Russellville 184, 228

S

Saleechie 149, 159, 220, 222, 226
Sand Mountain 181, 183
Saunders, Edmonds 276
Saunders, Ridge, Alex 128, 220, 222, 223, 264
Seminoles 126
Sequoyah 11, 78, 128, 207, 218, 219, 220, 225, 226, 253, 280
Sequoyah, George Gist 218
Sevier, John 223, 228, 243
Sevier, Valentine 223
Shawnee 50, 126, 127, 138, 224, 294
Shelby County 23
Sheridan, Richard C. 187
Ship Rock 279
Shoal Town 188, 198, 200, 206, 207, 208, 220, 221, 222, 224, 225, 226, 227, 244
Sipsey Wilderness Area 188, 278, 279, 280
Sipsie Trail 182, 189, 206
Smith, David 276
Southern Trail 182
Spillers, Amos 281
Staggs, Travis 293
Star Clan of Lower Muscogee Creek 293
Star Clan of Muscogee Creeks 292
Stewart, Joe 1
Stewart, Joseph "Two Eagles" 23, 293
Swimmer, Amanda 80

T

Tahlonteeskee 253
Tahlonteskee 221, 222, 225, 226, 227, 264
Tallapoosa 114, 238
Talo Tiske 220
Talohuskee 207, 219, 220, 221, 222, 225, 226, 253
Talohuskee Benge 207, 219, 220, 221, 225, 226, 264
Taluntuskee 223
Tecumseh 127, 238
Thomas, Edwin C. 222
Thornhill, Claud 293
Town Creek 1, 187, 188, 198, 201, 206, 207, 208, 220, 221, 226, 244
Trail of Tears 1, 66, 126, 189, 255, 266, 267, 294
Tukabachee 127
Tullis, Eddie L. 292
Turkey Town 117, 158, 181, 182, 183, 187, 225, 226, 228, 244, 253, 254, 264, 265, 295
Tuscaloosa 50, 114, 182, 187, 188, 189, 206, 276
Tuscumbia 50, 240
Tuskaloosa 114
Tuskegee 218
Tuskiahooto 149, 159, 220, 222, 226
Twisters Clan (*Long Hair*) 170

U

United Cherokee Aniyunwiya 160, 292, 295
United Cherokee Tribe of Alabama 23

V

Vann 223

Vinemont 182

W

Walker County 22
Walker, Rickey Butch 1, 277
Wallace, George 294
Wambles, Deal 293
Ward, Nancy 51
Warrior Mountains ... 24, 52, 80, 117, 158, 181, 184, 186, 189, 208, 221, 225, 226, 243, 244, 253, 254, 255, 264, 266, 267, 276, 277, 278, 279, 280, 281, 282, 283
Washington, George 220, 223
Waterloo Shoals 36, 101, 102
Watts, John 11, 218, 219, 220, 227
Watts, John Jr. 11, 218, 219, 220, 227
Watts, Wurteh 11, 207, 218, 219, 220
Weatherford, William 224, 238
Whisnant, Glenn 280
Wilburn, Authur 277
Wild Potato Clan 22, 170
Williams, Bill 293
Williamson, Gina 295
Willstown 218, 223, 227, 295
Winston County 22, 182, 189
Wolf Clan 22, 170
Woodland 33, 37, 38, 189, 208, 209
Wright, Johnny 294
Wright, Penny 294
Wurteh 11, 207, 218, 219

Y

Yuchi 50, 126, 127, 138

Bluewater Publications is a multi-faceted publishing company capable of meeting all of your reading and publishing needs. Our two-fold aim is to:
1) Provide the market with educationally enlightening and inspiring research and reading materials.
2) Make the opportunity of being published available to any author and or researcher who desires to be published.

We are passionate about preserving history; whether through the re-publishing of an out-of-print classic, or by publishing the research of historians and genealogists. Bluewater Publications is the *Peoples' Choice Publisher*.

For company information or information about how you can be published through Bluewater Publications, please visit:

www.BluewaterPublications.com

Also check Amazon.com to purchase any of the books that we publish.

Confidently Preserving Our Past,
Bluewater Publications.com
Formerly known as Heart of Dixie Publishing

www.ingramcontent.com/pod-product-compliance
Lightning Source LLC
Chambersburg PA
CBHW082026300426

44117CB00015B/2363